T. R. MALTHUS
AN ESSAY ON
THE PRINCIPLE OF POPULATION
VOLUME II

# T. R. MALTHUS
# AN ESSAY ON THE PRINCIPLE OF POPULATION;

or

A View of its past and present Effects on Human Happiness;

With an Inquiry into our Prospects respecting the future Removal or Mitigation of the Evils which it occasions

The version published in 1803, with the variora of 1806, 1807, 1817 and 1826

EDITED BY

PATRICIA JAMES

## VOLUME II

The right of the University of Cambridge to print and sell all manner of books was granted by Henry VIII in 1534. The University has printed and published continuously since 1584.

CAMBRIDGE UNIVERSITY PRESS

CAMBRIDGE

NEW YORK    PORT CHESTER

MELBOURNE    SYDNEY

FOR THE ROYAL ECONOMIC SOCIETY

CAMBRIDGE UNIVERSITY PRESS
Cambridge, New York, Melbourne, Madrid, Cape Town, Singapore, São Paulo

Cambridge University Press
The Edinburgh Building, Cambridge CB2 8RU, UK

Published in the United States of America by Cambridge University Press, New York

www.cambridge.org
Information on this title: www.cambridge.org/9780521323635

First published 1989
This digitally printed version 2008

*A catalogue record for this publication is available from the British Library*

*Library of Congress Cataloguing in Publication data*
Malthus, T. R. (Thomas Robert), 1766–1834.
An essay on the principle of population, or a
view of its past and present effects on human happiness.
"The version published in 1803, with the variora of
1806, 1807, 1817 and 1826, edited by Patricia James."
Includes index.
1. Population. I. James Patricia, 1933–
II. Title.
HB861.E7   1987   304.6   87–9372

ISBN 978-0-521-32360-4 hardback (volume I)
ISBN 978-0-521-07134-5 paperback (volume I)

ISBN 978-0-521-32363-5 hardback (volume II)
ISBN 978-0-521-07132-1 paperback (volume II)

# CONTENTS

## VOLUME II

# BOOK II

## CHAPTER IV(b)

## *On the fruitfulness of Marriages*[1]

It would be extremely desirable to be able to deduce from the rate of increase, the actual population, and the registers of births, deaths, and marriages, in different countries, the real prolificness[2] of marriages, and the true proportion of the born which lives to marry. Perhaps the problem may not be capable of an accurate solution, but we shall make some approximation towards it, and be able to account for some of the difficulties which appear in many registers, if we attend to the following considerations.

It should be premised however, that in the registers of most countries there is some reason to believe that the omissions in the births and deaths are greater than in the marriages; and consequently that the proportion of marriages is almost always given too great. In the enumeration which lately took place in this country, while it is supposed with reason that the registry of marriages is nearly correct, it is known with certainty that there are very great omissions in the births and deaths; and it is probable that similar omissions, though not perhaps to the same extent, prevail in other countries.

[In 1826 (Vol. I, p. 472) the following three paragraphs were inserted here:

If we suppose a country where the population is stationary, where there are no emigrations, immigrations, or illegitimate children, and where the registers of births, deaths, and marriages are accurate, and continue always in the same proportion to the population, then the proportion of the annual births to the annual marriages will express the number of children born to each marriage, including second and third marriages, and when corrected for second and third marriages, it will also express the proportion of the born which lives to marry, once or oftener; while the annual mortality will accurately express the expectation of life.

But if the population be either increasing or decreasing, and the births, deaths, and

---

[1] [This revised chapter: 'On the fruitfulness of marriages' was chapter ix of Book II in 1806; in 1817, after the new chapters on France and England had been added, it became chapter xi.]

[2] [In 1826 (Vol. I, p. 471) this chapter began:

It would be extremely desirable to be able to deduce from the registers of births, deaths, and marriages in different countries, and the actual population with the rate of increase, the real prolificness ...

marriages increasing or decreasing in the same ratio, such a movement will necessarily disturb all the proportions, because the events which are contemporary in the registers are not contemporary in the order of nature, and an increase or decrease must have been taking place in the interval.

In the first place, the births of any year cannot in the order of nature have come from the contemporary marriages, but must have been derived principally from the marriages of preceding years.

To form a judgment of the prolificness of marriages, taken as they occur, including second and third marriages, let us cut off a certain period of the registers of any country, 30 years for instance, and inquire what is the number of births which have been produced by all the marriages included in the period cut off. It is evident that with the marriages at the beginning of the period will be arranged a number of births proceeding from marriages not included in the period; and at the end, a number of births produced by the marriages included in the period will be found arranged with the marriages of a succeeding period. Now if we could subtract the former number, and add the latter, we should obtain exactly all the births produced by the marriages of the period, and of course the real prolificness of those marriages. If the population be stationary, the number of births to be added would exactly equal the number to be subtracted, and the proportion of births to marriages, as found in the registers, would exactly represent the real prolificness of marriages. But if the population be either increasing or decreasing, the number to be added would never be equal to the number to be subtracted, and the proportion of births to marriages in the registers would never truly represent the prolificness of marriages. In an increasing population the number to be added would evidently be greater than the number to be subtracted, and of course the proportion of births to marriages, as found in the registers, would always be too small to represent the true prolificness of marriages. And the contrary effect would take place in a decreasing population. The question therefore is what we are to add, and what to subtract, when the births and deaths are not equal.

The average proportion of births to marriages in Europe is about 4 to 1. Let us suppose, for the sake of illustration, that each marriage yields four children, one every other year.[3] In this case it is evident that, wherever you begin your period[4] in the registers, the marriages of the preceding eight years

---

[3] In the statistical account of Scotland, it is said that the average distance between the children of the same family has been calculated to be about two years.

[4] [In 1826 (Vol. I, p. 474) this was altered to:
    ... whenever we begin the period ...

will only have produced half of their births, and the other half will be arranged with the marriages included in the period, and ought to be subtracted from them. In the same manner, the marriages of the last eight years of the period will only have produced half of their births, and the other half ought to be added. But half of the births of any eight years may be considered as nearly equal to all the births of the succeeding $3\frac{3}{4}$ years. In instances of the most rapid increase it will rather exceed the births of the next $3\frac{1}{2}$ years, and in cases of slow increase approach towards the births of the next 4 years. The mean therefore may be taken at $3\frac{3}{4}$ years.[5] Consequently if we subtract the births of the first $3\frac{3}{4}$ years of the period, and add the births of the $3\frac{3}{4}$ years subsequent to the period, we shall have a number of births nearly equal to the births produced by all the marriages included in the period, and of course the prolificness of these marriages. But if the population of a country be increasing regularly, and the births, deaths, and marriages continue always to bear the same proportion to each other, and to the whole population, it is evident that all the births of any period will bear the same proportion to all the births of any other period of the same extent, taken a certain number of years later, as the births of any single year to the births of a single year taken the same number of years later;[6] and the same will be true with regard to the marriages. And consequently, to estimate the prolificness of marriages, we have only to compare the marriages of the present or any other year with the births of a subsequent year taken $3\frac{3}{4}$ years later.

We have supposed in the present instance, that each marriage yields four births; but the average proportion of births to marriages in Europe is 4 to 1,[7] and as the population of Europe is known to be increasing at present, the prolificness of marriages must be greater than 4. If, allowing for this circumstance, we take the distance of 4 years instead of $3\frac{3}{4}$ years, we shall probably be not far from the truth. And though undoubtedly the period will differ in different countries, yet it will not differ so much as we might at first imagine; because in countries where the marriages are more prolific, the births generally follow at shorter intervals, and where they are less prolific at

---

[5] According to the rate of increase which is now taking place in England, the period by calculation would be about $3\frac{3}{4}$ years.

[In 1817 (Vol. II, p. 137) '1802' was inserted in brackets, after ... taking place in England ...

[6] [In 1817 (Vol. II, pp. 137–8) this was changed:

... as the births of any single year, or an average of five years, to the births of a single year, or an average of five years, taken the same number of years later; ...

[7] [In 1807 (Vol. II, p. 510) a footnote was added here:

I think the proportion is probably greater, as there is reason to believe that in all registers the omissions in the births and deaths are more numerous than in the marriages.

[In 1826 (Vol. II, p. 475) this was altered to:

The true proportion will be greater if, as before stated, there is reason to believe ...

longer intervals; and with different degrees of prolificness, the length of the period might still remain the same.[8]

It will follow from these observations, that the more rapid is the increase of population, the more will the real prolificness of marriages exceed the proportion of births to marriages in the registers.

The rule which has been here laid down attempts to estimate the prolificness of marriages taken as they occur, but this prolificness should be carefully distinguished from the prolificness of first marriages and of married women, and still more from the natural prolificness of women in general, taken at the most favourable age. It is probable that the natural prolificness of women is nearly the same in most parts of the world; but the prolificness of marriages is liable to be affected by a variety of circumstances peculiar to each country; and particularly by the number of late marriages. In all countries the second and third marriages alone form a most important consideration, and materially influence the average proportions. According to Sussmilch, in all Pomerania, from 1748 to 1756 both included, the number of persons who married were 56 956, and of these 10 586 were widows and widowers.[9] According to Busching, in Prussia and Silesia for the year 1781, out of 29 308 persons who married, 4841 were widows and widowers,[10] and consequently the proportion of marriages will be given full one sixth too much. In estimating the prolificness of married women, the number of illegitimate births[11] would tend, though in a very slight degree, to counterbalance the overplus of marriages; and as it is found that the number of widowers who marry again is greater than the number of widows, the whole of the correction should not on this account be applied; but in estimating the proportion of the born which lives to marry from a comparison of the marriages and deaths, which is what we are now about to proceed to, the whole of this correction is always necessary.

[12]●To find the proportion of the born which lives to marry, we must first subtract one sixth from the marriages, and then compare the marriages of any year so corrected, with the deaths in the registers, at such a distance from

---

[8] In places where there are many exports and imports of people, the calculations will of course be disturbed. In towns, particularly where there is a frequent change of inhabitants, and where it so often happens that the marriages of the people in the neighbouring country are celebrated, the inferences from the proportion of births to marriages are not to be depended upon.

[In 1826 (Vol. I, p. 476) this was changed to:

In places where there are many migrations of people ...

[9] Gottliche Ordnung, vol. i. tables, p. 98.        [10] Sussmilch, vol. iii. tables, p. 95.

[11] In France before the revolution the proportion of illegitimate births was $\frac{1}{47}$ of the whole number. Probably it is less in this country.

them as is equal to the difference between the average age of marriage and the average age of death.

Thus, for example, if the proportion of marriages to deaths were as 1 to 3, then subtracting one sixth from the marriages this proportion would be as 5 to 18, and the number of persons marrying annually the first time would be to the number of annual deaths as 10 to 18. Supposing in this case the mean age of death to be ten years later than the mean age of marriage, in which ten years the deaths would increase $\frac{1}{9}$, then the number of persons marrying annually the first time, compared with the number of annual deaths, at the distance of the difference between the age of marriage and the age of death, would be as 10 to 20; from which it would follow that exactly half of the born lived to marry.

The grounds of this rule will appear from the following observations on registers in general.

In a country in which the population is stationary, the contemporary deaths compared with the births will be equal, and will of course represent the deaths of all the born; and the marriages, or more properly the number of married persons compared with both the births and deaths will, when a proper allowance has been made for second and third marriages, represent the true proportion of the born which lives to marry. But if the population be either increasing or decreasing, and the births, deaths, and marriages increasing or decreasing in the same ratio, then the deaths compared with the births, and the marriages compared with the births and deaths, will cease to express what they did before, unless the events which are contemporary in the registers are also contemporary in the order of nature.

In the first place it is evident that death cannot be contemporary with birth, but must on an average be always at such a distance from it as is equal to the expectation of life, or the mean age of death. Consequently, though the deaths of all the born are, or will be, in the registers, where there are no emigrations, yet, except when the population is stationary, the contemporary periods of births and deaths never show this; and we can only expect to find the deaths equal to the births if the deaths be taken at such a distance from the births in the registers as is equal to the expectation of life. And in fact, thus taken, the births and deaths will always be found equal.● [12]

Secondly, the marriages of any year can never be contemporary with the births from which they have resulted, but must always be at such a distance from them as is equal to the average age of marriage. If the population be increasing, the marriages of the present year have resulted from a smaller number of births than the births of the present year, and of course the marriages, compared with the contemporary births, will always be too few to represent the proportion of the born which lives to marry; and the contrary

---

[12] [These five paragraphs were expunged in 1826 (Vol. I, p. 477) and the next paragraph began thus:
It is obvious, in the second place, that the marriages . . .

will take place if the population be decreasing; and to find this proportion, we must compare the marriages of any year with the births of a previous year at the distance of the average age of marriage.

Thirdly, the average age of marriage will almost always be much nearer to the average age of death than marriage is to birth;[13] and consequently the annual marriages compared with the contemporary annual deaths will much more nearly represent the true proportion of the born living to marry, than the marriages compared with the births.[14] The marriages compared with the births, after a proper allowance has been made for second and third marriages, can never represent the true proportion of the born living to marry, unless when the population is absolutely stationary; but although the population be increasing or decreasing according to any ratio,[15] yet the average age of marriage may still be equal to the average of death; and in this case the marriages in the registers compared with the contemporary deaths, after the correction for second and third marriages, will represent the true proportion of the born living to marry.[16] Generally, however, when an

---

[13] [In 1826 (Vol. I, p. 478) this paragraph began thus:

But on account of the distance of this period, it may be often more convenient, though it is not essentially so correct, to compare the marriages with the contemporary deaths. The average age of marriage will almost always be much nearer to the average age of death ...

[14] Dr. Price very justly says (Observ. on Revers Pay. vol. i. p. 269. 4th edit.) 'that the general effect of an increase while it is going on in a country is to render the proportion of persons marrying annually, to the annual deaths *greater* and to the annual births *less* than the true proportion marrying out of any given number born. This proportion generally lies between the other two proportions, but always nearest the first.' In these observations I entirely agree with him, but in a note to this passage he appears to me to fall into an error. He says that if the prolificness of marriages be increased (the *probabilities of life* and *the encouragement to marriage* remaining the same) both the annual births and burials would increase in proportion to the annual weddings. That the proportion of annual births would increase is certainly true, and I here acknowledge my error in differing from Dr. Price on this point in my last edition; but I still think that the proportion of burials to weddings would not necessarily increase under the circumstances here supposed.

The reason why the proportion of births to weddings increases is, that the births occurring in the order of nature considerably prior to the marriages which result from them, their increase will affect the register of births much more than the contemporary register of marriages. But the same reason by no means holds with regard to the deaths, the average age of which is generally later than the age of marriage. And in this case, after the first interval between birth and marriage, the permanent effect would be, that the register of marriages would be more affected by the increase of births, than the contemporary register of deaths; and consequently the proportion of the burials to the weddings would be rather decreased than increased. From not attending to the circumstance that the average age of marriage may often be considerably earlier than the mean age of death, the general conclusion also which Dr. Price draws in this note does not appear to be strictly correct.

[15] [In 1817 (Vol. II, p. 146) the words *according to any ratio* were deleted.]

[16] The reader will be aware, that as all the born must die, deaths may in some cases be taken as synonymous with births. If we had the deaths registered of all the births which had taken.

increase of population is going forwards, the average age of marriage is less than the average of death, and then the proportion of marriages, compared with the contemporary deaths, will be too great to represent the true proportion of the born living to marry, and to find this proportion we must compare the marriages of any particular year with the deaths of a subsequent year, at such a distance from it in the registers as is equal to the difference between the average age of marriage and the average age of death.

There is no absolutely[17] necessary connection between the average age of marriage and the average age of death. In a country the resources of which will allow of a rapid increase of population, the expectation of life, or the average age of death, may be extremely high, and yet the age of marriage be very early, and the marriages then, compared with the contemporary deaths in the registers, would (even after the correction for second and third marriages) be very much too great to represent the true proportion of the born living to marry. In such a country we might suppose the average age of death to be 40, and the age of marriage only 20; and in this case, which however would be a rare one, the distance between marriage and death would be the same as between birth and marriage.

If we apply these observations to registers in general, though we shall seldom be able to obtain accurately the true proportion of the born living to marry, on account of our not knowing the average age of marriage, yet we may draw many useful inferences from the information which they contain, and reconcile many of the difficulties with which they are accompanied;[18] and it will generally be found, that in those countries where the marriages bear a very large proportion to the deaths, we shall see reason to believe that the age of marriage is much earlier than the average age of death.

In the Russian table for the year 1799, produced by Mr. Tooke, and referred to volume I, p. 179, the proportion of marriages to deaths appeared to be as, 100 to 210. When corrected for second and third marriages, by subtracting one sixth from the marriages, it will be as 100 to 252. From which it would seem to follow that out of 252 births 200 of them had lived to marry; but we can scarcely conceive any country to be so healthy, as that 200 out of 252

---

place in a country during a certain period, distinguishing the married from the unmarried, it is evident that the number of those who died married, compared with the whole number of deaths, would accurately express the proportion of the *births* which had lived to marry.

17  [In 1826 (Vol. I, p. 480) the word *absolutely* was deleted.]

18  [In 1826 (Vol. I, p. 481) this paragraph began thus:

If we apply these observations to registers in general, though we shall seldom be able to obtain the true proportion of the born living to marry, on account of the proportions of births, deaths and marriages not remaining the same, and of our not knowing the average age of marriage, yet we may draw many useful inferences from the information which they contain, and reconcile some apparent contradictions; and it will generally be found ...

should live to marry.[19] If however we suppose, what seems to be probable, that the age of marriage in Russia is 15 years earlier than the expectation of life or the average age of death, then, in order to find the proportion which lives to marry, we must compare the marriages of the present year with the deaths 15 years later. Supposing the births to deaths to be (as stated volume I, p. 181) 183 to 100, and the mortality 1 in 50, the yearly increase will be about $\frac{1}{60}$ of the population; and consequently in 15 years the deaths will have increased a little above .28; and the result will be, that the marriages compared with the deaths 15 years later, will be as 100 to 322. Out of 322 births it will appear that 200 live to marry, which, from the known healthiness of children in Russia, and the early age of marriage, is not an improbable proportion.[20] The proportion of marriages to births, being as 100 to 385, the prolificness of marriages, according to the rule laid down, will be as 100 to 411, or each marriage will on an average, including second and third marriages, produce 4.11 births.

The lists given in the earlier part of the chapter on Russia are probably not correct. It is suspected, with reason, that there are considerable omissions both in the births and deaths, but particularly in the deaths, and consequently the proportion of marriages is given too great. There may also be a further reason for this large proportion of marriages in Russia. The Empress Catherine, in her instructions for a new code of laws, notices a custom prevalent among the peasants, of parents obliging their sons, while actually children, to marry full-grown women in order to save the expense of buying female slaves. These women, it is said, generally become the mistresses of the father, and the custom is particularly reprobated by the Empress as prejudicial to population. This practice would naturally occasion a more than usual number of second and third marriages, and of course more than usually increase the proportion of marriages to births in the registers.

In the transactions of the society at Philadelphia, (vol. iii. No. vii. p. 25) there is a paper by Mr. Barton, entitled *Observations on the probability of life in the United States*, in which it appears that the proportion of marriages to births is as 1 to $4\frac{1}{2}$. He mentions indeed $6\frac{1}{2}$, but his numbers give only $4\frac{1}{2}$. As, however, this proportion was taken principally from towns, it is probable that the births are given too low, and I think we may very safely take as many as five for the average of towns and country. According to the same authority, the mortality is about 1 in 45, and if the population doubles every 25 years,

---

[19] [In 1817 (Vol. II, p. 148) this was changed to:
    ... but we cannot conceive any country to be so healthy as that 200 out of 252 should live to marry.
[20] [In 1826 (Vol. I, p. 482) this was altered:
    ... early age of marriage, is a possible proportion.

the births would be about 1 in 20. The proportion of marriages to deaths would on these suppositions be as 1 to $2\frac{2}{9}$; and corrected for second and third marriages as 1 to 2.7 nearly. But we cannot suppose that out of 27 births 20 should live to marry. If however the age of marriage be ten years earlier than the mean age of death, which is highly probable, we must compare the marriages of the present year with the deaths ten years later, in order to obtain the true proportion of the born which lives to marry. According to the progress of population here stated, the increase of the deaths in ten years would be a little above .3, and the result will be that 200 out of 351, or about 20 out of 35, instead of 20 out of 27 will live to marry.[21] The marriages compared with the births 4 years later, according to the rule laid down, will in this case give 5.58 for the prolificness of marriages. The calculations of Mr. Barton, respecting the age to which half of the born live, cannot possibly be applicable to America in general. The registers on which they are founded are taken from Philadelphia, and one or two small towns and villages, which do not appear to be so healthy as the moderate towns of Europe, and therefore can form no criterion for the country in general.

In England the average proportion of marriages to births appears of late years to have been about 100 to 350. If we add $\frac{1}{7}$ to the births, instead of $\frac{1}{6}$, which in the chapter on *the Checks to Population in England* I conjectured might be nearly the amount of the omissions in the births and deaths, this will allow for the circumstance of illegitimate births; and the marriages will then be to

---

[21] If the proportions mentioned by Mr. Barton be just, the expectation of life in America is considerably less than in Russia, which is the reason that I have taken only 10 years for the difference between the age of marriage and the age of death, instead of 15 years, as in Russia. According to the mode adopted by Dr. Price, (vol. i. p. 272) of estimating the expectation of life in countries the population of which is increasing, this expectation in Russia would be about 38, (births $\frac{1}{20}$, deaths $\frac{1}{50}$, mean $\frac{1}{38}$), and supposing the age of marriage to be 23, the difference would be 15.

In America the expectation of life would, upon the same principles be only $32\frac{1}{2}$, (births $\frac{1}{20}$, deaths $\frac{1}{45}$, mean $\frac{1}{32}\frac{1}{2}$), and supposing the age of marriage $22\frac{1}{2}$ the difference would be 10.

[In 1826 (Vol. 1, p. 484) Malthus added to this note:

Since this was written, I have seen reason to believe, from some calculations by Mr. Milne, actuary to the Sun Life Assurance Society, that Dr. Price's mode of estimating the expectation of life in countries that are increasing is by no means correct, and that the true expectation of life in such countries lies very much nearer the proportion of the annual mortality, than a mean between the annual mortality and the proportion of annual births; but I retain the mean proportion in the calculations of this chapter, because I find that this mean expresses more nearly the period when the deaths will equal the present births, or accord with the present marriages, than the distance of the expectation of life. In a progressive country, where the annual births considerably exceed the annual deaths, the period at which the annual deaths will equal the present annual births is less distant than the expectation of life.

the births as 1 to 4, to the deaths as 1 to 3.[22] Corrected for second and third marriages, the proportion of marriages to deaths will be as 1 to 3.6. Supposing the age of marriage in England about 7 years earlier than the mean age of death, the increase in these 7 years according to the present progress of population of $\frac{1}{120}$ yearly would be .06, and the proportion living to marry would be 200 out of 381, or rather more than half.[23] The marriages compared with the births 4 years later will give 4.136 for the prolificness of marriages.

These instances will be sufficient to show the mode of applying the rules which have been given, in order to form a judgment, from registers, of the prolificness of marriages, and the proportion of the born which lives to marry.[24]

It will be observed how very important the correction for second and third marriages is. Supposing each marriage to yield 4 births, and the births and deaths to be equal, it would at first appear necessary that in order to produce this effect, exactly half of the born should live to marry; but if on account of the second and third marriages we subtract $\frac{1}{6}$ from the marriages, and then compare them with the deaths, the proportion will be as 1 to $4\frac{4}{5}$, and it will appear that instead of one half it will only be necessary that 2 children out of $4\frac{4}{5}$ should live to marry. Upon the same principle if the births were to the marriages as 4 to 1, and exactly half of the born live to marry, it might be supposed at first that the population would be stationary; but if we subtract $\frac{1}{6}$ from the marriages, and then take the proportion of deaths to marriages as 4 to 1, we shall find that the deaths in the registers, compared with the

---

[22] [In 1817 (Vol. II, p. 153) a footnote was added here:
This applies to the state of population before 1800.

[23] Births $\frac{1}{30}$, deaths $\frac{1}{40}$, mean $\frac{1}{35}$, and on the supposition that the age of marriage is 28, the difference would be 7. With regard to the allowance which I have made here and in a former chapter for the omissions in the births and deaths, I wish to observe that as I had no very certain and satisfactory grounds on which to proceed, it may be incorrect, and perhaps too great, though assuming this allowance the mortality appears to be extraordinarily small considering the circumstances of the country. It should be remarked, however, that in countries which are different in their rates of increase, the annual mortality is a very incorrect criterion of their comparative healthiness. When an increase is going forward the portion of the population which becomes extinct every year is very different from the expectation of life, as has appeared very clearly in the cases of Russia and America just noticed. And as the increase of population in England has of late years been more rapid than in France, this circumstance will undoubtedly contribute in part to the great difference in the annual mortality.
[In 1826 (Vol. I, p. 485) the whole of this footnote was expunged except for the first sentence.]

[24] [In 1826 (Vol. I, p. 486) a sentence was added here:
... lives to marry; but it must still be remembered that they are only approximations, and intended rather to explain apparent difficulties than to obtain results which can be depended upon as correct.

marriages, would only be as $3\frac{1}{3}$ to 1; and the births would be to the deaths as 4 to $3\frac{1}{3}$, or 12 to 10, which is a tolerably fast rate of increase.

[In 1807 (Vol. I, pp. 525–6) a paragraph and a footnote were added here:

It should be further observed, that as a much greater number of widowers marry again than of widows, if we wish to know the proportion of males which lives to marry, we must subtract full $\frac{1}{5}$ from the marriages instead of $\frac{1}{7}$.[a] According to this correction, if each marriage yielded 4 births, it would only be necessary that two male children out of 5 should live to marry in order to keep up the population; and if each marriage yielded 5 births, less than one-third would be necessary for this purpose; and so for the other calculations. In estimating the proportion of males living to marry, some allowance ought also to be made for the greater proportion of male births.

Three causes appear to operate in producing an excess of the births above the deaths, 1. the prolificness of marriages; 2. the proportion of the born which lives to marry, and 3. the earliness of these marriages compared with the expectation of life, or the shortness of a generation by marriage and birth, compared with the passing away of a generation by death. This latter cause Dr. Price seems to have omitted to consider. For though he very justly says that the rate of increase, supposing the prolific powers the same, depends upon the encouragement to marriage, and the expectation of a child just born; yet in explaining himself, he seems to consider an increase in the expectation of life merely as it affects the increase of the number of persons who reach maturity and marry, and not as it affects, besides, the distance between the age of marriage and the age of death. But it is evident that if there be any principle of increase, that is, if one marriage in the present generation yields more than one in the next, including second and third marriages, the quicker these generations are repeated, compared with the passing away of a generation by death, the more rapid will be the increase.

A favourable change in either of these three causes, the other two remaining the same, will clearly produce an effect upon population, and occasion a greater excess of the births above the deaths in the registers. With regard to the two first causes, though an increase in either of them will produce the same kind of effect on the proportion of births to deaths, yet their effects on the proportion of marriages to births will be in opposite directions.

---

[a] Of 28 473 marriages in Pomerania, 5964 of the men were widowers. Sussmilch, vol. i. tables, p. 98. And according to Busching, of 14 759 marriages in Prussia and Silesia, 3071 of the men were widowers, Sussmilch, vol. iii. tables, p. 95. Muret calculates that 100 men generally marry 110 women. Mémoires par la Société Economique de Berne. Année 1766, première partie, p. 30.

The greater is the prolificness of marriages the greater will be the proportion of births to marriages; and the greater is the number of the born which lives to be married, the less will be the proportion of births to marriages.[25] Consequently, if within certain limits the prolificness of marriages, and the number of the born living to marry, increases at the same time, the proportion of births to marriages in the registers may still remain unaltered. And this is the reason why the registers of different countries with respect to births and marriages are often found the same under very different rates of increase.

The proportion of births to marriages, indeed, forms no criterion whatever by which to judge of the rate of increase. The population of a country may be stationary or declining with a proportion as 5 to 1, and may be increasing with some rapidity with a proportion as 4 to 1. But given the rate of increase, which may be obtained from other sources, it is clearly desirable to find in the registers a small rather than a large proportion of births to marriages; because the smaller this proportion is, the greater must be the proportion of the born which lives to marry, and of course the more healthy must be the country.

Crome[26] observes that when the marriages of a country yield less than 4 births, the population is in a very precarious state, and he estimates the prolificness of marriages by the proportion of yearly births to marriages. If this observation were just, the population of many countries of Europe would be in a precarious state, as in many countries the proportion of births to marriages in the registers is rather below than above 4 to 1. It has been shown in what manner this proportion in the registers should be corrected, in order to make it a just representation of the prolificness of marriages, and if a large part of the born live to marry, and the age of marriage be considerably

---

[25] Dr. Price himself has insisted strongly upon this, (vol. i. p. 270, 4th edit.) and yet he says, (p. 275) that healthfulness and prolificness are probably causes of increase seldom separated, and refers to registers of births and weddings as a proof of it. But though these causes may undoubtedly exist together, yet if Dr. Price's reasoning be just, such coexistence cannot possibly be inferred from the lists of births and weddings. Indeed the two countries, Sweden and France, to the registers of which he refers as showing the prolificness of their marriages, are known to be by no means remarkably healthy; and the registers of towns to which he alludes, though they may show, as he intends, a want of prolificness, yet, according to his previous reasoning, show at the same time great healthiness, and therefore ought not to be produced as a proof of the absence of both. The general fact that Dr. Price wishes to establish may still remain true, that country situations are both more healthy and more prolific than towns; but this fact certainly cannot be inferred merely from lists of births and marriages. With regard to the different countries of Europe, it will generally be found that those are the most healthy which are the least prolific, and those the most prolific which are the least healthy. The earlier age of marriage in unhealthy countries is the obvious reason of this fact.

[26] Ueber die Bevölkerung der Europais. Staat. p. 91.

earlier than the expectation of life, such a proportion in the registers is by no means inconsistent with a rapid increase. In Russia it has appeared that the proportion of births to marriages is less than 4 to 1, and yet its population increases faster than that of any other nation in Europe. In England the population increases more rapidly than in France, and yet in England the proportion of births to marriages, when allowance has been made for omissions, is about 4 to 1, in France $4\frac{4}{5}$ to 1. To occasion so rapid a progress as that which has taken place in America, it will indeed be necessary that all the causes of increase should be called into action; and if the prolificness of marriages be very great, the proportion of births to marriages will certainly be above 4 to 1; but in all ordinary cases, where the whole power of procreation has not room to expand itself, it is surely better that the actual increase should arise from that degree of healthiness in the early stages of life, which causes a great proportion of the born to live to maturity and to marry, than from a great degree of prolificness accompanied by a great mortality. And consequently in all ordinary cases a proportion of births to marriages as 4, or less than 4, to 1, cannot be considered as an unfavourable sign.

It should be observed that it does not follow that the marriages of a country are early, or that the preventive check to population does not prevail, because the greater part of the born lives to marry. In such countries as Norway and Switzerland, where half of the born live to above 40, it is evident that, though rather more than half live to marry, a large portion of the people between the ages of 20 and 40 would be living in an unmarried state, and the preventive check would appear to prevail to a great degree. In England it is probable that half of the born live to above 35,[27] and though rather more than half live to marry, the preventive check might prevail considerably (as we know it does), though not to the same extent as in Norway and Switzerland.

The preventive check is perhaps best measured by the smallness of the proportion of yearly births to the whole population. The proportion of yearly marriages to the population is only a just criterion in countries similarly circumstanced, but is incorrect where there is a difference in the prolificness of marriages, or in the proportion of the population under the age of puberty, and in the rate of increase. If all the marriages of a country, be they few or many, take place young, and be consequently prolific, it is evident that, to produce the same proportion of births, a smaller proportion of marriages will be necessary; or with the same proportion of marriages a greater proportion of births will be produced. This latter case seems to be applicable to France, where both the births and deaths are greater than in Sweden, though the

---

[27] [In 1826 (Vol. 1, p. 491) Malthus added a footnote here:
    At present (1825), and for the last ten, or even twenty years, there is reason to believe that half of the born live to 45 years.

proportion of marriages is nearly the same or rather less. And when, in two countries compared, one of them has a much greater part of its population under the age of puberty than the other, it is evident that any general proportion of the yearly marriages to the whole population will not imply the same operation of the preventive check among those of a marriageable age.

It is, in part, the small proportion of the population under the age of puberty, as well as the influx of strangers, that occasions in towns a greater proportion of marriages than in the country, although there can be little doubt that the preventive check prevails most in towns. The converse of this will also be true; and consequently in such a country as America, where half of the population is under sixteen, the proportion of yearly marriages will not accurately express how little the preventive check really operates.

But on the supposition of nearly the same natural prolificness in the women of most countries, the smallness of the proportion of births will generally indicate, with tolerable exactness, the degree in which the preventive check prevails, whether arising principally from late, and consequently unprolific marriages, or from a large proportion of the population above the age of puberty dying unmarried.

That the reader may see at once the rate of increase, and the period of doubling, which would result from any observed proportion of births to deaths, and of these to the whole population, I subjoin two tables from Sussmilch, calculated by Euler, which I believe are very correct. The first is confined to the supposition of a mortality of 1 in 36, and therefore can only be applied to countries where such a mortality is known to take place. The other is general, depending solely upon the proportion which the excess of the births above the burials bears to the whole population, and therefore may be applied universally to all countries, whatever may be the degree of their mortality.

[In 1826 (Vol. II, p. 494) Malthus continued this paragaph:
... mortality. I have now also (1825) added a third table as convenient on account of the custom of decennial enumerations in this and some other countries. It is calculated by the Rev. B. Bridge, of Peter House, Cambridge, and shows the rate of increase or period of doubling, from the observed percentage increase of any ten years, supposing such rate of increase to continue.
[For this 'Table III' see p. 17]

It will be observed that, when the proportion between the births and burials is given, the period of doubling with be shorter, the greater the mortality; because the births as well as deaths are increased by this supposition, and they both bear a greater proportion to the whole population than if the mortality were smaller, and there were a greater number of people in advanced life.

The mortality of Russia, according to Mr. Tooke, is 1 in 58, and the proportion of births 1 in 26. Allowing for the omissions in the burials, if we assume the mortality to be 1 in 52, then the births will be to the deaths as 2 to 1, and the proportion which the excess of births bears to the whole population will be $\frac{1}{52}$.[28] According to Table II the period of doubling will, in this case, be about 36 years. But if we were to keep the proportion of births to deaths as 2 to 1, and suppose a mortality of 1 in 36, as in Table I the excess of births above the burials would be $\frac{1}{36}$ of the whole population, and the period of doubling would be only 25 years.

Table I *When in any country there are* 100 000[29] *persons living, and the mortality is* 1 *in* 36

| If the proportion of deaths to births be as | Then the excess of the births will be | The proportion of the excess of the births, to the whole population, will be | And therefore the period of doubling will be |
|---|---|---|---|
| 10: 11 | 277 | $\frac{1}{360}$ | 250 years |
| 12 | 555 | $\frac{1}{180}$ | 125 |
| 13 | 833 | $\frac{1}{120}$ | $83\frac{1}{2}$ |
| 14 | 1110 | $\frac{1}{90}$ | $62\frac{3}{4}$ |
| 15 | 1388 | $\frac{1}{72}$ | $50\frac{1}{4}$ |
| 16 | 1666 | $\frac{1}{60}$ | 42 |
| 17 | 1943 | $\frac{1}{51}$ | $35\frac{3}{4}$ |
| 18 | 2221 | $\frac{1}{45}$ | $31\frac{2}{3}$ |
| 19 | 2499 | $\frac{1}{40}$ | 28 |
| 20 | 2777 | $\frac{1}{36}$ | $25\frac{3}{10}$ |
| 22 | 3332 | $\frac{1}{30}$ | $21\frac{1}{8}$ |
| 25 | 4165 | $\frac{1}{24}$ | 17 |
| 30 | 5554 | $\frac{1}{18}$ | $12\frac{4}{5}$ |

[28] The proportions here mentioned are different from those which have been taken from the additional table in Mr. Tooke's second edition; but they are assumed here as more easily and clearly illustrating the subject.

[29] [This figure was given in 1803 (see 'Table II' in chapter iv(a) of Vol. I, p. 191) and was repeated in 1806. In 1807 (Vol. I, p. 535), it was corrected to 103 000.]

## Table II *The fruitfulness of marriages*[30]

| The proportion of the excess of births above the deaths, to the whole of the living | Periods of doubling in years, and ten thousandth parts | The proportion of the excess of births above the deaths, to the whole of the living | Periods of doubling in years, and ten thousandth parts |
|---|---|---|---|
| 1: { 10 | 7.2722 | 1: { 110 | 76.5923 |
| 11 | 7.9659 | 120 | 83.5230 |
| 12 | 8.6595 | 130 | 90.4554 |
| 13 | 9.3530 | 140 | 97.3868 |
| 14 | 10.0465 | 150 | 104.3183 |
| 15 | 10.7400 | 160 | 111.2598 |
| 16 | 11.4333 | 170 | 118.1813 |
| 17 | 12.1266 | 180 | 125.1128 |
| 18 | 12.8200 | 190 | 132.0448 |
| 19 | 13.5133 | 200 | 138.9757 |
| 20 | 14.2066 | | |
| 1: { 21 | 14.9000 | 1: { 210 | 145.9072 |
| 22 | 15.5932 | 220 | 152.8387 |
| 23 | 16.2864 | 230 | 159.7702 |
| 24 | 16.9797 | 240 | 166.7017 |
| 25 | 17.6729 | 250 | 173.6332 |
| 26 | 18.3662 | 260 | 180.5647 |
| 27 | 19.0594 | 270 | 187.4961 |
| 28 | 19.7527 | 280 | 194.4275 |
| 29 | 20.4458 | 290 | 201.3590 |
| 30 | 21.1391 | 300 | 208.2905 |
| 1: { 32 | 22.5255 | 1: { 310 | 215.2220 |
| 34 | 23.9119 | 320 | 222.1535 |
| 36 | 25.2983 | 330 | 229.0850 |
| 38 | 26.6847 | 340 | 236.0164 |
| 40 | 28.0711 | 350 | 242.9479 |
| 42 | 29.4574 | 360 | 249.8794 |
| 44 | 30.8438 | 370 | 256.8109 |
| 46 | 32.2302 | 380 | 263.7425 |
| 48 | 33.6165 | 390 | 270.6740 |
| 50 | 35.0029 | 400 | 277.6055 |
| 1: { 55 | 38.4687 | 1: { 410 | 284.5370 |
| 60 | 41.9345 | 420 | 291.4685 |
| 65 | 45.4003 | 430 | 298.4000 |
| 70 | 48.8661 | 440 | 305.3314 |
| 75 | 52.3318 | 450 | 312.2629 |
| 80 | 55.7977 | 460 | 319.1943 |
| 85 | 59.2634 | 470 | 326.1258 |
| 90 | 62.7292 | 480 | 333.0573 |
| 95 | 66.1950 | 490 | 339.9888 |
| 100 | 69.6607 | 500 | 346.9202 |
| | | 1: 1000 | 693.49 |

[30] [This 'Table II' of 1806 is the same as 'Table III' of 1803. It appeared in all the editions published during Malthus's lifetime in two parts; the proportions from 1:10 to 1:30 were on one page, the proportions from 1:32 to 1:500 on the next. When this table was reproduced in the Everyman edition on a single page (Vol. I, p. 293) the first part of the table, just as it was printed, was simply stuck on top of the continuation, which must surely have puzzled the conscientious reader.]

## Table III

| I Percentage increase in ten years | II Period of doubling | I Percentage increase in ten years | II Period of doubling | I Percentage increase in ten years | II Period of doubling |
|---|---|---|---|---|---|
|  | Years. |  | Years. |  | Years. |
| 1 | 696.60 | 16 | 46.70 | 30.5 | 26.03 |
| 1.5 | 465.55 | 16.5 | 45.38 | 31 | 25.67 |
| 2 | 350.02 | 17 | 44.14 | 31.5 | 25.31 |
| 2.5 | 280.70 | 17.5 | 42.98 | 32 | 24.96 |
| 3 | 234.49 | 18 | 41.87 | 32.5 | 24.63 |
| 3.5 | 201.48 | 18.5 | 40.83 | 33 | 24.30 |
| 4 | 176.73 | 19 | 39.84 | 33.5 | 23.99 |
| 4.5 | 157.47 | 19.5 | 38.91 | 34 | 23.68 |
| 5 | 142.06 | 20 | 38.01 | 34.5 | 23.38 |
| 5.5 | 129.46 |  |  | 35 | 23.09 |
| 6 | 118.95 | 20.5 | 37.17 | 35.5 | 22.81 |
| 6.5 | 110.06 | 21 | 36.36 | 36 | 22.54 |
| 7 | 102.44 | 21.5 | 35.59 | 36.5 | 22.27 |
| 7.5 | 95.84 | 22 | 34.85 | 37 | 22.01 |
| 8 | 90.06 | 22.5 | 34.15 | 37.5 | 21.76 |
| 8.5 | 84.96 | 23 | 33.48 | 38 | 21.52 |
| 9 | 80.43 | 23.5 | 32.83 | 38.5 | 21.28 |
| 9.5 | 76.37 | 24 | 32.22 | 39 | 21.04 |
| 10 | 72.72 | 24.5 | 31.63 | 39.5 | 20.82 |
|  |  | 25 | 31.06 | 40 | 20.61 |
| 10.5 | 69.42 | 25.5 | 30.51 |  |  |
| 11 | 66.41 | 26 | 29.99 | 41 | 20.17 |
| 11.5 | 63.67 | 26.5 | 29.48 | 42 | 19.76 |
| 12 | 61.12 | 27 | 28.99 | 43 | 19.37 |
| 12.5 | 58.06 | 27.5 | 28.53 | 44 | 19.00 |
| 13 | 56.71 | 28 | 28.07 | 45 | 18.65 |
| 13.5 | 54.73 | 28.5 | 27.65 | 46 | 18.31 |
| 14 | 52.90 | 29 | 27.22 | 47 | 17.99 |
| 14.5 | 51.19 | 29.5 | 26.81 | 48 | 17.68 |
| 15 | 49.59 | 30 | 26.41 | 49 | 17.38 |
| 15.5 | 48.10 |  |  | 50 | 17.06 |

# BOOK II

## CHAPTER VI(b)

## *Effects of Epidemics on Registers of Births, Deaths, and Marriages*[1]

[The new matter in 1806 began on p. 40 of Vol. II. The last sentence on p. 39 (p. 208 of Vol. I in this edition) read thus:

... But the number of annual births is not very different during the whole period, though in this time the population had more than doubled itself; and therefore the *proportion* of births to the whole population, at first and at last, must have changed in an extraordinary degree.

It will appear therefore how liable we should be to err in assuming a given proportion of births for the purpose of estimating the past population of any country. In the present instance, it would have led to the conclusion that the population was scarcely diminished by the plague, although from the number of deaths it was known to be diminished one third.

Variations of the same kind, though not in the same degree, appear in the proportions of births, deaths, and marriages, in all the tables which Sussmilch has collected; and as writers on these subjects have been too apt to form calculations for past and future times from the proportions of a few years, it may be useful to draw the attention of the reader to a few more instances of such variations.

In the churmark of Brandenburgh,[2] during 15 years ending with 1712, the proportion of births to deaths was nearly 17 to 10. For 6 years, ending with 1718, the proportion sunk to 13 to 10; for 4 years, ending with 1752, it was only 11 to 10, and for 4 years ending with 1756, 12 to 10. For 3 years ending

---

[1] [This is the revised version of the latter part of chapter vi(a) of Book II of the quarto, there called 'Effects of Epidemics on Tables of Mortality': see in this edition Vol. I, pp. 203–14. 'Table IV' in the quarto became 'Table III' in 1806. Also in 1806 this chapter, like that 'On the Prolificness of Marriages', was placed much later on in Book II, following all the accounts of the checks to population 'in the different States of Modern Europe'. In 1806 and 1807 'Effects of Epidemics' was chapter x; in 1817 and 1826 it became chapter xii.]

[2] Sussmilch's Gottliche Ordnung, vol. i. Tables, p. 88.

with 1759, the deaths very greatly exceeded the births. The proportion of the births to the whole population is not given; but it is not probable that the great variations observable in the proportion of births to deaths should have arisen solely from the variations in the deaths. The proportion of births to marriages is tolerably uniform, the extremes being only 38 to 10, and 35 to 10, and the mean about 37 to 10. In this table no very great epidemics occur till the 3 years beginning with 1757, and beyond this period the lists are not continued.

In the dukedom of Pomerania,[3] the average proportion of births to deaths for 60 years, from 1694 to 1756, both included, was 138 to 100; but in some of the periods of six years it was as high as 177 to 100, and 155 to 100. In others it sunk as low as 124 to 100 and 130 to 100. The extremes of the proportions of births to marriages in the different periods of 5 and 6 years were 36 to 10 and 43 to 10, and the mean of the 60 years about 38 to 10. Epidemic years appear to have occurred occasionally, in three of which the deaths exceeded the births; but this temporary diminution of population produced no corresponding diminution of births; and the two individual years which contain the greatest proportion of marriages, in the whole table, occur one the year after, and the other two years after epidemics. The excess of deaths however was not great till the 3 years ending with 1759, with which the table concludes.

In the neumark of Brandenburgh,[4] for 60 years from 1695 to 1756, both included, the average proportion of births to deaths in the first 30 years was 148 to 100, in the last 30 years 127 to 100, in the whole 60 years 136 to 100. In some periods of 5 years it was as high as 171 and 167 to 100. In others as low as 118 and 128 to 100. For 5 years ending with 1726, the yearly average of births was 7012; for 5 years ending with 1746 it was 6927; from which, judging by the births, we might infer that the population had decreased in this interval of 20 years; but it appears, from the average proportion of births and deaths during this period, that it must have considerably increased, notwithstanding the intervention of some epidemic years. The proportion of births to the whole population must therefore have decidedly changed. Another interval of 20 years in the same table gives a similar result, both with regard to the births and the marriages. The extremes of the proportions of births to marriages are 34 to 10, and 42 to 10, and the mean about 38 to 10. The 3 years beginning with 1757 were, as in the other tables, very fatal years.

In the dukedom of Magdeburgh,[5] during 64 years ending with 1756, the average proportion of births to deaths was 123 to 100; in the first 28 years of the period 142 to 100, and in the last 34 years only 112 to 100; during one period of 5 years it was as high as 170 to 100, and in two periods the deaths

---

[3] Sussmilch, vol. i. tables, p. 91.    [4] Id. Gottliche Ordnung, vol. i. tables, p. 99.
[5] Id. vol. i. tables, p. 103.

exceeded the births. Slight epidemics appear to be interspersed rather thickly throughout the table. In the two instances where three or four occur in successive years, and diminish the population, they are followed by an increase of marriages and births. The extremes of the proportions of births to marriages are 42 to 10, and 34 to 10, and the mean of the 64 years 39 to 10. On this table Sussmilch remarks, that though the average number of deaths shows an increased population of one third from 1715 or 1720, yet the births and marriages would prove it to be stationary or even declining. In drawing this conclusion, however, he adds the three epidemic years ending with 1759, during which both the marriages and births seem to have diminished.

In the principality of Halberstadt,[5] the average proportion of births to deaths for 68 years, ending with 1756, was 124 to 100; but in some periods of 5 years it was as high as 160 to 100, and in others as low as 110 to 100. The increase in the whole 68 years was considerable, and yet for 5 years, ending with 1723, the average number of births was 2818; and for 4 years ending with 1750, 2628, from which it would appear that the population in 27 years had considerably diminished. A similar appearance occurs with regard to the marriages, during a period of 32 years. In the 5 years ending with 1718, they were 727; in the 5 years ending with 1750, 689. During both these periods the proportion of deaths would have shown a considerable increase. Epidemics seem to have occurred frequently; and in almost all the instances in which they were such as for the deaths to exceed the births, they were immediately succeeded by a more than usual proportion of marriages, and in a few years by an increased proportion of births. The greatest number of marriages in the whole table occurs in the year 1751, after an epidemic in the year 1750, in which the deaths had exceeded the births above one third, and the four or five following years contain the largest proportion of births. The extremes of the proportions of births to marriages are 42 to 10, and 34 to 10, the mean of the 68 years 38 to 10.

The remaining tables contain similar results; but these will be sufficient to show the variations which are continually occurring in the proportions of the births and marriages, as well as of the deaths, to the whole population.

It will be observed that the least variable of the proportions is that which the births and marriages bear to each other; and the obvious reason is, that this proportion nearly expresses the prolificness of marriages, which will not of course be subject to great changes. We can hardly indeed suppose that the prolificness of marriages should vary so much as the extremes which have been mentioned.[7] Nor is it necessary that it should, as another cause will

---

[6] Sussmilch, vol. i. Tables, p. 108.
[7] [In 1807 (Vol. I, p. 551) this was changed to:
. . . vary so much as the different proportions of births to marriages in the tables.

contribute to produce the same effect. The births which are contemporary with the marriages of any particular year belong principally to marriages which had taken place some years before; and therefore, if for four or five years a large proportion of marriages were to take place, and then accidentally for one or two years a small proportion, the effect would be a large proportion of births to marriages in the registers during these one or two years; and on the contrary, if for four or five years few marriages comparatively were to take place, and then for one or two years a great number, the effect would be a small proportion of births to marriages in the registers. This was strikingly illustrated in the table for Prussia and Lithuania, and would be confirmed by an inspection of all the other tables collected by Sussmilch; in which it appears that the extreme proportions of births to marriages are generally more affected by the number of marriages than the number of births, and consequently arise more from the variations in the disposition or encouragement to matrimony, than from the variations in the prolificness of marriages.

The common epidemical years that are interspersed throughout these tables will not, of course, have the same effects on the marriages and births as the great plague in the table for Prussia; but in proportion to their magnitude, their operation will in general be found to be similar. From the registers of many other countries, and particularly of towns, it appears that the visitations of the plague were frequent at the latter end of the 17th and the beginning of the 18th centuries ...

[The final paragraph of this revised chapter is not reprinted here, as it is the same as that of 1803: see in this edition Vol. i, pp. 213–14.]

# BOOK III

## CHAPTER A

# *Of the Agricultural System*[1]

As it is the nature of agriculture to produce subsistence for a greater number of families than can be employed in the business of cultivation, it might perhaps be supposed that a nation which strictly pursued an agricultural system would always have more food than was necessary for its inhabitants, and that its population could never be checked from the want of the means of subsistence.

It is indeed obviously true that the increase of such a country is not immediately checked, either by the want of power to produce, or even by the deficiency of the actual produce of the soil compared with the population. Yet if we examine the condition of its labouring classes, we shall find that the real wages of their labour are such as essentially to check and regulate their increase, by checking and regulating their command over the means of subsistence.

A country under certain circumstances of soil and situation, and with a deficient capital, may find it advantageous to purchase foreign commodities with its raw produce rather than manufacture them at home: and in this case it will necessarily grow more raw produce than it consumes. But this state of things is very little connected either with the permanent condition of the lower classes of the society or the rate of their increase; and in a country where the agricultural system entirely predominates, and the general mass of its industry is directed towards the land, the condition of the people is subject to almost every degree of variation.

Under the agricultural system perhaps are to be found the two extremes in the condition of the poor; instances where they are in the best state, and instances where they are in the worst state of any of which we have accounts.

In a country where there is an abundance of good land, where there are no difficulties in the way of its purchase and distribution, and where there is an

---

[1] [The six chapters here designated A–F replaced in 1817 the four chapters in Book III which were numbered vii–x in previous editions; in 1817 and 1826 these six re-written chapters were numbered viii–xiii.]

easy foreign vent for raw produce, both the profits of stock and the wages of labour will be high. These high profits and high wages, if habits of economy pretty generally prevail, will furnish the means of a rapid accumulation of capital and a great and continued demand for labour, while the rapid increase of population which will ensue will maintain undiminished the demand for produce, and check the fall of profits. If the extent of territory be considerable, and the population comparatively inconsiderable, the land may remain understocked both with capital and people for some length of time, notwithstanding a rapid increase of both; and it is under these circumstances of the agricultural system that labour is able to command the greatest portion of the necessaries of life, and that the condition of the labouring classes of society is the best.

The only drawback to the wealth of the labouring classes under these circumstances is the relatively low value of the raw produce.

If a considerable part of the manufactured commodities used in such a country be purchased by the export of its raw produce, it follows as a necessary consequence that the relative value of its raw produce will be lower, and of its manufactured produce higher, than in the countries with which such a trade is carried on. But where a given portion of raw produce will not command so much of manufactured and foreign commodities as in other countries, the condition of the labourer cannot be exactly measured by the quantity of raw produce which falls to his share. If, for instance, in one country the yearly earnings of a labourer amount in money value to fifteen quarters of wheat, and in another to nine, it would be incorrect to infer that their relative condition, and the comforts which they enjoy, were in the same proportion, because the whole of a labourer's earnings are not spent in food; and if that part which is not so spent will, in the country where the value of fifteen quarters is earned, not go near so far in the purchase of clothes and other conveniences as in the countries where the value of nine quarters is earned, it is clear that altogether the situation of the labourer in the latter country may approach nearer to that of the labourer in the former than might at first be supposed.

At the same time it should be recollected that *quantity* always tends powerfully to counterbalance any deficiency of value; and the labourer who earns the greatest number of quarters may still command the greatest quantity of necessaries and conveniences combined, though not to the extent implied by the proportions of the raw produce.

America affords a practical instance of the agricultural system in a state the most favourable to the condition of the labouring classes. [2] The nature of the country has been such as to make it answer to employ a very large proportion of its capital in agriculture; and the consequence has been a very rapid increase of stock. This rapid increase of stock has kept up a steady and continued demand for labour.●² The labouring classes have in consequence been peculiarly well paid. They have been able to command an unusual quantity of the necessaries of life, and the progress of population has been unusually rapid.

Yet even here, some little drawback has been felt from the relative cheapness of corn. As America till the late war imported the greatest part of its manufactures from England, and as England imported flour and wheat from America, the value of food in America compared with manufactures must have been decidedly less than in England. Nor would this effect take place merely with relation to the foreign commodities imported into America, but also to those of its home manufactures, in which it has no particular advantage. In agriculture, the abundance of good land would counterbalance the high wages of labour and high profits of stock, and keep the price of corn moderate, notwithstanding the great expense of these two elements of price. But in the production of manufactured commodities they must necessarily tell, without any particular advantage to counterbalance them, and must in general occasion in home goods, as well as foreign, a high price compared with food.

Under these circumstances, the condition of the labouring classes of society cannot in point of conveniences and comforts be so much better than that of the labourers of other countries as the relative quantity of food which they earn might seem to indicate; and this conclusion is sufficiently confirmed by experience. In some very intelligent Travels through a great part of England, written in 1810 and 1811 by Mr. Simond, a French gentleman, who had resided above twenty years in America, the author seems to have been evidently much struck with the air of convenience and comfort in the houses of our peasantry, and the neatness and cleanliness of their dress. In some parts of his tour he saw so many neat cottages, so much good clothing, and so little appearance of poverty and distress, that he could not help wondering where the poor of England and their dwellings were concealed. These observations, coming from an able, accurate and apparently most impartial observer, just landed from America and visiting England for the first time, are curious and instructive; and the facts which they notice, though they may arise in part from the different habits and modes of life prevailing in the two countries, must be occasioned in a considerable degree by the causes above mentioned.

---

² [In 1826 (Vol. II, p. 121) this passage was altered:

The nature of the country is such as to make it answer to employ a very large proportion of its capital in agriculture; and the consequence has been a very rapid increase of it. This rapid increase both of the quantity and value of capital has kept up a steady and continued demand for labour.

A very striking instance of the disadvantageous effect of a low relative price of food on the consumption of the poor may be observed in Ireland. ³●In Ireland the funds for the maintenance of labour have increased so rapidly during the last century, and so large a portion of that sort of food which forms the principal support of the lower classes of society has been awarded to them, that the increase of population has been more rapid that in almost any known country,●³ except America. The Irish labourer paid in potatoes has earned perhaps the means of subsistence for double the number of persons that could be supported by the earnings of an English labourer paid in wheat; and the increase of population in the two countries during the last century has been nearly in proportion to the relative quantity of the customary food awarded to the labourers in each. But their general condition with respect to conveniences and comforts are very far indeed from being in a similar proportion. The great quantity of food which land will bear when planted with potatoes, and the consequent cheapness of the labour supported by them, tends rather to raise than to lower the rents of land, and as far as rent goes, to keep up the price of the materials of manufactures and all other sorts of raw produce, except potatoes. ⁴●In the raw materials of home manufactures, therefore, a great relative disadvantage will be suffered, and a still greater both in the raw and manufactured produce of foreign countries. The exchangeable value of the food which the Irish labourer earns,●⁴ above what he and his family consume, will go but a very little way in the purchase of clothing, lodging and other conveniences; and the consequence is that his condition in these respects is extremely miserable, at the same time that his means of subsistence, such as they are, may be comparatively abundant.

In Ireland the money price of labour is not much more than the half of what it is in England. The quantity of food earned by no means makes up for its deficient value.⁵ A certain portion, therefore, of the Irish labourer's wages (a fourth or a fifth for instance) will go but a very little way in the purchase of

---

³ [In 1826 (Vol. II, p. 123) this sentence was changed:

The food of Ireland has increased so rapidly during the last century, and so large a portion of that which forms the principal support of the lower classes of society has been obtained by them, that the increase of population has been more rapid than in almost any known country ...

⁴ [In 1826 (Vol. II, pp. 123–4) this passage was altered:

The indolence and want of skill which usually accompany such a state of things tend further to render all wrought commodities comparatively dear. In home manufactures, therefore, a great relative disadvantage will be suffered, and a still greater both in the raw and manufactured produce of foreign countries. The value of the food which the Irish labourer earns ...

⁵ [In 1826 (Vol. II, p. 124) *deficient value* was changed to:

... very low price.

manufactures and foreign produce. In America,[6] on the other hand, even the money wages of labour are nearly double those of England. Though the American labourer, therefore, cannot purchase manufactures and foreign produce with the food that he earns so cheap as the English labourer, yet the greater quantity of this food makes up for its deficiency of relative value.[7] His condition, compared with the labouring classes of England, though it may not be so much superior as their relative means of subsistence might indicate, must still on the whole have decidedly the advantage; and altogether, perhaps, America[8] may be produced as an instance of the agricultural system in which the condition of the labouring classes is the best of any that we know.

The instances where, under the agricultural system, the condition of the lower classes of society is very wretched, are more frequent. When the accumulation of capital stops, whatever may be the cause, the population, before it comes to a stand, will always be pressed on as near to the limits of the actual means of subsistence as the habits of the lower classes of the society will allow; that is, the real wages of labour will sink till they are only just sufficient to maintain a stationary population. Should this happen, as it frequently does, while land is still in abundance and capital scarce, the profits of stock will naturally be high; but corn will be very cheap, owing to the goodness and plenty of the land, and the stationary demand for it, notwithstanding the high profits of stock; while these high profits, together with the usual want of skill and proper division of labour, which attend a scanty capital,[9] will render all domestic manufactured commodities comparatively very dear. This state of things will naturally be unfavourable to the generation of those habits of prudential restraint which most frequently arise· from the custom of enjoying conveniences and comforts, and it is to be expected that the population will not stop till the wages of labour, estimated even in food, are very low. But in a country where the wages of labour estimated in food are low, and that food is relatively of a very low value, both with regard to domestic and foreign manufactures, the condition of the labouring classes of society must be the worst possible.

Poland, and some parts of Russia, Siberia and European Turkey, afford instances of this kind. In Poland the population seems to be almost stationary

---

6 [In 1826 (Vol. II, p. 124) 'the United States' was substituted for *America*.]

7 [In 1826 (Vol. II, p. 124) this sentence was altered:

... English labourer, yet the greater quantity of this food more than makes up for its lower price.

8 [In 1826 (Vol. II, p. 125) *America* was again changed to 'the United States'.]

9 [In 1826 (Vol. II, p. 125) this was altered to:

... while these high profits, together with the want of skill and proper division of labour, which usually attend a scanty capital ...

or very slowly progressive; and as both the population and produce are scanty, compared with the extent of territory, we may infer with certainty that its capital is scanty, and yet slowly progressive. It follows, therefore, that the demand for labour increases very slowly, and that the real wages of labour, or the command of the labouring classes over the necessaries and conveniences of life, are such as to keep the population down to the level of the slowly increasing quantity that is awarded to them. And as from the state of the country the peasantry cannot have been much accustomed to conveniences and comforts, the checks to its population are more likely to be of the positive than of the preventive kind.

Yet here corn is in abundance, and great quantities of it are yearly exported. [10]●But it appears clearly that it is not either the power of the country to produce food, or even what it actually produces, that limits and regulates the progress of population, but the quantity which in the actual state of things is awarded to the labourer, and the rate at which the funds so appropriated increase.●[10]

In the present case the demand for labour is very small; and though the population is inconsiderable, it is greater than the scanty capital of the country can fully employ; the condition of the labourer therefore is depressed by his being able to command only such a quantity of food as will maintain a stationary or very slowly increasing population. It is further depressed by the low relative value of the food that he earns, which gives to any surplus he may possess a very small power in the purchase of manufactured commodities or foreign produce.

Under these circumstances, we cannot be surprised that all accounts of Poland should represent the condition of the lower classes of society as extremely miserable; and the other parts of Europe, which resemble Poland in the state of their land and capital, resemble it in the condition of their people.

In justice, however, to the agricultural system, it should be observed that the premature check to the capital and the demand for labour, which occurs in some of the countries of Europe, while land continues in considerable plenty, is not occasioned by the particular direction of their industry, but by the vices of the government and the structure of the society, which prevent its full and fair development in that direction.

Poland is continually brought forward as an example of the miserable

---

[10] [In 1826 (Vol. II, p. 126) this sentence was re-written:

Hence it appears that it is not either the power of the country to produce food, or even what it actually produces, that limits and regulates the progress of population, but the quantity and value of the food which in the actual state of things is awarded to the labourer, and the rate at which these funds appropriated increase.

effects of the agricultural system. But nothing surely can be less fair. The misery of Poland does not arise from its directing its industry chiefly to agriculture, but from the little encouragement given to industry of any kind, owing to the state of property and the servile condition of the people. While the land is cultivated by boors, the produce of whose exertions belongs entirely to their masters, and the whole society consists mainly of these degraded beings and the lords and owners of great tracts of territory, there will evidently be no class of persons possessed of the means either of furnishing an adequate demand at home for the surplus produce of the soil, or of accumulating fresh capital and increasing the demand for labour. In this miserable state of things, the best remedy would unquestionably be the introduction of manufactures and commerce; because the introduction of manufactures and commerce could alone liberate the mass of the people from slavery and give the necessary stimulus to industry and accumulation. But were the people already free and industrious, and landed property easily divisible and alienable, it might still answer to such a country as Poland to purchase its finer manufactures from foreign countries by means of its raw products, and thus to continue agricultural for many years. Under these new circumstances, however, it would present a totally different picture from that which it exhibits at present; and the condition of the people would more resemble that of the inhabitants of the United States of America than of the inhabitants of the unimproved countries of Europe.

Indeed America is perhaps the only modern instance of the fair operation of the agricultural system. In every country of Europe, and in most of its colonies in other parts of the world, formidable obstacles still exist to the employment of capital upon the land, arising from the remains of the feudal system. But these obstacles, which have essentially impeded cultivation, have been very far indeed from proportionably encouraging other branches of industry. Commerce and manufactures are necessary to agriculture; but agriculture is still more necessary to commerce and manufactures. It must ever be true that the surplus produce of the cultivators, taken in its most enlarged sense, measures and limits the growth of that part of the society which is not employed upon the land. Throughout the whole world the number of manufacturers, of merchants, of proprietors and of persons engaged in the various civil and military professions, must be exactly proportioned to this surplus produce, and cannot in the nature of things increase beyond it.

If the earth had been so niggardly of her produce as to oblige all her inhabitants to labour for it, no manufacturers or idle persons could ever have existed. But her first intercourse with man was a voluntary present, not very large indeed, but sufficient as a fund for his subsistence till he could procure a greater. And the power to procure a greater was given to him in that quality of the earth by which it may be made to yield a much larger quantity of food, and of the materials of clothing and lodging, than is necessary to feed, clothe and lodge the persons employed in the cultivation of the soil. This quality is the foundation of that surplus produce which peculiarly distinguishes the industry employed upon the land. In proportion as the labour and ingenuity of man exercised upon the land have increased this surplus produce, leisure has been given to a greater number of persons to employ themselves in all the inventions which embellish civilized life; while the desire to profit by these inventions has continued to stimulate the cultivators to increase their surplus produce. This desire indeed may be considered as almost absolutely necessary to give it its proper value, and to encourage its further extension; but still the order of precedence is, strictly speaking, the surplus produce; because the funds for the subsistence of the manufacturer must be advanced to him before he can complete his work; and no step can be taken in any other sort of industry unless the cultivators obtain from the soil more than they themselves consume.

If in asserting the peculiar productiveness of the labour employed upon the land, we look only to the clear moneyed rent yielded to a certain number of proprietors, we undoubtedly consider the subject in a very contracted point of view. In the advanced stages of society, this rent forms indeed the most prominent portion of the surplus produce here meant; but it may exist equally in the shape of high wages and profits during the earlier periods of cultivation, when there is little or no rent. The labourer who earns a value equal to fifteen[11] quarters of corn in the year may have only a family of three or four children, and not consume in kind above five or six quarters; and the owner of the farming stock, which yields high profits, may consume but a very moderate proportion of them in food and raw materials. All the rest, whether in the shape of wages and profits, or of rents, may be considered as a surplus produce from the soil, which affords the means of subsistence and the materials of clothing and lodging to a certain number of people according to its extent, some of whom may live without manual exertions, and others employ themselves in modifying the raw materials obtained from the earth into the forms best suited to the gratification of man.[12]

It will depend of course entirely upon its answering to a country to exchange a part of the surplus produce for foreign commodities, instead of consuming it at home, whether it is to be considered as mainly agricultural or otherwise. And such an exchange of raw produce for manufactures, or peculiar foreign products, may for a period of some extent suit a state which

---

[11] [In 1826 (Vol. II, p. 131) Malthus altered this to:
    ... fifteen or twenty quarters of corn in the year ...
[12] [Malthus repeats this in chapter C, n.2.]

might resemble Poland in scarcely any other feature but that of exporting corn.

It appears, then, that countries in which the industry of the inhabitants is principally directed towards the land, and in which corn continues to be exported, may enjoy great abundance or experience great want, according to the particular circumstances in which they are placed. They will in general not be much exposed to the temporary evils of scarcity arising from the variations of the seasons; but the quantity of food permanently awarded to the labourer may be such as not to allow of an increase of population; and their state, in respect to their being progressive, stationary or declining, will depend upon other causes than that of directing their attention principally to agriculture.

# CHAPTER B

## *Of the Commercial System*

A country which excels in commerce and manufactures may purchase corn from a great variety of others; and it may be supposed perhaps that, proceeding upon this system, it may continue to purchase an increasing quantity, and to maintain a rapidly increasing population, till the lands of all the nations with which it trades are fully cultivated. As this is an event necessarily at a great distance, it may appear that the population of such a country will not be checked from the difficulty of procuring subsistence till after the lapse of a great number of ages.

There are, however, causes constantly in operation, which will occasion the pressure of this difficulty long before the event here contemplated has taken place, and while the means of raising food in the surrounding countries may still be comparatively abundant.

In the first place, advantages which depend exclusively upon capital and skill, and the present possession of particular channels of commerce, cannot in their nature be permanent. We know how difficult it is to confine improvements in machinery to a single spot; we know that it is the constant object, both of individuals and countries, to increase their capital; and we know, from the past history of commercial states, that the channels of trade are not unfrequently taking a different direction. It is unreasonable therefore to expect that any one country, merely by the force of skill and capital, should remain in possession of markets uninterrupted by foreign competition. But, when a powerful foreign competition takes place, the exportable commodities of the country in question must soon fall to prices which will essentially reduce profits; and the fall of profits will diminish both the power and the will to save. Under these circumstances the accumulation of capital will be slow, and the demand for labour proportionably slow, till it comes nearly to a stand; while perhaps the new competitors, either by raising their own raw materials or by some other advantages, may still be increasing their capitals and population with some degree of rapidity.

But secondly, even if it were possible for a considerable time to exclude any formidable foreign competition, it is found that domestic competition produces almost unavoidably the same effects. If a machine be invented in a particular country, by the aid of which one man can do the work of ten, the.

possessors of it will of course at first make very unusual profits; but as soon as the invention is generally known, so much capital and industry will be brought into this new and profitable employment as to make its products greatly exceed both the foreign and domestic demand at the old prices. These prices, therefore, will continue to fall, till the stock and labour employed in this direction cease to yield unusual profits. In this case it is evident that, though in an early period of such a manufacture, the product of the industry of one man for a day might have been exchanged for such a portion of food as would support forty or fifty persons; yet, at a subsequent period, the product of the same industry might not purchase the support of ten.

In the cotton trade of this country, which has extended itself so wonderfully during the last twenty-five years, very little effect has hitherto been produced by foreign competition.[1] The very great fall which has taken place in the prices of cotton goods has been almost exclusively owing to domestic competition; and this competition has so glutted both the home and foreign markets, that the present capitals employed in the trade, notwithstanding the very peculiar advantages which they possess from the saving of labour, have ceased to possess any advantage whatever in the general rate of their profits. Although, by means of the admirable machinery used in the spinning of cotton, one boy or girl can now do as much as many grown persons could do formerly; yet neither the wages of the labourer, nor the profits of his master, are higher than in those employments where no machinery is used, and no saving of labour accomplished.

The country has, however, in the mean time, been very greatly benefited. Not only have all its inhabitants been enabled to obtain a superior fabric for clothing, at a less expense of labour and property, which must be considered as a great and permanent advantage; but the high temporary profits of the trade have occasioned a great accumulation of capital, and consequently a great demand for labour; while the extending markets abroad and the new values thrown into the market at home, have created such a demand for the products of every species of industry, agricultural and colonial, as well as commercial and manufacturing, as to prevent a fall of profits.

This country, from the extent of its lands, and its rich colonial possessions, has a large *arena* for the employment of an increasing capital; and the general rate of its profits are not, as it appears, very easily and rapidly reduced by accumulation. But a country, such as we are considering, engaged principally in manufactures, and unable to direct its industry to the same variety of pursuits, would sooner find its rate of profits diminished by an increase of

---

[1] 1816.

capital, and no ingenuity in machinery[2] could save it, after a certain period, from low profits and low wages, and their natural consequences, a check to population.

Thirdly, a country which is obliged to purchase both the raw materials of its manufactures, and the means of subsistence for its population, from foreign countries, is almost entirely dependent for the increase of its wealth and population on the increasing wealth and demands of the countries with which it trades.

It has been sometimes said that a manufacturing country is no more dependent upon the country which supplies it with food and raw materials, than the agricultural country is on that which manufactures for it; but this is really an abuse of terms. A country with great resources in land may find it decidedly for its advantage to employ the main part of its capital in cultivation and to import its manufactures. In so doing, it will often employ the whole of its industry most productively, and most rapidly increase its stock. But, if the slackness of its neighbours in manufacturing, or any other case, should either considerably check or altogether prevent the importation of manufactures, a country with food and raw materials provided at home cannot be long at a loss. For a time it would not certainly be so well supplied; but manufacturers and artisans would soon be found, and would soon acquire tolerable skill;[3] and though the capital and population of the country might not, under the new circumstances in which it was placed, increase so rapidly as before, it would still have the power of increasing in both to a great and almost undefinable extent.[4]

On the other hand, if food and raw materials were denied to a nation merely manufacturing, it is obvious that it could not longer exist. But not only does the absolute existence of such a nation, on an extreme supposition, depend upon its foreign commerce, but its progress in wealth must be almost entirely measured by the progress and demand of the countries which deal with it. However skilful, industrious and saving such a nation might be, if its customers, from indolence and want of accumulation, would not or could not take off a yearly increasing value of its commodities, the effects of its skill and machinery would be but of very short duration.

That the cheapness of manufactured commodities, occasioned by skill and machinery in one country, is calculated to encourage an increase of raw produce in others, no person can doubt; but we know at the same time that high profits may continue for a considerable period in an indolent and

---

[2] [In 1826 (Vol. II, p. 136) a clause was inserted here:
    ... no ingenuity in machinery which was not continually progressive could save it ...
[3] This has been fully exemplified in America (1816).
[4] [In 1826 (Vol. II, p. 137) the words *and almost undefinable* were deleted.]

ill-governed state, without producing an increase of wealth; yet, unless such an increase of wealth and demand were produced in the surrounding countries, the increasing ingenuity and exertions of the manufacturing and commercial state would be lost in continually falling prices. It would not only be obliged, as its skill and capital increased, to give a larger quantity of manufactured produce for the raw produce which it received in return; but it might be unable, even with the temptation of reduced prices, to stimulate its customers to such purchases as would allow of an increasing importation of food and raw materials; and without such an increasing importation, it is quite obvious that the population must become stationary.

It would come to the same thing, whether this inability to obtain an increasing quantity of food were occasioned by the advancing money price of corn or the falling money price of manufactures. In either case the effect would be the same; and it is certain that this effect might take place in either way, from increasing competition and accumulation in the manufacturing nation, and the want of them in the agricultural, long before any essential increase of difficulty had occurred in the production of corn.

Fourthly. A nation which is obliged to purchase from others nearly the whole of its raw materials, and the means of its subsistence, is not only dependent entirely upon the demands of its customers, as they may be variously affected by indolence, industry or caprice, but it is subjected to a necessary and unavoidable diminution of demand in the natural progress of these countries towards that proportion of skill and capital which they may reasonably be expected after a certain time to possess. It is generally an accidental and temporary, not a natural and permanent division of labour, which constitutes one state the manufacturer and the carrier of others. While in these landed nations agricultural profits continue very high, it may fully answer to them to pay others as their manufacturers and carriers; but when the profits on land fall, or the tenures on which it can be held are not such as to encourage the investment of an accumulating capital, the owner of this capital will naturally look towards commerce and manufactures for its employment; and, according to the just reasoning of Adam Smith and the Economists,[5] finding at home both the materials of manufactures, the means of subsistence, and the power of carrying on their own trade with foreign countries, they will probably be able to conduct the business of manufacturing and carrying for themselves at a cheaper rate than if they allowed it to continue in the hands of others. As long as the agricultural nations continued to apply their increasing capital principally to the land, this increase of capital would be of the greatest possible advantage to the manufacturing and

---

[5] [Malthus here means the French *Economistes* or *Physiocrates*: see DUPONT in the Alphabetical List.]

commercial nation. It would be indeed the main cause and great regulator of its progress in wealth and population. But after they had turned their attention to manufactures and commerce, their further increase of capital would be the signal of decay and destruction to the manufactures and commerce which they had before supported. And thus, in the natural progress of national improvement, and without the competition of superior skill and capital, a purely commercial state must be undersold and driven out of the markets by those who possess the advantage of land.

In the distribution of wealth during the progress of improvement, the interests of an independent state are essentially different from those of a province, a point which has not been sufficiently attended to.[6] If agricultural capital increases and agricultural profits diminish in Sussex, the overflowing stock will go to London, Manchester, Liverpool, or some other place where it can probably be engaged in manufactures or commerce more advantageously than at home. But if Sussex were an independent kingdom, this could not take place; and the corn which is now sent to London must be withdrawn to support manufacturers and traders living within its confines. If England, therefore, had continued to be separated into the seven kingdoms of the Heptarchy, London could not possibly have been what it is; and that distribution of wealth and population which takes place at present, and which we may fairly presume is the most beneficial to the whole of the realm, would have been essentially changed, if the object had been to accumulate the greatest quantity of wealth and population in particular districts instead of the whole island. But at all times the interest of each independent state is to accumulate the greatest quantity of wealth within its limits. Consequently, the interest of an independent state, with regard to the countries with which it trades, can rarely be the same as the interest of a province with regard to the empire to which it belongs; and the accumulation of capital which would occasion the withdrawing of the exports of corn in the one case, would leave them perfectly undisturbed in the other.

If, from the operation of one or more of the causes above enumerated, the importation of corn into a manufacturing and commercial country should be essentially checked, and should either actually decrease, or be prevented from increasing, it is quite evident that its population must be checked nearly in the same proportion.

Venice presents a striking instance of a commercial state at once stopped

---

[6] [In 1826 (Vol. II, pp. 140–1) this sentence was altered:

In the distribution of wealth during the progress of improvement, the interests of an independent state in relation to others are essentially different from those of a particular province, in relation to the kingdom to which it belongs, a point which has not been sufficiently attended to.

in its progress to wealth and population by foreign competition. The discovery made by the Portuguese of a passage to India by the Cape of Good Hope completely turned the channel of the Indian trade. The high profits of the Venetians, which had been the foundation of their rapidly increasing wealth and of their extraordinary preponderance as a naval and commercial power, were not only suddenly reduced; but the trade itself, on which these high profits had been made, was almost annihilated, and their power and wealth were shortly contracted to those more confined limits which suited their natural resources.

In the middle of the 15th century, Bruges in Flanders was the great *entrepôt* of the trade between the north and the south of Europe. Early in the 16th century its commerce began to decline under the competition of Antwerp. Many English and foreign merchants in consequence left the declining city, to settle in that which was rapidly increasing in commerce and wealth. About the middle of the 16th century Antwerp was at the zenith of its power. It contained above a hundred thousand inhabitants, and was universally allowed to be the most illustrious mercantile city, and to carry on the most extensive and richest commerce of any in the north of Europe.

The rising greatness of Amsterdam was favoured by the unfortunate siege and capture of Antwerp by the duke of Parma; and the competition of the extraordinary industry and persevering exertions of the Hollanders not only prevented Antwerp from recovering her commerce, but gave a severe blow to the foreign trade of almost all the other Hanse Towns.[7]

The subsequent decline of the trade of Amsterdam itself was caused partly by the low profits arising from home competition and abundance of capital; partly by excessive taxation, which raised the price of the necessaries of life; but more than either, perhaps, by the progress of other nations possessing greater natural advantages, and being able, even with inferior skill, industry and capital, beneficially to carry on much of that trade which had before fallen almost exclusively into the hands of the Dutch.

As early as 1669 and 1670, when Sir William Temple was in Holland, the

---

[7] [The siege and capture of Antwerp in 1585, by the Duke of Parma, was 'unfortunate' because it represented a victory for Roman Catholic Spain over the Protestant inhabitants. The reasons for the decline of Antwerp were many: by the Treaty of Münster in 1648 the United Provinces became independent of Spain, but the river Scheldt was closed to navigation; this meant that Antwerp ceased to be an international port (until it was re-opened by the French in 1795) and towns with better access to the sea naturally increased in prosperity at Antwerp's expense.

The Hanseatic League was a medieval *ad hoc* confederation of cities, headed by Lübeck; in the fourteenth century it monopolised the Baltic trade, and later it maintained agencies all over Europe, and as far east as Novgorod. It gradually became less important after the discovery of America, and the last formal Assembly of the Hansa at Lübeck took place in 1669.]

effects of abundance of capital and domestic competition were such that most of the foreign trades were losing ones, except the Indian, and that none of them gave a profit of more than two or three per cent.[8] In such a state of things both the power and the will to save must be greatly diminished. The accumulation of capital must have been either stationary or declining, or at the best very slowly progressive. In fact, Sir William Temple gives it as his opinion that the trade of Holland had for some years passed its meridian, and begun sensibly to decay.[9] Subsequently, when the progress of other nations was still more marked, it appeared from undoubted documents that most of the trades of Holland, as well as its fisheries, had decidedly fallen off, and that no branch of its commerce had retained its former vigour, except the American and African trades, and that of the Rhine and Maese, which are independent of foreign power and competition.

In 1669, the whole population of Holland and West Friezeland was estimated by John de Witt at 2 400 000.[10] In 1778, the population of the seven provinces was estimated only at 2 000 000;[11] and thus, in the course of above a hundred years, the population, instead of increasing, as is usual, had greatly diminished.

In all these cases of commercial states, the progress of wealth and population seems to have been checked by one or more of the causes above mentioned, which must necessarily affect more or less the power of commanding the means of subsistence.

Universally it may be observed that if, from any cause or causes whatever, the funds for the maintenance of labour in any country cease to be progressive, the effective demand for labour will also cease to be progressive; and wages will be reduced to that sum which, under the existing prices of provisions, and the existing habits of the people, will just keep up, and no more than keep up, a stationary population. A state so circumstanced is under a moral impossibility of increasing, whatever may be the plenty of corn, or however high may be the profits of stock in other countries.[12] It may indeed at a subsequent period, and under new circumstances, begin to increase again. If by some happy invention in mechanics, the discovery of some new channel of trade, or an unusual increase of agricultural wealth and population in the surrounding countries, its exports, of whatever kind, were

---

[8] Temple's Works, vol. i. p. 69 fol.    [9] Id. p. 67.    [10] Interest of Holland, vol. i. p. 9.
[11] Richesse de la Hollande, vol. ii. p. 349.
[See under this title in the Alphabetical List.]
[12] It is a curious fact, that among the causes of the decline of the Dutch trade, Sir William Temple reckons the cheapness of corn, which, he says, 'has been for these dozen years, or more, general in these parts of Europe'. (vol. i. p. 69) This cheapness, he says, impeded the vent of spices and other Indian commodities among the Baltic nations, by diminishing their power of purchasing.

to become unusually in demand, it might again import an increasing quantity of corn, and might again increase its population. But as long as it is unable to make yearly additions to its imports of food, it will evidently be unable to furnish the means of support to an increasing population; and it will necessarily experience this inability when, from the state of its commercial transactions, the funds for the maintenance of its labour become stationary or begin to decline.

# CHAPTER C

## *Of Systems of Agriculture and Commerce combined*

In a country the most exclusively confined to agriculture, some of its raw materials will always be worked up for domestic use. In the most commercial state, not absolutely confined to the walls of a town, some part of the food of its inhabitants, or of its cattle, will be drawn from the small territory in its neighbourhood. But, in speaking of systems of agriculture and commerce combined, something much further than this kind of combination is intended; and it is meant to refer to countries where the resources in land, and the capitals employed in commerce and manufactures, are both considerable, and neither preponderating greatly over the other.

A country so circumstanced possesses the advantages of both systems, while at the same time it is free from the peculiar evils which belong to each, taken separately.

The prosperity of manufactures and commerce in any state implies at once that it has freed itself from the worst parts of the feudal system. It shows that the great body of the people are not in a state of servitude; that they have both the power and the will to save; that when capital accumulates it can find the means of secure employment, and consequently that the government is such as to afford the necessary protection to property. Under these circumstances, it is scarcely possible that it should ever experience that premature stagnation in the demand for labour, and the produce of the soil, which at times has marked the history of most of the nations of Europe. In a country in which manufactures and commerce flourish, the produce of the soil will always find a ready market at home; and such a market is peculiarly favourable to the progressive increase of capital. But the progressive increase of capital, and of the funds for the maintenance of labour, is the great cause of a demand for labour, and of high corn wages,[1] while the high relative price of corn, occasioned by the improved machinery and extended capital employed in manufactures, together with the prosperity of foreign commerce, enables

---

[1] [In 1826 (Vol. II, p. 147) this sentence was amended thus:
    But the progressive increase of capital, and particularly of the quantity and value of the funds for the maintenance of labour, is the great cause of a demand for labour, and of good corn wages, ...

the labourer to exchange any given portion of his earnings in corn for a large proportion both of domestic and foreign conveniences and luxuries. Even when the effective demand for labour begins to slacken, and the corn wages to be reduced, still the high relative value of corn keeps up comparatively the condition of the labouring classes; and though their increase is checked, yet a very considerable body of them may still be well lodged and well clothed, and able to indulge themselves in the conveniences and luxuries of foreign produce. Nor can they ever be reduced to the miserable condition of the poor in those countries where, at the same time that the demand for labour is stationary, the value of corn, compared with manufactures and foreign commodities, is extremely low.

All the peculiar disadvantages therefore of a purely agricultural country are avoided by the growth and prosperity of manufactures and commerce.

In the same manner it will be found that the peculiar disadvantages attending states merely manufacturing and commercial will be avoided by the possession of resources in land.

A country which raises its own food cannot by any sort of foreign competition be reduced at once to a necessarily declining population. If the exports of a merely commercial country be essentially diminished by foreign competition, it may lose, in a very short time, its power of supporting the same number of people; but if the exports of a country which has resources in land be diminished, it will merely lose some of its foreign conveniences and luxuries; and the great and most important of all trades, the domestic trade carried on between the towns and the country, will remain comparatively undisturbed. It may indeed be checked in the rate of its progress, for a time, by the want of the same stimulus; but there is no reason for its becoming retrograde; and there is no doubt that the capital thrown out of employment by the loss of foreign trade will not lie idle. It will find some channel in which it can be employed with advantage, though not with the same advantage as before; and will be able to maintain an increasing population, though not increasing at the same rate as under the stimulus of a prosperous foreign trade.

The effects of home competition will in like manner be very different in the two states we are comparing.

In a state merely manufacturing and commercial, home competition and abundance of capital may so reduce the price of manufactured compared with raw produce, that the increased capital employed in manufactures may not procure in exchange an increased quantity of food. In a country where there are resources in land this cannot happen; and though from improvements in machinery and the decreasing fertility of the new land taken into cultivation, a greater quantity of manufactures will be given for raw produce, yet the mass of manufactures can never fall in value, owing to a competition of capital in this species of industry, unaccompanied by a correspondent competition of capital on land.

It should also be observed that in a state, the revenue of which consists solely in profits and wages, the diminution of profits and wages may greatly impair its disposable income. The increase in the amount of capital and in the number of labourers may in many cases not be sufficient to make up for the diminished rate of profits and wages. But where the revenue of the country consists of rents as well as profits and wages, a great part of what is lost in profits and wages is gained in rents, and the disposable income remains comparatively unimpaired.

Another eminent advantage possessed by a nation which is rich in land, as well as in commerce and manufactures, is, that the progress of its wealth and population is in a comparatively slight degree dependent upon the state and progress of other countries. A nation, whose wealth depends exclusively on manufactures and commerce, cannot increase without an increase in the raw products of the countries with which it trades; or taking away a share of what they have been in the habit of actually consuming, which will rarely be parted with; and thus the ignorance and indolence of others may not only be prejudicial, but fatal to its progress.

A country with resources in land can never be exposed to these inconveniences; and if its industry, ingenuity and economy increase, its wealth and population will increase, whatever may be the situation and conduct of the nations with which it trades. When its manufacturing capital becomes redundant, and manufactured commodities are too cheap, it will have no occasion to wait for the increasing raw products of its neighbours. The transfer of its own redundant capital to its own land will raise fresh products, against which its manufactures may be exchanged, and by the double operation of diminishing comparatively the supply, and increasing the demand, enhance their price. A similar operation, when raw produce is too abundant, will restore the level between the profits of agriculture and manufactures. And upon the same principle, the stock of the country will be distributed through its various and distant provinces, according to the advantages presented by each situation for the employment either of agricultural or manufacturing capital.

A country in which in this manner agriculture, manufactures, and commerce, and all the different parts of a large territory, act and re-act upon each other in turn, might evidently go on increasing in riches and strength, although surrounded by Bishop Berkeley's wall of brass. Such a country would naturally make the most of its foreign commerce, whatever might be the actual state of it; and its increase or decrease would be the addition or removal of a powerful stimulus to its own produce; but still the increase of this produce, to a very considerable extent, would be independent of foreign countries; and though it might be retarded by a failure of foreign commerce, it could not either be stopped or be made retrograde.

A fourth advantage derived from the union of agriculture and manufactures, particularly when they are nearly balanced, is that the capital and population of such a country can never be forced to make a retrograde movement, merely by the natural progress of other countries to that state of improvement to which they are all constantly tending.

According to all general principles, it will finally answer to most landed nations, both to manufacture for themselves, and to conduct their own commerce. That raw cottons should be shipped in America, carried some thousands of miles to another country, unshipped there, to be manufactured and shipped again for the American market, is a state of things which cannot be permanent. That it may last for some time, there can be no doubt; and I am very far from meaning to insinuate that an advantage, while it lasts, should not be used, merely because it will not continue for ever. But if the advantage be in its nature temporary, it is surely prudent to have this in view, and to use it in such a way that when it ceases it may not have been productive, on the whole, of more evil than good.

If a country, owing to temporary advantages of this kind, should have its commerce and manufactures so greatly preponderate as to make it necessary to support a large portion of its people on foreign corn, it is certain that the progressive improvement of foreign countries in manufactures and commerce might, after a time, subject it to a period of poverty and of retrograde movements in capital and population, which might more than counterbalance the temporary benefits before enjoyed. While a nation in which the commercial and manufacturing population continued to be supported by its agriculture might receive a very considerable stimulus to both, from such temporary advantages, without being exposed to any essential evil on their ceasing.

The countries which thus unite great landed resources with a prosperous state of commerce and manufactures, and in which the commercial part of the population never essentially exceeds the agricultural part, are eminently secure from sudden reverses. Their increasing wealth seems to be out of the reach of all common accidents; and there is no reason to say that they might not go on increasing in riches and population for hundreds, nay, almost thousands of years.

We must not, however, imagine that there is no limit to this progress though it is distant, and has certainly not been attained by any large landed nation yet known.

We have already seen that the limit to the population of commercial nations is the period when, from the actual state of foreign markets, they are unable regularly to import an increasing quantity of food. And the limit to the population of a nation which raises the whole of its food on its own territory is when the land has been so fully occupied and worked, that the employment of another labourer on it will not on an average raise an additional quantity of food sufficient to support a family of such a size as will admit of an increase of population.

This is evidently the extreme practical limit to the progress of population, which no nation has ever yet reached, nor indeed ever will; since no allowance has been here made either for other necessaries besides food, or for the profits of stock, both of which, however low, must always be something not inconsiderable.

Yet even this limit is very far short of what the earth is capable of producing, if all were employed upon it who were not employed in the production of other necessaries; that is, if soldiers, sailors, menial servants and all the artificers of luxuries, were made to labour upon the land. They would not indeed produce the support of a family, and ultimately not even of themselves; but till the earth absolutely refused to yield any more, they would continue to add something to the common stock and by increasing the means of subsistence, would afford the means of supporting an increasing population. The whole people of a country might thus be employed during their whole time in the production of mere necessaries, and no leisure be left for other pursuits of any kind. But this state of things could only be effected by the forced direction of the national industry into one channel by public authority. Upon the principle of private property, which it may be fairly presumed will always prevail in society, it could never happen. With a view to the individual interest, either of a landlord or farmer, no labourer can ever be employed on the soil who does not produce more than the value of his wages; and if these wages be not on an average sufficient to maintain a wife, and rear two children to the age of marriage, it is evident that both the population and produce must come to a stand. Consequently, at the most extreme practical limit of population, the state of the land must be such as to enable the last employed labourers to produce the maintenance of as many, probably, as four persons.

And it is happy for mankind that such are the laws of nature. If the competition for the necessaries of life, in the progress of population, could reduce the whole human race to the necessity of incessant labour for them, man would be continually tending to a state of degradation; and all the improvements which had marked the middle stages of his career would be completely lost at the end of it; but in reality, and according to the universal principle of private property, at the period when it will cease to answer to employ more labour upon the land, the excess of raw produce, not actually consumed by the cultivators, will, in the shape of rents, profits, and wages, particularly the first, bear nearly as great a proportion to the whole as at any previous period, and, at all events, sufficient to support a large part of the society living either without manual labour, or employing themselves in modifying the raw materials of the land into the forms best suited to the gratification of man.[2]

When we refer therefore to the practical limits of population, it is of great importance to recollect that they must be always very far short of the utmost power of the earth to produce food.

It is also of great importance to recollect that, long before this practical limit is attained in any country, the rate of the increase of population will gradually diminish. When the capital of a country becomes stationary from bad government, indolence, extravagance, or a sudden shock to commerce, it is just possible that the check to population may in some degree be sudden, though in that case it cannot take place without a considerable convulsion. But when the capital of a country comes to a stop from the continued progress of accumulation and the exhaustion of the cultivable land, both the profits of stock and the wages of labour must have been gradually diminishing for a long period, till they are both ultimately so low as to afford no further encouragement to an increase of stock, and no further means for the support of an increasing population. If we could suppose that the capital employed upon the land was, at all times, as great as could possibly be applied with the same profit, and there were no agricultural improvements to save labour, it is obvious that, as accumulation proceeded, profits and wages would regularly fall, and the diminished rate in the progress of population would be quite regular. But practically this can never happen; and various causes, both natural and artificial, will concur to prevent this regularity, and occasion great variations at different times in the rate at which the population proceeds towards its final limit.

In the first place, land is practically almost always understocked with capital. This arises partly from the usual tenures on which farms are held, which, by discouraging the transfer of capital from commerce and manufactures, leaves it principally to be generated on the land; and partly from the very nature of much of the soil of almost all large countries, which is such that the employment of a small capital upon it may be little productive, while the employment of a large capital in draining, or in changing the character of the soil by a sufficient quantity of natural and artificial manures, may be productive in a high degree; and partly also from the circumstance that, after every fall of profits and wages there will often be room for the employment of a much greater capital upon the land than is at the command of those who, by being in the actual occupation of farms, can alone so employ it.

---

[2] [This is a repetition of what Malthus has said before; see chapter A, n.12.]

Secondly; improvements in agriculture. If new and superior modes of cultivation be invented, by which not only the land is better managed, but is worked with less labour, it is obvious that inferior land may be cultivated at higher profits than could be obtained from richer land before; and an improved system of culture, with the use of better instruments, may, for a long period, more than counterbalance the tendency of an extended cultivation and a great increase of capital to yield smaller proportionate returns.

Thirdly; improvements in manufactures. When by increased skill and the invention of improved machinery in manufactures one man becomes capable of doing as much as eight or ten could before, it is well known that, from the principle of home competition and the consequent great increase of quantity, the prices of such manufactures will greatly fall; and, as far as they include the necessaries and accustomed conveniences of labourers and farmers, they must tend to diminish that portion of the value of the whole produce which is consumed necessarily on the land, and leave a larger remainder. From this larger remainder may be drawn a higher rate of profits, notwithstanding the increase of capital and extension of cultivation.

Fourthly; the prosperity of foreign commerce. If from a prosperous foreign commerce our labour and domestic commodities rise considerably in price, while foreign commodities are advanced comparatively very little, an event which is very common, it is evident that the farmer or labourer will be able to obtain the tea, sugar, cottons, linens, leather, tallow, timber, &c., which he stands in need of, for a smaller quantity of corn or labour than before; and this increased power of purchasing foreign commodities will have precisely the same effect, in allowing the means of an extended cultivation without a fall of profits, as the improvements in manufactures just referred to.

Fifthly; a temporary increase in the relative price of raw produce from increased demand. Allowing, what is certainly not true, that a rise in the price of raw produce will, after a certain number of years, occasion a proportionate rise in labour[3] and other commodities; yet, during the time that the price of raw produce takes the lead, it is obvious that the profits of cultivation may increase under an extended agriculture and a continued accumulation of capital. And these intervals, it should be observed, must be of infinite importance in the progress of the wealth of a landed nation, particularly with reference to the causes of deficient capital upon the land before mentioned. If the land, for the most part, generates the new capital which is employed in extending its cultivation; and if the employment of a

---

[3] A rise, which is occasioned exclusively by the increased quantity of labour which may be required in the progress of society to raise a given quantity of corn on the last land taken into cultivation must, of course, be peculiar to raw produce, and will not be communicated to those commodities in the production of which there is no increase of labour.

considerable capital for a certain period will often put land in such a state that it can be cultivated afterwards at comparatively little expense; a period of high agricultural profits, though it may last only eight or ten years, may often be the means of giving to a country what is equivalent to a fresh quantity of land.

Though it is unquestionably and necessarily true, therefore, that the *tendency* of a continually increasing capital and extending cultivation is to occasion a progressive fall both of profits and wages; yet the causes above enumerated are evidently sufficient to account for great and long irregularities in this progress.

We see in consequence, in all the states of Europe, great variations at different periods in the progress of their capital and population. After slumbering for years in a state almost stationary, some countries have made a sudden start, and have begun increasing at a rate almost approaching to new colonies.[4] Russia and parts of Prussia have afforded instances of this kind, and have continued this rate of progress after the accumulation of capital and the extension of cultivation had been proceeding with great rapidity for many years.

From the operation of the same causes we have seen similar variations in our own country. About the middle of last century the interest of money was at 3 per cent.; and we may conclude that the profits of stock were nearly in proportion. At that time, as far as can be collected from the births and marriages, the population was increasing but slowly. From 1720 to 1750, a period of 30 years, the increase is calculated to have been only about 900 000 on a population of 5 565 000.[5] Since this period it cannot be doubted that the capital of the country has been prodigiously enlarged, and its cultivation very greatly extended; yet, during the last twenty years, we have seen the interest of money at above 5 per cent., with profits in proportion; and, from 1800 to 1811, an increase of population equal to 1 200 000 on 9 287 000, a rate of increase about two and a half times as great as at the former period.

But, notwithstanding these causes of irregularity in the progress of capital and population, it is quite certain that they cannot reach their necessary practical limit but by a very gradual process. Before the accumulation of capital comes to a stop from *necessity*, the profits of stock must, for a long time, have been so low as to afford scarcely any encouragement to an excess of saving above expenditure; and before the progress of population is finally stopped, the real wages of labour must have been gradually diminishing till,

---

[4] [In 1826 (Vol. II, p. 160) this was amended to:
  ... increasing at a rate almost approaching to that of new colonies.
[5] Population Abstracts, Preliminary Observations, table, p. xxv.
  [This reference is to the volume published in 1812; see RICKMAN in the Alphabetical List.]

under the existing habits of the people, they could only support such families as would just keep up, and no more than keep up, the actual population.

It appears then, that it is the union of the agricultural and commercial systems, and not either of them taken separately, that is calculated to produce the greatest national prosperity; that a country with an extensive and rich territory, the cultivation of which is stimulated by improvements in agriculture, manufactures and foreign commerce, has such various and abundant resources that it is extremely difficult to say when they will reach their limits. That there is, however, a limit which, if the capital and population of a country continue increasing, they must ultimately reach, and cannot pass; and that this limit, upon the principle of private property, must be far short of the utmost power of the earth to produce food.

# CHAPTER D

# Of Corn-Laws. Bounties upon Exportation

It has been observed that some countries, with great resources in land, and an evident power of supporting a greatly increased population from their own soil, have yet been in the habit of importing large quantities of foreign corn, and have become dependent upon other states for a great part of their supplies.

The causes which may lead to this state of things seem to be chiefly the following:

First; any obstacles which the laws, constitutions and customs of a country present to the accumulation of capital on the land, which do not apply with equal force to the increasing employment of capital in commerce and manufactures.

In every state in which the feudal system has prevailed there are laws and customs of this kind, which prevent the free division and alienation of land like other property, and render the preparations for an extension of cultivation often both very difficult and very expensive. Improvements in such countries are chiefly carried on by tenants, a large part of whom have not leases, or at least leases of any length; and though their wealth and respectability have of late years very greatly increased, yet it is not possible to put them on a footing with enterprising owners, and to give them the same independence, and the same encouragement to employ their capitals with spirit, as merchants and manufacturers.

Secondly; a system of direct or indirect taxation, of such a nature as to throw a weight upon the agriculture of a country, which is either unequal, or, from peculiar circumstances, can be better borne by commerce and manufactures.

It is universally allowed that a direct tax on corn grown at home, if not counterbalanced by a corresponding tax on the importation of it, might be such as to destroy at once the cultivation of grain, and make a country import the whole of its consumption; and a partial effect of the same kind would follow if, by a system of indirect taxation, the general price of labour were raised, and yet by means of drawbacks on home and foreign commodities, by an abundance of colonial produce, and by those peculiar articles,[1] the

---

[1] A rise in the price of labour in China would certainly increase the returns which it receives for its teas.

demand for which abroad would not be much affected by the increase of price, the value of the whole of the exports, though not the quantity, might admit of increase.

Thirdly; improved machinery, combined with extensive capital and a very advantageous division of labour.

If in any country, by means of capital and machinery, one man be enabled to do the work of ten, it is quite obvious that before the same advantages are extended to other countries, a rise in the price of labour will but very little interfere with the power of selling those sorts of commodities in the production of which the capital and machinery are so effectively applied. It is quite true that an advance in the necessary wages of labour, which increases the expense of raising corn, may have the same effect upon many commodities besides corn; and if there were no others, no encouragement would be given to the importation of foreign grain, as there might be no means by which it could be purchased cheaper abroad.

But a large class of the exportable commodities of a commercial country are of a different description. They are either articles in a considerable degree peculiar to the country and its dependencies, or such as have been produced by superior capital and machinery, the prices of which are determined rather by domestic than foreign competition. All commodities of this kind will evidently be able to support without essential injury an advance in the price of labour, some permanently, and others for a considerable time. The rise in the price of the commodity so occasioned, or rather the prevention of that fall which would otherwise have taken place, may always indeed have the effect of decreasing in some degree the *quantity* of the commodity exported; but it by no means follows that it will diminish the whole of its bullion value in the foreign country, which is precisely what determines the bullion value, and generally the quantity of the returns. If cottons in this country were now to fall to half their present price, we should undoubtedly export a greater quantity than we do at present; but I very much doubt whether we should export double the quantity,[2] and yet we must do this to enable us to command as much foreign produce as before. In this case, as in numerous others of the same kind, quantity and value go together to a certain point, though not at an equal pace; but, beyond this point, a further increase of quantity only diminishes the whole value produced, and the amount of the returns that can be obtained for it.

It is obvious then that a country, notwithstanding a high comparative price of labour and of materials, may easily stand a competition with

---

[2] [In 1826 (Vol. II, p. 165) Malthus qualified this:
    ... but I very much doubt whether we should export double the quantity, at least for many years, and yet we must ...

foreigners in those commodities to which it can apply a superior capital and machinery with great effect; although such a price of labour and materials might give an undisputed advantage to foreigners in agriculture and some other sorts of produce, where the same saving of labour cannot take place. Consequently such a country may find it cheaper to purchase a considerable part of its supplies of grain from abroad, with its manufactures and peculiar products, than to grow the whole at home.

If, from all or any of these causes, a nation becomes habitually dependent on foreign countries for the support of a considerable portion of its population, it must evidently be subjected, while such dependence lasts, to some of those evils which belong to a nation purely manufacturing and commercial. In one respect, indeed, it will still continue to have a great superiority. It will possess resources in land which may be resorted to when its manufactures and commerce, either from foreign competition or any other causes, begin to fail. But, to balance this advantage, it will be subjected, during the time that large importations are necessary, to much greater fluctuations in its supplies of corn, than countries wholly manufacturing and commercial. The demands of Holland and Hamburgh may be known with considerable accuracy by the merchants who supply them. If they increase, they increase gradually; and, not being subject from year to year to any great and sudden variations, it might be safe and practicable to make regular contracts for the average quantity wanted. But it is otherwise with such countries as England and Spain. Their wants are necessarily very variable, from the variableness of the seasons; and if the merchants were to contract with exporting countries for the quantity required in average years, two or three abundant seasons might ruin them. They must necessarily wait to see the state of the crops in each year, in order safely to regulate their proceedings; and though it is certainly true that it is only the deficiency from the average crop, and not the whole deficiency, which may be considered altogether in the light of a new demand in Europe; yet the largeness and previous uncertainty of this whole deficiency, the danger of making contracts for a stated quantity annually, and the greater chance of hostile combinations against large and warlike states, must greatly aggravate the difficulties of procuring a steady supply; and if it be true that unfavourable seasons are not unfrequently general, it is impossible to conceive that they should not occasionally be subject to great variations of price.

It has been sometimes stated that scarcities are partial, not general, and that a deficiency in one country is always compensated by a plentiful supply in others. But this seems to be quite an unfounded supposition. In the evidence brought before the Committee of the House of Commons in 1814, relating to the corn-laws, one of the corn merchants being asked whether it frequently happened that crops in the countries bordering upon the Baltic failed, when they failed here, replied: 'When crops are unfavourable in one part of Europe, it generally happens that they are more or less so in another.'[3] If any person will take the trouble to examine the contemporaneous prices of corn in the different countries of Europe for some length of time, he will be convinced that the answer here given is perfectly just. In the last hundred and fifty years, above twenty will be found in which the rise of prices is common to France and England, although there was seldom much intercourse between them in the trade of corn: and Spain and the Baltic nations, as far as their prices have been collected, appear frequently to have shared in the same general deficiency. Even within the last five years, two have occurred, the years 1811–12, and 1816–17, in which, with extraordinary high prices in this country, the imports have been comparatively inconsiderable; which can only have arisen from those scarcities having been general over the greatest part of Europe.

Under these circumstances let us suppose that two million quarters of foreign grain were the average quantity annually wanted in this country, and suppose, at the same time, that a million quarters were deficient from a bad season; the whole deficiency to be supplied would then be three millions.

If the scarcity were general in Europe, it may fairly be concluded that some states would prohibit the export of their corn entirely, and others tax it very highly; and if we could obtain a million or fifteen hundred thousand quarters, it is probably as much as we could reasonably expect. We should then, however, be two millions or fifteen hundred thousand quarters deficient. On the other hand, if we had habitually grown our own consumption, and were deficient a million of quarters from a bad season, it is scarcely probable that, notwithstanding a general scarcity, we should not be able to obtain three or four hundred thousand quarters in consequence of our advanced prices; particularly if the usual prices of our corn and labour were higher than in the rest of Europe. And in this case the sum of our whole deficiency would only be six or seven hundred thousand quarters, instead of fifteen hundred thousand or two millions of quarters. If the present year (1816–17) had found us in a state in which our growth of corn had been habitually far short of our consumption, the distresses of the country would have been dreadfully aggravated.

To provide against accidents of this kind, and to secure a more abundant and, at the time, a more steady supply of grain, a system of corn-laws has been recommended, the object of which is to discourage by duties or prohibitions the importation of foreign corn, and encourage by bounties the exportation of corn of home growth.

---

[3] Report, p. 93.

[See CORN LAWS (1) in the Alphabetical List.]

A system of this kind was completed in our own country in 1688,[4] the policy of which has been treated of at some length by Adam Smith.

In whatever way the general question may be finally decided, it must be allowed, by all those who acknowledge the efficacy of the great principle of supply and demand, that the line of argument taken by the author of the *Wealth of Nations* against the system is essentially erroneous.

He first states that, whatever extension of the foreign market can be occasioned by the bounty, must in every particular year be altogether at the expense of the home market, as every bushel of corn which is exported by means of the bounty, and which would not have been exported without the bounty, would have remained in the home market to increase the consumption, and to lower the price of that commodity.[5]

In this observation he evidently misapplies the term market. Because, by selling a commodity lower, it is easy to get rid of a greater quantity of it, in any particular market, than would have gone off otherwise, it cannot justly be said that by this process such a market is proportionally extended. Though the removal of the two taxes mentioned by Adam Smith as paid on account of the bounty would certainly increase the power of the lower classes to purchase, yet in each particular year the consumption must ultimately be limited by the population, and the increase of consumption from the removal of these taxes would by no means be sufficient to give the same encouragement to cultivation as the addition of the foreign demand. If the price of British corn in the home market rise in consequence of the bounty, before the price of production is increased (and an immediate rise is distinctly acknowledged by Adam Smith), it is an unanswerable proof that the effectual demand for British corn is extended by it; and that the diminution of demand at home, whatever it may be, is more than counterbalanced by the extension of demand abroad.

Adam Smith goes on to say that the two taxes paid by the people on account of the bounty, namely, the one to the government to pay this bounty,

---

[4] Though the object here stated may not have been the specific object of the law of 1688, it is certainly the object for which the system has been subsequently recommended.

[This footnote is difficult to understand. There had been corn laws in England since the time of Richard II (1377–99) to facilitate exports and prevent cheap imports, in the interest of both the farmers and the sovereign: armies could not be raised without a plentiful supply of home-grown food, and the insurrections which followed a scarcity were a threat to the throne.

A systematic bounty on the export of corn was first introduced during the reign of Charles II (1660–85) and made permanent after the Glorious Revolution of 1688: the subsidy on the export of wheat was 5s. a quarter, as long as the home price of wheat did not exceed 48s., which it seldom did during the eighteenth century, but the object of the scheme was to encourage farmers to keep land in tillage and to help them to 'dump' their surplus grain abroad in the event of a glut.]

[5] Vol. ii. b. iv. c. 5.

and the other paid in the advanced price of the commodity, must either reduce the subsistence of the labouring poor, or occasion an augmentation in their pecuniary wages proportioned to that in the pecuniary price of their subsistence. So far as it operates in the one way, it must reduce the ability of the labouring poor to educate and bring up their children, and must so far tend to restrain the population of the country. So far as it operates in the other, it must reduce the ability of the employers of the poor to employ so great a number as they otherwise might do, and must so far tend to restrain the industry of the country.

It will be readily allowed that the tax occasioned by the bounty will have the one or the other of the effects here contemplated; but it cannot be allowed that it will have both. Yet it is observed, that though the tax, which that institution imposes upon the whole body of the people be very burdensome to those who pay it, it is of very little advantage to those who receive it. This is surely a contradiction. If the price of labour rise in proportion to the price of wheat, as is subsequently asserted, how is the labourer rendered less competent to support a family? If the price of labour do not rise in proportion to the price of wheat, how is it possible to maintain that the landlords and farmers are not able to employ more labourers on their land? Yet in this contradiction the author of the *Wealth of Nations* has had respectable followers; and some of those who have agreed with him in his opinion that corn regulates the prices of labour, and of all other commodities, still insist on the injury done to the labouring classes of society by a rise in the price of corn, and the benefit they would derive from a fall.

The main argument, however, which Adam Smith adduces against the bounty, is that as the money price of corn regulates that of all other home-made commodities, the advantage to the proprietor from the increase of money price is merely apparent, and not real; since what he gains in his sales he must lose in his purchases.

This position, though true to a certain extent, is by no means true to the extent of preventing the movement of capital to or from the land, which is the precise point in question. The money price of corn in a particular country is undoubtedly by far the most powerful ingredient in regulating the price of labour, and of all other commodities; but it is not enough for Adam Smith's position that it should be the most powerful ingredient; it must be shown that, other causes remaining the same, the price of every article will rise and fall exactly in proportion to the price of corn, and this is very far from being the case. Adam Smith himself excepts all foreign commodities; but when we reflect upon the vast amount of our imports, and the quantity of foreign articles used in our manufactures, this exception alone is of the greatest importance. Wool and raw hides, two most important materials of home growth, do not, according to Adam Smith's own reasonings (Book I. c. xi.

p. 363, et seq.) depend much upon the price of corn and the rent of land; and the prices of flax, tallow, and leather, are of course greatly influenced by the quantity we import. But woollen cloths, cotton and linen goods, leather, soap, candles, tea, sugar &c., which are comprehended in the above-named articles, form almost the whole of the clothing and luxuries of the industrious classes of society.

It should be further observed that in all countries, the industry of which is greatly assisted by fixed capital, the part of the price of the wrought commodity which pays the profits of such capital will not necessarily rise in consequence of an advance in the price of corn, except as it requires gradual renovation; and the advantage derived from machinery which has been constructed before the advance in the price of labour will naturally last for some years.

In the case also of great and numerous taxes on consumption, a rise or fall in the price of corn, though it would increase or decrease that part of the wages of labour which resolves itself into food, evidently would not increase or decrease that part which is destined for the payment of taxes.

It cannot then be admitted as a general position that the money price of corn in any country is a just measure of the real value of silver in that country. But all these considerations, though of great weight to the owners of land, will not influence the farmers beyond the present leases. At the expiration of a lease, any particular advantage which a farmer had received from a favourable proportion between the price of corn and of labour would be taken from him, and any disadvantage from an unfavourable proportion be made up to him. The sole cause which would determine the proportion of capital employed in agriculture, would be the extent of the effectual demand for corn; and if the bounty had really enlarged this demand, which it certainly would have done, it is impossible to suppose that more capital would not be employed upon the land.

When Adam Smith says that the nature of things has stamped upon corn a real value, which cannot be altered by merely altering the money price, and that no bounty upon exportation, no monopoly of the home market, can raise that value, nor the freest competition lower it, it is obvious that he changes the question from the profits of the growers of corn, or of the proprietors of the land, to the physical and absolute value of corn itself.[6] I certainly do not mean to say that the bounty alters the physical value of corn, and makes a bushel of it support equally well a greater number of labourers than it did before; but I certainly do mean to say that the bounty to the British cultivator does, in the actual state of things, really increase the demand for British corn,

---

[6] [In 1826 (Vol. II, p. 174) this read:
... to the physical value of corn itself.

and thus encourage him to sow more than he otherwise would do, and enables him in consequence to employ more bushels of corn in the maintenance of a greater number of labourers.

If Adam Smith's theory were true, and the real price of corn were unchangeable,[7] or not capable of experiencing a relative increase or decrease of value compared with labour and other commodities, agriculture would indeed be in an unfortunate situation. It would be at once excluded from the operation of that principle so beautifully explained in the *Wealth of Nations*, by which capital flows from one employment to another, according to the various and necessarily fluctuating wants of society. But surely we cannot doubt that the real price of corn varies, though it may not vary so much as the real price of other commodities; and that there are periods when all wrought commodities are cheaper, and periods when they are dearer, in proportion to the price of corn; and in the one case capital flows from manufactures to agriculture, and in the other from agriculture to manufactures. To overlook these periods, or consider them of slight importance, is not allowable; because in every branch of trade these periods form the grand encouragement to an increase of supply. Undoubtedly the profits of trade in any particular branch of industry can never long remain higher than in others; but how are they lowered except by the influx of capital occasioned by these high profits? It never can be a national object permanently to increase the profits of any particular set of dealers. The national object is the increase of supply; but this object cannot be attained except by previously increasing the profits of these dealers, and thus determining a greater quantity of capital to this particular employment. The ship-owners and sailors of Great Britain do not make greater profits now than they did before the Navigation Act;[8] but the object of the nation was not to increase the profits of ship-owners and sailors, but the quantity of shipping and seamen; and this could not be done but by a law which, by increasing the demand for them, raised the profits of the capital before employed in this way, and determined a greater quantity to flow into the same channel. The object of a nation in the establishment of a bounty is, not to increase the profits of the farmers or the rents of the landlords, but to determine a greater quantity of the national capital to the land, and consequently to increase supply; and though, in the case of an advance in the price of corn from an increased demand, the rise of wages, the rise of rents and the fall of silver tend, in some degree, to obscure our view of the subject; yet we cannot refuse to acknowledge that the real price of corn

---

[7] [In 1826 (Vol. II, p. 175) this paragraph began:
    If Adam Smith's theory were true, and what he calls the real price of corn were unchangeable ...

[8] [For a note on the Navigation Acts see Book III, ch. xi, n.18(b) in Vol. I, p. 421.]

varies during periods sufficiently long to affect the determination of capital, or we shall be reduced to the dilemma of owning that no possible degree of demand can encourage the growth of corn.

It must be allowed then that the peculiar argument relating to the nature of corn brought forward by Adam Smith upon this occasion cannot be maintained; and that a bounty upon the exportation of corn must enlarge the demand for it and encourage its production in the same manner, if not in the same degree, as a bounty upon the exportation of any other commodity.

But it has been urged further, that this increased production of corn must necessarily occasion permanent cheapness; and a period of considerable length, during the first 64 years of the last century, while a bounty was in full operation in this country, has been advanced as a proof of it. In this conclusion, however, it may be reasonably suspected that an effect, in its nature temporary, though it may be of some duration, has been mistaken for one which is necessarily permanent.

According to the theory of demand and supply, the bounty might be expected to operate in the following manner:

It is frequently stated in the *Wealth of Nations* that a great demand is followed by a great supply; a great scarcity by a great plenty; an unusual dearness by an unusual cheapness. A great and indefinite demand is indeed generally found to produce a supply more than proportioned to it. This supply as naturally occasions unusual cheapness; but this cheapness, when it comes, must in its turn check the production of the commodity; and this check, upon the same principle, is apt to continue longer than necessary, and again to occasion a return to high prices.

This appears to be the manner in which a bounty upon the exportation of corn, if granted under circumstances favourable to its efficiency, might be expected to operate, and this seems to have been the manner in which it really did operate in the only instance where it has been fairly tried.

Without meaning to deny the concurrence of other causes, or attempting to estimate the relative efficiency of the bounty, it is impossible not to acknowledge that when the growing price of corn was, according to Adam Smith, only 28 shillings a quarter, and the corn-markets of England were as low as those of the continent, a premium of five shillings a quarter upon exportation must have occasioned an increase of real price, and given encouragement to the cultivation of grain. But the changes produced in the direction of capital to or from the land will always be slow. Those who have been in the habit of employing their stock in mercantile concerns do not readily turn it into the channel of agriculture; and it is a still more difficult and slower operation to withdraw capital from the soil, to employ it in commerce. For the first 25 years after the establishment of the bounty in this country the price of corn rose 2 or 3 shillings in the quarter; but owing probably to the wars of William and Anne, to bad seasons, and a scarcity of money, capital seems to have accumulated slowly on the land, and no great surplus growth was effected. It was not till after the peace of Utrecht[9] that the capital of the country began in a marked manner to increase; and it is impossible that the bounty should not gradually have directed a larger portion of this accumulation to the land than would otherwise have gone to it. A surplus growth, and a fall of price for thirty or forty years, followed.

It will be said that this period of low prices was too long to be occasioned by a bounty, even according to the theory just laid down. This is perhaps true, and in all probability the period would have been shorter if the bounty alone had operated; but in this case other causes powerfully combined with it.

The fall in the price of British corn was accompanied by a fall of prices on the continent. Whatever were the general causes which produced this effect in foreign countries, it is probable that they were not wholly inoperative in England. At all events nothing could be so powerfully calculated to produce cheapness, and to occasion a slow return to high prices, as a considerable surplus growth, which was unwillingly received, and only at low prices, by other nations. When such a surplus growth had been obtained, some time would necessarily be required to destroy it by cheapness, particularly as the moral stimulus of the bounty would probably continue to act long after the fall of prices had commenced. If to these causes we add that a marked fall in the rate of interest, about the same time, evinced an abundance of capital, and a consequent difficulty of finding a profitable employment for it; and consider further the natural obstacles to the moving of capital from the land; we shall see sufficient reason why even a long period might elapse without any essential alteration in the comparative abundance and cheapness of corn.

Adam Smith attributes this cheapness to a rise in the value of silver. The fall in the price of corn which took place in France and some other countries about the same time might give some countenance to the conjecture. But the accounts we have lately had of the produce of the mines during the period in question does not sufficiently support it; and it is much more probable that it arose from the comparative state of peace in which Europe was placed after the termination of the wars of Louis XIV, which facilitated the accumulation of capital on the land, and encouraged agricultural improvements.

With regard to this country, indeed, it is observed by Adam Smith

---

9  [The Peace of Utrecht, in the spring of 1713, ended the War of the Spanish Succession, and virtually established a balance of power (as far as Europe was concerned) which lasted until the revolutionary wars at the end of the eighteenth century.]

himself, that labour[10] and other articles were rising; a fact very unfavourable to the supposition of an increased value of the precious metals. Not only the money price of corn fell, but its value relative to other articles was lowered, and this fall of relative value, together with great exportations, clearly pointed to a relative abundance of corn, in whatever way it might be occasioned, as the main course of the facts observed, rather than a scarcity of silver. This great fall in the British corn-market, particularly during the ten years from 1740 to 1750, accompanied by a great fall in the continental markets, owing in some degree perhaps to the great exportations of British corn, especially during the years 1748, 1749, and 1750, must necessarily have given some check to its cultivation, while the increase of the real price of labour must at the same time have given a stimulus to the increase of population. The united operation of these two causes is exactly calculated first to diminish and ultimately to destroy a surplus of corn; and as, after 1764,[11] the wealth and manufacturing population of Great Britain increased more rapidly than those of her neighbours, the returning stimulus to agriculture, considerable as it was, arising almost exclusively from a home demand, was incapable of producing a surplus; and not being confined, as before, to British cultivation, owing to the alteration in the corn-laws, was inadequate even to effect an independent supply. Had the old corn-laws remained in full force, we should still probably have lost our surplus growth, owing to the causes above mentioned, although, from their restrictive clauses, we should certainly have been nearer the growth of an independent supply immediately previous to the scarcity of 1800.

It is not therefore necessary, in order to object to the bounty, to say with Adam Smith that the fall in the price of corn which took place during the first half of the last century must have happened in spite of the bounty, and could not possibly have happened in consequence of it. We may allow, on the contrary, what I think we ought to allow according to all general principles, that the bounty, when granted under favourable circumstances, is really calculated, after going through a period of dearness, to produce the surplus

---

[10] [In 1826 (Vol. II, p. 180) Malthus added a footnote here:

It is certainly a very remarkable fact, that although Adam Smith repeatedly states, in the most distinct manner, that labour alone is the true measure of the value of silver and of all other commodities, he should suppose that silver was rising at the very time when he says the money price of labour was rising. There cannot be a more decided contradiction.

[11] [This date is the last given in Adam Smith's table of the prices of wheat (per quarter measure) from 1202 to 1764, twelve years before the publication of the *Wealth of Nations* in 1776; he did not trouble to bring the figures up to date in subsequent editions. The table may be easily found at the very end of Book I of the *Wealth of Nations*; the most important references to it are in the 'Digression concerning the Variations in the Value of Silver during the Course of the Four last Centuries'.]

and the cheapness which its advocates promise,[12] but according to the same general principles we must allow that this surplus and cheapness, from their operating at once as a check to produce and an encouragement to population, cannot be for any great length of time maintained.

The objection then to a bounty on corn, independently of the objections to bounties in general, is that, when imposed under the most favourable circumstances, it cannot produce permanent cheapness: and if it be imposed under unfavourable circumstances; that is, if an attempt be made to force exportation by an adequate bounty at a time when the country does not fully grow its own consumption; it is obvious not only that the tax necessary for the purpose must be a very heavy one, but that the effect will be absolutely prejudicial to the population, and the surplus growth will be purchased by a sacrifice very far beyond its worth.

But notwithstanding the strong objections to bounties on general grounds, and their inapplicability in cases which are not unfrequent, it must be acknowledged that while they are operative (that is, while they produce an exportation which would not otherwise have taken place) they unquestionably encourage an increased growth of corn in the countries in which they are established, or maintain it at a point to which it would not otherwise have attained.

Under peculiar and favourable circumstances a country might maintain a considerable surplus growth for a great length of time, with an inconsiderable increase of the growing price of corn; and perhaps little or no increase of the average price, including years of scarcity.[13] If from any period during the last century, when an average excess of growth for exportation had been obtained by the stimulus of a bounty, the foreign demand for our corn had increased at the same rate as the domestic demand, our surplus growth might have become permanent. After the bounty had ceased to stimulate to fresh exertions, its influence would by no means be lost. For some years it would have given the British grower an absolute advantage over the foreign grower. This advantage would of course gradually diminish; because it is the nature of all effectual demand to be ultimately supplied, and oblige the producers to sell at the lowest price they can afford consistently with the general rate of

---

[12] As far as the bounty might tend to force the cultivation of poorer land, so far no doubt it would have a tendency to raise the price of corn; but we know from experience that the rise of price naturally occasioned in this way is continually counteracted by improvements in agriculture. As a matter of fact it must be allowed that, during the period of the last century when corn was falling, more land must have been taken into cultivation.

[13] The average price is different from the growing price. Years of scarcity, which must occasionally occur, essentially affect the average price; and the growth of a surplus quantity of corn, which tends to prevent scarcity, will tend to lower this average, and make it approach nearer to the growing price.

profits. But, after having experienced a period of decided encouragement, the British grower would find himself in the habit of supplying a larger market than his own upon equal terms with his competitors. And if the foreign and British markets continued to extend themselves equally, he would continue to proportion his supplies to both; because, unless a particular increase of demand were to take place at home, he could never withdraw his foreign supply without lowering the price of his whole crop; and the nation would thus be in possession of a constant store for years of scarcity.

But even supposing that by a bounty, combined with the most favourable state of prices in other countries, a particular state could maintain permanently an average excess of growth for exportation, it must not of course be imagined that its population would not still be checked by the difficulty of procuring subsistence. It would indeed be less exposed to the particular pressure arising from years of scarcity; but in other respects it would be subject to the same checks as those already described in the preceding chapters; and whether there was an habitual exportation or not, the population would be regulated by the real wages of labour, and would come to a stand when the necessaries which these wages could command were not sufficient, under the actual habits of the people, to encourage an increase of numbers.

# CHAPTER E

## *Of Corn-Laws. Restrictions upon Importation*

The laws which prohibit the importation of foreign grain, though by no means unobjectionable, are not open to the same objections as bounties, and must be allowed to be adequate to the object they have in view – the maintenance of an independent supply. A country with landed resources, which determines never to import corn but when the price indicates an approach towards a scarcity, will necessarily, in average years, supply its own wants. Though we may reasonably therefore object to restrictions upon the importation of foreign corn, on the grounds of their tending to prevent the most profitable employment of the national capital and industry, to check population, and to discourage the export of our manufactures; yet we cannot deny their tendency to encourage the growth of corn at home, and to procure and maintain an independent supply. A bounty, it has appeared, sufficient to make it answer its purpose in forcing a surplus growth, would, in many cases, require so very heavy a direct tax, and would bear so large a proportion to the whole price of the corn, as to make it in some countries next to impracticable. Restrictions upon importation impose no direct tax upon the people. On the contrary, they might be made, if it were thought advisable, sources of revenue to the government, and they can always, without difficulty, be put in execution, and be made infallibly to answer their express purpose of securing, in average years, a sufficient growth of corn for the actual population.

We have considered, in the preceding chapters, the peculiar disadvantages which attend a system either almost exclusively agricultural or exclusively commercial, and the peculiar advantages which attend a system in which they are united and flourish together. It has further appeared that, in a country with great landed resources, the commercial population may, from particular causes, so far predominate as to subject it to some of the evils which belong to a state purely commercial and manufacturing, and to a degree of fluctuation in the price of corn greater than is found to take place in such a state. It is obviously possible, by restrictions upon the importation of foreign corn, to maintain a balance between the agricultural and commercial classes. The question is not a question of the efficiency or inefficiency of the measure proposed, but of its policy or impolicy. The object can certainly be accomplished, but it may be purchased too dear; and to those who do not at once reject all inquiries on points of this kind, as impeaching a principle which they hold sacred, the question whether a balance between the agricultural and commercial classes of society, which would not take place naturally, ought, under certain circumstances, to be maintained artificially, must appear to be the most important practical question in the whole compass of political economy.[1]

One of the objections to the admission of the doctrine, that restrictions upon importation are advantageous, is that it cannot possibly be laid down as a general rule that every state ought to raise its own corn. There are some states so circumstanced that the rule is clearly and obviously inapplicable to them.

In the first place there are many states which have made some figure in history, the territories of which have been perfectly inconsiderable compared with their main town or towns, and utterly incompetent to supply the actual population with food. In such communities, what is called the principal internal trade of a large state, the trade which is carried on between the towns and the country, must necessarily be a foreign trade, and the importation of foreign corn is absolutely necessary to their existence. They may be said to be born without the advantage of land, and to whatever risks and disadvantages a system merely commercial and manufacturing may be exposed, they have no power of choosing any other. All that they can do is to make the most of their own situation, compared with the situation of their neighbours, and to endeavour by superior industry, skill, and capital, to make up for so important a deficiency. In these efforts, some states of which we have accounts have been wonderfully successful; but the reverses to which they, have been subject have been almost as conspicuous as the degree of their prosperity compared with the scantiness of their natural resources.

Secondly, restrictions upon the importation of foreign corn are evidently not applicable to a country which, from its soil and climate, is subject to very great and sudden variations in its home supplies, from the variations of the seasons. A country so circumstanced will unquestionably increase its chance of a steady supply of grain by opening as many markets for importation and exportation as possible, and this will probably be true, even though other countries occasionally prohibit or tax the exports of their grain. The peculiar evil to which such a country is subject can only be mitigated by encouraging the freest possible foreign trade in corn.

Thirdly, restrictions upon importation are not applicable to a country which has a very barren territory, although it may be of some extent. An

---

[1] [In 1826 (Vol. II, p. 186) this was altered to:
 ... must appear to be a most important practical question.

attempt fully to cultivate and improve such a territory by forcibly directing capital to it would probably, under any circumstances, fail; and the actual produce obtained in this way might be purchased by sacrifices which the capital and industry of the nation could not possibly continue to support. Whatever advantages those countries may enjoy, which possess the means of supporting a considerable population from their own soil, such advantages are not within the reach of a state so circumstanced. It must either consent to be a poor and inconsiderable community, or it must place its chief dependence on other resources than those of land. It resembles in many respects those states which have a very small territory; and its policy, with regard to the importation of corn, must of course be nearly the same.

In all these cases there can be no doubt of the impolicy of attempting to maintain a balance between the agricultural and commercial classes of society which would not take place naturally.

Under other and opposite circumstances, however, this impolicy is by no means so clear.

If a nation possesses a large territory consisting of land of an average quality, it may without difficulty support from its own soil a population fully sufficient to maintain its rank in wealth and power among the countries with which it has relations either of commerce or of war. Territories of a certain extent must ultimately in the main support their own population. As each exporting country approaches towards that complement of wealth and population to which it is naturally tending, it will gradually withdraw the corn which for a time it had spared to its more manufacturing and commercial neighbours, and leave them to subsist on their own resources. The peculiar products of each soil and climate are objects of foreign trade which can never, under any circumstances, fail. But food is not a peculiar product; and the country which produces it in the greatest abundance may, according to the laws which govern the progress of population, have nothing to spare for others. An extensive foreign trade in corn beyond what arises from the variableness of the seasons in different countries is rather a temporary and incidental trade, depending chiefly upon the different stages of improvement which different countries may have reached, and on other accidental circumstances, than a trade which is in its nature permanent, and the stimulus to which will remain in the progress of society unabated. In the wildness of speculation it has been suggested (of course more in jest than in earnest) that Europe ought to grow its corn in America, and devote itself solely to manufactures and commerce, as the best sort of division of the labour of the globe. But even on the extravagant supposition that the natural course of things might lead to such a division of labour for a time, and that by such means Europe could raise a population greater than its lands could possibly support, the consequences ought justly to be dreaded. It is an.

unquestionable truth that it must answer to every territorial state, in its natural progress to wealth, to manufacture for itself, unless the countries from which it had purchased its manufactures possess some advantages peculiar to them besides capital and skill. But when upon this principle America began to withdraw its corn from Europe, and the agricultural exertions of Europe were inadequate to make up for the deficiency, it would certainly be felt that the temporary advantages of a greater degree of wealth and population (supposing them to have been really attained) had been very dearly purchased by a long period of retrograde movements and misery.

If then a country be of such a size that it may fairly be expected finally to supply its own population with food; if the population which it can thus support from its own resources in land be such as to enable it to maintain its rank and power among other nations; and further, if there be reason to fear not only the final withdrawing of foreign corn used for a certain time, which might be a distant event, but the immediate effects that attend a great predominance of a manufacturing population, such as increased unhealthiness, increased turbulence, increased fluctuations in the price of corn, and increased variableness in the wages of labour; it may not appear impolitic artificially to maintain a more equal balance between the agricultural and commercial classes by restricting the importation of foreign corn, and making agriculture keep pace with manufactures.

Thirdly, if a country be possessed of such a soil and climate, that the variations in its annual growth of corn are less than in most other countries, this may be an additional reason for admitting the policy of restricting the importation of foreign corn. Countries are very different in the degree of variableness to which their annual supplies are subject; and though it is unquestionably true that if all were nearly equal in this respect, and the trade in corn *really* free, the steadiness of price in a particular state would increase with an increase in the number of the nations connected with it by the commerce of grain; yet it by no means follows that the same conclusion will hold good when the premises are essentially different; that is, when some of the countries taken into the circle of trade are subject to very great comparative variations in their supplies of grain, and when this defect is aggravated by the acknowledged want of real freedom in the foreign trade of corn.

Suppose, for instance, that the extreme variations above and below the average quantity of corn grown, were in England $\frac{1}{4}$ and in France $\frac{1}{3}$, a free intercourse between the two countries would probably increase the variableness of the English markets. And if, in addition to England and France, such a country as Bengal could be brought near, and admitted into the circle – a country in which, according to Sir George Colebrook, rice is sometimes sold four times as cheap in one year as in the succeeding without famine or scarcity;[2] and where, notwithstanding the frequency of abundant harvests, deficiencies sometimes occur of such extent as necessarily to destroy a considerable portion of the population; it is quite certain that the supplies both of England and France would become very much more variable than before the accession.

In point of fact, there is reason to believe that the British isles, owing to the nature of their soil and climate, are peculiarly free from great variations in their annual produce of grain. If we compare the prices of corn in England and France from the period of the commencement of the Eton tables to the beginning of the revolutionary war, we shall find that in England the highest price of the quarter of wheat of 8 bushels during the whole of that time was $3l.$ $15s.$ $6\frac{3}{4}d.$ (in 1648), and the lowest price $1l.$ $2s.$ $1d.$ (in 1743), while in France the highest price of the septier was 62 francs 78 centimes (in 1662), and the lowest price 8 francs 89 centimes (in 1718).[3] In the one case the difference is a little above $3\frac{1}{4}$ times, and in the other very nearly 7 times. In the English tables, during periods of ten or twelve years, only two instances occur of a variation amounting to as much as 3 times; in the French tables, during periods of the same length, one instance occurs of a variation of above 6 times, and three instances besides of a variation of 4 times or above.[4]

These variations may, perhaps, have been aggravated by a want of freedom in the internal trade of corn, but they are strongly confirmed by the calculations of Turgot, which relate solely to variations of produce, without reference to any difficulties or obstructions in its free transport from one part of the country to another.

On land of an average quality he estimates the produce at seven septiers the arpent in years of great abundance, and three septiers the arpent in years of great scarcity; while the medium produce he values at five septiers the arpent.[5] These calculations he conceives are not far removed from the truth;

---

[2] Husbandry of Bengal, p. 108. Note. He observes in the text of the same page that the price of corn fluctuates much more than in Europe.

[3] Garnier's Edition of the Wealth of Nations vol. ii. Table, p. 188.

[The Eton tables are taken from the accounts of Eton College, originally a religious foundation, but later an expensive boarding-school for boys: their provisions included what Adam Smith called 'the best wheat at Windsor market'. It was not necessary for Malthus to give a reference here to the *Wealth of Nations* for the English figures, but obviously his readers would have been less familiar with the prices in France, included by Garnier in his copious addenda to Smith's original work.]

[4] [In 1826 (Vol. II, p. 193) this was corrected to:
... in the French tables, during periods of the same length, one instance occurs of a variation of 4 times or above.

[5] Oeuvres de Turgot, tom. vi, p. 143. Edit. 1808.

[An *arpent*, before the French adopted the metric system in 1791, was a portion of land roughly equal to one and a quarter English acres, or 0.5 hectares; the word still survives in

and proceeding on these grounds he observes that, in a very abundant year, the produce will be five months above its ordinary consumption, and in a very scarce year as much below. These variations are, I should think, much greater than those which take place in this country, at least if we may judge from prices, particularly as in a given degree of scarcity in the two countries there is little doubt that, from the superior riches of England, and the extensive parish relief which it affords to the poorer classes in times of dearth, its prices would rise more above the usual average than those of France.

If we look to the prices of wheat in Spain during the same period, we shall find, in like manner, much greater variations than in England. In a table of the prices of the fanega of wheat in the market of Seville from 1675 to 1764 inclusive, published in the Appendix to the Bullion Report,[6] the highest price is 48 reals vellon (in 1677), and the lowest price 7 reals vellon (in 1720), a difference of nearly seven times; and in periods of ten or twelve years the difference is, in two or three instances, as much as four times. In another table, from 1788 to 1792 inclusive, relating to the towns of Old Castille, the highest price in 1790 was 109 reals vellon the fanega, and in 1792 the lowest price was only 16 reals vellon the fanega. In the market of Medina del Rio Seco, a town of the kingdom of Leon, surrounded by a very fine corn country, the price of the load of four fanegas of wheat was, in May, 1800, 100 reals vellon, and in May, 1804, 600 reals vellon, and these were both what are called *low prices*, as compared with the highest prices of the year. The difference would be greater if the high prices were compared with the low prices. Thus, in 1799, the low price of the four fanegas was 88 reals vellon, and in 1804 the high price of the four fanegas was 640 reals vellon – a difference of above seven times in so short a period as six years.[7]

In Spain, foreign corn is freely admitted; yet the variation of price, in the towns of Andalusia, a province adjoining the sea, and penetrated by the river Guadalquiver, though not so great as those just mentioned, seem to show that the coasts of the Mediterranean by no means furnish very steady supplies. It is known, indeed, that Spain is the principal competitor of England in the purchase of grain in the Baltic; and as it is quite certain that what may be called the growing or usual price of corn in Spain is much lower

---

*arpentage*, which means land-surveying. *Septier* is no longer used as a measure of capacity; it equalled about four English bushels, half a 'quarter' of corn. A quarter equalled 2.9 hectolitres, but the comparison is irrelevant today, since grain is now sold by weight and not capacity. With the passing of the Weights and Measures Act of 1963, it became illegal to use the old bushel for trading purposes.]

[6] Appendix, p. 182.

[See BULLION REPORT in the Alphabetical List.]

[7] Bullion Report. Appendix, p. 185.

than in England, it follows that the difference between the prices of plentiful and scarce years must be very considerable.

I have not the means of ascertaining the variations in the supplies and prices of the northern nations. They are, however, occasionally great, as it is well known that some of these countries are at times subject to very severe scarcities. But the instances already produced are sufficient to show, that a country which is advantageously circumstanced with regard to the steadiness of its home supplies may rather diminish than increase this steadiness by uniting its interests with a country less favourably circumstanced in this respect; and this steadiness will unquestionably be still further diminished, if the country which is the most variable in its supplies is allowed to inundate the other with its crops when they are abundant, while it reserves to itself the privilege of retaining them in a period of slight scarcity, when its commercial neighbour happens to be in the greatest want.[8]

Thirdly, if a nation be possessed of a territory, not only of sufficient extent to maintain under its actual cultivation a population adequate to a state of the first rank, but of sufficient unexhausted fertility to allow of a very great increase of population, such a circumstance would of course make the measure of restricting the importation of foreign corn more applicable to it.

A country which, though fertile and populous, had been cultivated nearly to the utmost, would have no other means of increasing its population than by the admission of foreign corn. But the British isles show at present no symptoms whatever of this species of exhaustion. The necessary accompaniments of a territory worked to the utmost are very low profits and interest, a very slack demand for labour, low wages, and a stationary population. Some of these symptoms may indeed take place without an exhausted territory; but an exhausted territory cannot take place without all these symptoms. Instead, however, of such symptoms, we have seen in this country, during the twenty years previous to 1814, a high rate of profits and interest, a very great demand for labour, good wages, and an increase of population more rapid, perhaps, than during any period of our history. The capitals which have been laid out in bringing new land into cultivation, or improving the old, must necessarily have yielded good returns, or, under the actual rate of general profits, they would not have been so employed; and although it is strictly true that, as capital accumulates upon the land, its profits must ultimately diminish; yet owing to the increase of agricultural skill, and other causes noticed in a former chapter, these two effects of progressive cultivation do not by any means always keep pace with each

---

[8] These two circumstances essentially change the premises on which the question of a free importation, as applicable to a particular state, must rest.

other.[9] Though they must finally unite and terminate the career of their progress together, they are often, during the course of their progress, separated for a considerable time and at a considerable distance. In some countries, and some soils, the quantity of capital which can be absorbed before any essential diminution of profits necessarily takes place is so great that its limit is not easily calculated; and certainly, when we consider what has actually been done in some districts of England and Scotland, and compare it with what remains to be done in other districts, we must allow that no near approach to this limit has yet been made. On account of the high money price of labour, and of the materials of agricultural capital, occasioned partly by direct and indirect taxation, and partly, or perhaps chiefly, by the great prosperity of our foreign commerce,[10] new lands cannot be brought into cultivation, nor great improvements made on the old, without a high money price of grain; but these lands, when they have been so brought into cultivation, or improved, have by no means turned out unproductive. The quantity and value of their produce have borne a full and fair proportion to the quantity of capital and labour employed upon them; and they were cultivated with great advantage both to individuals and the state, as long as the same, or nearly the same, relations between the value of produce and the cost of production, which prompted this cultivation, continued to exist.

In such a state of the soil, the British empire[11] might unquestionably be able, not only to support from its own agricultural resources its present population, but double, and in time, perhaps, even treble the number; and consequently a restriction upon the importation of foreign corn, which might be thought greatly objectionable in a country which had reached nearly the end of its resources, might appear in a very different light in a country capable of supporting from its own lands a very great increase of population.

But it will be said that, although a country may be allowed to be capable of

---

[9] [In 1826 (Vol. II, p. 197) this was altered to:
   ... these two events do not by any means keep pace with each other.
[10] [In 1826 (Vol. II, p. 198) Malthus added a footnote here:
   No restrictions upon the importation of grain, however absurdly severe, could permanently maintain our corn and labour at a much higher price than in the rest of Europe, if such restrictions were essentially to interfere with the prosperity of our foreign commerce. When the money price of labour is high in any country, or, what is the same thing, when the value of money is low, nothing can prevent it from going out to find its level, but some comparative advantages, either natural or acquired, which enable such country to maintain the abundance of its exports, notwithstanding the high money price of its labour.
[11] [It is important to remember in this connection that for Malthus 'the British empire' meant England and Wales, Scotland and Ireland. Overseas settlements and possessions were not included in the term *British Empire* until about the middle of the nineteenth century, to be replaced roughly a hundred years later by 'the British Commonwealth of Nations', now simply 'the Commonwealth'.]

maintaining from its own soil not only a great, but an increasing population; yet if it be acknowledged that, by opening its ports for the free admission of foreign corn, it may be made to support a greater and more rapidly increasing population, it is unjustifiable to go out of our way to check this tendency, and to prevent that degree of wealth and population which would naturally take place.

This is unquestionably a powerful argument; and granting fully the premises, (which however may admit of some doubt)[12] it cannot be answered upon the principles of political economy solely. I should say, however, that if it could be clearly ascertained that the addition of wealth and population so acquired would subject the society to a greater degree of uncertainty in its supplies of corn, greater fluctuations in the wages of labour, greater unhealthiness and immorality owing to a larger proportion of the population being employed in manufactories, and a greater chance of long and depressing retrograde movements occasioned by the natural progress of those countries from which corn had been imported; I should have no hesitation in considering such wealth and population as much too dearly purchased. The happiness of a society is, after all, the legitimate end even of its wealth, power, and population. It is certainly true that with a view to the structure of society most favourable to this happiness, and an adequate stimulus to the production of wealth from the soil, a very considerable admixture of commercial and manufacturing population with the agricultural is absolutely necessary; but there is no argument so frequently and obviously fallacious as that which infers that what is good to a certain extent is good to any extent; and though it will be most readily admitted that, in a large landed nation, the evils which belong to the manufacturing and commercial system are much more than counterbalanced by its advantages, as long as it is supported by agriculture; yet, in reference to the effect of the excess which is not so supported, it may fairly be doubted whether the evils do not decidedly predominate.

It is observed by Adam Smith, that the 'capital which is acquired to any country by commerce and manufactures is all a very uncertain and precarious possession, till some part of it has been secured and realized in the cultivation and improvement of its lands'.[13]

It is remarked in another place, that the monopoly of the colony trade, by raising the rate of mercantile profit, discourages the improvement of the soil, and retards the natural increase of that great original source of revenue – the rent of land.[14]

---

[12] [In 1826 (Vol. II, p. 199) this significant parenthesis was omitted.]

[13] Vol. ii. b. iii. c. 4. p. 137.

[14] Id. b. iv. c. 8. p. 495.

Now it is certain that, at no period, have the manufactures, commerce and colony trade of the country been in a state to absorb so much capital as during the twenty years ending with 1814. From the year 1764 to the peace of Amiens, it is generally allowed that the commerce and manufactures of the country increased faster than its agriculture, and that it became gradually more and more dependent on foreign corn for its support. Since the peace of Amiens the state of its colonial monopoly and of its manufactures has been such as to demand an unusual quantity of capital; and if the peculiar circumstances of the subsequent war, the high freights and insurance, and the decrees of Buonaparte, had not rendered the importation of foreign corn extremely difficult and expensive, we should at this moment, according to all general principles, have been in the habit of supporting a much larger portion of our population upon it, than at any former period of our history. The cultivation of the country would be in a very different state from what it is at present. Very few or none of those great improvements would have taken place which may be said to have purchased fresh land for the state that no fall of price can destroy. And the peace, or accidents of different kinds, might have curtailed essentially both our colonial and manufacturing advantages, and destroyed or driven away our capital before it had spread itself on the soil, and become national property.

As it is, the practical restrictions thrown in the way of importing foreign corn during the war have forced our steam-engines and our colonial monopoly to cultivate our lands; and those very causes which, according to Adam Smith, tend to draw capital from agriculture, and would certainly have so drawn it if we could have continued to purchase foreign corn at the market prices of France and Holland, have been the means of giving such a spur to our agriculture, that it has not only kept pace with a very rapid increase of commerce and manufactures, but has recovered the distance at which it had for many years been left behind, and now marches with them abreast.

But restrictions upon the importation of foreign corn, in a country which has great landed resources, not only tend to spread every commercial and manufacturing advantage possessed, whether permanent or temporary, on the soil, and thus, in the language of Adam Smith, secure and realize it; but also tend to prevent those great oscillations in the progress of agriculture and commerce which are seldom unattended with evil.

It is to be recollected, and it is a point of great importance to keep constantly in our minds, that the distress which has been experienced among almost all classes of society from the sudden fall of prices, except as far as it has been aggravated by the state of the currency, has been occasioned by *natural*, not *artificial*, causes.

There is a tendency to an alternation in the rate of the progress of agriculture and manufactures in the same manner as there is a tendency to an alternation in the rate of the progress of food and population. In periods of peace and uninterrupted trade, these alternations, though not favourable to the happiness and quiet of society, may take place without producing material evil; but the intervention of war is always liable to give them a force and rapidity that must unavoidably produce a convulsion in the state of property.

The war that succeeded to the peace of Amiens found us dependent upon foreign countries for a very considerable portion of our supplies of corn; and we now grow our own consumption, notwithstanding an unusual increase of population in the interval. This great and sudden change in the state of our agriculture could only have been effected by very high prices occasioned by an inadequate home supply and the great expense and difficulty of importing foreign corn. But the rapidity with which this change has been effected must necessarily create a glut in the market as soon as the home growth of corn became fully equal or a little in excess above the home consumption; and, aided only by a small foreign importation, must inevitably occasion a very sudden fall of prices. If the ports had continued open for the free importation of foreign corn, there can be little doubt that the price of corn in 1815 would have been still considerably lower. This low price of corn, even if by means of lowered rents our present state of cultivation could be in a great degree preserved, must give such a check to future improvement that, if the ports were to continue open, we should certainly not grow a sufficiency at home to keep pace with our increasing population; and at the end of ten or twelve years we might be found by a new war in the same state that we were at the commencement of the present. We should then have the same career of high prices to pass through, the same excessive stimulus to agriculture[15] followed by the same sudden and depressing check to it, and the same enormous loans borrowed with the price of wheat at 90 or 100 shillings a quarter, and the monied incomes of the landholders and industrious classes of society nearly in proportion, to be paid when wheat is at 50 or 60 shillings a quarter, and the incomes of the landlords and industrious classes of society greatly reduced – a state of things which cannot take place without an excessive aggravation of the difficulty of paying taxes, and particularly that invariable monied amount which pays the interest of the national debt.

---

[15] According to the evidence before the House of Lords (Reports, p. 49), the freight and insurance alone on a quarter of corn were greater by 48 shillings in 1811 than in 1814. Without any artificial interference then, it appears that war alone may occasion unavoidably a prodigious increase of price. [See CORN LAWS: 2 in the Alphabetical List.]

On the other hand a country which so restricts the importations of foreign corn as on an average to grow its own supplies, and to import merely in periods of scarcity, is not only certain of spreading every invention in manufactures and every peculiar advantage it may possess from its colonies or general commerce on the land, and thus of fixing them to the spot and rescuing them from accidents; but is necessarily exempt from those violent and distressing convulsions of property which almost unavoidably arise from the coincidence of a general war and an insufficient home supply of corn.

If the late war had found us independent of foreigners for our average consumption, not even our paper currency could have made the prices of our corn approach to the prices which were at one time experienced.[16] And if we had continued, during the course of the contest, independent of foreign supplies, except in an occasional scarcity, it is impossible that the growth of our own consumption, or a little above it, should have produced at the end of the war so universal a feeling of distress.

The chief practical objection to which restrictions on the importation of corn are exposed is a glut from an abundant harvest, which cannot be relieved by exportation. And in the consideration of that part of the question which relates to the fluctuations of prices this objection ought to have its full and fair weight. But the fluctuation of prices arising from this cause has sometimes been very greatly exaggerated. A glut which might essentially distress the farmers of a poor country, might be comparatively little felt by the farmers of a rich one; and it is difficult to conceive that a nation with an ample capital, and not under the influence of a great shock to commercial confidence, as this country was in 1815, would find much difficulty in reserving the surplus of one year to supply the wants of the next or some future year. It may fairly indeed be doubted whether, in such a country as our own, the fall of price arising from this cause would be so great as that which would be occasioned by the sudden pouring in of the supplies from an abundant crop in Europe, particularly from those states which do not regularly export corn. If our ports were always open, the existing laws of France would still prevent such a supply as would equalize prices; and French corn would only come in to us in considerable quantities in years of

---

[16] It will be found upon examination, that the prices of our corn led the way to the excess and diminution of our paper currency, rather than followed, although the prices of corn could never have been either so high or so low if this excess and diminution had not taken place. [In 1826 (Vol. II, p. 205) Malthus added a sentence at the beginning of this footnote:

According to Mr. Tooke (High and Low Prices, p. 215), if the last war had found us with a growth beyond our consumption, we should have witnessed a totally different set of phenomena connected with prices. It will be found upon examination ...

great abundance, when we were the least likely to want it, and when it was most likely to occasion a glut.[17]

But if the fall of price occasioned in these two ways would not be essentially different, as it is quite certain that the rise of price in years of general scarcity would be less in those countries which habitually grow their own supplies; it must be allowed that the range of variation will be the least under such a system of restrictions as, without preventing importation when prices are high, will secure in ordinary years a growth equal to the consumption.[18]

One objection, however, to systems of restriction, must always remain. They are essentially unsocial. I certainly think that, in reference to the interests of a particular state, a restriction upon the importation of foreign corn may sometimes be advantageous; but I feel still more certain that in reference to the interests of Europe in general the most perfect freedom of trade in corn, as well as in every other commodity, would be the most advantageous. Such a perfect freedom, however, could hardly fail to be followed by a more free and equal distribution of capital, which, though it would greatly advance the riches and happiness of Europe, would unquestionably render some parts of it poorer and less populous than they are at present; and there is little reason to expect that individual states will ever consent to sacrifice the wealth within their own confines to the wealth of the world.

It is further to be observed that, independently of more direct regulations, taxation alone produces a system of discouragements and encouragements which essentially interferes with the natural relations of commodities to each other; and as there is no hope of abolishing taxation, it may sometimes be only by a further interference that these natural relations can be restored.

A perfect freedom of trade therefore is a vision which it is to be feared can never be realized. But still it should be our object to make as near approaches to it as we can. It should always be considered as the great general rule. And when any deviations from it are proposed, those who propose them are bound clearly to make out the exception.

---

[17] Almost all the corn merchants who gave their evidence before the committees of the two houses in 1814 seemed fully aware of the low prices likely to be occasioned by an abundant crop in Europe, if our ports were open to receive it.

[18] [In 1826 (Vol. II, pp. 207–9) a long footnote was added here:

[1825.] In the sixth number of the Westminster Review, in which prodigious stress is laid upon the necessary effect of the corn laws in occasioning great fluctuations in the price of corn, a table, said to be from the very highest mercantile authority, is given of the average prices of wheat at Rotterdam for each of the ten years ending with 1824. The purpose for which the table is produced is to show the average price of wheat in Holland during these ten years; but it incidentally shows that, even in Holland, which in many respects must be peculiarly favourable to steady prices, a free trade in corn can by no means secure them.

In the year 1817, the price per last of 86 Winchester bushels was 574 guilders; and in 1824, it was only 147 guilders; a difference of nearly four times. During the same period of ten years the greatest variation in the average price of each year in England was between 94*s*. 9*d*., which was the price in 1817, and 43*s*. 9*d*., which was the price in 1822 (Appendix to Mr. Tooke's work on High and Low Prices. Table xii. p. 31) – a difference short of $2\frac{1}{5}$!!

It is repeated over and over again, apparently without the slightest reference to facts, that the freedom of the trade in corn would infallibly secure us from the possibility of a scarcity. The writer of the article *Corn Laws* in the supplement to the Encyclopædia Britannica goes so far as to say, 'it is constantly found that when the crops of one country fail, plenty reigns in some other quarter ... There is always abundance of food in the world. To enjoy a constant plenty, we have only to lay aside our prohibitions and restrictions, and cease to counteract the benevolent wisdom of Providence.' The same kind of language is repeated in the Review above adverted to: 'If there be a bad harvest', it is said, 'in one country, there is a good one in another, and the surplus produce of the latter supplies the deficiency of the former', etc., etc. Now there are the best reasons for believing that these statements are decidedly contradicted by the most enlarged experience. In the first place, if they were true, and if the general plenty alluded to were only prevented by the want of a free trade in corn, we should necessarily see a great rise in prices in one country contemporaneous with a great fall in others; but a slight glance at the prices of corn in the countries of the commercial world for the last one or two centuries will be sufficient to convince any impartial person that, on the contrary, there is a very remarkable sympathy of prices at the same periods, which is absolutely inconsistent with the truth of the above statements. Secondly, all travellers who have paid any attention to the seasons, agree in stating that the same sort of weather often prevails in different countries at the same time. The peculiar and excessive heats of the very last summer not only prevailed generally over the greatest part of Europe, but extended even to America. Mr. Tooke, On High and Low Prices (p. 247, 2nd edit.), quotes a passage from Mr. Lowe's work on the Present State of England, in which he observes that 'The Public, particularly the untravelled part of the public, are hardly aware of the similarity of temperature prevailing throughout what may be called the corn-country of Europe, we mean Great Britain, Ireland, the north of France, the Netherlands, Denmark, the north-west of Germany, and in some measure Poland and the north-east of Germany.' He then goes on to state instances of scarcity in different countries of Europe at the same time. And in the justness of these remarks, on the prevalence of a general similarity of seasons in Europe within certain latitudes, Mr. Tooke says he perfectly concurs. Many of the corn-merchants examined before the Committees of the two Houses, both in 1814 and 1821, expressed similar opinions; and I do not recollect a single instance of the opinion that good and bad harvests generally balance each other in different countries being stated by any person who had been in a situation to observe the facts. Such statements, therefore, must be considered as mere assertions quite unsupported by the least shadow of proof.

I am very far, however, from meaning to say that the circumstance of different countries having often an abundance or deficiency of corn at the same time, though it must prevent the possibility of steady prices, is a decisive reason against the abolition or alteration of the corn-laws. The most powerful of all the arguments against restrictions is their unsocial tendency, and the acknowledged injury which they must do to the interests of the commercial world in general. The weight of this argument is increased rather than diminished by the numbers which may suffer from scarcity at the same time. And at a period when our ministers are most laudably setting an example of a more liberal system of commercial policy, it would be greatly desirable that foreign nations should not have so marked an exception as our present corn-laws to cast in our teeth. A duty on importation not too high, and a bounty nearly such as was recommended by Mr. Ricardo, would probably be best suited to our present situation, and best secure steady prices. A duty on foreign corn would resemble the duties laid by other countries on our manufactures as objects of taxation, and would not in the same manner impeach the principles of free trade.

But whatever system we may adopt, it is essential to a sound determination, and highly useful in preventing disappointments, that all the arguments both for and against corn-laws should be thoroughly and impartially considered; and it is because on a calm, and, as far as I can judge, an impartial review of the arguments of this chapter, they still appear to me of weight sufficient to deserve such consideration, and not as a kind of protest against the abolition or change of the corn-laws, that I republish them in another edition.

[For the *Westminster Review* see MILL, JOHN STUART, in the Alphabetical List; for the *Supplement to the Encyclopædia Britannica*, see McCULLOCH, JOHN RAMSAY.]

# CHAPTER F

*Of increasing Wealth, as it affects the Condition of the Poor*

The professed object of Adam Smith's *Inquiry* is *the Nature and Causes of the Wealth of Nations*. There is another, however, still more interesting, which he occasionally mixes with it – the causes which affect the happiness and comfort of the lower orders of society, which in every nation form the most numerous class. These two subjects are, no doubt, nearly connected; but the nature and extent of this connexion, and the mode in which increasing wealth operates on the condition of the poor, have not been stated with sufficient correctness and precision.

Adam Smith, in his chapter on the wages of labour, considers every increase in the stock or revenue of the society as an increase in the funds for the maintenance of labour; and having before laid down the position that the demand for those who live by wages can only increase in proportion to the increase of the funds for the payment of wages, the conclusion naturally follows that every increase of wealth tends to increase the demand for labour, and to improve the condition of the lower classes of society.[1]

Upon a nearer examination, however, it will be found that the funds for the maintenance of labour do not necessarily increase with the increase of wealth, and very rarely increase in *proportion* to it; and that the condition of the lower classes of society does not depend exclusively upon the increase of the funds for the maintenance of labour, or the power of supporting a greater number of labourers.

Adam Smith defines the wealth of a state to be the annual produce of its land and labour. This definition evidently includes manufactured produce as well as the produce of the land. Now, upon the supposition that a nation, from peculiar situation and circumstances, was unable to procure an additional quantity of food, it is obvious that the produce of its labour would not necessarily come to a stand, although the produce of its land or its power of importing corn were incapable of further increase. If the materials of manufactures could be obtained either at home or from abroad, improved skill and machinery might work them up to a greatly increased amount with

---

[1] Vol. i. book i. c. 8.

the same number of hands, and even the number of hands might be considerably increased by an increased taste for manufactures, compared with war and menial service, and by the employment consequently of a greater proportion of the whole population in manufacturing and commercial labour.

That such a case does not frequently occur will be most readily allowed. It is not only however possible, but forms the specific limit to the increase of population in the natural progress of cultivation, with which limit, the limit to the further progress of wealth is obviously not contemporary. But though cases of this kind do not often occur, because these limits are seldom reached; yet approximations to them are constantly taking place, and in the usual progress of improvement the increase of wealth and capital is rarely accompanied with a proportionately increased power of supporting an additional number of labourers.

Some ancient nations which, according to the accounts we have received of them, possessed but an inconsiderable quantity of manufacturing and commercial capital, appear to have cultivated their lands highly by means of an agrarian division of property, and were unquestionably very populous. In such countries, though full of people already, there would evidently be room for a very great increase of capital and riches; but, allowing all the weight that is in any degree probable to the increased production or importation of food occasioned by the stimulus of additional capital, there would evidently not be room for a proportionate increase of the means of subsistence.

If we compare the early state of our most flourishing European kingdoms with their present state, we shall find this conclusion confirmed almost universally by experience.

Adam Smith, in treating of the different progress of opulence in different nations, says that England, since the time of Elizabeth, has been continually advancing in commerce and manufactures. He then adds: 'The cultivation and improvement of the country has no doubt been gradually advancing. But it seems to have followed slowly and at a distance the more rapid progress of commerce and manufactures. The greater part of the country must probably have been cultivated before the reign of Elizabeth, and a very great part of it still remains uncultivated, and the cultivation of the far greater part is much inferior to what it might be.'[2] The same observation is applicable to most of the other countries of Europe. The best land would naturally be the first occupied. This land, even with that sort of indolent cultivation and great waste of labour which particularly marked the feudal times, would be capable of supporting a considerable population; and on the increase of

---

[2] Vol. ii. book iv. c. 4, p. 133.

capital, the increasing taste for conveniences and luxuries, combined with the decreasing power of production in the new land to be taken into cultivation, would naturally and necessarily direct the greatest part of this new capital to commerce and manufactures, and occasion a more rapid increase of wealth than of population.

The population of England accordingly in the reign of Elizabeth appears to have been nearly five millions, which would not be very far short of the half of what it is at present;[3] but when we consider the very great proportion which the products of commercial and manufacturing industry now bear to the quantity of food raised for human consumption, it is probably a very low estimate to say that the mass of wealth or the stock and revenue of the country must, independently of any change in the value of the circulating medium, have increased above four times. Few of the other countries in Europe have increased to the same extent in commercial and manufacturing wealth as England; but as far as they have proceeded in this career, all appearances clearly indicate that the progress of their general wealth has been greater than the progress of their means of supporting an additional population.

That every increase of the stock or revenue of a nation cannot be considered as an increase of the real funds for the maintenance of labour will appear in a striking light in the case of China.

Adam Smith observes, that China has probably long been as rich as the nature of her laws and institutions will admit; but intimates that, with other laws and institutions, and if foreign commerce were held in honour, she might still be much richer.

If trade and foreign commerce were held in great honour in China, it is evident that, from the great number of her labourers and the cheapness of her labour, she might work up manufactures for foreign sale to a great amount. It is equally evident that, from the great bulk of provisions and the prodigious extent of her inland territory, she could not in return import such a quantity as would be any sensible addition to her means of subsistence. Her immense amount of manufactures, therefore, she would either consume at home, or exchange for luxuries collected from all parts of the world. At present the country appears to be overpeopled compared with what its stock can employ, and no labour is spared in the production of food. An immense capital could not be employed in China in preparing manufactures for foreign trade, without altering this state of things, and taking off some labourers from agriculture, which might have a tendency to diminish the produce of the

---

[3] [In 1826 (Vol. II, p. 214) Malthus inserted '(1811)' here, to show that he had not taken into account the census returns of 1821. He had already added a note about this census to chapter xi of Book II: 'Of the checks to population in England (continued)'; see Vol. I, pp. 276–80.]

country. Allowing, however, that this would be made up, and indeed more than made up, by the beneficial effects of improved skill and economy of labour in the cultivation of the poorest lands, yet, as the quantity of subsistence could be but little increased, the demand for manufactures, which would raise the price of labour, would necessarily be followed by a proportionate rise in the price of provisions, and the labourer would be able to command but little more food than before. The country would, however, obviously be advancing in wealth; the exchangeable value of the annual produce of its land and labour would be annually augmented; yet the real funds for the maintenance of labour would be nearly stationary. The argument perhaps appears clearer when applied to China, because it is generally allowed that its wealth has been long stationary, and its soil cultivated nearly to the utmost.[4]

In all these cases, it is not on account of any undue preference given to commerce and manufactures, compared with agriculture, that the effect just described takes place, but merely because the powers of the earth in the production of food have narrower limits than the skill and tastes of mankind in giving value to raw materials, and consequently in the approach towards the limits of subsistence there is naturally more room, and consequently more encouragement, for the increase of the one species of wealth than of the other.

It must be allowed then, that the funds for the maintenance of labour do not *necessarily* increase with the increase of wealth, and very *rarely* increase in *proportion* to it.

But the condition of the lower classes of society certainly does not depend exclusively upon the increase of the funds for the maintenance of labour, or the means of supporting more labourers. That these means form always a very powerful ingredient in the condition of the poor, and the main ingredient in the increase of population, is unquestionable. But, in the first place, the comforts of the lower classes of society do not depend solely upon food, nor even upon strict necessaries; and they cannot be considered as in a good state unless they have the command of some conveniences and even luxuries. Secondly, the tendency in population fully to keep pace with the means of subsistence must in general prevent the increase of these means from having a great and permanent effect in improving the condition of the poor. And, thirdly, the cause which has the most lasting effect in improving

---

[4] How far this latter opinion is to be depended upon it is not very easy to say. Improved skill and a saving of labour would certainly enable the Chinese to cultivate some lands with advantage which they cannot cultivate now, but the more general use of horses instead of men might prevent this extended cultivation from giving any encouragement to an increase of people.

the situation of the lower classes of society depends chiefly upon the conduct and prudence of the individuals themselves, and is therefore not immediately and necessarily connected with an increase in the means of subsistence.

With a view, therefore, to the other causes which affect the condition of the labouring classes, as well as the increase of the means of subsistence, it may be desirable to trace more particularly the mode in which increasing wealth operates, and to state both the disadvantages as well as the advantages with which it is accompanied.

In the natural and regular progress of a country to a state of great wealth and population, there are two disadvantages to which the lower classes of society seem necessarily to be subjected. The first is, a diminished power of supporting children under the existing habits of the society with respect to the necessaries of life. And the second – the employment of a larger proportion of the population in occupations less favourable to health, and more exposed to fluctuations of demand and unsteadiness of wages.

A diminished power of supporting children is an absolutely unavoidable consequence of the progress of a country towards the utmost limits of its population. If we allow that the power of a given quantity of territory to produce food has some limit, we must allow that as this limit is approached, and the increase of population becomes slower and slower, the power of supporting children will be less and less, till finally, when the increase of produce stops, it becomes only sufficient to maintain, on an average, families of such a size as will not allow of a further addition of numbers. This state of things is generally accompanied by a fall in the *corn* price of labour; but should this effect be prevented by the prevalence of prudential habits among the lower classes of society, still the result just described must take place; and though, from the powerful operation of the preventive check to increase, the wages of labour estimated even in corn might not be low, yet it is obvious that in this case the power of supporting children would rather be nominal than real; and the moment this power began to be exercised to its apparent extent, it would cease to exist.

The second disadvantage to which the lower classes of society are subjected in the progressive increase of wealth is, that a larger portion of them is engaged in unhealthy occupations, and in employments in which the wages of labour are exposed to much greater fluctuations than in agriculture, and the simpler kinds of domestic trade.

On the state of the poor employed in manufactories with respect to health, and the fluctuations of wages, I will beg leave to quote a passage from Dr. Aikin's Description of the Country round Manchester:

'The invention and improvements of machines to shorten labour have had a surprising influence to extend our trade, and also to call in hands from all parts, particularly children for the cotton-mills. It is the wise plan of

Providence, that in this life there shall be no good without its attendant inconvenience. There are many which are too obvious in these cotton-mills, and similar factories, which counteract that increase of population usually consequent on the improved facility of labour. In these, children of a very tender age are employed, many of them collected from the work-houses in London and Westminster, and transported in crowds as apprentices to masters resident many hundred miles distant, where they serve unknown, unprotected and forgotten by those to whose care nature or the laws had consigned them. These children are usually too long confined to work in close rooms, often during the whole night. The air they breathe from the oil, &c., employed in the machinery, and other circumstances, is injurious; little attention is paid to their cleanliness; and frequent changes from a warm and dense to a cold and thin atmosphere are predisposing causes to sickness and debility, and particularly to the epidemic fever which is so generally to be met with in these factories. It is also much to be questioned if society does not receive detriment from the manner in which children are thus employed during their early years. They are not generally strong to labour, or capable of pursuing any other branch of business when the term of their apprenticeship expires. The females are wholly uninstructed in sewing, knitting, and other domestic affairs requisite to make them notable and frugal wives and mothers. This is a very great misfortune to them and to the public, as is sadly proved by a comparison of the families of labourers in husbandry and those of manufacturers in general. In the former we meet with neatness, cleanliness and comfort; in the latter with filth, rags and poverty, although their wages may be nearly double to those of the husbandman. It must be added that the want of early religious instruction and example, and the numerous and indiscriminate association in these buildings, are very unfavourable to their future conduct in life.'[5]

In the same work it appears that the register for the collegiate church of Manchester, from Christmas, 1793, to Christmas, 1794, showed a decrease of 168 marriages, 538 christenings, and 250 burials. In the parish of Rochdale, in the neighbourhood, a still more melancholy reduction in proportion to the

---

[5] P. 219. Dr. Aikin says that endeavours have been made to remedy these evils, which in some factories have been attended with success. And it is very satisfactory to be able to add that, since this account was written, the situation of the children employed in the cotton-mills has been further very essentially improved, partly by the interference of the legislature, and partly by the humane and liberal exertions of individuals.
[This footnote is quite different from the corresponding one of 1803; see Bk III, ch. viii, n.11 for information about Factory Acts. The individuals whom Malthus has in mind here would most likely have been Robert Owen (see ch. iii(b) of Bk III) and before him Sir Robert Peel the elder (1750–1830) who was responsible for the Health and Morals of Apprentices Act of 1802.]

number of people took place. In 1792 the births were 746, the burials 646, and the marriages 389. In 1794 the births were 373, the burials 671, and the marriages 199. The cause of this sudden check to population was the failure of demand and of commercial credit which occurred at the commencement of the war, and such a check could not have taken place in so sudden a manner without the most severe distress, occasioned by the sudden reduction of wages.

In addition to the fluctuations arising from the changes from peace to war and from war to peace, it is well known how subject particular manufactures are to fail from the caprices of taste. The weavers of Spitalfields were plunged into the most severe distress by the fashion of muslins instead of silks; and great numbers of workmen in Sheffield and Birmingham were for a time thrown out of employment owing to the adoption of shoe strings and covered buttons, instead of buckles and metal buttons. Our manufactures, taken in the mass, have increased with prodigious rapidity, but in particular places they have failed; and the parishes where this has happened are invariably loaded with a crowd of poor in the most distressed and miserable condition.

In the evidence brought before the House of Lords during the inquiries which preceded the Corn-Bill of 1815, various accounts are produced from different manufactories, intended to show that the high price of corn has rather the effect of lowering than of raising the price of manufacturing labour.[6] Adam Smith has clearly and correctly stated that the money price of labour depends upon the money price of provisions, and the state of the demand and the supply of labour. And he shows how much he thinks it is occasionally affected by the latter cause, by explaining in what manner it may vary in an opposite direction from the price of provisions during the pressure of a scarcity. The accounts brought before the House of Lords are a striking illustration of this part of his proposition; but they certainly do not prove the incorrectness of the other part of it, as it is quite obvious that, whatever may take place for a few years, the supply of manufacturing labour cannot possibly be continued in the market unless the natural or necessary price, that is, the price necessary to continue it in the market be paid, and this of course is not done unless the money price be so proportioned to the price of provisions, that labourers are enabled to bring up families of such a size as will supply the number of hands required.

But though these accounts do not in any degree invalidate the usual doctrines respecting labour, or the statements of Adam Smith, they show very clearly the great fluctuations to which the condition of the manufacturing labourer is subjected.

---

[6] Reports, p. 51. [See CORN LAWS: 2 in the Alphabetical List.]

In looking over these accounts, it will be found that in some cases the price of weaving has fallen a third, or nearly one-half, at the same time that the price of wheat has risen a third, or nearly one half; and yet these proportions do not always express the full amount of the fluctuations, as it sometimes happens that when the price is low, the state of the demand will not allow of the usual number of hours of working; and when the price is high, it will admit of extra hours.

That from the same causes there are sometimes variations of a similar kind in the price of task-work in agriculture will be readily admitted; but, in the first place, they do not appear to be nearly so considerable; and secondly, the great mass of agricultural labourers is employed by the day, and a sudden and general fall in the money price of agricultural day-labour is an event of extremely rare occurrence.[7]

It must be allowed then, that in the natural and usual progress of wealth, the means of marrying early and supporting a family are diminished, and a greater proportion of the population is engaged in employments less favourable to health and morals, and more subject to fluctuations in the price of labour, than the population employed in agriculture.

These are no doubt considerable disadvantages, and they would be sufficient to render the progress of riches decidedly unfavourable to the condition of the poor, if they were not counteracted by advantages which nearly, if not fully, counterbalance them.

And first, it is obvious that the profits of stock are that source of revenue from which the middle classes are chiefly maintained; and the increase of capital, which is both the cause and effect of increasing riches, may be said to be the efficient cause of the emancipation of the great body of society from a dependence on the landlords. In a country of limited extent, consisting of fertile land divided into large properties, as long as the capital remains inconsiderable, the structure of society is most unfavourable to liberty and good government. This was exactly the state of Europe in the feudal times. The landlords could in no other way spend their incomes than by maintaining a great number of idle followers; and it was by the growth of capital in all the employments to which it is directed that the pernicious power of the landlords was destroyed, and their dependent followers were turned into merchants, manufacturers, tradesmen, farmers, and independent labourers – a change of prodigious advantage to the great body of society, including the labouring classes.

---

[7] Almost the only instance on record in this country is that which has lately taken place (1815 and 1816), occasioned by an unparalleled fall in the exchangeable value of the raw produce, which has necessarily disabled the holders of it from employing the same quantity of labour at the same price.

Secondly; in the natural progress of cultivation and wealth, the production of an additional quantity of corn will require more labour, while, at the same time, from the accumulation and better distribution of capital, the continual improvements made in machinery, and the facilities opened to foreign commerce, manufactures and foreign commodities will be produced or purchased with less labour; and consequently a given quantity of corn will command a much greater quantity of manufactures and foreign commodities than while the country was poor. Although, therefore, the labourer may earn less corn than before, the superior value which every portion which he does not consume in kind will have in the purchase of conveniences may more than counterbalance this diminution. He will not indeed have the same power of maintaining a large family; but with a small family he may be better lodged and clothed, and better able to command the decencies and comforts of life.

Thirdly; it seems to be proved by experience, that the lower classes of society seldom acquire a decided taste for conveniences and comforts till they become plentiful compared with food, which they never do till food has become in some degree scarce. If the labourer can obtain the full support of himself and family by two or three days' labour; and if, to furnish himself with conveniences and comforts, he must work three or four days more, he will generally think the sacrifice too great compared with the objects to be obtained, which are not strictly necessary to him, and will therefore often prefer the luxury of idleness to the luxury of improved lodging and clothing. This is said by Humboldt to be particularly the case in some parts of South America, and to a certain extent prevails in Ireland, India, and all countries where food is plentiful compared with capital and manufactured commodities. On the other hand, if the main part of the labourer's time be occupied in procuring food, habits of industry are necessarily generated, and the remaining time, which is but inconsiderable compared with the commodities it will purchase, is seldom grudged. It is under these circumstances, particularly when combined with a good government, that the lower classes of society are most likely to acquire a decided taste for the conveniences and comforts of life; and this taste may be such as even to prevent, after a certain period, a further fall in the corn price of labour. But if the corn price of labour continues tolerably high while the relative value of commodities compared with corn falls very considerably, the labourer is placed in a most favourable situation. Owing to his decided taste for conveniences and comforts, the good corn wages of labour will not generally lead to early marriages; yet in individual cases, where large families occur, there will be the means of supporting them independently, by the sacrifice of the accustomed conveniences and comforts; and thus the poorest of the lower classes will rarely be stinted in food, while the great mass of them will not only have sufficient means of subsistence, but be able to command no inconsiderable quantity of those conveniences and comforts, which, at the same time that they gratify a natural or acquired want, tend unquestionably to improve the mind and elevate the character.

On an attentive review then of the effects of increasing wealth on the condition of the poor, it appears that, although such an increase does not imply a proportionate increase of the funds for the maintenance of mere labour,[8] yet it brings with it advantages to the lower classes of society which may fully counterbalance the disadvantages with which it is attended; and, strictly speaking, the good or bad condition of the poor is not *necessarily* connected with any particular stage in the progress of society to its full complement of wealth. A rapid increase of wealth indeed, whether it consists principally in additions to the means of subsistence or to the stock of conveniences and comforts, will always, *cæteris paribus*, have a favourable effect on the poor; but the influence even of this cause is greatly modified and altered by other circumstances, and nothing but the union of individual prudence with the skill and industry which produce wealth can permanently secure to the lower classes of society that share of it which it is on every account so desirable that they should possess.

---

[8] [In 1826 (Vol. ii, p. 228) the word *mere* was excised.]

# ESSAY, &c

## BOOK IV

### OF OUR FUTURE PROSPECTS RESPECTING THE REMOVAL OR MITIGATION OF THE EVILS ARISING FROM THE PRINCIPLE OF POPULATION

### CHAPTER I

*Of moral restraint, and the foundations of our obligation to practise this virtue*[1]

As it appears that, in the actual state of every society which has come within our review, the natural progress of population has been constantly and powerfully checked; and as it seems evident, that no improved form of government, no plans of emigration, no benevolent institutions, and no degree or direction of national industry, can prevent the continued action of a great check to population in some form or other; it follows that we must submit to it as an inevitable law of nature; and the only inquiry that remains is how it may take place with the least possible prejudice to the virtue and happiness of human society. The various[2] checks to population, which have been observed to prevail in the same and different countries, seem all to be resolvable into moral restraint, vice, and misery; and if our choice be confined to these three, we cannot long hesitate in our decision respecting which it would be most eligible to encourage.

In the former edition of this essay,[3] I observed that as, from the laws of

---

[1] [In 1806 this was altered to:
'Of moral restraint, and our obligation to practise this virtue'.
[2] [In 1806 (Vol. II, p. 302) this was changed to:
All the immediate checks to population ...
[3] [In 1806 (Vol. II, p. 302) this was altered to:
In the first edition of this essay ... [See the 1798 *Essay*, pp. 89–90.]

nature, it appeared that some check to population must exist, it was better that this check should arise from a foresight of the difficulties attending a family, and the fear of dependent poverty, than from the actual presence of want and sickness. This idea will admit of being pursued further; and I am inclined to think that, from the prevailing opinions respecting population, which undoubtedly originated in barbarous ages, and have been continued and circulated by that part of every community which may be supposed to be interested in their support, we have been prevented from attending to the clear dictates of reason and nature on this subject.

Natural and moral evil seem to be the instruments employed by the Deity in admonishing us to avoid any mode of conduct which is not suited to our being, and will consequently injure our happiness. If we be intemperate in eating and drinking, we are disordered;[4] if we indulge the transports of anger, we seldom fail to commit acts of which we afterwards repent; if we multiply too fast, we die miserably of poverty and contagious diseases. The laws of nature in all these cases are similar and uniform. They indicate to us that we have followed these impulses too far, so as to trench upon some other law which equally demands attention. The uneasiness we feel from repletion, the injuries that we inflict on ourselves or others in anger, and the inconveniences we suffer on the approach of poverty, are all admonitions to us to regulate these impulses better; and if we heed not this admonition, we justly incur the penalty of our disobedience, and our sufferings operate as a warning to others.

From the inattention of mankind, hitherto, to the consequences of increasing too fast, it must be presumed that these consequences are not so immediately and powerfully connected with the conduct which leads to them, as in the other instances; but the delayed knowledge of particular effects does not alter their nature, nor our obligation to regulate our conduct accordingly, as soon as we are satisfied of what this conduct ought to be. In many other instances, it has not been till after long and painful experience that the conduct most favourable to the happiness of man has been forced upon his attention. The kind of food, and the mode of preparing it, best suited to the purposes of nutrition and the gratification of the palate; the treatment and remedies of different disorders; the bad effects on the human frame of low and marshy situations; the invention of the most convenient and comfortable clothing; the construction of good houses; and all the advantages and extended enjoyments, which distinguish civilized life, were not pointed out to the attention of man at once; but were the slow and late result of experience, and of the admonitions received by repeated failures.

---

[4] [In 1817 (Vol. III, p. 65) this was amended to:
  If we be intemperate in eating and drinking, our health is disordered.

Diseases have been generally considered as the inevitable inflictions of Providence; but, perhaps, a great part of them may more justly be considered as indications that we have offended against some of the laws of nature. The plague at Constantinople, and in other towns of the East, is a constant admonition of this kind to the inhabitants. The human constitution cannot support such a state of filth and torpor; and as dirt, squalid poverty, and indolence are in the highest degree unfavourable to happiness and virtue, it seems a benevolent dispensation that such a state should, by the laws of nature, produce disease and death, as a beacon to others to avoid splitting on the same rock.

The prevalence of the plague in London till the year 1666 operated in a proper manner on the conduct of our ancestors; and the removal of nuisances, the construction of drains, the widening of the streets, and the giving more room and air to their houses, had the effect of eradicating completely this dreadful disorder, and of adding greatly to the health and happiness of the inhabitants.[5]

In the history of every epidemic it has almost invariably been observed that the lower classes of people, whose food was poor and insufficient, and who lived crowded together in small and dirty houses, were the principal victims. In what other manner can nature point out to us, that if we increase too fast for the means of subsistence, so as to render it necessary for a considerable part of the society to live in this miserable manner, we have offended against one of her laws? This law she has declared exactly in the same manner as she declares that intemperance in eating and drinking will be followed by ill health; and that, however grateful it may be to us at the moment to indulge these passions to excess,[6] this indulgence will ultimately produce unhappiness. It is as much a law of nature that repletion is bad for the human frame, as that eating and drinking, unattended with this consequence, are good for it.

An implicit obedience to the impulses of our natural passions would lead us into the wildest and most fatal extravagancies; and yet we have the strongest reasons for believing that all these passions are so necessary to our being, that they could not be generally weakened or diminished, without injuring our happiness. The most powerful and universal of all our desires is the desire of food, and of those things, such as clothing, houses, &c. which are immediately necessary to relieve us from the pains of hunger and cold. It is acknowledged by all, that these desires put in motion the greatest part of that

---

[5] [It should be remembered that all Malthus's own editions of the *Essay* appeared before the first outbreak of cholera in nineteenth-century Britain, in 1831–2; two more occurred after Malthus's death, in 1848 and 1865–6.]

[6] [In 1826 (Vol. ii, p. 259) *these passions* were changed to 'this propensity'.]

activity from which spring the multiplied improvements and advantages of civilized life;[7] and that the pursuit of these objects and the gratification of these desires form the principal happiness of the larger half of mankind, civilized or uncivilized, and are indispensably necessary to the more refined enjoyments of the other half. We are all conscious of the inestimable benefits that we derive from these desires when directed in a certain manner; but we are equally conscious of the evils resulting from them when not directed in this manner; so much so, that society has taken upon itself to punish most severely what it considers as an irregular gratification of them. And yet the desires in both cases are equally natural and, abstractedly considered, equally virtuous. The act of the hungry man, who satisfies his appetite by taking a loaf from the shelf of another, is in no respect to be distinguished from the act of him who does the same thing with a loaf of his own, but by its consequences. From the consideration of these consequences, we feel the most perfect conviction that, if people were not prevented from gratifying their natural desires with the loaves in the possession of others, the number of loaves would universally diminish. This experience is the foundation of the laws relating to property, and of the distinctions of virtue and vice, in the gratification of desires otherwise perfectly the same.

If the pleasure arising from the gratification of these propensities were universally diminished in vividness, violations of property would become less frequent; but this advantage would be greatly overbalanced by the narrowing of the sources of enjoyment. The diminution in the quantity of all those productions, which contribute to human gratification, would be much greater in proportion than the diminution of thefts; and the loss of general happiness on the one side would be beyond comparison greater than the gain to happiness on the other. When we contemplate the constant and severe toils of the greatest part of mankind, it is impossible not to be forcibly impressed with the reflection, that the sources of human happiness would be most cruelly diminished, if the prospect of a good meal, a warm house, and a comfortable fireside in the evening, were not incitements sufficiently vivid to give interest and cheerfulness to the labours and privations of the day.

After the desire of food, the most powerful and general of our desires is the passion between the sexes, taken in an enlarged sense. Of the happiness spread over human life by this passion, very few are unconscious. Virtuous love, exalted by friendship, seems to be that sort of mixture of sensual and intellectual enjoyment, particularly suited to the nature of man, and most powerfully calculated to awaken the sympathies of the soul, and produce the

---

[7] [In 1806 (Vol. ii, p. 309) this sentence was altered to:
... from which the multiplied improvements and advantages of civilized life are derived; ... .

most exquisite gratifications. Perhaps there is scarcely a man who has once experienced the genuine delight of virtuous love, however great his intellectual pleasures may have been, who does not look back to that period, as the sunny spot in his whole life, where his imagination loves most to bask, which he recollects and contemplates with the fondest regret, and which he would most wish to live over again.

It has been said by Mr. Godwin, in order to show the evident inferiority of the pleasures of sense: 'Strip the commerce of the sexes of all its attendant circumstances, and it would be generally despised.' He might as well say to a man who admired trees, strip them of their spreading branches and lovely foliage, and what beauty can you see in a bare pole? But it was the tree with the branches and foliage, and not without them, that excited admiration. It is 'the symmetry of person, the vivacity, the voluptuous softness of temper, the affectionate kindness of feeling, the imagination and the wit'[8] of a woman, which excite the passion of love, and not the mere distinction of her being a female.[9]

It is a very great mistake to suppose that the passion between the sexes only operates and influences human conduct when the immediate gratification of it is in contemplation. The formation and steady pursuit of some particular plan of life has been justly considered as one of the most permanent sources of happiness; but I am inclined to believe that there are not many of these plans formed which are not connected, in a considerable degree, with the prospect of the gratification of this passion, and with the support of children arising from it. The evening meal, the warm house, and the comfortable fireside, would lose half of their interest, if we were to exclude the idea of some object of affection with whom they were to be shared.

We have also great reason to believe that the passion between the sexes has the most powerful tendency to soften and meliorate the human character, and keep it more alive to all the kindlier emotions of benevolence and pity. Observations on savage life have generally tended to prove, that nations in which this passion appeared to be less vivid, were distinguished by a ferocious and malignant spirit; and particularly by tyranny and cruelty to the sex. If, indeed, this bond of conjugal affection were considerably weakened, it seems probable, either that the man would make use of his superior physical strength, and turn his wife into a slave, as among the generality of savages; or at best, that every little inequality of temper, which must necessarily occur between two persons, would produce a total alienation of affection; and this could hardly take place without a diminution of parental fondness and care, which would have the most fatal effect on the happiness of society.

---

[8] Political Justice, vol. i. b. i. c. v. p. 72. 8vo. [Third edition.]
[9] [This paragraph, and the one preceding it, are taken from pp. 211–15 of the 1798 *Essay*.]

It may be further remarked, that observations on the human character in different countries warrant us in the conclusion, that the passion is stronger, and its general effects in producing gentleness, kindness, and suavity of manners, much more powerful, where obstacles are thrown in the way of very early and universal gratification. In some of the southern countries where every impulse may be almost immediately indulged, the passion sinks into mere animal desire, is soon weakened and almost extinguished by excess; and its influence on the character is extremely confined. But in European countries where, though the women are not secluded, yet manners have imposed considerable restraints on this gratification, the passion not only rises in force, but in the universality and beneficial tendency of its effects, and has often the greatest influence in the formation and improvement of the character, where it is the least gratified.

Considering then the passion between the sexes in all its bearings and relations, and including the endearing engagement of parent and child resulting from it, few will be disposed to deny that it is one of the principal ingredients of human happiness. Yet experience teaches us that much evil flows from the irregular gratification of it; and though the evil be of little weight in the scale, when compared with the good; yet its absolute quantity cannot be inconsiderable, on account of the strength and universality of the passion. It is evident, however, from the general conduct of all governments in their distribution of punishments, that the evil resulting from this cause is not so great, and so immediately dangerous to society, as the irregular gratification of the desire of property; but placing this evil in the most formidable point of view, we should evidently purchase a diminution of it at a very high price, by the extinction or diminution of the passion which causes it; a change which would probably convert human life either into a cold and cheerless blank, or a scene of savage and merciless ferocity.

A careful attention to the remote as well as immediate effect of all the human passions, and all the general laws of nature, leads us strongly to the conclusion that, under the present constitution of things, few or none of them would admit of being greatly diminished without narrowing the sources of good more powerfully than the sources of evil. And the reason seems to be obvious. They are, in fact, the materials of all our pleasures, as well as of all our pains; of all our happiness, as well as of all our misery; of all our virtues, as well as of all our vices. It must therefore be regulation and direction that are wanted, not diminution or extinction.

It is justly observed by Dr. Paley that: 'Human passions are either necessary to human welfare, or capable of being made, and in a great majority of instances in fact made, conducive to its happiness. These passions are strong and general; and perhaps would not answer their purpose unless they were so. But strength and generality, when it is expedient that particular circumstances should be respected, become, if left to themselves, excess and misdirection. From which excess and misdirection the vices of mankind (the causes no doubt of much misery) appear to spring. This account, while it shows us the principle of vice, shows us at the same time, the province of reason and self-government.'[10]

Our virtue, therefore, as reasonable beings, evidently consists in educing, from the general materials which the Creator has placed under our guidance, the greatest sum of human happiness; and as all our[11] natural impulses are abstractedly considered good, and only to be distinguished by their consequences, a strict attention to these consequences, and the regulation of our conduct conformably to them, must be considered as our principal duty.

The fecundity of the human species is, in some respects, a distinct consideration from the passion between the sexes, as it evidently depends more upon the power of women in bearing children, than upon the strength or weakness of this passion. It is, however, a law, exactly similar in its great features to all the other laws of nature. It is strong and general, and apparently would not admit of any very considerable diminution, without being inadequate to its object; the evils arising from it are incidental to these necessary qualities of strength and generality; and these evils are capable of being very greatly mitigated and rendered comparatively light by human energy and virtue. We cannot but conceive, that it is an object of the Creator, that the earth should be replenished, at least to a considerable degree;[12] and it appears to me clear, that this could not be effected without a tendency in population to increase faster than food; and as, with the present law of increase, the peopling of the earth does not proceed very rapidly, we have undoubtedly some reason to believe that this law is not too powerful for its apparent object. The desire of the means of subsistence would be comparatively confined in its effects, and would fail of producing that general activity so necessary to the improvement of the human faculties, were it not for the strong and universal effort of population to increase with greater rapidity than its supplies. If these two tendencies were exactly balanced, I do not see what motive there would be sufficiently strong to overcome the acknowledged indolence of man, and make him proceed in the cultivation of the soil. The population of any large territory, however fertile, would be as likely to stop at five hundred, or five thousand, as at five millions, or fifty millions. Such a balance, therefore, would clearly defeat one great purpose of creation; and if the question be merely a question of degree, a question of a little more

---

[10] Natural Theology, c. xxvi. p. 547.

[11] [In 1806 (Vol. ii, p. 314) the word *all* was excised; in 1807 (Vol. ii, p. 238) *our natural impulses* was changed to 'natural impulses', *our* being excised.]

[12] [In 1806 (Vol. ii, p. 315) this qualification, *at least to a considerable degree*, was omitted.]

or a little less strength, we may fairly distrust our competence to judge of the precise quantity necessary to answer the object with the smallest sum of incidental evil. In the present state of things we appear to have under our guidance a great power, capable of peopling a desert region in a small number of years; and yet, under other circumstances, capable of being confined by human energy and virtue to any limits, however narrow, at the expense of a small comparative quantity of evil. The analogy of all the other laws of nature would be completely violated, if in this instance alone there were no provision for accidental failures, no resources against the vices of mankind, or the partial mischiefs resulting from other general laws. To effect the apparent object without any attendant evil, it is evident that a perpetual change in the law of increase would be necessary, varying with the varying circumstances of each country. But instead of this, it is not only more consonant to the analogy of the other parts of nature, but we have reason to think that it is more conducive to the formation and improvement of the human mind, that the law should be uniform, and the evils, incidental to it under certain circumstances, be left to be mitigated or removed by man himself. His duties in this case vary with his situation; he is thus kept more alive to the consequences of his actions; and his faculties have evidently greater play, and opportunity of improvement, than if the evil were removed by a perpetual change of the law according to circumstances.

Even if from passions too easily subdued, or the facility of illicit inter-course, a state of celibacy were a matter of indifference, and not a state of some privation, the end of nature in the peopling of the earth would be apparently liable to be defeated. It is of the very utmost importance to the happiness of mankind, that they[13] should not increase too fast; but it does not appear that the object to be accomplished would admit of any very considerable diminution in the desire of marriage. It is clearly the duty of each individual not to marry till he has a prospect of supporting his children; but it is at the same time to be wished that he should retain undiminished his desire of marriage, in order that he may exert himself to realize this prospect, and be stimulated to make provision for the support of greater numbers.

It is evidently, therefore, regulation and direction which are required with regard to the principle of population, not diminution or alteration. And if moral restraint be the only virtuous mode of avoiding the incidental evils arising from this principle, our obligation to practise it will evidently rest exactly upon the same foundation as our obligation to practise any of the other virtues, the foundation of utility.[14]

---

[13] [In 1817 (Vol. III, p. 82) this was altered to:
    ... that population should not increase too fast; ...
[14] [In 1817 (Vol. III, p. 83) *the foundation of utility* was excised.]

[15]●Whatever indulgence we may be disposed to allow to occasional failures in the discharge of a duty of acknowledged difficulty; yet of the strict line of duty, during the period of celibacy, whatever that may be, we cannot doubt. And with regard to the necessity of this celibacy in countries that have been long peopled, or our obligation not to marry till we have a fair prospect of being able to support our children, it will appear to deserve the attention of the moralist, if it can be proved that an attention to this obligation is of more effect in the prevention of misery than all the other virtues combined; and that if, in violation of this duty, it were the general custom to follow the first impulse of nature, and marry at the age of puberty, the universal prevalence of every known virtue in the greatest conceivable degree would fail of rescuing society from the most wretched and desperate state of want, and all the diseases and famines which usually accompany it.●[15]

---

[15] [This paragraph was revised twice. In 1806 (Vol. II, p. 318) it read:
   ... difficulty; yet of the strict line of duty we cannot doubt. Our obligation not to marry till we have a fair prospect of being able to support our children will appear to deserve the attention of the moralist, if it can be proved that an attention to this obligation ...
[In 1807 (Vol. II, p. 242) Malthus altered the original passage again:
   ... an attention to this obligation is of most powerful effect in the prevention of misery; and that if it were the general custom to follow the first impulse of nature ...
[The excision of the *period of celibacy* in 1806 may have been a concession to reviewers, who declared that it was an impossibility; the affirmation that delayed marriage might prevent misery more effectively than all the other virtues combined was possibly expunged in 1807 after theological discussions with friends, at the East India College and elsewhere.]

# CHAPTER II

## *Of the Effects which would result to Society from the general practice of this virtue*[1]

One of the principal reasons which has prevented an assent to the doctrine, of the constant tendency of population to increase beyond the means of subsistence, is a great unwillingness to believe that the Deity would, by the laws of nature, bring beings into existence which, by the laws of nature, could not be supported in that existence. But if, in addition to that general activity and direction of our industry put in motion by these laws, we further consider that the incidental evils arising from them are constantly directing our attention to the proper check to population, moral restraint; and if it appear that by a strict obedience to those duties which are pointed out to us by the light of nature and reason, and are confirmed and sanctioned by revelation, these evils may be avoided, the objection will, I trust, be removed, and all apparent imputation on the goodness of the Deity be done away.

The heathen moralists never represented happiness as attainable on earth, but through the medium of virtue; and among their virtues, prudence ranked in the first class, and by some was even considered as including every other. The Christian religion places our present as well as future happiness in the exercise of those virtues which tend to fit us for a state of superior enjoyment; and the subjection of the passions to the guidance of reason, which, if not the whole, is a principal branch of prudence, is in consequence most particularly inculcated.

If, for the sake of illustration, we might be permitted to draw a picture of society, in which each individual endeavoured to attain happiness by the strict fulfilment of those duties, which the most enlightened of the ancient philosophers deduced from the laws of nature, and which have been directly taught, and received such powerful sanctions in the moral code of Christianity, it would present a very different scene from that which we now contemplate. Every act which was prompted by the desire of immediate gratification, but which threatened an ultimate overbalance of pain, would be considered as a breach of duty; and, consequently no man, whose earnings

---

[1] [In 1806 (Vol. II, p. 320) this chapter was headed 'Of the Effects which would result to Society from the Prevalence of this Virtue'. In 1817 (Vol. III, p. 84) it was changed again to 'Of the Effects which would result to Society from the Prevalence of Moral Restraint'.]

were only sufficient to maintain two children, would put himself in a situation in which he might have to maintain four or five, however he might be prompted to it by the passion of love. This prudential restraint, if it were generally adopted, by narrowing the supply of labour in the market, would, in the natural course of things soon raise its price. The period of delayed gratification would be passed in saving the earnings which were above the wants of a single man, and in acquiring habits of sobriety, industry, and economy, which would enable him, in a few years, to enter into the matrimonial contract without fear of its consequences. The operation of the preventive check in this way, by constantly keeping the population within the limits of the food, though constantly following its increase, would give a real value to the rise of wages and the sums saved by labourers before marriage, very different from those forced advances in the price of labour, or arbitrary parochial donations which, in proportion to their magnitude and extensiveness, must of necessity be followed by a proportional advance in the price of provisions. As the wages of labour would thus be sufficient to maintain with decency a large family, and as every married couple would set out with a sum for contingencies, all squalid[2] poverty would be removed from society; or would at least be confined to a very few, who had fallen into misfortunes against which no prudence or foresight could provide.

The interval between the age of puberty and the period at which each individual might venture on marriage must, according to the supposition, be passed in strict chastity; because the law of chastity cannot be violated without producing evil. The effect of anything like a promiscuous intercourse, which prevents the birth of children, is evidently to weaken the best affections of the heart, and in a very marked manner to degrade the female character. And any other intercourse would, without improper arts, bring as many children into the society as marriage, with a much greater probability of their becoming a burden to it.

These considerations show that the virtue of chastity is not, as some have supposed, a forced produce of artificial society; but that it has the most real and solid foundation in nature and reason; being apparently the only virtuous means of avoiding the vice and misery which result[3] from the principle of population.

In such a society as we have been supposing, it might be necessary for both sexes[4] to pass many of the early years of life in the single state; and if this were

---

[2] [In 1817 (Vol. III, p. 87) *squalid* was changed to 'abject'.
[3] [In 1806 (Vol. II, p. 323) this was amended to:
... which result so often from the principle of population.
[4] [In 1817 (Vol. III, p. 88) Malthus altered this to:
... for some of both sexes ...

general, there would certainly be room for a much greater number to marry afterwards, so that fewer, upon the whole, would be condemned to pass their lives in celibacy. If the custom of not marrying early prevailed generally, and if violations of chastity were equally dishonourable in both sexes, a more familiar and friendly intercourse between them might take place without danger. Two young people might converse together intimately, without its being immediately supposed that they either intended marriage or intrigue; and a much better opportunity would thus be given to both sexes of finding out kindred dispositions, and of forming those strong and lasting attachments, without which the married state is generally more productive of misery than of happiness. The earlier years of life would not be spent without love, though without the full gratification of it. The passion, instead of being extinguished, as it now too frequently is by early sensuality, would only be repressed for a time, that it might afterwards burn with a brighter, purer, and steadier flame; and the happiness of the married state, instead of an opportunity of immediate indulgence,[5] would be looked forward to as the prize of industry and virtue, and the reward of a genuine and constant attachment.[6]

The passion of love is a powerful stimulus in the formation of character, and often prompts to the most noble and generous exertions; but this is only when the affections are centred in one object; and generally, when full gratification is delayed by difficulties.[7] The heart is perhaps never so much disposed to virtuous conduct, and certainly at no time is the virtue of chastity so little difficult to men, as when under the influence of such a passion. Late marriages taking place in this way would be very different from those of the

---

[5] [In 1817 (Vol. III, p. 89) this was altered to:
    ... instead of only affording the means of immediate indulgence, would be ...

[6] Dr. Currie, in his interesting observations on the character and condition of the Scotch Peasantry, which he has prefixed to his life of Burns, remarks, with a just knowledge of human nature, that 'in appreciating the happiness and virtue of a community, there is perhaps no single criterion on which so much dependence may be placed, as the state of the intercourse between the sexes. Where this displays ardour of attachment, accompanied by purity of conduct, the character and the influence of women rise, our imperfect nature mounts in the scale of moral excellence; and, from the source of this single affection, a stream of felicity descends, which branches into a thousand rivulets, that enrich and adorn the field of life. Where the attachment between the sexes sinks into an appetite, the heritage of our species is comparatively poor, and man approaches to the condition of the brutes that perish.' Vol. i. p. 18.

[7] Dr. Currie observes, that the Scottish peasant, in the course of his passion, often exerts a spirit of adventure, of which a Spanish cavalier need not be ashamed. Burns' Works, vol. i. p. 16. It is not to be doubted, that this kind of romantic passion, which, Dr. C. says, characterizes the attachments of the humblest of the people of Scotland, and which has been greatly fostered by the elevation of mind given to them by a superior education, has had a most powerful and most beneficial influence on the national character.

same name at present, where the union is too frequently prompted solely by interested views, and the parties meet, not unfrequently, with exhausted constitutions, and generally with exhausted affections. The late marriages at present are indeed principally confined to the men; and there are few, however advanced in life they may be, who, if they determine to marry, do not fix their choice on a very young wife.[8] A young woman without fortune, when she has passed her twenty-fifth year, begins to fear, and with reason, that she may lead a life of celibacy; and with a heart capable of forming a strong attachment, feels, as each year creeps on, her hopes of finding an object on which to rest her affections gradually diminishing, and the uneasiness of her situation aggravated by the silly and unjust prejudices of the world. If the general age of marriage among women were later, the period of youth and hope would be prolonged, and fewer would be ultimately disappointed.

That a change of this kind would be a most decided advantage to the more virtuous half of society, we cannot for a moment doubt. However impatiently the privation might be borne by the men, it would be supported by the women readily and cheerfully; and if they could look forwards with just confidence to marriage at twenty-eight or thirty,[9] I fully believe that, if the matter were left to their free choice, they would clearly prefer waiting till this period, to the being involved in all the cares of a large family at twenty-five. The most eligible age of marriage, however, could not be fixed; but must depend on circumstances and situation, and must be determined entirely by experience.[10] There is no period of human life at which nature more strongly prompts to an union of the sexes, than from seventeen or eighteen, to twenty. In every society above that state of depression which almost excludes reason and foresight, these early tendencies must necessarily be restrained; and if, in the actual state of things, such a restraint on the impulses of nature be found unavoidable, at what time can we be consistently released from it, but at that period, whatever it may be, when in the existing circumstances of the society a fair prospect presents itself of maintaining a family?

The difficulty of moral restraint, will perhaps be objected to this doctrine. To him who does not acknowledge the authority of the Christian religion, I have only to say that, after the most careful investigation, this virtue appears to be absolutely necessary, in order to avoid certain evils which would otherwise result from the general laws of nature. According to his own

---

[8] [In 1817 (Vol. III, p. 91) this was changed:
    ... men; of whom there are few, however advanced in life, who, if they determine to marry, do not fix their choice on a young wife.

[9] [In 1817 (Vol. III, p. 92) Malthus lowered the ages to
    ... twenty-seven or twenty-eight, ...

[10] [In 1806 (Vol. II, p. 327) this was altered to:
    ... but must depend entirely on circumstance and situation.

principles, it is his duty to pursue the greatest good consistent with these laws; and not to fail in this important end, and produce an overbalance of misery, by a partial obedience to some of the dictates of nature while he neglects others. The path of virtue, though it be the only path which leads to permanent happiness, has always been represented by the heathen moralists as of difficult ascent.

To the Christian I would say that the scriptures most clearly and precisely point it out to us as our duty, to restrain our passions within the bounds of reason; and it is a palpable disobedience of this law to indulge our desires in such a manner, as reason tells us, will unavoidably end in misery. The Christian cannot consider the difficulty of moral restraint as any argument against its being his duty; since in almost every page of the sacred writings, man is described as encompassed on all sides by temptations which it is extremely difficult to resist; and though no duties are enjoined which do not contribute to his happiness on earth as well as in a future state, yet an undeviating obedience is never represented as an easy task.

There is in general so strong a tendency to love in early youth, that it is extremely difficult, at this period, to distinguish a genuine from a transient passion. If the earlier years of life were passed by both sexes in moral restraint, from the greater facility that this would give to the meeting of kindred dispositions, it might even admit of a doubt whether more happy marriages would not take place, and consequently more pleasure from the passion of love, than in a state such as that of America, the circumstances of which allow of a very early union of the sexes. But if we compare the intercourse of the sexes in such a society as I have been supposing, with that which now exists in Europe, taken under all its circumstances, it may safely be asserted that, independently of the load of misery which would be removed by the prevalence of moral restraint,[11] the sum of pleasurable sensations from the passion of love would be increased in a very great degree.

If we could suppose such a system general, the accession of happiness to society in its internal economy would scarcely be greater than in its external relations. It might fairly be expected that war, that great pest of the human race, would, under such circumstances, soon cease to extend its ravages so widely and so frequently, as it does at present,[12] and might ultimately perhaps cease entirely.

One of its first causes and most powerful impulses was undoubtedly an insufficiency of room and food; and, greatly as the circumstances of mankind have changed since it first began, the same cause still continues to operate

---

[11] [In 1806 (Vol. II, p. 330) *by the prevalence of moral restraint* was excised.]

[12] [In 1806 (Vol. II, p. 330) this paragraph concluded with the words 'at present', the optimistic attitude being impossible to maintain while Napoleon was supreme in Europe.]

and to produce, though in a smaller degree, the same effects. The ambition of princes would want instruments of destruction, if the distresses of the lower classes of people did not drive them under their standards. A recruiting serjeant always prays for a bad harvest and a want of employment, or, in other words, a redundant population.

In the earlier ages of the world, when war was the great business of mankind, and the drains of population from this cause were, beyond comparison, greater than in modern times, the legislators and statesmen of each country, adverting principally to the means of offence and defence, encouraged an increase of people in every possible way, fixed a stigma on barrenness and celibacy, and honoured marriage. The popular religions followed these prevailing opinions. In many countries the prolific power of nature was the object of solemn worship. In the religion of Mahomet, which was established by the sword, and the promulgation of which, in consequence, could not be unaccompanied by an extraordinary destruction of its followers, the procreation of children to glorify the Creator was laid down as one of the principal duties of man; and he who had the most numerous offspring was considered as having best answered the end of his creation. The prevalence of such moral sentiments had naturally a great effect in encouraging marriage; and the rapid procreation which followed, was partly the effect and partly the cause of incessant war. The vacancies occasioned by former desolations made room for the rearing of fresh supplies; and the overflowing rapidity, with which these supplies followed, constantly furnished fresh incitements and fresh instruments for renewed hostilities. Under the influence of such moral sentiments, it is difficult to conceive how the fury of incessant war should ever abate.

It is a pleasing confirmation of the truth and divinity of the Christian religion, and of its being adapted to a more improved state of human society, that it places our duties respecting marriage and the procreation of children in a different light from that in which they were before beheld.

Without entering minutely into the subject, which would evidently lead too far, I think it will be admitted, that if we apply the spirit of St. Paul's declarations respecting marriage to the present state of society, and the known constitution of our nature, the natural inference seems to be that, when marriage does not interfere with higher duties, it is right; when it does, it is wrong.[13] According to the genuine principles of moral science: 'The method of coming at the will of God from the light of nature is to inquire into the tendency of the action to promote or diminish the general happiness.'[14] There are perhaps few actions that tend so directly to diminish the general

---

[13] [See PAUL OF TARSUS (1) in the Alphabetical List.]
[14] Paley's Moral Philosophy, vol. i. b. ii. c. iv. p. 65.

happiness as to marry without the means of supporting children. He who commits this act, therefore, clearly offends against the will of God; and having become a burden on the society in which he lives, and plunged himself and family into a situation in which virtuous habits are preserved with more difficulty than in any other, he appears to have violated his duty to his neighbours and to himself, and thus to have listened to the voice of passion in opposition to his higher obligations.

In a society such as I have supposed, all the members of which endeavour to attain happiness by obedience to the moral code, derived from the light of nature, and enforced by strong sanctions in revealed religion, it is evident that no such marriages could take place; and the prevention of a redundant population, in this way, would remove one of the principal causes, and certainly the principal means of offensive war;[15] and at the same time tend powerfully to eradicate those two fatal political disorders, internal tyranny and internal tumult, which mutually produce each other.

Weak in offensive war,[16] in a war of defence such a society would be strong as a rock of adamant. Where every family possessed the necessaries of life in plenty, and a decent portion of its comforts and conveniences, there could not exist that hope of change, or at best that melancholy and disheartening indifference to it, which sometimes prompts the lower classes of people to say, 'let what will come, we cannot be worse off than we are now'.[17] Every heart and hand would be united to repel an invader, when each individual felt the value of the solid advantages which he enjoyed, and a prospect of change presented only a prospect of being deprived of them.

As it appears, therefore, that it is in the power of each individual to avoid all the evil consequences to himself and society resulting from the principle of population, by the practice of a virtue clearly dictated to him by the light of nature, and expressly enjoined in revealed religion; and as we have reason to think that the exercise of this virtue to a certain degree would rather tend to increase than diminish individual happiness; we can have no reason to impeach the justice of the Deity because his general laws make this virtue necessary, and punish our offences against it by the evils attendant upon vice, and the pains that accompany the various forms of premature death. A

---

[15] [In 1806 (Vol. II, p. 333) this was changed to:
   ... remove one of the principal encouragements to offensive war; ...

[16] [In 1806 (Vol. II, p. 333) this was amended to:
   Indisposed to a war of offence, ...

[17] [This echoes a pamphlet of Malthus's tutor Gilbert Wakefield (1756–1801) who died of typhus after two years' imprisonment for writing it: *A Reply to some parts of the Bishop of Llandaff's Address to the People of Great Britain.* Wakefield affirmed that 'the lower orders of the community' would not fight a French invading army, because 'they cannot well be poorer, or made to work harder than they did before' (second edition, London, 1798, p. 33).]

really virtuous society, such as I have supposed, would avoid these evils. It is the apparent object of the Creator to deter us from vice by the pains which accompany it, and to lead us to virtue by the happiness that it produces. This object appears to our conceptions to be worthy of a benevolent Creator. The laws of nature respecting population tend to promote this object. No imputation, therefore, on the benevolence of the Deity can be founded on these laws, which is not equally applicable to any of the evils necessarily incidental to an imperfect state of existence.

# CHAPTER III

## *Of the only effectual mode of improving the condition of the Poor*

He who publishes a moral code, or system of duties, however firmly he may be convinced of the strong obligation on each individual strictly to conform to it, has never the folly to imagine that it will be universally or even generally practised. But this is no valid objection against the publication of the code. If it were, the same objection would always have applied; we should be totally without general rules; and to the vices of mankind arising from temptation would be added a much longer list, than we have at present, of vices from ignorance.

Judging merely from the light of nature, if we feel convinced of the misery arising from a redundant population on the one hand, and of the evils and unhappiness, particularly to the female sex, arising from promiscuous intercourse, on the other, I do not see how it is possible for any person, who acknowledges the principle of utility as the great foundation of morals,[1] to escape the conclusion that moral restraint, till we are in a condition to support a family, is the strict line of duty;[2] and when revelation is taken into the question, this duty undoubtedly receives very powerful confirmation. At the same time, I believe that few of my readers can be less sanguine in their expectations of any great change in the general conduct of men on this subject than I am;[3] and the chief reason why, in the last chapter, I allowed myself to suppose the universal prevalence of this virtue, was that I might endeavour to remove any imputation on the goodness of the Deity, by showing that the evils arising from the principle of population were exactly of the same nature as the generality of other evils which excite fewer complaints, that they were increased by human ignorance and indolence, and

---

[1] [In 1817 (Vol. III, p. 103) this was altered to:
  ... utility as the great criterion of moral rules, ...
[2] [In 1806 (Vol. II, p. 337) Malthus changed this to:
  ... moral restraint, or the abstaining from marriage till we are in a condition to support a family, with a perfectly moral conduct during that period, is the strict line of duty; ...
[3] [In 1817 (Vol. III, p. 103) this sentence began:
  At the same time I believe that few of my readers can be less sanguine than I am in their expectations of any sudden and great change in the general conduct of men on this subject; and the chief reason ...

diminished by human knowledge and virtue; and on the supposition, that each individual strictly fulfilled his duty, would be almost totally removed; and this without any general diminution of those sources of pleasure, arising from the regulated indulgence of the passions, which have been justly considered as the principal ingredients of human happiness.

If it will answer any purpose of illustration, I see no harm in drawing the picture of a society in which each individual is supposed strictly to fulfil his duties; nor does a writer appear to be justly liable to the imputation of being visionary, unless he make such universal or general obedience necessary to the practical utility of his system, and to that degree of moderate and partial improvement, which is all that can rationally be expected from the most complete knowledge of our duties.

But in this respect there is an essential difference between that improved state of society, which I have supposed in the last chapter, and most of the other speculations on this subject. The improvement there supposed, if we ever should make approaches towards it, is to be effected in the way in which we have been in the habit of seeing all the greatest improvements effected, by a direct application to the interest and happiness of each individual. It is not required of us to act from motives to which we are unaccustomed; to pursue a general good, which we may not distinctly comprehend, or the effect of which may be weakened by distance and diffusion. The happiness of the whole is to be the result of the happiness of individuals, and to begin first with them. No co-operation is required. Every step tells. He who performs his duty faithfully will reap the full fruits of it, whatever may be the number of others who fail. This duty is express, and intelligible to the humblest capacity.[4] It is merely that he is not to bring beings into the world for whom he cannot find the means of support. When once this subject is cleared from the obscurity thrown over it by parochial laws and private benevolence, every man must feel the strongest conviction of such an obligation. If he cannot support his children, they must starve; and if he marry in the face of a fair probability that he shall not be able to support his children, he is guilty of all the evils which he thus brings upon himself, his wife, and his offspring. It is clearly his interest, and will tend greatly to promote his happiness, to defer marrying till, by industry and economy, he is in a capacity to support the children that he may reasonably expect from his marriage; and as he cannot in the meantime gratify his passions without violating an express command of God, and running a great risk of injuring himself, or some of his fellow creatures,

---

[4] [In 1807 (Vol. II, p. 263) this was altered to:
  This duty is intelligible to the humblest capacity.

considerations of his own interest and happiness will dictate to him the strong obligation to moral restraint.[5]

However powerful may be the impulses of passion, they are generally in some degree modified by reason. And it does not seem entirely visionary to suppose that, if the true and permanent cause of poverty were clearly explained, and forcibly brought home to each man's bosom, it would have some, and perhaps not an inconsiderable, influence on his conduct; at least the experiment has never yet been fairly tried. Almost everything that has been hitherto done for the poor has tended, as if with solicitous care, to throw a veil of obscurity over this subject, and to hide from them the true cause of their poverty. When the wages of labour are hardly sufficient to maintain two children, a man marries and has five or six. He of course finds himself miserably distressed. He accuses the insufficiency of the price of labour to maintain a family. He accuses his parish for their tardy and sparing fulfilment of their obligation to assist him. He accuses the avarice of the rich, who suffer him to want what they can so well spare. He accuses the partial and unjust institutions of society, which have awarded him an inadequate share of the produce of the earth. He accuses perhaps the dispensations of Providence, which have assigned to him a place in society so beset with unavoidable distress and dependence. In searching for objects of accusation, he never adverts to the quarter from which all his misfortunes originate. The last person that he would think of accusing is himself, on whom, in fact, the whole of the blame lies,[6] except in as far as he has been deceived by the higher classes of society. He may perhaps wish that he had not married, because he now feels the inconveniences of it; but it never enters into his head that he can have done any thing wrong. He has always been told that to raise up subjects for his king and country is a very meritorious act. [7●]He has done this act, and yet is suffering for it. He naturally thinks that he is suffering for righteousness sake;[●7] and it cannot but strike him as most extremely unjust and cruel in his king and country, to allow him thus to suffer, in return, for giving them what they are continually declaring that they particularly want.

Till these erroneous ideas have been corrected, and the language of nature and reason has been generally heard on the subject of population, instead of the language of error and prejudice, it cannot be said that any fair experiment has been made with the understandings of the common people;

---

[5] [In 1806 (Vol. II, p. 340) Malthus changed this to:
    ... strong obligation to a moral conduct while he remains unmarried.
[6] [In 1806 (Vol. II, p. 341) this was modified:
    ... on whom, in fact, the principal blame lies, ...
[7] [In 1817 (Vol. III, p. 108) this passage was altered:
    He has done this, and yet is suffering for it; and it cannot but strike him ...

and we cannot justly accuse them of improvidence and want of industry, till they act as they do now, after it has been brought home to their comprehensions, that they are themselves the cause of their own poverty; that the means of redress are in their own hands, and in the hands of no other persons whatever; that the society in which they live, and the government which presides over it, are totally without power in this respect;[8] and that however ardently they may desire to relieve them, and whatever attempts they may make to do so, they are really and truly unable to execute what they benevolently wish, but unjustly promise; that when the wages of labour will not maintain a family, it is an incontrovertible sign that their king and country do not want more subjects, or at least that they cannot support them; that if they marry in this case, so far from fulfilling a duty to society, they are throwing a useless burden on it, at the same time that they are plunging themselves into distress; and that they are acting directly contrary to the will of God, and bringing down upon themselves various diseases, which might all, or in a great part,[9] have been avoided, if they had attended to the repeated admonitions which he gives, by the general laws of nature, to every being capable of reason.

Dr. Paley, in his Moral Philosophy, observes, that 'in countries in which subsistence is become scarce, it behoves the state to watch over the public morals with increased solicitude; for nothing but the instinct of nature, under the restraint of chastity, will induce men to undertake the labour, or consent to the sacrifice of personal liberty and indulgence, which the support of a family in such circumstances requires'.[10] That it is always the duty of a state to use every exertion, likely to be effectual, in discouraging vice and promoting virtue, and that no temporary circumstances ought to cause any relaxation in these exertions, is certainly true. The means therefore proposed are always good; but the particular end in view, in this case, appears to be absolutely criminal. We wish to force people into marriage when, from the acknowledged scarcity of subsistence, they will have little chance of being able to support their children. We might as well force people into the water who are unable to swim. In both cases we rashly tempt Providence. Nor have we more reason to believe that a miracle will be worked to save us from the misery and mortality resulting from our conduct, in the one case, than in the other.

---

[8] [In 1806 (Vol. ii, p. 342) this was changed to:
    ... over it, are without any direct power in this respect; ...
  [In 1817 (Vol. iii, p. 109) the word *direct* was italicised.]
[9] [In 1806 (Vol. ii, p. 343) this was changed to:
    ... which might all, or the greater part, have been avoided, ...
[10] Vol. ii. c. xi. p. 352.

The object of those who really wish to better the condition of the lower classes of society must be to raise the relative proportion between the price of labour and the price of provisions; so as to enable the labourer to command a larger share of the necessaries and comforts of life. We have hitherto principally attempted to attain this end by encouraging the married poor, and consequently increasing the number of labourers, and overstocking the market with a commodity which we still say that we wish to be dear. It would seem to have required no great spirit of divination to foretell the certain failure of such a plan of proceeding. There is nothing, however, like experience. It has been tried in many different countries, and for many hundred years, and the success has always been answerable to the nature of the scheme. It is really time now to try something else.

When it was found that oxygen, or pure vital air, would not cure consumptions, as was expected, but rather aggravated their symptoms, a trial was made of an air of the most opposite kind. I wish we had acted with the same philosophical[11] spirit in our attempts to cure the disease of poverty; and having found that the pouring in of fresh supplies of labour only tended to aggravate the symptoms, had tried what would be the effect of withholding a little these supplies.

In all old and fully-peopled states it is from this method, and this alone, that we can rationally expect any essential and permanent amelioration in the condition of the lower classes of people.[12]

In an endeavour to raise the proportion of the quantity of provisions to the number of consumers, in any country, our attention would naturally be first directed to the increasing of the absolute quantity of provisions; but finding that as fast as we did this, the number of consumers more than kept pace with it, and that, with all our exertions, we were still as far as ever behind, we should be convinced that our efforts, directed only in this way, would never succeed. It would appear to be setting the tortoise to catch the hare. Finding therefore that, from the laws of nature, we could not proportion the food to the population, our next attempt should naturally be to proportion the population to the food. If we can persuade the hare to go to sleep, the tortoise may have some chance of overtaking her.[13]

We are not, however, to relax our efforts in increasing the quantity of provisions, but to combine another effort with it; that of keeping the population, when once it has been overtaken, at such a distance behind as to effect the relative proportion which we desire; and thus unite the two grand

---

[11] [*Philosophical* at this period corresponded to the modern word 'scientific'.]
[12] [In 1826 (Vol. ii, p. 290) this was altered to:
    ... the condition of the labouring classes of the people.
[13] [See AESOP in the Alphabetical List.]

*desiderata*, a great actual population, and a state of society in which squalid poverty[14] and dependence are comparatively but little known; two objects which are far from being incompatible.

If we be really serious in what appears to be the object of such general research, the mode of essentially and permanently bettering the condition of the poor, we must explain to them the true nature of their situation, and show them that the withholding of the supplies of labour is the only possible way of really raising its price; and that they themselves, being the possessors of this commodity, have alone the power to do this.

I cannot but consider this mode of diminishing poverty as so perfectly clear in theory, and so invariably confirmed by the analogy of every other commodity which is brought to market, that nothing but its being shown to be calculated to produce greater evils than it proposes to remedy can justify us in not making the attempt to put it into execution.

---

[14] [In 1817 (Vol. III, p. 113) *squalid* was changed to 'abject'.

# CHAPTER IV

## *Objections to this mode considered*

One objection, which perhaps will be made to this plan, is that from which alone it derives its value – a market rather understocked with labour. This must undoubtedly take place in a certain degree; but by no means in such a degree as to affect the wealth and prosperity of the country. [1]●The way in which we are going on at present, and the enormous increase in the price of provisions which seems to threaten us, will tend much more effectually to enable foreigners to undersell us in the markets of Europe, than the plan now proposed. If the population of this country were better proportioned to its food, the nominal price of labour might be lower than it is now, and yet be sufficient to maintain a wife and six children.●[1] But putting this subject of a market understocked with labour in the most unfavourable point of view, if the rich will not submit to a slight inconvenience necessarily attendant on the attainment of what they profess to desire, they cannot really be in earnest in their professions. Their benevolence to the poor must be either childish play or hypocrisy; it must be either to amuse themselves, or to pacify the minds of the common people with a mere show of attention to their wants. To wish to better the condition of the poor, by enabling them to command a greater quantity of the necessaries and comforts of life, and then to complain of high wages, is the act of a silly boy who gives away his cake and then cries for it. A market overstocked with labour, and an ample remuneration to each labourer, are objects perfectly incompatible with each other. In the annals of the world they never existed together; and to couple them, even in imagination, betrays a gross ignorance of the simplest principles of political economy.

A second objection that may be made to this plan is the diminution of population that it would cause. It is to be considered, however, that this diminution is merely relative; and when once this relative diminution had been effected, by keeping the population stationary, while the supply of food had increased, it might then start afresh, and continue increasing for ages, with the increase of food, maintaining always the same relative proportion to

---

[1] [In 1817 (Vol. III, p. 115) these two sentences were omitted.]

it.[2] I can easily conceive that this country, with a proper direction of the national industry, might, in the course of some centuries, contain two or three times its present population, and yet every man in the kingdom be much better fed and clothed than he is at present. While the springs of industry continue in vigour, and a sufficient part of that industry is directed to agriculture, we need be under no apprehensions of a deficient population; and nothing perhaps would tend so strongly to excite a spirit of industry and economy among the poor, as a thorough knowledge that their happiness must always depend principally upon themselves; and that, if they obey their passions in opposition to their reason, or be not industrious and frugal while they are single men,[3] to save a sum for the common contingencies of the married state, they must expect to suffer the natural evils which Providence has prepared for those who disobey its repeated admonitions.

A third objection which may be started to this plan, and the only one which appears to me to have any kind of plausibility, is that, by endeavouring to urge the duty of moral restraint on the poor, we may increase the quantity of vice relating to the sex.

I should be most extremely sorry to say anything which could either directly or remotely be construed unfavourably to the cause of virtue: but I certainly cannot think that the vices which relate to the sex, are the only vices which are to be considered in a moral question; or that they are even the greatest and most degrading to the human character. They can rarely or never be committed without producing unhappiness somewhere or other, and therefore ought always to be strongly reprobated; but there are other vices, the effects of which are still more pernicious; and there are other situations which lead more certainly to moral offences than the refraining from marriage. Powerful as may be the temptations to a breach of chastity, I am inclined to think that they are impotent in comparison of the temptations arising from continued distress. A large class of women, and many men, I have no doubt, pass a considerable part of their lives in moral restraint;[4] but I believe there will be found very few, who pass through the ordeal of squalid and hopeless poverty, or even of long continued embarrassed circumstances, without a considerable[5] moral degradation of character.

In the higher and middle classes of society it is a melancholy and

---

[2] [In 1817 (Vol. III, p. 116) this read:
... always nearly the same relative proportion to it.
[3] [In 1817 (Vol. III, p. 117) the word *men* was excised.]
[4] [In 1806 (Vol. II, p. 351) *in moral restraint* was changed to:
... in chastity; ...
[In 1807 (Vol. II, p. 275) this was altered again to:
... pass a considerable part of their lives consistently with the laws of chastity; ...
[5] [In 1807 (Vol. II, p. 276) *considerable* was changed to 'great'.

distressing sight to observe, not unfrequently, a man of a noble and ingenuous disposition, once feelingly alive to a sense of honour and integrity, gradually sinking under the pressure of circumstances, making his excuses at first with a blush of conscious shame, afraid of seeing the faces of his friends from whom he may have borrowed money, reduced to the meanest tricks and subterfuges to delay or avoid the payment of his just debts; till ultimately grown familiar with falsehood, and at enmity with the world, he loses all the grace and dignity of man.

To the general prevalence of indigence, and the extraordinary encouragements which we afford in this country to a total want of foresight and prudence among the common people,[6] is to be attributed the principal part of those continual depredations on property, and other more atrocious crimes, which drives us to the painful resource of such a number of executions.[7] According to Mr. Colquhoun, above twenty thousand miserable individuals of various classes rise up every morning without knowing how, or by what means, they are to be supported during the passing day, or where, in many instances, they are to lodge on the succeeding night.[8] It is by these unhappy persons that the principal depredations on the public are committed; and supposing but few of them to be married, and driven to these acts from the necessity of supporting their children; yet still it will not cease to be true[9] that the too great frequency of marriage among the poorest classes is one of the principal causes of the temptations to these crimes. A considerable part of these unhappy wretches will probably be found to be the offspring of such marriages, educated in workhouses where every vice is propagated, or bred up at home in filth and rags, and with an utter ignorance of every moral obligation.[10] A still greater part perhaps consists of persons who, being unable for some time to get employment, owing to the full supply of labour,

---

[6] Mr. Colquhoun, speaking of the poor laws, observes that 'in spite of all the ingenious arguments which have been used in favour of a system, admitted to be wisely conceived in its origin, the effects it has produced incontestably prove that, with respect to the mass of the poor, there is something radically wrong in the execution. If it were not so, it is impossible that there could exist in the metropolis such an inconceivable portion of human misery amidst examples of munificence and benevolence unparalleled in any age or country.' Police of Metropolis, c. xiii. p. 359.

[7] In the effects of the poor laws, I fully agree with Mr. Colquhoun; but I cannot agree with him in admitting that the system was well conceived in its origin. I attribute still more evil to the original ill conception than to the subsequent ill execution.

Mr. Colquhoun observes, that: 'Indigence, in the present state of society, may be considered as a principal cause of the increase of crimes.' Police of Metropolis, c. xiii. p. 352.

[8] Id. c. xi. p. 313.

[9] [In 1817 (Vol. III, p. 131) this was changed to:
... yet still it is probably true that the too great frequency of marriage ...

[10] Police of Metropolis, c. xi. p. 313 and c. xii. p. 355, 370.

have been urged to these extremities by their temporary wants, and having thus lost their characters, are rejected even when their labour may be wanted by the well-founded caution of civil society.[11]

When indigence does not produce overt acts of vice, it palsies every virtue. Under the continued temptations to a breach of chastity, occasional failures may take place, and the moral sensibility, in other respects, not be very strikingly impaired; but the continued temptations which beset hopeless poverty, and the strong sense of injustice that generally accompanies it from an ignorance of its true cause, tend so powerfully to sour the disposition, to harden the heart, and deaden the moral sense that, generally speaking, virtue takes her flight clear away from the tainted spot, and does not often return.

Even with respect to the vices which relate to the sex, marriage has been found to be by no means a complete remedy. Among the higher classes, our Doctors Commons,[12] and the lives that many married men are known to

---

[11] Police of the Metropolis, c. xiii. p. 353. et seq. In so large a town as London, which must necessarily encourage a prodigious influx of strangers from the country, there must be always a great many persons out of work; and it is possible that some public institution for the relief of the casual poor, upon a plan similar to that proposed by Mr. Colquhoun (c. xiii. p. 371.) might, under very judicious management, produce more good than evil. But for this purpose it would be absolutely necessary that, if work were provided by the institution, the sum that a man could earn by it should be less than the worst paid common labour; otherwise the claimants would rapidly increase, and the funds would soon be inadequate to their object. In the institution at Hamburgh, which appears to have been the most successful of any yet established, the nature of the work was such that, though paid above the usual price, a person could not easily earn by it more than eighteen pence a week. It was the determined principle of the managers of the institution to reduce the support which they gave lower than what any industrious man or woman in such circumstances could earn. (Account of the management of the poor in Hamburgh, by C. Voght, p. 18.) And it is to this principle that they attribute their success. It should be observed, however, that neither the institution at Hamburgh, nor that planned by Count Rumford in Bavaria, has subsisted long enough for us to be able to pronounce on their permanent good effects. It will not admit of a doubt that institutions for the relief of the poor, on their first establishment, remove a great quantity of distress. The only question is whether, as succeeding generations arise, the increasing funds necessary for their support, and the increasing numbers that become dependent, are not greater evils than that which was to be remedied; and whether the country will not ultimately be left with as much mendicity as before, besides all the poverty and dependence accumulated in the public institutions. This seems to be nearly the case in England at present. I do not believe[(a)] that we should have more beggars if we had no poor laws.

[(a)] [In 1817 (Vol. III, p. 123) *I do not believe* was changed to:
    It may be doubted ...

[12] [*Doctors' Commons* originally meant the 'common table' (where simple set meals were provided) of the Association or College of Doctors of Civil Law in London, founded in 1509 and incorporated in 1768. In the buildings which became known as Doctors' Commons there were five 'courts'; they dealt with ecclesiastical law, including prosecution for heresy, Admiralty cases – frequently relating to prize money – and family matters such as the probate of wills, licences for marriage, and divorce suits.]

lead, sufficiently prove this; and the same kind of vice, though not so much heard of among the lower classes of people, owing to their indifference and want of delicacy on these subjects,[13] is probably not very much less frequent.

Add to this, that squalid poverty,[14] particularly when joined with idleness, is a state the most unfavourable to chastity that can well be conceived. The passion is as strong, or nearly so, as in other situations, and every restraint on it, from personal respect, or a sense of morality, is generally removed. There is a degree of squalid poverty, in which, if a girl was brought up, I should say that her being really modest at twenty was an absolute miracle. Those persons must have extraordinary minds indeed, and such as are not usually formed under similar circumstances, who can continue to respect themselves when no other person whatever respects them. If the children thus brought up were even to marry at twenty, it is probable that they would have passed some years in vicious habits before that period.

If after all, however, these arguments should appear insufficient; if we reprobate the idea of endeavouring to encourage the virtues of moral restraint and prudence among the poor,[15] from a fear of producing vice; and if we think that to facilitate marriage by all possible means is a point of the first consequence to the morality and happiness of the people; let us act consistently and, before we proceed, endeavour to make ourselves acquainted with the mode by which alone we can effect our object.

---

[13] [In 1817 (Vol. III, p. 124) these words were excised, and the passage read:
   ... lower classes of people, is probably in all our great towns not much less frequent.
[14] [In 1817 (Vol. III, p. 124) *squalid* was again changed to 'abject', as in ch. ii, n.2, and ch. iii, n.14.
[15] [In 1806 (Vol. II, p. 357) this was altered:
   ... to encourage the virtue of moral restraint among the poor, ...

# CHAPTER V

## *Of the consequences of pursuing the opposite mode*

It is an evident truth that, whatever may be the rate of increase in the means of subsistence, the increase of population must be limited by it, at least after the food has once been divided into the smallest shares that will support life. All the children born, beyond what would be required to keep up the population to this level, must necessarily perish, unless room be made for them by the deaths of grown persons. It has appeared indeed clearly, in the course of this work, that in all old states the marriages and births depend principally upon the deaths, and that there is no encouragement to early unions so powerful as a great mortality. To act consistently, therefore, we should facilitate, instead of foolishly and vainly endeavouring to impede the operations of nature, in producing this mortality; and if we dread the too frequent visitation of the horrid form of famine, we should sedulously encourage the other forms of destruction which we compel nature to use. Instead of recommending cleanliness to the poor, we should encourage contrary habits. In our towns we should make the streets narrower, crowd more people into the houses, and court the return of the plague. In the country we should build our villages near stagnant pools, and particularly encourage settlements in all marshy and unwholesome situations.[1] But above all, we should reprobate specific remedies for ravaging diseases, and those benevolent, but much mistaken men, who have thought they were doing a service to mankind by projecting schemes for the total extirpation of

---

[1] Necker, speaking of the proportion of the births in France, makes use of a new and instructive expression on this subject, though he hardly seems to be sufficiently aware of it himself. He says: 'Le nombre des naissances est a celui des habitans de un a vingt-trois et vingt-quatre dans le à lieux *contrariés par la nature, ou par des circonstances morales*: ce meme rapport dans la plus grande partie de la France, est de un a 25, $25\frac{1}{2}$, & 26.' Administ. des Finances, tom. i. c. ix. p. 254. 12mo. It would appear, therefore, that we had nothing more to do,[a] than to settle people in marshy situations, and oppress them by a bad government, in order to attain what politicians have hitherto considered as so desirable – a great proportion of marriages, and a great proportion of births. ['The proportion of births to the number of inhabitants is one to twenty-three or twenty-four in situations that are naturally unhealthy or socially unfavourable; the same ratio in the greater part of France is one to 25, $25\frac{1}{2}$ or 26.']

[a] [In 1826 (Vol. II, p. 301) this sentence began:

It appears, therefore, that we have nothing more to do ...

particular disorders. If by these, and similar means, the annual mortality were increased from 1 in 36 or 40, to 1 in 18 or 20, we might probably every one of us marry at the age of puberty, and yet few be absolutely starved.

If, however, we all marry at this age, and yet still continue our exertions to impede the operations of nature, we may rest assured that all our efforts will be vain. Nature will not, nor cannot, be defeated in her purposes. The necessary mortality must come in some form or other; and the extirpation of one disease will only be the signal for the birth of another, perhaps more fatal. We cannot lower the waters of misery by pressing them down in different places which must necessarily make them rise somewhere else: the only way in which we can hope to effect our purpose is by drawing them off. To this course nature is constantly directing our attention by the chastisements which await a contrary conduct. These chastisements are more or less severe, in proportion to the degree in which her admonitions produce their intended effect. In this country, at present, these admonitions are by no means entirely neglected. The preventive check to population prevails to a considerable degree, and her chastisements are in consequence moderate: but if we were all to marry at the age of puberty, they would be severe indeed. Political evils would probably be added to physical. A people goaded by constant distress, and visited by frequent returns of famine, could not be kept down but by a cruel despotism. We should approach to the state of the people in Egypt or Abyssinia; and I would ask whether, in that case, it is probable that we should be more virtuous?

Physicians have long remarked the great changes which take place in diseases; and that, while some appear to yield to the efforts of human care and skill, others seem to become in proportion more malignant and fatal. Dr. William Heberden published, not long since, some valuable observations on this subject deduced from the London bills of mortality. In his preface, speaking of these bills, he says: 'the gradual changes they exhibit in particular diseases correspond to the alterations which in time are known to take place in the channels through which the great stream of mortality is constantly flowing'.[2] In the body of his work afterwards, speaking of some particular diseases, he observes with that candour which always distinguishes true science: 'It is not easy to give a satisfactory reason for all the changes which may be observed to take place in the history of diseases. Nor is it any disgrace to physicians, if their causes are often so gradual in their operation, or so subtle, as to elude investigation.'[3]

I hope I shall not be accused of presumption, in venturing to suggest that, under certain circumstances, such changes must take place; and perhaps

---

[2] Observations on the Increase and Decrease of different Diseases. Preface, p. v. 4to. 1801.
[3] Id. p. 43.

without any alteration in those proximate causes which are usually looked to on these occasions. If this should appear to be true, it will not seem extraordinary that the most skilful and scientific physicians, whose business it is principally to investigate proximate causes, should sometimes search for these causes in vain.

In a country which keeps its population at a certain standard, if the average number of marriages and births be given, it is evident, that the average number of deaths will also be given; and, to use Dr. Heberden's metaphor, the channels through which the great stream of mortality is constantly flowing will always convey off a given quantity. Now if we stop up any of these channels, it is perfectly clear that the stream of mortality must run with greater force through some of the other channels; that is, if we eradicate some diseases, others will become proportionally more fatal. In this case the only distinguishable cause is the damming up a necessary outlet of mortality.[4] Nature, in the attainment of her great purposes, seems always to seize upon the weakest part. If this part be made strong by human skill, she seizes upon the next weakest part, and so on in succession; not like a capricious deity, with an intention to sport with our suffering and constantly to defeat our labours; but like a kind though sometimes severe instructor, with the intention of teaching us to make all parts strong, and to chase vice and misery from the earth. In avoiding one fault we are too apt to run into some other; but we always find Nature faithful to her great object, at every false step we commit ready to admonish us of our errors, by the infliction of some physical or moral evil. If the prevalence of the preventive check to population, in a sufficient degree, were to remove many of those diseases which now afflict us, yet be accompanied by a considerable increase of the vice of promiscuous intercourse; it is probable that the disorders and unhappiness, the physical and moral evils arising from this vice, would increase in strength and degree; and, admonishing us severely of our error, would point to the only line of conduct approved by nature, reason, and religion: abstinence from marriage till we can support our children, and chastity till that period arrives.

In the case just stated, in which the population and the number of marriages are supposed to be fixed, the necessity of a change in the mortality of some diseases, from the diminution or extinction of others, is capable of mathematical demonstration. The only obscurity which can possibly involve this subject arises from taking into consideration the effect that might be produced by a diminution of mortality in increasing the population, or in decreasing the number of marriages. That the removal of any of the

---

[4] The way in which it operates is probably by increasing poverty, in consequence of a supply of labour too rapid for the demand.

particular causes of mortality can have no further effect upon population than the means of subsistence will allow; and that it has little or no influence on these means of subsistence is a fact of which, I hope, the reader is already convinced.[5] Of its operation in tending to prevent marriage, by diminishing the demand for fresh supplies of children, I have no doubt; and there is reason to think that it had this effect, in no inconsiderable degree, on the extinction of the plague, which had so long and so dreadfully ravaged this country. Dr. Heberden draws a striking picture of the favourable change observed in the health of the people of England since this period; and justly attributes it to the improvements which have gradually taken place, not only in London, but in all great towns; and in the manner of living throughout the kingdom, particularly with respect to cleanliness and ventilation.[6] But these causes would not have been adequate to the effect observed,[7] if they had not been accompanied by an increase of the preventive check; and probably the spirit of cleanliness, and better mode of living, which then began to prevail, by spreading more generally a decent and useful pride, principally contributed to this increase. The diminution in the number of marriages, however, was not sufficient to make up for the great decrease of mortality from the extinction of the plague, and the striking reduction of the deaths in the dysentery.[8] While these and some other disorders become almost evanescent, consumption, palsy, apoplexy, gout, lunacy, and the small-pox, became more mortal.[9] The widening of these drains was necessary to carry off the population which still remained redundant, notwithstanding the increased operation of the preventive check, and the part which was annually disposed of and enabled to exist[10] by the increase of agriculture.

Dr. Haygarth, in the sketch of his benevolent plan for the extermination of the casual small-pox, draws a frightful picture of the mortality which has been occasioned by this distemper; attributes to it the slow progress of population; and makes some curious calculations on the favourable effects which would be produced, in this respect, by its extermination.[11] His conclusions, however, I fear, would not follow from his premises. I am far

---

[5] [In 1817 (Vol. III, pp. 133–4) this sentence was altered:

   ... than the means of subsistence will allow, and that it has no certain and necessary influence on these means of subsistence, are facts of which the reader must be already convinced.

[6] Observ. on Inc. and Dec. of Diseases, p. 35.

[7] [In 1806 (Vol. II, p. 365) this sentence began:

   But these causes would not have produced the effect observed, if they had not been accompanied ...

[8] Observ. on Inc. and Dec. of Diseases, p. 34.      [9] Id. p. 36 et seq.

[10] [In 1806 (Vol. II, p. 366) *exist* was changed to 'subsist'.

[11] Vol. i. part ii. sect. v. and vi.

from doubting that millions and millions of human beings have been destroyed by the small-pox. But were its devastations, as Dr. Haygarth supposes, many thousand degrees greater than the plague,[12] I should still doubt whether the average population of the earth had been diminished by them a single unit.[13] The small-pox is certainly one of the channels, and a very broad one, which nature has opened for the last thousand years, to keep down the population to the level of the means of subsistence; but had this been closed, others would have become wider, or new ones would have been formed. In ancient times the mortality from war and the plague was incomparably greater than in modern. On the gradual diminution of this stream of mortality, the generation and almost universal prevalence of the small-pox is a great and striking instance of one of those changes in the channels of mortality, which ought to awaken our attention, and animate us to patient and persevering investigation. For my own part, I feel not the slightest doubt that, if the introduction of the cow-pox should extirpate the small-pox, and yet the number of marriages continue the same, we shall find a very perceptible difference in the increased mortality of some other diseases. Nothing could prevent this effect but a sudden start in our agriculture; and should this take place, which I fear we have not much reason to expect, it will not be owing[14] to the number of children saved from death by the cow-pox inoculation, but to the alarms occasioned among the people of property by the late scarcities,[15] and to the increased gains of farmers, which have been so absurdly reprobated. I am strongly, however, inclined to believe that the number of marriages will not, in this case, remain the same; but that the gradual light which may be expected to be thrown on this interesting topic of human inquiry will teach us how to make the extinction of a mortal disorder a real blessing to us, a real improvement in the general health and happiness of the society.

If, on contemplating the increase of vice which might contingently follow an attempt to inculcate the duty of moral restraint, and the increase of misery that must necessarily follow the attempts to encourage marriage and population, we come to the conclusion not to interfere in any respect, but to leave every man to his own free choice, and responsible only to God for the evil which he does in either way; this is all I contend for; I would on no account do more; but I contend that at present we are very far from doing this.

---

[12] Vol. i. part ii. s. viii p 164.     [13] [In 1806 (Vol. ii, p. 366) *a single unit* was excised.]
[14] [In 1817 (Vol. iii, p. 137) this sentence was altered:
      ... agriculture; and if this should take place, it will not be so much owing ...
[15] [In 1817 (Vol. iii, p. 137) a footnote was added here:
      The scarce harvests of 1799 and 1800. The start here alluded to, certainly took place from 1801 to 1814, and provision was really made for the diminished mortality.

Among the lower classes,[16] where the point is of the greatest importance, the poor laws afford a direct, constant, and systematical encouragement to marriage, by removing from each individual that heavy responsibility, which he would incur by the laws of nature, for bringing beings into the world which he could not support. Our private benevolence has the same direction as the poor laws, and almost invariably tends to facilitate the rearing of families,[17] and to equalize, as much as possible, the circumstances of married and single men.

Among the higher classes of people, the superior distinctions which married women receive, and the marked inattentions to which single women of advanced age are exposed, enable many men, who are agreeable neither in mind or person, and are besides in the wane of life, to choose a partner among the young and fair instead of being confined, as nature seems to dictate, to persons of nearly their own age and accomplishments. It is scarcely to be doubted that the fear of being an old maid, and of that silly and unjust ridicule, which folly sometimes attaches to this name, drives many women into the marriage union with men whom they dislike or, at best to whom they are perfectly indifferent. Such marriages must to every delicate mind appear little better than legal prostitutions; and they often burden the earth with unnecessary children, without compensating for it by an accession of happiness and virtue to the parties themselves.

Throughout all the ranks of society, the prevailing opinions respecting the duty and obligation of marriage cannot but have a very powerful influence. The man who thinks that, in going out of the world without leaving representatives behind him, he shall have failed in an important duty to society, will be disposed to force rather than to repress his inclinations on this subject; and when his reason represents to him the difficulties attending a family, he will endeavour not to attend to these suggestions, will still determine to venture, and will hope that, in the discharge of what he conceives to be his duty, he shall not be deserted by Providence.

In a civilized country, such as England, where a taste for the decencies and comforts of life prevails among a very large class of people, it is not possible that the encouragements to marriage from positive institutions and prevailing opinions should entirely obscure the light of nature and reason on this subject; but still they contribute to make it comparatively weak and indistinct. And till this obscurity is entirely removed, and the poor are

---

[16] [In 1817 (Vol. III, p. 138) this was altered to:
  Among the lower classes of society, ...
[17] [In 1817 (Vol. III, p. 139) this was changed to:
  ... and almost invariably tends to encourage marriage, and to equalize, as much as possible, ...

undeceived with respect to the principal cause of their past poverty, and taught to know that their future happiness or misery must depend chiefly upon themselves, it cannot be said that, with regard to the great question of marriage or celibacy, we leave every man to his own free and fair choice.[18]

---

[18] [This sentence was amended three times. In 1806 (Vol. II, p. 371) Malthus omitted *or celibacy*, so that the final words were:

   ... with regard to the great question of marriage, we leave every man ...

[In 1817 (Vol. III, p. 141) the sentence began:

   And till this obscurity is removed, and the poor are undeceived with respect to the principal cause of their poverty, and taught to know ...

[In 1826 (Vol. II, p. 310) the word *future* was expunged, like the word *past* in 1817:

   ... taught to know that their happiness or misery must depend chiefly upon themselves, ...

# CHAPTER VI

## *Effect of the knowledge of the principal cause of poverty on Civil Liberty*[1]

It may appear, perhaps, that a doctrine, which attributes the greatest part of the sufferings of the lower classes of society exclusively to themselves, is unfavourable to the cause of liberty; as affording a tempting opportunity to governments of oppressing their subjects at pleasure, and laying the whole blame on the laws of nature and the imprudence of the poor. We are not, however, to trust to first appearances; and I am strongly disposed to believe that those who will be at the pains to consider this subject deeply, will be convinced that nothing would so powerfully contribute to the advancement of rational freedom as a thorough knowledge, generally circulated, of the principal cause of poverty; and that the ignorance of this cause, and the natural consequences of this ignorance, form, at present, one of the chief obstacles to its progress.

The pressure of distress on the lower classes of people, together with the habit of attributing this distress to their rulers, appears to me to be the rock of defence, the castle, the guardian spirit of despotism. It affords to the tyrant the fatal and unanswerable plea of necessity. It is the reason why every free government tends constantly to destruction; and that its appointed guardians become daily less jealous of the encroachments of power. It is the reason

---

[1] [The cherished British ideal of civil liberty was at this period a subject of violent debate. Civil liberty included free speech (which involved freedom of the press, freedom of association and assembly, and freedom to correspond overseas) as well as the equality of all classes before the law, and the old right of *Habeas Corpus*, which was interpreted as meaning no imprisonment without a public trial. The Act of Parliament embodying the principle of *Habeas Corpus* was passed in 1679; in times of emergency, such as the Jacobite rebellion of 1745, the Habeas Corpus Act was suspended.

British liberty was sustained by a hereditary House of Lords and a House of Commons elected by a very limited number of voters; their franchise was determined by the chances of local history even more than by a property qualification. Inevitably there was agitation for reform, and William Pitt, as Prime Minister, had tried in vain to effect a small re-distribution of seats in the Commons in 1785. The whole situation was transformed by the French Revolution of 1789; fears of invasion, and of insurrection at home, led to repressive measures by the government, and Pitt suspended the Habeas Corpus Act in 1794, for the first time since 1745. At the turn of the century a serious shortage of food intensified the general unrest, and bread riots were widespread. See also ch. v of Bk III, PORTLAND in the Alphabetical List, and n.17 of ch. ii of Bk. IV.]

why so many noble efforts in the cause of freedom have failed, and why almost every revolution, after long and painful sacrifices, has terminated in a military despotism. While any dissatisfied man of talents has power to persuade the lower classes of people that all their poverty and distress arise solely from the iniquity of the government, though perhaps the greatest part of what they suffer is totally unconnected with this cause, it is evident that the seeds of fresh discontent and fresh revolutions are continually sowing. When an established government has been destroyed, finding that their poverty is not removed, their resentment naturally falls upon the successors to power; and when these have been immolated without producing the desired effect, other sacrifices are called for, and so on without end. Are we to be surprised that, under such circumstances, the majority of well-disposed people, finding that a government with proper restrictions is unable to support itself against the revolutionary spirit, and weary and exhausted with perpetual change, to which they can see no end, should give up the struggle in despair, and throw themselves into the arms of the first power which can afford them protection against the horrors of anarchy?

A mob, which is generally the growth of a redundant population, goaded by resentment for real sufferings, but totally ignorant of the quarter from which they originate, is of all monsters the most fatal to freedom. It fosters a prevailing tyranny, and engenders one where it was not; and though, in its dreadful fits of resentment, it appears occasionally to devour its unsightly offspring; yet no sooner is the horrid deed committed, than, however unwilling it may be to propagate such a breed, it immediately groans with the pangs of[2] a new birth.

Of the tendency of mobs to produce tyranny, we may not be long[3] without an example in this country. As a friend to freedom, and an enemy to large standing armies, it is with extreme reluctance that I am compelled to acknowledge that, had it not been for the organized force in the country,[4] the distresses of the people during the late scarcities,[5] encouraged by the extreme ignorance and folly of many among the higher classes, might have driven them to commit the most dreadful outrages, and ultimately to involve the country in all the horrors of famine. Should such periods often recur (a recurrence which we have too much reason to apprehend from the present

---

[2] [In 1806 (Vol. II, p. 374) *the pangs of* were excised.]

[3] [In 1817 (Vol. III, p. 145) this was changed to:
    ... we may not, perhaps, be long without an example in this country.

[4] [In 1806 (Vol. II, p. 374) Malthus made two alterations to this sentence:
    As a friend to freedom, and naturally an enemy to large standing armies ... I am compelled
    to acknowledge that, had it not been for the great organized force in the country, ...

[5] [In 1817 (Vol. III, p. 145) a footnote was added here:
    1800 and 1801.

state of the country) the prospect which opens to our view is melancholy in the extreme. The English constitution will be seen hastening with rapid strides to the *Euthanasia* foretold by Hume, unless its progress be interrupted by some popular commotion; and this alternative presents a picture still more appalling to the imagination. If political discontents were blended with the cries of hunger, and a revolution were to take place by the instrumentality of a mob clamouring for want of food, the consequences would be unceasing change and unceasing carnage, the bloody career of which nothing but the establishment of some complete despotism could arrest.

We can scarcely believe that the appointed guardians of British liberty should quietly have acquiesced in those gradual encroachments of power, which have taken place of late years, but from the apprehension of these still more dreadful evils. Great as has been the influence of corruption, I cannot yet think so meanly of the country gentlemen of England as to believe that they would thus have given up a part of their birthright of liberty, if they had not been actuated by a real and genuine fear that it was then in greater danger from the people than from the crown. They appeared to surrender themselves to government on condition of being protected from the mob; but they never would have made this melancholy and disheartening surrender, if such a mob had not existed either in reality or in imagination. That the fears on this subject were artfully exaggerated, and increased beyond the limits of just apprehension, is undeniable; but I think it is also undeniable that the frequent declamation which was heard against the unjust institutions of society, and the delusive arguments on equality which were circulated among the lower classes, gave us just reason to suppose that, if the *vox populi* had been allowed to speak, it would have appeared to be the voice of error and absurdity instead of the *vox Dei*.[6]

---

[6] [*Vox populi, vox Dei*, the voice of the people is the voice of God, was a Latin maxim cited in England from the fifteenth century onwards.

The whole of the above paragraph is reminiscent of a pamphlet Malthus wrote in 1796 but never published, and of which only fragmentary quotations survive: it was called *The Crisis, a View of the Present Interesting State of Great Britain, by a Friend to the Constitution*. Malthus's younger colleague at the East India College, William Empson, referred to this pamphlet in his article on the 'Life, Writings and Character of Mr. Malthus' in the *Edinburgh Review* for January 1837, Vol. LXIV, p. 479. According to Empson, Malthus wrote that: 'In the country gentleman of 1796, it is impossible to recognize that old and noble character, the jealous guardian of British freedom.' Malthus went on:

It appears to me that nothing can save the Constitution but the revival of the true Whig principles in a body of the community sufficiently numerous and powerful to snatch the object of contention from the opposing factions. In the Portland party, it is in vain to look for a revival, fettered with blue ribbands, secretaryships and military commands: freedom of action may be as soon expected from prisoners in chains. ... The only hope that Great Britain has, is in the returning sense and reason of the country gentleman, and middle classes of society, which may influence the legislature to adopt the safe and enlightened .

To say that our conduct is not to be regulated by circumstances is to betray an ignorance of the most solid and incontrovertible principles of morality. Though the admission of this principle may sometimes afford a cloak to changes of opinion that do not result from the purest motives; yet the admission of a contrary principle would be productive of infinitely worse consequences. The phrase of 'existing circumstances' has, I believe, not unfrequently created a smile in the English House of Commons; but the smile should have been reserved for the application of the phrase, and not have been excited by the phrase itself. A very frequent repetition of it has indeed, of itself, rather a suspicious air; and its application should always be watched with the most jealous and anxious attention; but no man ought to be judged *in limine*[7] for saying that existing circumstances had obliged him to alter his opinions and conduct. The country gentlemen were perhaps too easily convinced that existing circumstances called upon them to give up some of the most valuable privileges of Englishmen; but, as far as they were really convinced of this obligation, they acted consistently with the clearest rule of morality.

The degree of power to be given to the civil government, and the measure of our submission to it, must be determined by general expediency; and in judging of this expediency, every circumstance is to be taken into consideration; particularly the state of public opinion, and the degree of ignorance and delusion prevailing among the common people. The patriot, who might be called upon by the love of his country to join with heart and hand in a rising of the people for some specific attainable object of reform, if he knew that they were enlightened respecting their own situation, and would stop short when they had attained their demand, would be called upon by the same motive to submit to very great oppression, rather than give the slightest countenance to a popular tumult, the members of which (at least the greater number of them) were persuaded that the destruction of the Parliament, the Lord Mayor, and the monopolizers, would make bread cheap, and that a revolution would enable them all to support their families. In this case, it is more the ignorance and delusion of the lower classes of people that occasions the oppression, than the actual disposition of the government to tyranny.

That there is, however, in all power a constant tendency to encroach is an incontrovertible truth, and cannot be too strongly inculcated. The checks which are necessary to secure the liberty of the subject will always, in some degree, embarrass and delay the operations of the executive government.

---

policy of removing the weight of the objections to our constitution by diminishing the truth of them.

See also PORTLAND in the Alphabetical List.]

[7] [*In limine* means literally 'on the threshold', but it was used in Latin for 'at the outset' or 'initially'.]

The members of this government feeling these inconveniences, while they are exerting themselves, as they conceive, in the service of their country, and conscious, perhaps, of no ill intention towards the people, will naturally be disposed on every occasion to demand the suspension or abolition of these checks; but if once the convenience of ministers be put into competition with the liberties of the people, and we get into a habit of relying on fair assurances and personal character, instead of examining, with the most scrupulous and jealous care, the merits of each particular case, there is an end of British freedom. If we once admit the principle that the government must know better with regard to the quantity of power which it wants, than we can possibly do with our limited means of information, and that therefore it is our duty to surrender up our private judgments, we may just as well, at the same time, surrender up the whole of our constitution. Government is a quarter in which liberty is not, nor cannot be, very faithfully preserved. If we are wanting to ourselves, and inattentive to our great interests in this respect, it is the height of folly and unreasonableness, to expect that government will attend to them for us. Should the British constitution ultimately lapse into a despotism, as has been prophesied, I shall think that the country gentlemen of England will have really[8] much more to answer for than the ministers.

To do the country gentlemen justice, however, I should readily acknowledge that, in the partial desertion of their posts as guardians of British freedom, which has already taken place, they have been actuated more by fear than treachery.[9] And the principal reason of this fear was, I conceive, the ignorance and delusions of the common people, and the prospective horrors which were contemplated if, in such a state of mind, they should by any revolutionary movement obtain an ascendant.

The circulation of Paine's Rights of Man, it is supposed, has done great mischief among the lower and middling classes of people in this country. This is probably true; but not because man is without rights, or that these rights ought not to be known; but because Mr. Paine has fallen into some fundamental errors respecting the principles of government, and in many important points has shown himself totally unacquainted with the structure of society, and the different moral effects to be expected from the physical difference between this country and America. Mobs, of the same description as those collections of people known by this name in Europe, could not exist in America. The number of people without property is there, from the physical state of the country, comparatively small; and therefore the civil power which is to protect property cannot require the same degree of strength. Mr. Paine very justly observes that whatever the apparent cause of

---

[8] [In 1817 (Vol. III, p. 151) the word *really* was excised.]
[9] [In 1806 (Vol. II, p. 380) *treachery* was replaced by 'corruption'.

any riots may be, the real one is always want of happiness; but when he goes on to say it shows that something is wrong in the system of government, that injures the felicity by which society is to be preserved, he falls into the common error of attributing all want of happiness to government. It is evident that this want of happiness might have existed, and from ignorance might have been the principal cause of the riots, and yet be almost wholly unconnected with any of the proceedings of government. The redundant population of an old state furnishes materials of unhappiness unknown to such a state as that of America; and if an attempt were to be made to remedy this unhappiness, by distributing the produce of the taxes to the poorer classes of society, according to the plan proposed by Mr. Paine, the evil would be aggravated a hundred fold, and in a very short time no sum that the society could possibly raise would be adequate to the proposed object.

Nothing would so effectually counteract the mischiefs occasioned by Mr. Paine's Rights of Man as a general knowledge of the real rights of man. What these rights are, it is not my business at present to explain; but there is one right which man has generally been thought to possess, which I am confident he neither does, nor can possess – a right to subsistence when his labour will not fairly purchase it. Our laws indeed say that he has this right, and bind the society to furnish employment and food to those who cannot get them in the regular market; but in so doing, they attempt to reverse the laws of nature; and it is in consequence to be expected, not only that they should fail in their object, but that the poor who were intended to be benefited, should suffer most cruelly from this inhuman deceit which is practised upon them.

[10]●A man who is born into a world already possessed, if he cannot get subsistence from his parents on whom he has a just demand, and if the society do not want his labour, has no claim of *right* to the smallest portion of food, and, in fact, has no business to be where he is. At nature's mighty feast there is no vacant cover for him. She tells him to be gone, and will quickly execute her own orders, if he do not work upon the compassion of some of her guests. If these guests get up and make room for him, other intruders immediately appear demanding the same favour. The report of a provision for all that come fills the hall with numerous claimants. The order and harmony of the feast is disturbed, the plenty that before reigned is changed into scarcity; and the happiness of the guests is destroyed by the spectacle of misery and dependence in every part of the hall, and by the clamorous importunity of those who are justly enraged at not finding the provision which they had been taught to expect. The guests learn too late their error, in counteracting those strict orders to all intruders, issued by the great mistress of the feast, who, wishing that all her guests should have plenty, and knowing

that she could not provide for unlimited numbers, humanely refused to admit fresh comers when her table was already full.●[10]

The Abbé Raynal has said, that: 'Avant toutes les loix sociales l'homme avoit le droit de subsister!'[11] He might with just as much propriety have said that, before the institution of social laws, every man had a right to live a hundred years. Undoubtedly he had then, and has still, a good right to live a hundred years, nay, a thousand *if he can*, without interfering with the right of others to live; but the affair in both cases is principally an affair of power, not of right. Social laws very greatly increase this power, by enabling a much greater number to subsist than could subsist without them, and so far very greatly enlarge *le droit de subsister*; but neither before nor after the institution of social laws could an unlimited number subsist; and before, as well as since, he who ceased to have the power ceased to have the right.

If the great truths on these subjects were more generally circulated, and the lower classes of people could be convinced that, by the laws of nature, independently of any particular institutions, except the great one of property, which is absolutely necessary in order to attain any considerable produce, no person has any claim of right[12] on society for subsistence, if his labour will not purchase it, the greatest part of the mischievous declamation on the unjust institutions of society would fall powerless to the ground. The poor are by no means inclined to be visionary. Their distresses are always real, though they are not attributed to the real causes. If these real causes were properly explained to them, and they were taught to know how small a part of their present distress was attributable to government, and how great a part to causes totally unconnected with it,[13] discontent and irritation among the lower classes of people would show themselves much less frequently than at present; and when they did show themselves, would be much less to be dreaded. The efforts of turbulent and discontented men in the middle classes of society might safely be disregarded, if the poor were so far enlightened respecting the real nature of their situation, as to be aware that, by aiding them in their schemes of renovation, they would probably be promoting the ambitious views of others without in any respect benefiting themselves. And the country gentlemen and men of property in England might securely return to a wholesome jealousy of the encroachments of power; and instead of daily

---

[10] [In 1806 (Vol. II, p. 383) this famous paragraph was omitted.]

[11] Raynal, Hist. des Indes, vol. x. s. x. p. 322. 8vo. 'Before any laws were made, man had the right to eat, to keep himself alive.'

[12] [In 1806 (Vol. II, p. 384) the word *right* was italicised.]

[13] [In 1817 (Vol. III, p. 156) this sentence began:

If these causes were properly explained to them, and they were taught to know what part of their present distress was attributable to government, and what part to causes totally unconnected with it, discontent and irritation . . .

sacrificing the liberties of the subject on the altar of public safety, might, without any just apprehension from the people, not only tread back their late steps, but firmly insist upon those gradual reforms which the lapse of time, and the storms of circumstances,[14] have rendered necessary, to prevent the gradual destruction of the British constitution.

All improvements in government must necessarily originate with persons of some education, and these will of course be found among the people of property. Whatever may be said of a few, it is impossible to suppose that the great mass of the people of property should be really interested in the abuses of government. They merely submit to them, from the fear that an endeavour to remove them might be productive of greater evils. Could we but take away this fear, reform and improvement would proceed with as much facility as the removal of nuisances,[15] or the paving and lighting of the streets. In human life we are continually called upon to submit to a lesser evil in order to avoid a greater; and it is the part of a wise man to do this readily and cheerfully; but no wise man will submit to any evil if he can get rid of it without danger. Remove all apprehension from the tyranny or folly of the people, and the tyranny of government could not stand a moment. It would then appear in its proper deformity, without palliation, without pretext, without protector. Naturally feeble in itself, when it was once stripped naked, and deprived of the support of public opinion, and of the great plea of necessity, it would fall without a struggle. Its few interested defenders would hide their heads abashed, and would be ashamed any longer to advocate a cause for which no human ingenuity could invent a plausible argument.

The most successful supporters of tyranny are without doubt those general declaimers, who attribute the distresses of the poor, and almost all the evils to which society is subject, to human institutions and the iniquity of governments. The falsity of these accusations, and the dreadful consequences that would result from their being generally admitted and acted upon, make it absolutely necessary that they should at all events be resisted; not only on account of the immediate revolutionary horrors to be expected from a movement of the people acting under such impressions (a consideration which must at all times have very great weight); but also on account of the extreme probability that such a revolution would terminate in a much worse despotism than that which it had destroyed. On these grounds, a genuine friend of freedom, a zealous advocate for the real rights of man, might be found among the defenders of a considerable degree of tyranny. A cause bad

---

[14] [In 1806 (Vol. II, p. 385) this was altered to:
... and the storms of the political world, ...

[15] [According to Dr Johnson's Dictionary, nuisances could consist of rotting vegetables and offal, as well as ordure.]

in itself, might be supported by the good and the virtuous, merely because that which was opposed to it was much worse; and because it was absolutely necessary at the moment to make a choice between the two. Whatever therefore may be the intention of those indiscriminate and wholesale accusations against governments,[16] their real effect undoubtedly is to add a weight of talents and principles to the prevailing power, which it never would have received otherwise.

It is a truth, which I trust has been sufficiently proved in the course of this work, that under a government constructed upon the best and purest principles, and executed by men of the highest talents and integrity, the most squalid poverty and wretchedness might universally prevail from the principle of population alone.[17] And as this cause of unhappiness has hitherto been so little understood, that the efforts of society have always tended rather to aggravate than to lessen it, we have the strongest reasons for supposing that, in all the governments with which we are acquainted, a very great part of the misery[18] to be observed among the lower classes of the people arises from this cause.

The inference therefore, which Mr. Paine and others have drawn against governments from the unhappiness of the people, is palpably unfair; and before we give a sanction to such accusations, it is a debt we owe to truth and justice, to ascertain how much of this unhappiness arises from the principle of population, and how much is fairly to be attributed to government. When this distinction has been properly made, and all the vague, indefinite, and false accusations removed, government would remain, as it ought to be, clearly responsible for the rest. ●A tenfold weight would be immediately given to the cause of the people, and every man of principle would join in asserting and enforcing, if necessary, their rights.●

[In 1806 (Vol. II, pp. 388–91) Malthus excised this last sentence and continued thus:

... clearly responsible for the rest; and the amount of this would still be such as to make the responsibility very considerable. Though government has but little power in the direct and immediate relief of poverty, yet its indirect influence on the prosperity of its subjects is striking and incontestable. And the reason is, that though it is comparatively impotent in its efforts to make the food of a country keep pace with an unrestricted increase of population, yet its influence is great in giving the best

---

[16] [In 1806 (Vol. II, p. 387) the words *and wholesale* were excised.]

[17] [In 1806 (Vol. II, p. 387) this was altered:
    ... squalid poverty and wretchedness might universally prevail from an inattention to the prudential check to population.

[18] [In 1806 (Vol. II, p. 388) the word *very* was excised.]

direction to those checks, which in some form or other must necessarily take place. It has clearly appeared in the former part of this work, that the most despotic and worst-governed countries, however low they might be in actual population, were uniformly the most populous in proportion to their means of subsistence; and the necessary effect of this state of things must of course be very low wages. In such countries the checks to population arise more from the sickness and mortality consequent on poverty, than from the prudence and foresight which restrain the frequency and universality of early marriages. The checks are more of the positive and less of the preventive kind.

The first grand requisite to the growth of prudential habits is the perfect security of property; and the next perhaps is that respectability and importance which are given to the lower classes by equal laws, and the possession of some influence in the framing of them. The more excellent therefore is the government, the more does it tend to generate that prudence and elevation of sentiment by which alone, in the present state of our being, poverty can be avoided.

It has been sometimes asserted that the only reason why it is advantageous that the people should have some share in the government is that a representation of the people tends best to secure the framing of good and equal laws; but that, if the same object could be attained under a despotism, the same advantage would accrue to the community. If however the representative system, by securing to the lower classes of society a more equal and liberal mode of treatment from their superiors, gives to each individual a greater personal respectability, and a greater fear of personal degradation; it is evident that it will powerfully co-operate with the security of property in animating the exertions of industry and in generating habits of prudence; and thus more powerfully tend to increase the riches and prosperity of the lower classes of the community than if the same laws had existed under a despotism.

But though the tendency of a free constitution and a good government to diminish poverty be certain; yet their effect in this way must necessarily be indirect and slow, and very different from the direct and immediate relief which the lower classes of people are too frequently in the habit of looking forward to as the consequence of a revolution. This habit of expecting too much, and the irritation occasioned by disappointment, continually give a wrong direction to their efforts in favour of liberty, and constantly tend to defeat the accomplishment of those gradual reforms in government, and that slow melioration of the condition of the lower classes of society, which are really attainable. It is of the very highest importance therefore, to know distinctly what government cannot do, as well as what it can. If I were called upon to name the cause, which, in my conception, . . .

I may be deceived; but I confess that if I were called upon to name the cause which, in my conception, had more than any other contributed to the very slow progress of freedom, so disheartening to every liberal mind, I should say that it was the confusion that had existed respecting the causes of the unhappiness and discontents which prevail in society; and the advantage which governments had been able to take, and indeed had been compelled to take, of this confusion, to confirm and strengthen their power. I cannot help thinking, therefore, that a knowledge generally circulated, that the principal cause of want and unhappiness is unconnected[19] with government, and totally beyond its power to remove, and that it depends upon the conduct of the poor themselves, would, instead of giving any advantage to governments, give a great additional weight to the popular side of the question, by removing the dangers with which from ignorance it is at present accompanied; and thus tend, in a very powerful manner, to promote the cause of rational freedom.

---

[19] [In 1806 (Vol. II, p. 391) this was changed to:
    ... is only indirectly connected with government, ...

# CHAPTER VII

## Continuation of the same Subject[1]

The reasonings of the foregoing chapter have been strikingly confirmed by the events of the last two or three years. Perhaps there never was a period when more erroneous views were formed by the lower classes of society of the effects to be expected from reforms in the government, when these erroneous views were more immediately founded on a total misapprehension of the principal cause of poverty, and when they more directly led to results unfavourable to liberty.

One of the main causes of complaint against the government has been, that a considerable number of labourers, who are both able and willing to work, are wholly out of employment, and unable consequently to command the necessaries of life.

That this state of things is one of the most afflicting events that can occur in civilized life, that it is a natural and pardonable cause of discontent among the lower classes of society, and that every effort should be made by the higher classes to mitigate it, consistently with a proper care not to render it permanent, no man of humanity can doubt. But that such a state of things may occur in the best-conducted and most economical government that ever existed is as certain as that governments have not the power of commanding, with effect, the resources of a country to be progressive, when they are naturally stationary or declining.

It will be allowed that periods of prosperity may occur in any well-governed state, during which an extraordinary stimulus may be given to its wealth and population which cannot in its nature be permanent. If, for instance, new channels of trade are opened, new colonies are possessed, new inventions take place in machinery, and new and great improvements are

---

[1] Written in 1817.
  [Malthus added this brief footnote in 1826 (Vol. II, p. 328). His additional chapter was inspired by widespread disturbances, caused partly by long-term industrial changes, which gave rise to outbursts of machine-breaking; there was also an exceptionally wet summer and bad harvest in 1816. These factors increased the distress which resulted from the cessation of the war-time demand for men and commodities, and led to renewed popular agitation for parliamentary reform; the government retaliated with strong repressive measures, in the name of law and order, and the Habeas Corpus Act was suspended again in 1817.]

made in agriculture, it is quite obvious that while the markets at home and abroad will readily take off at advantageous prices the increasing produce, there must be a rapid increase of capital, and an unusual stimulus given to the population. On the other hand, if subsequently these channels of trade are either closed by accident or contracted by foreign competition; if colonies are lost, or the same produce is supplied from other quarters; if the markets, either from glut or competition, cease to extend with the extension of the new machinery; and if the improvements in agriculture from any cause whatever cease to be progressive, it is as obvious that, just at the time when the stimulus to population has produced its greatest effect, the means of employing and supporting this population may, in the natural course of things, and without any fault whatever in the government, become deficient. This failure must unavoidably produce great distress among the labouring classes of society; but it is quite clear that no inference can be drawn from this distress that a radical change is required in the government; and the attempt to accomplish such a change might only aggravate the evil.

It has been supposed in this case that the government has in no respect, by its conduct, contributed to the pressure in question, a supposition which in practice perhaps will rarely be borne out by the fact. It is unquestionably in the power of a government to produce great distress by war and taxation, and it requires some skill to distinguish the distress which is the natural result of these causes from that which is occasioned in the way just described. In our own case unquestionably both descriptions of causes have combined, but the former in a greater degree than the latter. War and taxation, as far as they operate directly and simply, tend to destroy or retard the progress of capital, produce and population; but during the late war these checks to prosperity have been much more than overbalanced by a combination of circumstances which has given an extraordinary stimulus to production. That for this overbalance of advantages the country cannot be considered as much indebted to the government, is most certain. The government during the last twenty-five years has shown no very great love either of peace or liberty; and no particular economy in the use of the national resources. It has proceeded in a very straight-forward manner to spend great sums in war, and to raise them by very heavy taxes. It has no doubt done its part towards the dilapidation of the national resources. But still the broad fact must stare every impartial observer in the face, that at the end of the war in 1814 the national resources were not dilapidated; and that not only were the wealth and population of the country considerably greater than they were at the commencement of the war, but that they had increased in the interval at a more rapid rate than was ever experienced before.

Perhaps this may justly be considered as one of the most extraordinary facts in history; and it certainly follows from it, that the sufferings of the country since the peace have not been occasioned so much by the usual and most natural effects to be expected from war and taxation, as by the sudden ceasing of an extraordinary stimulus to production, the distresses consequent upon which, though increased no doubt by the weight of taxation, do not essentially arise from it, and are not directly therefore, and immediately, to be relieved by its removal.

That the labouring classes of society should not be fully aware that the main causes of their distress are to a certain extent and for a certain time, irremediable, is natural enough; and that they should listen much more readily and willingly to those who confidently promise immediate relief, rather than to those who can only tell them unpalatable truths, is by no means surprising. But it must be allowed that full advantage has been taken by the popular orators and writers of a crisis which has given them so much power.[2] Partly from ignorance, and partly from design, everything that could tend to enlighten the labouring classes as to the real nature of their situation, and encourage them to bear an unavoidable pressure with patience, has been either sedulously kept out of their view, or clamorously reprobated; and every thing that could tend to deceive them, to aggravate and encourage their discontents, and to raise unreasonable and extravagant expectations as to the relief to be expected from reform, has been as sedulously brought forward. If under these circumstances the reforms proposed had been accomplished, it is impossible that the people should not have been most cruelly disappointed; and under a system of universal suffrage and annual parliaments,[3] a general disappointment of the people would probably lead to every sort of experiment in government, till the career of change was stopped by a military despotism. The warmest friends of genuine liberty might justly feel alarmed at such a prospect. To a cause conducted upon such principles, and likely to be attended with such results, they could not of course, consistently with their duty, lend any assistance. And if with great difficulty, and against the sense of the great mass of petitioners, they were to effect a more moderate and more really useful reform, they could not but feel certain

---

[2] [The 'popular orators and writers' would have included Henry Hunt (1773–1835) known as 'Orator Hunt', who tried to organise nationwide petitions to the Prince Regent; at a great meeting in Spa Fields, on the outskirts of London, on 15 November 1816, Hunt appeared with an escort carrying a tricolour flag and a cap of liberty on a pike. William Cobbett (1763–1835) was an old enemy of Malthus, and constantly attacked him in his *Weekly Register*; he could well have been one of the 'popular' writers whom Malthus had in mind.]

[3] [Universal suffrage, at this period, meant manhood suffrage; annual general elections were intended to keep members of parliament properly subservient to their constituents. These suggestions for reform were particularly associated with Sir Francis Burdett (1770–1844); as M.P. for Westminster he unsuccessfully introduced in 1817 a motion for a committee to enquire into parliamentary representation.]

that the unavoidable disappointment of the people would be attributed to the half-measures which had been pursued; and that they would be either forced to proceed to more radical changes, or submit to a total loss of their influence and popularity by stopping short while the distresses of the people were unrelieved, their discontents unallayed, and the great *panacea* on which they had built their sanguine expectations untried.

These considerations have naturally paralyzed the exertions of the best friends of liberty; and those salutary reforms which are acknowledged to be necessary in order to repair the breaches of time, and improve the fabric of our constitution, are thus rendered much more difficult, and consequently much less probable.

But not only have the false expectations and extravagant demands suggested by the leaders of the people given an easy victory to government over every proposition for reform, whether violent or moderate, but they have furnished the most fatal instruments of offensive attack against the constitution itself. They are naturally calculated to excite some alarm, and to check moderate reform; but alarm, when once excited, seldom knows where to stop, and the causes of it are particularly liable to be exaggerated. There is reason to believe that it has been under the influence of exaggerated statements, and of inferences drawn by exaggerated fears from these statements, that acts unfavourable to liberty have been passed without an adequate necessity. But the power of creating these exaggerated fears, and of passing these acts, has been unquestionably furnished by the extravagant expectations of the people. And it must be allowed that the present times furnish a very striking illustration of the doctrine that an ignorance of the principal cause of poverty is peculiarly unfavourable, and that a knowledge of it must be peculiarly favourable, to the cause of civil liberty.

# CHAPTER VIII

*Plan of the gradual abolition of the Poor Laws proposed*

If the principles in the preceding chapters should stand the test of examination, and we should ever feel the obligation of endeavouring to act upon them, the next inquiry would be in what way we ought practically to proceed. The first grand obstacle which presents itself in this country is the system of the poor laws, which has been justly stated to be an evil in comparison of which the national debt, with all its magnitude of terror, is of little moment.[1] [2]●The extraordinary rapidity with which the poor's rates have increased of late years, presents us, indeed, with the prospect of a monstrous deformity in society, which, if it did not really exist to a great degree at present, and were not daily advancing in growth, would be considered as perfectly incredible. It presents us with the prospect of a great nation, flourishing in arts and arms and commerce, and with a government, which has generally been allowed to be the best, which has hitherto stood the test of experience, in any country, and yet the larger half of the people reduced to the condition of paupers.●[2]

Greatly as we may be shocked at such a prospect, and ardently as we may wish to remove it, the evil is now so deeply seated, and the relief given by the poor laws so widely extended, that no man of humanity could venture to propose their immediate abolition. To mitigate their effects, however, and stop their future increase, to which, if left to continue upon their present plan,

---

[1] Reports of the Society for bettering the condition of the poor, vol. iii. p. 21.
[See BERNARD, THOMAS, in the Alphabetical List.]

[2] [In 1806 (Vol. ii, pp. 393–4) this passage was altered:
The rapidity with which the poor's rates have increased of late years presents us indeed with the prospect of such an extraordinary proportion of paupers in the society as would seem to be incredible in a nation flourishing in arts, agriculture, and commerce, and with a government which has generally been allowed to be the best that has hitherto stood the test of experience.[a]

[a] It has been said, that, during the late scarcities, half of the population of the country received relief. If the poor's rates continue increasing as rapidly as they have done on the average of the last ten years, how melancholy are our future prospects! The system of the poor laws has been justly stated by the French to be *la plaie politique de l'Angleterre la plus dévorante*. (Comité de Mendicité.)
[This footnote was retained in all the editions, but in 1817 (Vol. iii, p. 176) the first sentence was omitted. See COMITÉ DE MENDICITÉ in the Alphabetical List for a note and translation.]

we can see no probable termination, it has been proposed to fix the whole sum to be raised at its present rate, or any other that might be determined upon; and to make a law that on no account this sum should be exceeded. The objection to this plan is that a very large sum would be still to be raised, and a great number of people to be supported; the consequence of which would be, that the poor would not be easily able to distinguish the alteration that had been made. Each individual would think that he had as good a right to be supported when he was in want as any other person; and those who unfortunately chanced to be in distress when the fixed sum had been collected, would think themselves particularly ill-used on being excluded from all assistance, while so many others were enjoying this advantage. If the sum collected were divided among all that were in want, however their numbers might increase, though such a plan would be perfectly fair, with regard to those who became dependent after the sum had been fixed,[3] it would undoubtedly be rather hard upon those who had been in the habit of receiving a more liberal supply, and had done nothing to justify its being taken from them.

[In 1806 (Vol. II, p. 395) Malthus added to this paragraph:
... justify its being taken from them: and in both cases it would certainly be unjust in the society to undertake the support of the poor, and yet, if their numbers increased, to feed them so sparingly that they must necessarily die of hunger and disease.

I have reflected much on the subject of the poor laws and hope, therefore, that I shall be excused in venturing to suggest a mode of their gradual abolition, to which I confess that at present I can see no material objection. Of this, indeed, I feel nearly convinced: that should we ever become sufficiently sensible[4] of the wide-spreading tyranny, dependence, indolence, and unhappiness which they create, as seriously to make an effort to abolish them, we shall be compelled[5] to adopt the principle, if not the plan, which I shall mention. It seems impossible to get rid of so extensive a system of support, consistently with humanity, without applying ourselves directly to its vital principle, and endeavouring to counteract that deeply-seated cause, which occasions the rapid growth of all such establishments, and invariably renders them inadequate to their object.

---

[3] [In 1806 (Vol. II, p. 395) this was altered to:
    ... though such a plan would not be so unfair with regard to those who became dependent after the sum had been fixed ...
[4] [In 1826 (Vol. II, p. 337) *sufficiently sensible* was replaced by 'so fully sensible.'
[5] [In 1806 (Vol. II, p. 396) Malthus wrote:
    ... we shall be compelled by a sense of justice to adopt the principle, if not the plan ...

[In 1806 (Vol. II, p. 396) a short paragraph was inserted here:

As a previous step even to any considerable alteration in the present system, which would contract or stop the increase of the relief to be given, it appears to me that we are bound in justice and honour formally to disclaim the *right* of the poor to support.

To this end, I should propose a regulation to be made, declaring that no child born from any marriage taking place after the expiration of a year from the date of the law, and no illegitimate child born two years from the same date, should ever be entitled to parish assistance. And to give a more general knowledge of this law, and to enforce it more strongly on the minds of the lower classes of people, the clergyman of each parish should, previously to the solemnization of a marriage, read a short address to the parties,[6] stating the strong obligation on every man to support his own children; the impropriety, and even immorality, of marrying without a fair prospect[7] of being able to do this; the evils which had resulted to the poor themselves, from the attempt which had been made to assist, by public institutions, in a duty which ought to be exclusively appropriated to parents; and the absolute necessity which had at length appeared, of abandoning all such institutions, on account of their producing effects totally opposite to those which were intended.

This would operate as a fair, distinct, and precise notice, which no man could well mistake; and, without pressing hard on any particular individuals, would at once throw off the rising generation from that miserable and helpless dependence upon the government and the rich, the moral as well as physical consequences of which are almost incalculable. [8]●When the poor are in the habit of constantly looking to these sources, for all the good or evil they enjoy or suffer, their minds must almost necessarily be under a continual state of irritation against the higher classes of society whenever they feel distressed from the pressure of circumstances.

I have often heard great surprise expressed that the poor in this country should be with such difficulty persuaded to take to any substitutes during a period of scarcity; but I confess that this fact never surprised me in the least. The poor are told that the parish is obliged to provide for them. This, they naturally conceive, is a rich source of supply; and when they are offered any kind of food to which they are not accustomed, they consider it as a breach of obligation in the parish, and as proceeding not from the hard law of necessity, from which there is no appeal; but from the injustice and hardheartedness of the higher classes of society, against which they would

---

[6] [In 1806 (Vol. II, p. 397) this was altered to:

... should, after the publication of banns, read a short address, stating ...

[See BOOK OF COMMON PRAYER (1) in the Alphabetical List.]

[7] [In 1807 (Vol. II, p. 321) the word *fair* was excised.]

wish to appeal to the right of the strongest. The language which they generally make use of upon these occasions is: 'See what stuff *they* want to make us eat, I wonder how *they* would like it *themselves*. I should like to see some of *them* do a day's work upon it.' The words *they* and *them* generally refer to Parliament, the Lord Mayor, the Justices, the Parish, and in general to all the higher classes of society. Both the irritation of mind and the helplessness in expedients, during the pressure of want, arise in this instance from the wretched system of governing too much. When the poor were once taught, by the abolition of the poor laws, and a proper knowledge of their real situation, to depend more upon themselves, we might rest secure that they would be fruitful enough in resources, and that the evils which were absolutely irremediable they would bear with the fortitude of men and the resignation of Christians.●[8]

After the public notice which I have proposed had been given, and the system of poor laws had ceased with regard to the rising generation, if any man chose to marry, without a prospect of being able to support a family, he should have the most perfect liberty so to do. Though to marry, in this case, is in my opinion clearly an immoral act, yet it is not one which society can justly take upon itself to prevent or punish; because the punishment provided for it by the laws of nature falls directly and most severely upon the individual who commits the act, and, through him, only more remotely and feebly on the society. When nature will govern and punish for us, it is a very miserable ambition to wish to snatch the rod from her hands, and draw upon ourselves the odium of executioner. To the punishment, therefore, of nature he should be left, the punishment of severe want.[9] He has erred in the face of a most clear and precise warning, and can have no just reason to complain of any person but himself when he feels the consequences of his error. All parish assistance should be most rigidly denied him: and if the hand of private charity be stretched forth in his relief, the interests of humanity imperiously require that it should be administered very sparingly.[10] He should be taught to know that the laws of nature, which are the laws of God, had doomed him and his family to starve[11] for disobeying their repeated admonitions; that he

---

[8] [In 1806 (Vol. II, p. 397) this sentence and the whole of the following paragraph were expunged.]

[9] [In 1806 (Vol. II, p. 398) the word *severe* was omitted.]

[10] [In 1806 (Vol. II, p. 398) this read:

All parish assistance should be denied him: ... private charity ... should be administered sparingly.

[In 1817 (Vol. III, p. 181) this sentence was altered again:

All parish assistance should be denied him, and he should be left to the uncertain support of private charity.

[11] [In 1806 (Vol. II, p. 398) *starve* was changed to 'suffer'.

had no claim of right on society for the smallest portion of food, beyond that which his labour would fairly purchase; and that if he and his family were saved from suffering the utmost extremities of hunger,[12] he would owe it to the pity of some kind benefactor, to whom, therefore, he ought to be bound by the strongest ties of gratitude.

If this system were pursued, we need be under no apprehensions whatever[13] that the number of persons in extreme want would be beyond the power and the will of the benevolent to supply. The sphere for the exercise of private charity would, I am confident, be less than it is at present; and the only difficulty would be, to restrain the hand of benevolence from assisting those in distress in so liberal[14] a manner as to encourage indolence and want of foresight in others.

With regard to illegitimate children, after the proper notice had been given, they should on no account whatever be allowed to have any claim to parish assistance.[15] If the parents desert their child, they ought to be made answerable for the crime. The infant is, comparatively speaking, of no value[16] to the society, as others will immediately supply its place. Its principal value is on account of its being the object of one of the most delightful passions in human nature – parental affection. But if this value be disregarded by those who are alone in a capacity to feel it, the society cannot be called upon to put itself in their place; and has no further business in its protection than, in the case of its murder or intentional ill-treatment, to follow the general rules in punishing such crimes; which rules, for the interests of morality, it is bound to pursue, whether the object, in the particular instance, be of value to the state or not.[17]

---

[12] [This sentence was altered twice. In 1806 (Vol. II, p. 399) the word *utmost* was excised.]
[In 1817 (Vol. III, p. 181) it read:
... if he and his family were saved from feeling the natural consequences of his imprudence, he would owe it to the pity of some kind benefactor ...

[13] [In 1806 (Vol. II, p. 399) the word *whatever* was excised.]

[14] [In 1806 (Vol. II, p. 399) *liberal* was changed to 'indiscriminate'.
[In 1817 (Vol. III, p. 182) the sentence was altered:
The sphere for the exercise of private charity would, probably, not be greater than it is at present; and the principal difficulty would be to restrain the hand of benevolence from assisting those in distress in so indiscriminate a manner as to encourage ...

[15] [In 1806 (Vol. II, p. 399) this sentence was altered:
... had been given, they should not be allowed to have any claim to parish assistance, but be left entirely to the support of private charity.

[16] [In 1806 (Vol. II, p. 399) *no value* was amended to 'little value'.]

[17] [In 1806 (Vol. II, p. 400) this was changed:
... in their place; and has no further business in its protection than to punish the crime of desertion or intentional ill-treatment in the persons whose duty it is to provide for it.

At present the child is taken under the protection of the parish,[18] and generally dies, at least in London, within the first year. The loss to the society, if it be one, is the same;[19] but the crime is diluted by the number of people concerned, and the death passes as a visitation of Providence, instead of being considered as the necessary consequence of the conduct of its parents, for which they ought to be held responsible to God and to society.

The desertion of both parents, however, is not so common as the desertion of one. When a servant or labouring man has an illegitimate child, his running away is perfectly a matter of course; and it is by no means uncommon for a man with a wife and large family to withdraw into a distant county, and leave them to the parish; indeed, I once heard a hard-working good sort of man propose to do this, as the best mode of providing for a wife and six children.[20] If the simple fact of these frequent desertions were related in some countries, a strange inference would be drawn against the English character; but the wonder would cease when our public institutions were explained.

By the laws of nature, a child is confided directly and exclusively to the protection of its parents. By the laws of nature, the mother of a child is confided almost as strongly and exclusively to the man who is the father of it. If these ties were suffered to remain in the state in which nature has left them, and the man were convinced that the woman and the child depended solely upon him for support, I scarcely believe that there are ten men breathing so atrocious as to desert them. But our laws, in opposition to the laws of nature, say that if the parents forsake their child, other persons will undertake to support it; or, if the man forsake the woman, that she shall still meet with protection elsewhere; that is, we take all possible pains to weaken and render null the ties of nature, and then say that men are unnatural. But the fact is, that the society itself, in its body politic, is the unnatural character, for framing laws that thus counteract the laws of nature and give premiums to the violation of the best and most honourable feelings of the human heart.

It is a common thing in most parishes, when the father of an illegitimate child can be seized, to endeavour to frighten him into marriage by the terrors of a jail; but such a proceeding cannot surely be too strongly reprobated. In the first place, it is almost shallow policy in the parish officers; for if they succeed the effect, upon the present system, will generally be that of having

---

[18] I fully agree with Sir F. M. Eden, in thinking that the constant public support which deserted children receive is the cause of their very great numbers in the two most opulent countries of Europe, France and England. State of the Poor, vol. i. p. 339.

[19] [In 1806 (Vol. ii, p. 400) the words *if it be one* were omitted.]

[20] 'That many of the poorer classes of the community avail themselves of the liberality of the law, and leave their wives and children on the parish, the reader will find abundant proof in the subsequent part of this work.' Sir F. M. Eden on the State of the Poor, vol. i. p. 339.

three or four children to provide for, instead of one. And, in the next place, it is difficult to conceive a more gross and scandalous profanation of a religious ceremony. Those who believe that the character of the woman is salved by such a forced engagement,[21] or that the moral worth of the man is enhanced by affirming a lie before God, have, I confess, very different ideas of delicacy and morality from those which I have been taught to consider as just. If a man deceive a woman into a connexion with him under a promise of marriage, he has undoubtedly been guilty of a most atrocious act; and there are few crimes which merit a more severe punishment: but the last that I should choose is that which will oblige him to affirm another falsehood, which will probably render the woman that he is to be joined to miserable, and will burden the society with a family of paupers.

The obligation on every man to support his children, whether legitimate or illegitimate, is so clear and strong, that it would be just to arm society with any power to enforce it which would be likely to answer the purpose. But I am inclined to believe that no exercise of the civil power, however rigorous, would be half so effectual as a knowledge generally circulated, that children were in future to depend solely for support upon their parents, and would perhaps starve if they were deserted.[22]

It may appear to be hard that a mother and her children, who had been guilty of no particular crime themselves, should suffer for the ill-conduct of the father; but this is one of the invariable laws of nature; and knowing this, we should think twice upon the subject, and be very sure of the ground on which we go, before we presume *systematically* to counteract it.

I have often heard the goodness of the Deity impeached on account of that part of the decalogue, in which he declares that he will visit the sins of the father upon the children;[23] but the objection has not perhaps been sufficiently considered. Without a most complete and fundamental change in the whole constitution of human nature; without making man an angel, or at least something totally different from what he is at present; it seems absolutely necessary that such a law should prevail. Would it not require a perpetual miracle, which is perhaps a contradiction in terms, to prevent children from being affected in their moral and civil condition by the conduct of their parents? What man is there, that has been brought up by his parents, who is not at the present moment enjoying something from their virtues, or

---

[21] [In 1817 (Vol. III, p. 186) *salved* was replaced by 'restored'.
[22] [In 1806 (Vol. II, p. 403) this was altered:
  ... upon their parents, and would be left only to casual charity if they were deserted.
[23] [Malthus is here referring to the second of the Ten Commandments, in the words he would have learned as a child in the Anglican Catechism. See BOOK OF COMMON PRAYER (2) in the Alphabetical List.]

suffering something from their vices; who, in his moral character, has not been elevated in some degree by their prudence, their justice, their benevolence, their temperance, or depressed by the contraries; who, in his civil condition, has not been raised by their reputation, their foresight, their industry, their good fortune; or lowered by their want of character, their imprudence, their indolence, and their adversity? And how much does a knowledge of this transmission of blessings contribute to excite and invigorate virtuous exertion? Proceeding upon this certainty, how ardent and incessant are the efforts of parents to give their children a good education, and to provide for their future situation in the world! If a man could neglect or desert his wife and children without their suffering any injury, how many individuals there are who, not being very fond of their wives, or being tired of the shackles of matrimony, would withdraw from household cares and difficulties, and resume their liberty and independence as single men! But the consideration that children may suffer for the faults of their parents has a strong hold even upon vice, and many who are in such a state of mind as to disregard the consequences of their habitual course of life, as far as relates to themselves, are yet greatly anxious that their children should not suffer from their vices and follies. In the moral government of the world, it seems evidently necessary that the sins of the fathers should be visited upon the children; and if in our overweening vanity we imagine that we can govern a private society better by endeavouring *systematically* to counteract this law, I am inclined to believe that we shall find ourselves very greatly mistaken.

If the plan which I have proposed were adopted, the poor's rates in a few years would begin very rapidly to decrease, and in no great length of time would be completely extinguished; and yet, as far as it appears to me at present, no individual would be either deceived or injured, and consequently no person could have a just right to complain.

The abolition of the poor-laws, however, is not of itself sufficient; and the obvious answer to those who lay too much stress upon this system is to desire them to look at the state of the poor in some other countries, where such laws do not prevail, and to compare it with their condition in England. But this comparison, it must be acknowledged, is in many respects unfair; and would by no means decide the question of the utility or inutility of such a system. England possesses very great natural and political advantages in which, perhaps, the countries that we should in this case compare with her would be found to be palpably deficient. The nature of her soil and climate is such, that those almost universal failures in the crops of grain, which are known in some countries, never occur in England. Her insular situation and extended commerce are peculiarly favourable for importation. Her numerous manufactures employ all the hands that are not engaged in agriculture,[24] and afford the means of a regular distribution of the annual produce of the land and labour to the whole of her inhabitants. But above all, throughout a very large class of the people, a decided taste for the conveniences and comforts of life, a strong desire of bettering their condition (that master-spring of public prosperity) and, in consequence, a most laudable spirit of industry and foresight, are observed to prevail. These dispositions, so contrary to the hopeless indolence remarked in despotic countries, are probably generated, in great measure, by the constitution of the English government,[25] and the excellence of its laws, which secure to every individual the produce of his industry. When, therefore, on a comparison with other countries, England appears to have the advantage in the state of her poor, the superiority is entirely to be attributed to these favourable circumstances, and not to the poor laws. A woman with one bad feature may greatly excel in beauty some other who may have this individual feature tolerably good; but it would be rather strange to assert, in consequence, that the superior beauty of the former was occasioned by this particular deformity. [26]●The poor laws have constantly tended, in the most powerful manner, to counteract the natural and acquired advantages of this country. Fortunately these advantages have been so considerable that, though greatly weakened, they could not be entirely overcome; and to these advantages, and these alone, it is owing, that England has been able to bear up so long against this pernicious system. I am so strongly of this opinion, that I do not think that any other country in the world, except perhaps Holland before the revolution, could have acted upon it so completely, for the same period of time, without utter ruin.●[26]

It has been proposed by some, to establish poor laws in Ireland; but, from the wretched and degraded state of the common people, and the total want of that decent pride, which in England prevents so many from having recourse to parish assistance,[27] there is little reason to doubt that, on the estab-

---

[24] [In 1806 (Vol. II, p. 407) Malthus altered this to:
   ... manufactures employ nearly all the hands that are not engaged in agriculture, ...
[25] [In 1806 (Vol. II, p. 407) this was changed to:
   These dispositions ... are generated by the constitution of the English government, ...
[26] [In 1806 (Vol. II, p. 408) this passage was modified:
   The poor-laws have constantly tended to counteract the natural and acquired advantages of this country. Fortunately these advantages have been so considerable that, though weakened, they could not be overcome; and to these advantages, together with the checks to marriage which the laws themselves create, it is owing that England has been able to bear up so long against this pernicious system. Probably there is not any other country in the world, except perhaps Holland before the revolution, which could have acted upon it ...
[27] [In 1817 (Vol. III, p. 193) this was amended to:
   ... but, from the depressed state of the common people, there is little reason to doubt ...

lishment of such laws, the whole of the landed property would very soon be absorbed, or the system be given up in despair.

In Sweden, from the dearths which are not unfrequent, owing to the general failure of crops in an unpropitious climate, and the impossibility of great importations in a poor country, an attempt to establish a system of parochial relief such as that in England (if it were not speedily abandoned from the physical impossibility of executing it) would level the property of the kingdom from one end to the other, and convulse the social system in such a manner, as absolutely to prevent it from recovering its former state on the return of plenty.

Even in France, with all her advantages of situation and climate, the tendency to population is so great, and the want of foresight among the lower classes of the people so conspicuous,[28] that if poor laws were established, the landed property would soon sink under the burden, and the wretchedness of the people at the same time be increased. On these considerations the committee *de Mendicité*, at the beginning of the revolution, very properly and judiciously rejected the establishment of such a system which had been proposed.

The exception of Holland, if it were an exception, would arise from very particular circumstances – her extensive foreign trade, and her numerous colonial emigrations, compared with the smallness of her territory, together with the extreme unhealthiness of a great part of the country, which occasions a much greater average mortality than is common in other states. These, I conceive, were the unobserved causes which principally contributed to render Holland so famous for the management of her poor, and able to employ and support all who applied for relief.

No part of Germany is sufficiently rich to support an extensive system of parochial relief; but I am inclined to think that, from the absence of it, the lower classes of the people in some parts of Germany are in a better situation than those of the same class in England. In Switzerland for the same reason their condition, before the late troubles, was perhaps universally superior. And in a journey through the dutchies of Holstein and Sleswick belonging to Denmark, the houses of the lower classes of people appeared to me to be neater and better, and in general there were fewer indications of poverty and wretchedness among them, than among the same ranks in this country.[29]

Even in Norway, notwithstanding the disadvantage of a severe and uncertain climate, from the little that I saw in a few weeks residence in the country, and the information that I could collect from others, I am inclined to think that the poor were, on the average, better off than in England. Their

---

[28] [In 1817 (Vol. III, p. 193) *conspicuous* was changed to 'remarkable'.
[29] [See *The Travel Diaries of T. R. Malthus* (Cambridge University Press, 1966) pp. 40–7.]

houses and clothing were superior and, though they had no white bread, they had much more meat, fish, and milk than our labourers; and I particularly remarked that the farmers' boys were much stouter and healthier looking lads than those of the same description in England. This degree of happiness, superior to what could be expected from the soil and climate, arises almost exclusively from the degree in which the preventive check to population operates;[30] and the establishment of a system of poor-laws, which would destroy this check, would at once sink the lower classes of the people into a state of the most miserable poverty and wretchedness; would diminish their industry, and consequently the produce of the land and labour of the country; would weaken the resources of ingenuity in times of scarcity; and ultimately involve the country in all the horrors of continual famines.

If, as in Ireland, and in Spain, and many of the southern countries, the people be in so degraded a state as to propagate their species like brutes, totally regardless of consequences,[31] it matters little whether they have poor-laws or not. Misery in all its various forms must be the predominant check to their increase. Poor-laws, indeed, will always tend to aggravate the evil, by diminishing the general resources of the country, and in such a state of things could [32]● exist only for a very short time; but with or without them, no stretch of human ingenuity and exertion could ●[32] rescue the people from the most extreme poverty and wretchedness.

---

[30] [See *The Travel Diaries of T. R. Malthus*, pp. 117–18, 124, 133–4, 139–40, 142, 145, 175, 202. In 1817 (Vol. III, p. 195) Malthus rather surprisingly changed the past to the present tense:
... the poor are, on the average, better off... Their houses and clothing are often superior; and though they have no white bread, they have much more meat, fish and milk ...

[31] [In 1817 (Vol. III, p. 196) this was altered:
If, as in Ireland, Spain, and many countries of the more southern climates, the people are in so degraded a state as to propagate their species without regard to consequences, it matters little ...

[32] [In 1817 (Vol. III, p. 197) *could* was replaced by 'can':
... can exist only for a very short time ... no stretch of human ingenuity and exertion can rescue the people ...

# CHAPTER IX

## *Of the modes of correcting the prevailing opinions on the subject of*[1] *Population*

It is not enough to abolish all the positive institutions which encourage population; but we must endeavour, at the same time, to correct the prevailing opinions which have the same or perhaps even a more powerful effect. This must necessarily be a work of time; and can only be done by circulating juster notions on these subjects in writings and conversation; and by endeavouring to impress as strongly as possible on the public mind that it is not the duty of man simply to propagate his species, but to propagate virtue and happiness; and that, if he has not a tolerably fair prospect of doing this, he is by no means called upon to leave descendants.

[2]•The merits of the childless, and of those who have brought up large families, should be compared without prejudice, and their different influence on the general happiness of society justly appreciated.

The matron who has reared a family of ten or twelve children, and whose sons, perhaps, may be fighting the battles of their country, is apt to think that society owes her much; and this imaginary debt society is, in general, fully inclined to acknowledge. But if the subject be fairly considered, and the respected matron weighed in the scales of justice against the neglected old maid, it is possible that the matron might kick the beam. She will appear rather in the character of a monopolist than of a great benefactor to the state. If she had not married and had so many children, other members of the society might have enjoyed this satisfaction; and there is no particular reason for supposing that her sons would fight better for their country than the sons of other women. She has therefore rather subtracted from, than added to, the happiness of the other parts of society. The old maid, on the contrary, has exalted others by depressing herself. Her self-denial has made room for another marriage, without any additional distress; and she has not, like the generality of men, in avoiding one error, fallen into its opposite. She has really and truly contributed more to the happiness of the rest of the society arising from the pleasures of marriage, than if she had entered in this union herself, and had besides portioned twenty maidens with a hundred pounds

---

[1] [In 1806 (Vol. II, p. 413) the words *the subject of* were omitted.]

each; whose particular happiness would have been balanced either by an increase in the general difficulties of rearing children and getting employment, or by the necessity of celibacy in twenty other maidens somewhere else. Like the truly benevolent man in an irremediable scarcity, she has diminished her own consumption, instead of raising up a few particular people by pressing down the rest. On a fair comparison, therefore, she seems to have a better founded claim to the gratitude of society than the matron. Whether we could always completely sympathize with the motives of her conduct has not much to do with the question. The particular motive which influenced the matron to marry was certainly not the good of her country. To refuse a proper tribute of respect to the old maid, because she was not directly influenced in her conduct by the desire of conferring on society a certain benefit which, though it must undoubtedly exist, must necessarily be so diffused as to be invisible to her, is in the highest degree impolitic and unjust. It is expecting a strain of virtue beyond humanity. If we never reward any persons with our approbation but those who are exclusively influenced by motives of general benevolence, this powerful encouragement to good actions will not be very often called into exercise.

There are very few women who might not have married in some way or other. The old maid, who has either never formed an attachment, or has been disappointed in the object of it, has, under the circumstances in which she has been placed, conducted herself with the most perfect propriety; and has acted a much more virtuous and honourable part in society than those women who marry without a proper degree of love, or at least of esteem, for their husbands; a species of immorality which is not reprobated as it deserves.

If, in comparisons of this kind, we should be compelled to acknowledge that, in considering the general tendency of population to increase beyond the means of subsistence, the conduct of the old maid had contributed more to the happiness of the society than that of the matron; it will surely appear not only unjust, but strikingly impolitic, not to proportion our tribute of honour and estimation more fairly according to their respective merits. Though we should not go so far as to reward single women with particular distinctions; yet the plainest principles of equity and policy require that the respect which they might claim from their personal character should, in no way whatever, be impeded by their particular situation; and that, with regard to rank, precedence, and the ceremonial attentions of society, they should be completely on a level with married women.

It is still however true that the life of a married person with a family is of more consequence to society than that of a single person; because, when there is a family of children already born, it is of the utmost importance that they should be well taken care of and well educated; and of this there is very seldom so fair a probability when they have lost their parents. Our object should be merely to correct the prevailing opinions with regard to the duty of marriage; and, without positively discouraging it, to prevent any persons from being attracted or driven into this state by the respect and honour which await the married dame, and the neglect and inconveniences attendant on the single woman.

It is perfectly absurd, as well as unjust, that a giddy girl of sixteen should, because she is married, be considered by the forms of society as the protector of women of thirty, should come first into the room, should be assigned the highest place at table, and be the prominent figure to whom the attentions of the company are more particularly addressed. Those who believe that these distinctions (added to the very long confinement of single women to the parental roof, and their being compelled on all occasions to occupy the background of the picture) have not an influence in impelling many young women into the married state against their natural inclinations, and without a proper degree of regard for their intended husbands, do not as I conceive reason with much knowledge of human nature. And till these customs are changed, as far as circumstances will admit, and the respect and liberty which women enjoy are made to depend more upon personal character and propriety of conduct, than upon their situation as married or single; it must be acknowledged that among the higher ranks of life we encourage marriage by considerable premiums.●[2]

It is not, however, among the higher ranks of society, that we have most reason to apprehend the too great frequency of marriage.[3] Though the circulation of juster notions on this subject might, even in this part of the community, do much good, and prevent many unhappy marriages; yet whether we make particular exertions for this purpose or not, we may rest assured that the degree of proper pride and spirit of independence, almost invariably connected with education and a certain rank in life, will secure the operation of the preventive check[4] to a considerable extent. All that the society can reasonably require of its members is that they should not have families without being able to support them. [5]●This may be fairly enjoined as a solemn duty. Every restraint beyond this, though in many points of view

---

[2] [In 1806 (Vol. ii, p. 413) the previous six paragraphs were expunged, possibly in consequence of Malthus's own marriage in 1804.]

[3] [In 1806 (Vol. ii, p. 413) this sentence was altered to take account of the previous long excision:

Among the higher ranks of society we have not much reason to apprehend the too great frequency of marriage.

[4] [In 1806 (Vol. ii, p. 414) this was changed to:

... the operation of the prudential check to marriage ...

highly desirable, must be considered as a matter of choice and taste;●[5] but from what we already know of the habits which prevail among the higher ranks of life, we have reason to think that little more is wanted to attain the object required than to award a greater degree of respect and of personal liberty to single women, and to remove the distinctions in favour of married women, so as to place them exactly upon a level;[6] a change which, independently of any particular purpose in view, the plainest principles of equity seem to demand.

If, among the higher classes of society, the object of securing the operation of the preventive check to population[7] to a sufficient degree appear to be attainable without much difficulty, the obvious mode of proceeding with the lower classes of society, where the point is of the principal importance, is, to endeavour to infuse into them a portion of that knowledge and foresight which so much facilitates the attainment of this object in the educated part of the community.

The fairest chance of accomplishing this end would probably be by the establishment of a system of parochial education upon a plan similar to that proposed by Dr. Smith.[8] In addition to the usual subjects of instruction, and those which he has mentioned, I should be disposed to lay considerable stress on the frequent explanation of the real state of the lower classes of society, as affected by the principle of population, and their consequent dependence on themselves, for the chief part of their happiness or misery.

[In 1806 (Vol. II, p. 415) Malthus added the following passage here, to conclude the paragraph:
... happiness or misery. It would be by no means necessary or proper in these explanations to underrate, in the smallest degree, the desirableness of marriage. It should always be represented as, what it really is, a state peculiarly suited to the nature of man, and calculated greatly to advance his happiness and remove the temptations to vice; but, like property or any other desirable object, its advantages should be shown to be unattainable except under certain conditions. And a strong conviction in a young man of the great desirableness of marriage, with a conviction at the same time, that the power of supporting a family was the only condition which would enable him really to enjoy its blessings, would be the most effectual motive imaginable to industry and sobriety before marriage, and would powerfully urge him

---

[5] [In 1806 (Vol. II, p. 414) Malthus made two more alterations here:
    This may be fairly enjoined as a positive duty. Every restraint beyond this must be considered as a matter of choice and taste; but from what we already know ...
[6] [In 1806 (Vol. II, p. 414) this was altered:
    ... single women, and place them nearer upon a level with married women; – a change which, ...
[7] [In 1806 (Vol. II, p. 414) this was changed to:
    ... the operation of the prudential check to marriage ...
[8] Wealth of Nations, vol. iii. b. v. c. i. p. 187.

to save that superfluity of income which single labourers necessarily possess for the accomplishment of a rational and desirable object, instead of dissipating it, as is now usually done, in idleness and vice.

If, in the course of time, a few of the simplest principles of political economy could be added to these instructions,[9] the benefit to society would be almost incalculable.[10] In some conversations with labouring men, during the late scarcities,[11] I confess that I was to the last degree disheartened at observing their inveterate prejudices on the subject of grain; and I felt very strongly the almost absolute incompatibility of a government really free with such a degree of ignorance. The delusions are of such a nature that, if acted

---

[9] [In 1806 (Vol. II, p. 416) this was altered to:
    ... added to the instruction given in these schools, the benefit to society ...

[10] Dr. Smith proposes that the elementary parts of geometry and mechanics should be taught in these parish schools; and I cannot help thinking that the common principles by which markets are regulated might be made sufficiently clear to be of considerable use. It is certainly a subject that, as it interests the lower classes of people nearly, would be likely to attract their attention. At the same time it must be confessed that it is impossible to be in any degree sanguine on this point, recollecting how very ignorant in general the educated part of the community is of these principles. If, however, political economy cannot be taught to the common people, I really think that it ought to form a branch of a university education. Scotland has set us an example in this respect, which we ought not to be so slow to imitate. It is of the utmost importance that the gentlemen of the country, and particularly the clergy, should not from ignorance aggravate the evils of scarcity every time that it unfortunately occurs. During the late dearths, half of the gentlemen and clergymen in the kingdom richly deserved to have been prosecuted for sedition. After inflaming the minds of the common people against the farmers and corn-dealers, by the manner in which they talked of them or preached about them, it was but a feeble antidote to the poison which they had infused coldly to observe that, however the poor might be oppressed or cheated, it was their duty to keep the peace. It was little better than Anthony's repeated declaration that the conspirators were all honourable men, which did not save either their houses or their persons from the attacks of the mob. Political economy is perhaps the only science of which it may be said that the ignorance of it is not merely a deprivation of good, but produces great evil. [For Anthony, see SHAKESPEARE (4) in the Alphabetical List.]
[In 1826 (Vol. II, pp. 354–5) Malthus added to this note:
    [1825.] This note was written in 1803; and it is particularly gratifying to me, at the end of the year 1825, to see that what I stated as so desirable twenty-two years ago, seems to be now on the eve of its accomplishment. The increasing attention which in the interval has been paid generally to the science of political economy; the lectures which have been given at Cambridge, London, and Liverpool; the chair which has lately been established at Oxford; the projected University in the Metropolis; and, above all, the Mechanic's Institution, open the fairest prospect that, within a moderate period of time, the fundamental principles of political economy will, to a very useful extent, be known to the higher, middle, and a most important portion of the working classes of society in England.
    [For the Cambridge lectures, see PRYME in the Alphabetical List; for those given in London and Liverpool, see McCULLOCH; for the Oxford Chair, see DRUMMOND; for the projected University of London and the Mechanics' Institution, see BROUGHAM.]
[11] [In 1817 (Vol. III, p. 203) a note was added here:
    1800 and 1801.

upon, they must at all events be repressed by force; and it is extremely difficult to give such a power to the government as will be sufficient at all times for this purpose, without the risk of its being employed improperly and endangering the liberty of the subject. [12]●And this reflection cannot but be disheartening to every friend to freedom.●[12]

We have lavished immense sums on the poor, which we have every reason to think have constantly tended to aggravate their misery. But in their education, and in the circulation of those important political truths that most nearly concern them, which are perhaps the only means in our power of really raising their condition, and of making them happier men and more peaceable subjects, we have been miserably deficient. It is surely a great national disgrace, that the education of the lower classes of people in England should be left merely to a few Sunday schools, supported by a subscription from individuals, who of course[13] can give to the course of instruction in them any kind of bias which they please. And even the improvement of Sunday schools, for objectionable as they are in some points of view, and imperfect in all, I cannot but consider them as an improvement, is of very late date.[14]

The arguments which have been urged against instructing the people appear to me to be not only illiberal, but to the last degree, feeble; and they ought, on the contrary, to be extremely forcible, and to be supported by the most obvious and striking necessity, to warrant us in withholding the means of raising the condition of the lower classes of people, when they are in our power. Those who will not listen to any answer to these arguments drawn from theory cannot, I think, refuse the testimony of experience; and I would ask whether the advantage of superior instruction, which the lower classes of people in Scotland are known to possess, has appeared to have any tendency towards creating a spirit of tumult and discontent amongst them. And yet from the natural inferiority of its soil and climate, the pressure of want is more constant, and the dearths are not only more frequent but more dreadful than in England. In the case of Scotland, the knowledge circulated among the common people, though not sufficient essentially to better their condition by increasing, in an adequate degree, their habits of prudence and foresight, has yet the effect of making them bear with patience the evils they suffer, from being aware of the folly and inefficacy of turbulence. The quiet and peaceable habits of the instructed Scotch peasant, compared with the

---

[12] [In 1806 (Vol. II, p. 418) this sentence was omitted, the paragraph concluding with the words:
　... liberty of the subject.
[13] [In 1817 (Vol. III, p. 204) the words *of course* were excised.]
[14] [In 1817 (Vol. III, p. 204) there was a footnote here:
　Written in 1803.

turbulent disposition of the ignorant Irishman, ought not to be without effect upon every impartial reasoner.

The principal argument which I have heard advanced against a system of national education in England is, that the common people would be put in a capacity to read such works as those of Paine, and that the consequences would probably be fatal to government. But, on this subject, I agree most cordially with Dr. Smith[15] in thinking that an instructed and well-informed people would be much less likely to be led away by inflammatory writings, and much better able to detect the false declamation of interested and ambitious demagogues, than an ignorant people. One or two readers in a parish are sufficient to circulate any quantity of sedition; and if these be gained to the democratic side, they will probably have the power of doing much more mischief, by selecting the passages best suited to their hearers, and choosing the moments when their oratory is likely to have the most effect, than if each individual in the parish had been in a capacity to read and judge of the whole work himself; and, at the same time, to read and judge of the opposing arguments, which we may suppose would also reach him.

But in addition to this, a double weight would undoubtedly be added to the observation of Dr. Smith, if these schools were made the means of instructing the people in the real nature of their situation; if they were taught, what is really true, that without an increase of their own industry and prudence, no change of government could essentially better their condition; that, though they might get rid of some particular grievance, yet in the great point of supporting their families they would be but little or perhaps not at all benefited; that a revolution would not alter in their favour the proportion of the supply of labour to the demand, or the quantity of food to the number of the consumers; and that, if the supply of labour were greater than the demand, and the demand for food greater than the supply, they might suffer the utmost severity of want under the freest, the most perfect, and best executed government that the human imagination could conceive.

A knowledge of these truths so obviously tends to promote peace and quietness, to weaken the effect of inflammatory writings, and to prevent all unreasonable and ill-directed opposition to the constituted authorities, that those who would still object to the instruction of the people may fairly be suspected of a wish to encourage their ignorance, as a pretext for tyranny, and an opportunity of increasing the power and the influence of the executive government.

Besides correcting the prevailing opinions respecting marriage, and explaining the real situation of the lower classes of society, as depending

---

[15] Wealth of Nations, vol. iii. b. v. c. i. p. 192.

almost entirely upon themselves for their happiness or misery,[16] the parochial schools would, by early instruction and the judicious distribution of rewards, have the fairest chance of training up the rising generation in habits of sobriety, industry, independence, and prudence, and in a proper discharge of their religious duties; which would raise them from their present degraded state, and approximate them in some degree to the middle classes of society, whose habits, generally speaking, are certainly superior.

In most countries, among the lower classes of people, there appears to be something like a standard of wretchedness, a point below which they will not continue to marry and propagate their species. This standard is different in different countries, and is formed by various concurring circumstances of soil, climate, government, degree of knowledge, and civilization, &c. The principal circumstances which contribute to raise it are liberty, security of property, the spread of knowledge,[17] and a taste for the conveniences and the comforts of life. Those which contribute principally to lower it are despotism and ignorance.

In an attempt to better the condition of the lower classes of society,[18] our object should be to raise this standard as high as possible, by cultivating a spirit of independence, a decent pride, and a taste for cleanliness and comfort [19]•among the poor. These habits would be best inculcated by a system of general education and, when strongly fixed, would be the most powerful means of preventing their marrying with the prospect of being obliged to forfeit such advantages; and would consequently raise them nearer to the middle classes of society.•[19]

---

[16] [In 1806 (Vol. II, p. 422) this was altered to:
    Besides explaining the real situation of the lower classes of society, as depending principally upon themselves for their happiness or misery, the parochial schools would ...
[17] [In 1817 (Vol. III, p. 209) *spread* was changed to 'diffusion'.
[18] [In 1826 (Vol. II, p. 359) *lower classes* was changed to 'labouring classes'.
[19] [In 1806 (Vol. II, p. 423) the words *among the poor* were omitted, and the chapter concluded thus:
    ... and a taste for cleanliness and comfort. The effect of a good government in increasing the prudential habits and personal respectability of the lower classes of society has already been insisted on; but certainly this effect will always be incomplete without a good system of education; and, indeed, it may be said that no government can approach to perfection that does not provide for the instruction of the people. The benefits derived from education are among those which may be enjoyed without restriction of numbers; and, as it is in the power of governments to confer these benefits, it is undoubtedly their duty to do it.

# CHAPTER X

## *Of the direction of our charity*

An important and interesting inquiry yet remains, relating to the mode of directing our private charity so as not to interfere with the great object in view, of ameliorating the condition of the lower classes of people[1] by preventing the population from pressing too hard against the limits of the means of subsistence.

The emotion which prompts us to relieve our fellow creatures in distress is, like all our other natural passions, general, and in some degree indiscriminate and blind. Our feelings of compassion may be worked up to a higher pitch by a well-wrought scene in a play, or a fictitious tale in a novel, than by almost any events in real life; and if, among ten petitioners, we were to listen only to the first impulses of our feelings, without making further inquiries, we should undoubtedly give our assistance to the best actor of the party. It is evident, therefore, that the impulse of benevolence, like the impulses of love, of anger, of ambition, of eating and drinking,[2] or any other of our natural propensities, must be regulated by experience, and frequently brought to the test of utility, or it will defeat its intended purpose.

The apparent object of the passion between the sexes is the continuation of the species, and the formation of such an intimate union of views and interests between two persons as will best promote their happiness, and at the same time secure the proper degree of attention to the helplessness of infancy and the education of the rising generation; but if every man were to obey at all times the impulses of nature in the gratification of this passion, without regard to consequences, the principal part of these important objects would not be attained, and even the continuation of the species might be defeated by a promiscuous intercourse.

The apparent end of the impulse of benevolence is to draw the whole human race together, but more particularly that part of it which is of our own nation and kindred, in the bonds of brotherly love; and by giving men an

---

[1] [In 1826 (Vol. II, p. 361) *lower classes of people* was changed to:
... labouring classes of people ...
[2] [In 1806 (Vol. II, p. 425) this was altered to:
... of ambition, the desire of eating and drinking, or any other ...

interest in the happiness and misery of their fellow creatures, to prompt them, as they have power, to mitigate some of the partial evils arising from general laws, and thus to increase the sum of human happiness; but if our benevolence be indiscriminate, and the degree of apparent distress be made the sole measure of our liberality, it is evident that it will be exercised almost exclusively upon common beggars, while modest unobtrusive merit, struggling with unavoidable difficulties, yet still maintaining some slight appearances of decency and cleanliness, will be totally neglected. We shall raise the worthless above the worthy; we shall encourage indolence and check industry; and, in the most marked manner subtract from the sum of human happiness.

Our experience has, indeed, informed us that the impulse of benevolence is not so strong as the passion between the sexes, and that, generally speaking, there is much less danger to be apprehended from the indulgence of the former than of the latter; but, independently of this experience, and of the moral codes founded upon it, [3]●a youth of eighteen would be as completely justified in indulging the sexual passion with every object capable of exciting it, as in following indiscriminately every impulse of his benevolence.●[3] They are both natural passions, excited by their appropriate objects, and to the gratification of which we are prompted by the pleasurable sensations which accompany them. As animals, or till we know their consequences, our only business is to follow these dictates of nature; but, as reasonable beings, we are under the strongest obligations to attend to their consequences; and if they be evil to ourselves or others, we may justly consider it as an indication that such a mode of indulging these passions is not suited to our state or conformable to the will of God. As moral agents, therefore, it is clearly our duty to restrain their indulgence in these particular directions: and by thus carefully examining the consequences of our natural passions, and frequently bringing them to the test of utility, gradually to acquire a habit of gratifying them only in that way which, being unattended with evil, will clearly add to the sum of human happiness and fulfil the apparent purpose of the Creator.

Though utility, therefore, can never be the immediate excitement to the gratification of any passion, it is the test by which alone we can know whether it ought or ought not to be indulged;[4] and is, therefore, the surest

---

[3] [In 1817 (Vol. III, p. 214) this was altered:
    ... founded upon it, we should be as much justified in a general indulgence of the former passion as in following indiscriminately every impulse of our benevolence.
[4] [In 1817 (Vol. III, p. 215) Malthus made an important insertion here:
    ... by which alone we can know, independently of the revealed will of God, whether it ought or ought not ...

foundation of all morality[5] which can be collected from the light of nature. All the moral codes which have inculcated the subjection of the passions to reason have been, as I conceive, really built upon this foundation, whether the promulgators of them were aware of it or not.

I remind the reader of these truths in order to apply them to the habitual direction of our charity; and, if we keep the criterion of utility constantly in view, we may find ample room for the exercise of our benevolence without interfering with the great purpose which we have to accomplish.

One of the most valuable parts of charity is its effect upon the giver. It is more blessed to give than to receive. Supposing it to be allowed that the exercise of our benevolence in acts of charity is not, upon the whole, really beneficial to the poor, yet we could never sanction any endeavour to extinguish an impulse, the proper gratification of which has so evident a tendency to purify and exalt the human mind. But it is particularly satisfactory and pleasing to find that the mode of exercising our charity which, when brought to the test of utility, will appear to be most beneficial to the poor, is precisely that which will have the best and most improving effect on the mind of the donor.

The quality of charity like that of mercy,

> is not strained;
> It droppeth as the gentle rain from heaven
> Upon the earth beneath.[6]

The immense sums distributed to the poor in this country, by the parochial laws, are improperly called charity. They want its most distinguishing attribute; and, as might be expected, from an attempt to force that which loses its essence the moment that it ceases to be voluntary, their effects upon those from whom they are collected are as prejudicial as on those to whom they are distributed. On the side of the receivers of this miscalled charity, instead of real relief, we find accumulated distress and more extended poverty; on the side of the givers, instead of pleasurable sensations, unceasing discontent and irritation.

In the great charitable institutions supported by voluntary contributions, many[7] of which are certainly of a prejudicial tendency, the subscriptions, I am inclined to fear, are sometimes given grudgingly, and rather because they are expected by the world from certain stations, and certain fortunes, than because they are prompted by motives of genuine benevolence; and as the greater part of the subscribers do not interest themselves in the management

---

[5] [In 1817 (Vol. II, p. 215) *the surest foundation of all morality* was changed to 'the surest criterion of moral rules'.

[6] [See SHAKESPEARE (5) in the Alphabetical List.]

[7] [In 1806 (Vol. II, p. 429) Malthus changed *many* to 'some'.

of the funds, or in the fate of the particular objects relieved, it is not to be expected that this kind of charity should have any strikingly beneficial influence on the minds of the majority who exercise it.

Even in the relief of common beggars, we shall find that we are more frequently influenced by the desire of getting rid of the importunities of a disgusting object than by the pleasure of relieving it.[8] We wish that it had not fallen in our way, rather than rejoice in the opportunity given us of assisting a fellow-creature. We feel a painful emotion at the sight of so much apparent misery; but the pittance we give does not relieve it. We know that it is totally inadequate to produce any essential effect. We know, besides, that we shall be addressed in the same manner at the corner of the next street; and we know that we are liable to the grossest impositions. We hurry therefore sometimes by them,[9] and shut our ears to their importunate demands. We give no more than we can help giving without doing actual violence to our feelings. Our charity is in some degree forced and, like forced charity, it leaves no satisfactory impression on the mind, and cannot therefore have any very beneficial and improving effect on the heart and affections.

But it is far otherwise with that voluntary and active charity, which makes itself acquainted with the objects which it relieves; which seems to feel, and to be proud of, the bond which unites the rich with the poor; which enters into their houses; informs itself not only of their wants, but of their habits and dispositions; checks the hopes of clamorous and obstrusive poverty, with no other recommendation but rags; and encourages with adequate relief the silent and retiring sufferer, labouring under unmerited difficulties. This mode of exercising our charity presents a very different picture from that of any other; and its contrast with the common mode of parish relief cannot be better described than in the words of Mr. Townsend, in the conclusion of his admirable dissertation on the Poor Laws: Nothing in nature can be more disgusting than a parish pay-table, attendant upon which, in the same objects of misery, are too often found combined snuff, gin, rags, vermin, insolence, and abusive language; nor in nature can any thing be more beautiful than the mild complacency of benevolence hastening to the humble cottage to relieve the wants of industry and virtue, to feed the hungry, to clothe the naked, and to soothe the sorrows of the widow with her tender orphans; nothing can be more pleasing, unless it be their sparkling eyes, their bursting tears, and their uplifted hands, the artless expressions of

---

[8] [In 1806 (Vol. II, p. 430) this was altered:
   ... we shall find that we are often as much influenced by the desire of getting rid ... of a disgusting object as by the pleasure of relieving it.
[9] [In 1826 (Vol. II, p. 366) *them* was changed to 'such objects'.

unfeigned gratitude for unexpected favours. Such scenes will frequently occur whenever men shall have power to dispose of their own property.'

I conceive it to be almost impossible, that any person could be much engaged in such scenes without daily making advances in virtue. No exercise of our affections can have a more evident tendency to purify and exalt the human mind. It is almost exclusively this species of charity that blesseth him that gives; and, in a general view, it is almost exclusively this species of charity which blesseth him that takes; at least it may be asserted that there is no other mode of exercising our charity[10] in which large sums can be distributed without a greater chance of producing evil than good.

The discretionary power of giving or withholding relief, which is, to a certain extent, vested in parish officers and justices, is of a very different nature, and will have a very different effect from the discrimination which may be exercised by voluntary charity. Every man in this country, under certain circumstances, is entitled by law to parish assistance; and unless his disqualification is clearly proved, has a right to complain if it be withheld. The inquiries necessary to settle this point, and the extent of the relief to be granted, too often produce evasion and lying on the part of the petitioner, and afford an opening to partiality and oppression in the overseer. If the proposed relief be given, it is of course received with unthankfulness; and if it be denied, the party generally thinks himself severely aggrieved, and feels resentment and indignation at his treatment.

In the distribution of voluntary charity, nothing of this kind can take place. The person who receives it is made the proper subject of the pleasurable sensation of gratitude; and those who do not receive it cannot possibly conceive themselves in the slightest degree injured. Every man has a right to do what he will with his own; and cannot, in justice, be called upon to render a reason why he gives in the one case and abstains from it in the other. This kind of despotic power, essential to voluntary charity, gives the greatest facility to the selection of worthy objects of relief, without being accompanied by any ill consequences; and has further a most beneficial effect from the degree of uncertainty which must necessarily be attached to it. It is, in the highest degree, important to the general happiness of the poor that no man should look to charity as a fund on which he may confidently depend. He should be taught that his own exertions, his own industry and foresight, are his only just ground of dependence; that if these fail, assistance in his distresses could only be the subject of rational hope; and that even the

---

[10] [This was modified twice. In 1806 (Vol. II, p. 432) it was changed to:
    ... that there is hardly any other mode of exercising our charity ...
    [In 1817 (Vol. III, p. 220) Malthus wrote:
    ... that there are but few other modes of exercising our charity ...

foundation of this hope must be in his own good conduct,[11] and the consciousness that he had not involved himself in these difficulties by his indolence or imprudence.

That, in the distribution of our charity, we are under a strong moral obligation to inculcate this lesson on the poor, by a proper discrimination, is a truth of which I cannot feel a doubt. If all could be completely relieved, and poverty banished from the country, even at the expense of three-fourths of the fortunes of the rich, I would be the last person to say a single syllable against relieving all, and making the degree of distress alone the measure of our bounty. But as experience has proved, I believe without a single exception, that poverty and misery have always increased in proportion to the quantity of indiscriminate charity; are we not bound to infer, reasoning as we usually do from the laws of nature, that it is an intimation that such a mode of distribution is not the proper office of benevolence?

The laws of nature say, with St. Paul: 'If a man will not work, neither shall he eat.'[12] They also say that he is not rashly to trust to Providence. They appear indeed to be constant and uniform for the express purpose of telling him what he is to trust to, and that if he marry, without being able to support a family, he must expect severe want.[13] These intimations appear from the constitution of human nature to be absolutely necessary, and to have a strikingly beneficial tendency. If in the direction either of our public or our private charity we say that though a man will not work, yet he shall eat; and though he marry, without being able to support a family, yet his family shall be supported; it is evident that we do not merely endeavour to mitigate some of the partial evils arising from general laws, but regularly and systematically to counteract the obviously beneficial effects of these general laws themselves.[14] And we cannot easily conceive that the Deity should implant any passion in the human breast for such a purpose.

In the great course of human events, the best-founded expectations will sometimes be disappointed; and industry, prudence, and virtue, not only fail of their just reward, but be involved in unmerited calamities. Those who are thus suffering in spite of the best-directed endeavours to avoid it, and from causes which they could not be expected to foresee, are the genuine objects of charity. In relieving these, we exercise the appropriate office of benevolence,

---

[11] [In 1817 (Vol. III, p. 222) this was altered:
    ... and that even the foundation of this hope will depend in a considerable degree on his own good conduct, ...
[12] [See PAUL OF TARSUS (2) in the Alphabetical List.]
[13] [In 1817 (Vol. III, p. 224) this was modified:
    ... if he marry without a reasonable prospect of supporting a family, he must expect to suffer want.
[14] [In 1817 (Vol. III, p. 224) Malthus italicised *regularly* and *systematically*.]

that of mitigating some of[15] the partial evils arising from general laws; and in this direction of our charity, therefore, we need not apprehend any ill consequences. Such objects ought to be relieved according to our means liberally and adequately, even though the worthless were starving.[16]

When indeed this first claim on our benevolence was satisfied, we might then turn our attention to the idle and improvident: but the interests of human happiness most clearly require, that the relief which we afford them should be very scanty.[17] We may perhaps take upon ourselves, with great caution, to mitigate in some degree[18] the punishments which they are suffering from the laws of nature; but on no account to remove them entirely. They are deservedly at the bottom in the scale of society; and if we raise them from this situation, we not only palpably defeat the end of benevolence, but commit a most glaring injustice to those who are above them. They should on no account be enabled to command so much of the necessaries of life as can be obtained by the worst-paid common labour.[19] [20]●The brownest bread, with the coarsest and scantiest apparel, is the utmost which they should have the means of purchasing.●[20]

It is evident that these reasonings do not apply to those cases of urgent distress arising from disastrous accidents, unconnected with habits of indolence and improvidence. If a man break a leg or an arm, we are not to stop to inquire into his moral character before we lend him our assistance; but in this case we are perfectly consistent, and the touchstone of utility completely justifies our conduct. By affording the most indiscriminate assistance in this way, we are in little danger of encouraging people to break their arms and legs. According to the touchstone of utility, the high approbation which Christ gave to the conduct of the good Samaritan, who followed the immediate impulse of his benevolence in relieving a stranger, in the urgent distress of an accident, does not in the smallest degree contradict the expression of St. Paul, 'If a man will not work, neither shall he eat.'[21]

---

[15] [In 1806 (Vol. II, p. 436) the words *some of* were omitted.]

[16] [In 1817 (Vol. III, p. 225) this was changed to:
... even though the worthless were in much more severe distress.

[17] [In 1806 (Vol. II, p. 436) the word *very* was excised.]
[In 1817 (Vol. III, p. 225) this was altered again to:
... the relief which we afford them should not be abundant.

[18] [In 1806 (Vol. II, p. 437) the words *in some degree* were omitted.]

[19] [In 1817 (Vol. III, p. 226) this was altered to:
... can be obtained by the wages of common labour.

[20] [In 1817 (Vol. III, p. 226) this sentence was omitted.]

[21] [Jesus Christ's parable of the good man of Samaria may be found in the tenth chapter of St Luke's Gospel (vv.25–37). It was to illustrate the commandment that, after loving God, a man should love his neighbour as himself. In reply to the question: 'Who is my neighbour?' Christ told the story of a traveller who was attacked by robbers and left half dead on the

We are not, however, in any case, to lose a present opportunity of doing good from the mere supposition that we may possibly meet with a worthier object. In all doubtful cases, it may safely be laid down as our duty to follow the natural impulse of our benevolence; but when in fulfilling our obligation, as reasonable beings, to attend to the consequences of our actions, we have from our own experience and that of others drawn the conclusion that the exercise of our benevolence in one mode is prejudicial, and in another is beneficial in its effects; we are certainly bound, as moral agents, to check our natural propensities in the one direction, and to encourage them and acquire the habits of exercising them in the other.

---

road. Two later travellers saw him lying there, and each in turn passed by on the other side; a third traveller, a Samaritan, had pity on the injured man, bound up his wounds, and took him to an inn, where he paid the landlord to care for him. The good Samaritan was obviously 'neighbour unto him that fell among thieves', and Christ concluded with the words, 'Go and do thou likewise' (Bible of 1611). See GODWIN in the Alphabetical List: in 1801, in his pamphlet on *Dr Parr's Spital Sermon*, Godwin pointed out (p. 43) that Christ had not merely justified, but applauded, the good Samaritan; presumably Malthus had Godwin in mind when he wrote this paragraph.]

# CHAPTER XI

## *Of the errors in different plans which have been proposed, to improve the condition of the Poor*[1]

In the distribution of our charity, or in any efforts which we may make to better the condition of the lower classes of society, there is another point relating to the main argument of this work to which we must be particularly attentive. We must on no account do anything which tends directly to encourage marriage; or to remove, in any regular and systematic manner, that inequality of circumstances which ought always to exist between the single man and the man with a family. The writers who have best understood the principle of population appear to me all to have fallen into very important errors on this point.

Sir James Steuart, who is fully aware of what he calls vicious procreation, and of the misery that attends a redundant population, recommends, notwithstanding, the general establishment of foundling hospitals; the taking of children, under certain circumstances, from their parents, and supporting them at the expense of the state; and particularly laments the inequality of condition between the married and single man, so ill-proportioned to their respective wants.[2] He forgets, in these instances, that if, without the encouragement to multiplication of foundling hospitals, or of public support for the children of some married persons, and under the discouragement of great pecuniary disadvantages on the side of the married man, population be still redundant; which is evinced by the inability of the poor to maintain all their children; it is a clear proof that the funds destined for the maintenance of labour cannot properly support a greater population; and that, if further encouragements to multiplication be given, and discouragements removed, the result must be an increase, somewhere or other, of that vicious procreation which he so justly reprobates.

Mr. Townsend, who in his Dissertation on the Poor Laws has treated this subject with great skill and perspicuity, appears to me to conclude with a proposal which violates the principles on which he had reasoned so well. He wishes to make the benefit clubs or friendly societies, which are now

---

[1] [In 1806 (Vol. ii, p. 439) this heading was changed to:
   Different plans of improving the condition of the Poor considered.
[2] Political Oeconomy, vol. i. b. i. c. xii.

voluntarily established in many parishes, compulsory and universal; and proposes, as a regulation, that an unmarried man should pay a fourth part of his wages, and a married man with four children not more than a thirtieth part.[3]

I must first remark that the moment these subscriptions are made compulsory, they will necessarily operate exactly like a direct tax upon labour, which, as Dr. Smith justly states, will always be paid, and in a more expensive manner, by the consumer. The landed interest, therefore, would receive no[4] relief from this plan, but would pay the same sum as at present, only in the advanced price of labour and of commodities, instead of in the parish rates. A compulsory subscription of this kind would have almost all the ill effects[5] of the present system of relief and, though altered in name, would still possess the essential spirit of the poor laws.

Dean Tucker, in some remarks on a plan of the same kind, proposed by Mr. Pew, observed that, after much talk and reflection on the subject, he had come to the conclusion that they must be voluntary associations and not compulsory assemblies. A voluntary subscription is like a tax upon a luxury, and does not necessarily raise the price of labour.

It should be recollected, also, that in a voluntary association of a small extent, over which each individual member can exercise a superintendence, it is highly probable that the original agreements will all be strictly fulfilled, or if they be not, every man may at least have the redress of withdrawing himself from the club. But in an universal compulsory subscription, which must necessarily become a natural concern, there would be no security whatever for the fulfilment of the original agreements; and when the funds failed, which they certainly would do, when all the idle and dissolute were included, instead of some of the most industrious and provident, as at present, a larger subscription would probably be demanded, and no man would have the right to refuse it. The evil would thus go on increasing as the poor rates do now. If, indeed, the assistance given were always specific, and on no account to be increased, as in the present voluntary associations, this would certainly be a striking advantage; but the same advantage might be completely attained by a similar distribution of the sums collected by the parish rates. On the whole, therefore, it appears to me that, if the friendly societies were made universal and compulsory, it would be merely a different mode of collecting parish rates; and any particular mode of distribution might be as well adopted upon one system as upon the other.

With regard to the proposal of making single men pay a fourth part of their

---

[3] Dissertation on the Poor Laws, p. 89. 2d edit. 1787.
[4] [In 1826 (Vol. II, p. 376) *no* was changed to 'little'.
[5] [In 1817 (Vol. III, p. 230) *ill effects* was changed to 'bad effects'.

earnings weekly, and married men with families only a thirtieth part, it would evidently operate as a heavy fine upon bachelors and a high bounty upon children; and is therefore directly adverse to the general spirit in which Mr. Townsend's excellent dissertation is written. Before he introduces this proposal, he lays it down as a general principle that no system for the relief of the poor can be good, which does not regulate population by the demand for labour;[6] but this proposal clearly tends to encourage population without any reference to the demand for labour, and punishes a young man for his prudence in refraining from marriage at a time, perhaps, when this demand is so small[7] that the wages of labour are totally inadequate to the support of a family. I should be averse to any compulsory system whatever for the poor; but certainly if single men were compelled to pay a contribution for the future contingencies of the married state, they ought in justice to receive a benefit proportioned to the period of their privation; and the man who had contributed a fourth of his earnings for merely one year ought not to be put upon a level with him who has contributed this proportion for ten years.

Arthur Young, in most of his works, appears clearly to understand the principle of population, and is fully aware of the evils which must necessarily result from an increase of people beyond the demand for labour and the means of comfortable subsistence. In his Tour through France he has particularly laboured this point, and shown most forcibly the misery which results, in that country, from the excess of population occasioned by the too great division of property. Such an increase he justly calls merely a multiplication of wretchedness. 'Couples marry and procreate on the idea, not the reality, of a maintenance; they increase beyond the demand of towns and manufactures; and the consequence is distress, and numbers dying of diseases arising from insufficient nourishment.'[8]

In another place he quotes a very sensible passage from the report of the Committee on Mendicity which, alluding to the evils of overpopulation, concludes thus: 'Il faudroit enfin necessairement que le prix de travail baissat par la plus grand concurrence de travailleurs, d'ou resulteroit un indigence complette pour ceux qui ne trouveroient pas de travail, et une subsistence incomplette pour ceux mêmes aux quels il ne seroit pas refusé.'[9] And in remarking upon this passage, he observes: 'France itself affords an irrefragable proof of the truth of these sentiments; for I am clearly of opinion, from the observations I made in every province of the kingdom, that her population is

---

[6] P. 84.    [7] [In 1817 (Vol. III, p. 233) *is so small* was changed to 'may be so small'.
[8] Travels in France, vol. i. c. xii. p. 408.
[9] ['Excessive competition among labourers must in the end necessarily lower the wages of labour, which will result in utter poverty for those who cannot find work, and an inadequate subsistence for those who can.']

so much beyond the proportion of her industry and labour, that she would be much more powerful and infinitely more flourishing if she had five or six millions less of inhabitants. From her too great population she presents, in every quarter, such spectacles of wretchedness as are absolutely inconsistent with that degree of national felicity which she was capable of attaining, even under the old government. A traveller much less attentive than I was to objects of this kind must see at every turn most unequivocal signs of distress. That these should exist, no one can wonder, who considers the price of labour and provisions, and the misery into which a small rise in the price of wheat throws the lower classes.'[10]

'If you would see', he says, 'a district with as little distress in it as is consistent with the political system of the old government of France, you must assuredly go where there are no little properties at all. You must visit the great farms in Beauce, Picardy, part of Normandy, and Artois, and there you will find no more population than what is regularly employed and regularly paid; and if in such districts you should, contrary to this rule, meet with much distress, it is twenty to one but that it is in a parish which has some commons, which tempt the poor to have cattle – to have property – and in consequence misery. When you are engaged in this political tour, finish it by seeing England, and I will shew you a set of peasants well clothed, well nourished, tolerably drunken from superfluity, well lodged, and at their ease; and yet, amongst them not one in a thousand has either land or cattle.'[11] A little further on, alluding to encouragements to marriage, he says of France: 'the predominant evil of the kingdom is the having so great a population that she can neither employ nor feed it; why then encourage marriage? Would you breed more people, because you have more already than you know what to do with? You have so great a competition for food, that your people are starving or in misery; and you would encourage the production of more to encrease that competition. It may almost be questioned whether the contrary policy ought not to be embraced; whether difficulties should not be laid on the marriage of those who cannot make it appear that they have the prospect of maintaining the children that shall be the fruit of it? But why encourage marriages, which are sure to take place in all situations in which they ought to take place? There is no instance to be found of plenty of regular employment being first established where marriages have not followed in a proportionate degree. The policy therefore, at best, is useless, and may be pernicious.'

After having once so clearly understood the principle of population as to express these and many other sentiments on the subject, equally just and

---

[10] Travels in France, vol. i. c. xvii. p. 469.     [11] Id. p. 471.

important, it is not a little surprising to find Mr. Young in a pamphlet, intitled, *The Question of Scarcity plainly stated, and Remedies considered, (published in* 1800), observing that 'the means which would of all others perhaps tend most surely to prevent future scarcities so oppressive to the poor as the present, would be to secure to every country labourer in the kingdom, that has three children and upwards, half an acre of land for potatoes, and grass enough to feed one or two cows[12] .... If each had his ample potatoe ground and a cow, the price of wheat would be of little more consequence to them than it is to their brethren in Ireland.

Every one admits the system to be good, but the question is, how to enforce it.'

I was by no means aware that the excellence of the system had been so generally admitted. For myself I strongly protest against being included in the general term of *every one*, as I should consider the adoption of this system as the most cruel and fatal blow to the happiness of the lower classes of people in this country, that they had ever received.

Mr. Young, however, goes on to say that: 'The magnitude of the object should make us disregard any difficulties, but such as are insuperable: none such would probably occur if something like the following means were resorted to:

I Where there are common pastures, to give to a labouring man having children, a right to demand an allotment proportioned to the family, to be set out by the parish officers, &c. ... and a cow bought. Such labourer to have both for life, paying 40s. a year till the price of the cow, &c. was reimbursed: at his death to go to the labourer having the most numerous family, for life, paying [oo] shillings a week to the widow of his predecessor.

II Labourers thus demanding allotments by reason of their families to have land assigned, and cows bought, till the proportion so allotted amounts to one [o^{th}] of the extent of the common.

III In parishes where there are no commons, and the quality of the land adequate, every cottager having [oo] children, to whose cottage there is not within a given time land sufficient for a cow, and half an acre of potatoes, assigned at a fair average rent, subject to appeal to the sessions, to have a right to demand [oo] shillings per week of the parish for every child, till such land be assigned; leaving to landlords and tenants the means of doing it. Cows to be found by the parish, under an annual reimbursement.'[13]

'The great object is, by means of milk and potatoes, to take the mass of the country poor from the consumption of wheat, and to give them substitutes

---

[12] P. 77.    [13] P. 78.

equally wholesome and nourishing, and as independent of scarcities, natural and artificial, as the providence of the Almighty will admit.'[14]

Would not this plan operate, in the most direct manner, as an encouragement to marriage and a bounty on children, which Mr. Young has with so much justice reprobated in his travels in France? and does he seriously think that it would be an eligible thing, to feed the mass of the people in this country on milk and potatoes, and make them as independent of the price of corn, and of the demand for labour, as their brethren in Ireland?

The specific cause of the poverty and misery of the lower classes of people in France and Ireland is that, from the extreme subdivision of property in the one country, and the facility of obtaining a potatoe ground in the other,[15] a population is brought into existence, which is not demanded by the quantity of capital and employment in the country; and the consequence of which must therefore necessarily be, as is very justly expressed in the report of the Committee on Mendicity before mentioned, to lower in general the price of labour by too great competition; from which must result complete indigence to those who cannot find employment, and an incomplete subsistence even to those who can.

The obvious tendency of Mr. Young's plan is, by encouraging marriage and furnishing a cheap food, independent of the price of corn, and of course of the demand for labour, to place the lower classes of people exactly in this situation.

It may perhaps be said that our poor laws, at present, regularly encourage marriage and children by distributing relief in proportion to the size of families; and that this plan, which is proposed as a substitute, would merely do the same thing in a less objectionable manner. But surely, in endeavouring to get rid of the evil of the poor laws, we ought not to retain their most pernicious quality: and Mr. Young must know as well as I do that the principal reason why poor laws have invariably been found ineffectual in the relief of the poor is, that they tend to encourage a population which is not regulated by the demand for labour. Mr. Young himself, indeed, expressly takes notice of this effect in England, and observes that, notwithstanding the unrivalled prosperity of her manufactures, 'population is sometimes too active, as we see clearly by the dangerous increase of poor's rates in country villages'.[16]

But the fact is, that Mr. Young's plan would be incomparably more powerful in encouraging a population beyond the demand for labour than

---

[14] P. 79.
[15] [In 1806 (Vol. II, p. 451) this was altered to:
... and the facility of obtaining a cabin and potatoes in the other ...
[16] Travels in France, vol. i. c. xvii. p. 470.

our present poor laws. A laudable repugnance to the receiving of parish relief, arising partly from a spirit of independence not yet extinct, and partly from the disagreeable mode in which the relief is given, undoubtedly deters many from marrying with a certainty of falling on the parish; and the proportion of marriages to the whole population, which has before been noticed, clearly proves that the poor laws, though they have undoubtedly a considerable influence in this respect, do not encourage marriage so much as might be expected from theory.[17] But the case would be very different if, when a labourer had an early marriage in contemplation, the terrific forms of workhouses and parish officers, which might disturb his resolution, were to be exchanged for the fascinating visions of land and cows. If the love of property, as Mr. Young has repeatedly said, will make a man do much, it would be rather strange if it would not make him marry; an action to which, it appears from experience that he is by no means disinclined.

The population which would be thus called into being would be supported by the extended cultivation of potatoes, and would of course go on without any reference to the demand for labour. In the present state of things, notwithstanding the flourishing condition of our manufactures and the numerous checks to our population, there is no practical problem so difficult as to find employment for the poor; but this difficulty would evidently be aggravated a hundred fold under the circumstances here supposed.

In Ireland, or in any other country where the common food is potatoes, and every man who wishes to marry may obtain a piece of ground sufficient, when planted with this root, to support a family, prizes may be given till the treasury is exhausted for essays on the best means of employing the poor; but till some stop to the progress of population naturally arising from this state of things take place, the object in view is really a physical impossibility.[18]

Mr. Young has intimated that if the people were fed upon milk and potatoes, they would be more independent of scarcities than at present; but why this should be the case I really cannot comprehend. Undoubtedly people who live upon potatoes will not be much affected by a scarcity of

---

[17] [In 1806 (Vol. II, p. 452) this was amended:
   ... falling on the parish; and the proportion of births and marriages to the whole population, which has before been noticed, clearly proves that the poor-laws do not encourage marriage so much as might be expected from theory.

[18] Dr. Crumpe's prize essay on the best means of finding employment for the people is an excellent treatise, and contains much valuable information;[(a)] but, till the capital of the country is better proportioned to its population, it is perfectly chimerical to expect success in any project of the kind. I am also strongly disposed to believe that the indolent and turbulent habits of the lower Irish can never be corrected while the potatoe system enables them to increase so much beyond the regular demand for labour.

[(a)] [In 1807 (Vol. II, p. 378 n.) Malthus subtly altered this to:
   most valuable information.

wheat; but is there any contradiction in the supposition of a failure in the crops of potatoes? I believe it is generally understood that they are more liable to suffer damage during the winter than grain. From the much greater quantity of food yielded by a given piece of land, when planted with potatoes, than under any other kind of cultivation, it would naturally happen that, for some time after the introduction of this root as the general food of the lower classes of people,[19] a greater quantity would be grown than was demanded, and they would live in plenty. Mr. Young, in his travels through France, observes, that: 'In districts which contain immense quantities of waste land of a certain degree of fertility, as in the roots of the Pyrenees, belonging to communities ready to sell them, economy and industry, animated with the views of settling and marrying, flourish greatly; in such neighbourhoods something like an American increase takes place and, if the land be cheap, little distress is found. But as procreation goes on rapidly under such circumstances, the least check to subsistence is attended with great misery; as wastes becoming dearer, or the best portions being sold, or difficulties arising in the acquisition; all which circumstances I met with in those mountains. The moment that any impediment happens, the distress of such people will be proportioned to the activity and vigour which had animated population.'[20]

This description will apply exactly to what would take place in this country, on the distribution of small portions of land to the common people, and the introduction of potatoes as their general food. For a time the change might appear beneficial, and of course the idea of property would make it, at first, highly acceptable to the poor; but, as Mr. Young in another place says: 'You presently arrive at the limit beyond which the earth, cultivate it as you please, will feed no more mouths; yet those simple manners which instigate to marriage still continue; what then is the consequence but the most dreadful misery imaginable?'[21]

When the commons were all divided and difficulties began to occur in procuring potato-grounds, the habit of early marriages, which had been introduced, would occasion the most complicated distress; and when, from the increasing population and diminishing sources of subsistence, the average growth of potatoes was not more than the average consumption, a scarcity of potatoes would be, in every respect, as probable as a scarcity of wheat at present, and when it did arrive it would be, beyond all comparison, more dreadful.

When the common people of a country live principally upon the dearest

---

[19] [In 1826 (Vol. II, p. 387) this was changed to:
... labouring classes of people. ...
[20] Travels in France, vol. i. c. xvii. p. 470.     [21] Ibid, c. xii. p. 409.

grain, as they do in England on wheat, they have great resources in a scarcity; and barley, oats, rice, cheap soups, and potatoes, all present themselves as less expensive yet at the same time wholesome means of nourishment; but when their habitual food is the lowest in this scale, they appear to be absolutely without resource, except in the bark of trees, like the poor Swedes; and a great portion of them must necessarily be starved. [22]●Wheaten bread, roast beef, and turbot, which might not fail at the same time, are indeed in themselves unexceptionable substitutes for potatoes, and would probably be accepted as such, without murmuring, by the common people; but the misfortune is that a large population, which had been habitually supported by milk and potatoes, would find it difficult to obtain these substitutes in sufficient quantities, even if the whole benevolence of the kingdom were called into action for the purpose.●[22]

The wages of labour will always be regulated by the proportion of the supply to the demand.[23] And as, upon the potato system, a supply more than adequate to the demand would very soon take place, and this supply might be continued at a very cheap rate, on account of the cheapness of the food which would furnish it, the common price of labour would soon be regulated principally by the price of potatoes, instead of the price of wheat, as at present; and the rags and wretched cabins of Ireland would follow of course.

When the demand for labour occasionally exceeds the supply, and wages are regulated by the price of the dearest grain, they will generally be such as to yield something besides mere food, and the common people may be able to obtain decent houses and decent clothing. If the contrast between the state of the French and English labourers, which Mr. Young has drawn, be in any degree near the truth, the advantage on the side of England has been occasioned precisely and exclusively by these two circumstances; and if, by the adoption of milk and potatoes as the general food of the common people, these circumstances were totally altered, so as to make the supply of labour constantly in a great excess above the demand for it, and regulate wages by the price of the cheapest food, the advantage would be immediately lost, and no efforts of benevolence could prevent the most general and abject poverty.

Upon the same principle, it would by no means be eligible that the cheap soups of Count Rumford should be adopted as the general food of the common people. They are excellent inventions for public institutions, and as occasional resources; but if they were once universally adopted by the poor, it would be impossible to prevent the price of labour from being regulated by

---

[22] [In 1817 (Vol. III, p. 249) this passage was expunged.]

[23] [In 1826 (Vol. II, p. 389) this sentence read:
  The wages of labour will always be regulated mainly by the proportion of the supply of labour to the demand.

them; and the labourer, though at first he might have more to spare for other expenses besides food, would ultimately have much less to spare than before.

The desirable thing, with a view to the happiness of the common people, seems to be that their habitual food should be dear, and their wages regulated by it; but that, in a scarcity, or other occasional distress, the cheaper food should be readily and cheerfully adopted.[24] With a view of rendering this transition easier, and at the same time of making a useful distinction between these who are dependent on parish relief, and those who are not, I should think that one plan which Mr. Young proposes would be extremely eligible. This is 'to pass an act prohibiting relief, so far as subsistence is concerned, in any other manner than by potatoes, rice, and soup, not merely as a measure of the moment, but permanently'.[25] I do not think that this plan would necessarily introduce these articles as the common food of the lower classes; and if it merely made the transition to them in periods of distress easier, and at the same time drew a more marked line than at present between dependence and independence, it would have a very beneficial effect.

As it is acknowledged that the introduction of milk and potatoes, or of cheap soups, as the general food of the lower classes of people, would lower the price of labour, perhaps some cold politician might propose to adopt the system, with a view of underselling foreigners in the markets of Europe. I should not envy the feelings which could suggest such a proposal. I really cannot conceive anything much more detestable than the idea of knowingly condemning the labourers of this country to the rags and wretched cabins of Ireland, for the purpose of selling a few more broadcloths and calicoes.[26] The

---

[24] It is certainly to be wished that every cottage in England should have a garden to it, well stocked with vegetables. A little variety of food is in every point of view highly useful. Potatoes are undoubtedly a most valuable subsidiary, though I should be very sorry ever to see them the principal dependence of our labourers.

[25] Question of Scarcity, &c. p. 80. This might be done, at least, with regard to workhouses. In assisting the poor at their own homes, it might be subject to some practical difficulties.

[26] In this observation, I have not the least idea of alluding to Mr. Young who, I firmly believe, ardently wishes to ameliorate the condition of the lower classes of people, though I do not think that his plan would effect the object in view. He either did not see those consequences which I apprehend from it; or he has a better opinion of the happiness of the common people in Ireland than I have. In his Irish tour he seemed much struck with the plenty of potatoes which they possessed, and the absence of all apprehension of want. Had he travelled in 1800 and 1801, his impressions would by all accounts have been very different. From the facility which has hitherto prevailed in Ireland of procuring potatoe grounds, scarcities have certainly been rare, and all the effects of the system have not yet been felt, though certainly enough to make it appear very far from desirable.

Mr. Young has since pursued his idea more in detail, in a pamphlet entitled *An Inquiry into the Propriety of applying Wastes to the better Maintenance and Support of the Poor*. But the impression on my mind is still the same; and it appears to me calculated to assimilate the condition of

wealth and power of nations are, after all, only desirable as they contribute to happiness. In this point of view, I should be very far from undervaluing them, considering them, in general, as absolutely necessary means to attain the end; but if any particular case should occur, in which they appeared to be in direct opposition to each other, we cannot rationally doubt which ought to be postponed.[27]

Fortunately, however, even on the narrowest political principles, the adoption of such a system would not answer. It has always been observed that those who work chiefly on their own property, work very indolently and unwillingly when employed for others; and it must necessarily happen when, from the general adoption of a very cheap food, the population of a country increases considerably beyond the demand for labour, that habits of idleness and turbulence will be generated, most peculiarly unfavourable to a flourishing state of manufactures. In spite of the cheapness of labour in Ireland, there are few manufactures which can be prepared in that country for foreign sale so cheap as in England: and this is evidently owing[28] to the want of those industrious habits which can only be produced by regular employment.

---

the labourers of this country to that of the lower classes of the Irish. Mr. Young seems, in a most unaccountable manner, to have forgotten all his general principles on this subject. He has treated the question of a provision for the poor as if it was merely, How to provide in the cheapest and best manner for a *given number* of people? If this had been the sole question, it would never have taken so many hundred years to resolve. But the real question is, How to provide for those who are in want in such a manner as to prevent a continual accumulation of their numbers? and it will readily occur to the reader, that a plan of giving them land and cows cannot promise much success in this respect. If, after all the commons had been divided, the poor laws were still to continue in force, no good reason can be assigned why the rates should not in a few years be as high as they are at present, independently of all that had been expended in the purchase of land and stock.

[27] [In 1817 (Vol. III, p. 254) this was changed:
    ... but if any particular case should occur, where they appear to be in direct opposition to each other, we cannot rationally doubt which ought to be preferred.

[28] [In 1806 (Vol. II, p. 463) this was altered to:
    ... and this is in a great measure owing ...

# CHAPTER XII

## *Continuation of the same Subject*[1]

The increasing portion of the society which has of late years become either wholly or partially dependent upon parish assistance, together with the increasing burden of the poor's rates on the landed property, has for some time been working a gradual change in the public opinion respecting the benefits resulting to the labouring classes of society, and to society in general, from a legal provision for the poor. But the distress which has followed the peace of 1814, and the great and sudden pressure which it has occasioned on the parish rates, have accelerated this change in a very marked manner. More just and enlightened views on the subject are daily gaining ground; the difficulties attending a legal provision for the poor are better understood, and more generally acknowledged; and opinions are now seen in print, and heard in conversation, which twenty years ago would almost have been considered as treason to the interests of the state.

This change of public opinion, stimulated by the severe pressure of the moment, has directed an unusual portion of attention to the subject of the poor-laws; and as it is acknowledged that the present system has essentially failed, various plans have been proposed either as substitutes or improvements. It may be useful to inquire shortly how far the plans which have already been published are calculated to accomplish the ends which they propose. It is generally thought that some measure of importance will be the result of the present state of public opinion. To the permanent success of any such measure, it is absolutely necessary that it should apply itself in some degree to the real source of the difficulty. Yet there is reason to fear, that notwithstanding the present improved knowledge on the subject, this point may be too much overlooked.

Among the plans which appear to have excited a considerable degree of the public attention, is one of Mr. Owen. I have already adverted to some views of Mr. Owen in a chapter on Systems of Equality, and spoken of his experience with the respect which is justly due to it. If the question were

---

[1] [This chapter was added in 1817 (Vol. III, p. 256) and in the edition of 1826 (Vol. II, p. 394) there was a footnote:
Written in 1817.

merely how to accommodate, support and train, in the best manner, societies of 1200 people, there are perhaps few persons more entitled to attention than Mr. Owen: but in the plan which he has proposed, he seems totally to have overlooked the nature of the problem to be solved. This problem is, *How to provide for those who are in want, in such a manner as to prevent a continual increase of their numbers, and of the proportion which they bear to the whole society.* And it must be allowed that Mr. Owen's plan not only does not make the slightest approach towards accomplishing this object, but seems to be peculiarly calculated to effect an object exactly the reverse of it, that is, to increase and multiply the number of paupers.

If the establishments which he recommends could really be conducted according to his apparent intentions, the order of nature and the lessons of providence would indeed be in the most marked manner reversed; and the idle and profligate would be placed in a situation which might justly be the envy of the industrious and virtuous. The labourer or manufacturer who is now ill lodged and ill clothed, and obliged to work twelve hours a day to maintain his family, could have no motive to continue his exertions, if the reward for slackening them, and seeking parish assistance, was good lodging, good clothing, the maintenance and education of all his children, and the exchange of twelve hours hard work in an unwholesome manufactory for four or five hours of easy agricultural labour on a pleasant farm. Under these temptations, the numbers yearly falling into the new establishments from the labouring and manufacturing classes, together with the rapid increase by procreation of the societies themselves, would very soon render the first purchases of land utterly incompetent to their support. More land must then be purchased, and fresh settlements made; and if the higher classes of society were bound to proceed in the system according to its apparent spirit and intention, there cannot be a doubt that the whole nation would shortly become a nation of paupers with a community of goods.

Such a result might not perhaps be alarming to Mr. Owen. It is just possible indeed that he may have had this result in contemplation when he proposed his plan, and have thought that it was the best mode of quietly introducing that community of goods which he believes is necessary to complete the virtue and happiness of society. But to those who totally dissent from him as to the effects to be expected from a community of goods; to those who are convinced that even his favourite doctrine, that a man can be trained to produce more than he consumes, which is no doubt true at present, may easily cease to be true, when cultivation is pushed beyond the bounds prescribed to it by private property,[2] the approaches towards a system of this

---

[2] See vol. ii b. iii. ch. x [Vol. II, p. 44 in this edition.]

kind will be considered as approaches towards a system of universal indolence, poverty and wretchedness.

Upon the supposition, then, that Mr. Owen's plan could be effectively executed, and that the various pauper societies scattered over the country could at first be made to realize his most sanguine wishes, such might be expected to be their termination in a moderately short time, from the natural and necessary action of the principle of population.

But it is probable that the other grand objection to all systems of common property would even at the very outset confound the experience of Mr. Owen, and destroy the happiness to which he looks forward. In the society at the Lanerk Mills, two powerful stimulants to industry and good conduct are in action, which would be totally wanting in the societies proposed. At Lanerk, the whole of every man's earnings is his own; and his power of maintaining himself, his wife and children, in decency and comfort, will be in exact proportion to his industry, sobriety and economy. At Lanerk, also, if any workman be perseveringly indolent and negligent, if he get drunk and spoil his work, or if in any way he conduct himself essentially ill, he not only naturally suffers by the diminution of his earnings, but may at any time be turned off, and the society be relieved from the influence and example of a profligate and dangerous member. On the other hand, in the pauper establishments proposed in the present plan, the industry, sobriety and good conduct of each individual would be very feebly indeed connected with his power of maintaining himself and family comfortably; and in the case of persevering idleness and misconduct, instead of the simple and effective remedy of dismission, recourse must be had to a system of direct punishment of some kind or other, determined, and enforced by authority, which is always painful and distressing, and generally inefficient.

I confess it appears to me that the most successful experience, in such an establishment as that of Lanerk, furnishes no ground whatever to say what could be done towards the improvement of society in an establishment where the produce of all the labour employed would go to a common stock, and dismissal, from the very nature and object of the institution, would be impossible. If under such disadvantages the proper management of these establishments were within the limits of possibility, what judgment, what firmness, what patience, would be required for the purpose! But where are such qualities to be found in sufficient abundance to manage one or two millions of people?

On the whole, then, it may be concluded that Mr. Owen's plan would have to encounter obstacles that really appear to be insuperable, even at its first outset; and that if these could by any possible means be overcome, and the most complete success attained, the system would, without some most unnatural and unjust laws to prevent the progress of population, lead to a state of universal poverty and distress, in which, though all the rich might be made poor, none of the poor could be made rich – not even so rich as a common labourer at present.

The plan for bettering the condition of the labouring classes of the community, published by Mr. Curwen, is professedly a slight sketch; but principles, not details, are what it is our present object to consider; and the principles on which he would proceed are declared with sufficient distinctness, when he states the great objects of his design to be,

1. Meliorating the present wretched condition of the lower orders of the people.

2. Equalizing by a new tax the present poor's rates, which *must* be raised for their relief.

3. And giving to all those, who may think proper to place themselves under its protection, a voice in the local management and distribution of the fund destined for their support.

The first proposition is, of course, or ought to be, the object of every plan proposed. And the two last may be considered as the modes by which it is intended to accomplish it.

But it is obvious that these two propositions, though they may be both desirable on other accounts, not only do not really touch, but do not even propose to touch, the great problem. We wish to check the increase and diminish the proportion of paupers, in order to give greater wealth, happiness and independence to the mass of the labouring classes. But the equalization of the poor's rates, simply considered, would have a very strong tendency to increase rather than to diminish the number of the dependent poor. At present the parochial rates fall so very heavily upon one particular species of property, that the persons whose business it is to allow them have in general a very strong interest indeed to keep them low; but if they fell equally on all sorts of property, and particularly if they were collected from large districts, or from counties, the local distributors would have comparatively but very feeble motives to reduce them, and they might be expected to increase with great rapidity.

It may be readily allowed, however, that the peculiar weight with which the poor's rates press upon land is essentially unfair. It is particularly hard upon some country parishes, where the births greatly exceed the deaths, owing to the constant emigrations which are taking place to towns and manufactories, that, under any circumstances, a great portion of these emigrants should be returned upon them, when old, disabled, or out of work. Such parishes may be totally without the power of furnishing either work or support for all the persons born within their precincts. In fact, the same number would not have been born in them unless these emigrations had taken place. And it is certainly hard, therefore, that parishes so circumstanced should be obliged to receive and maintain all who may return to them in distress. Yet, in the present state of the country, the most pressing evil is not the weight upon the land, but the increasing proportion of paupers. And, as the equalization of the rates would certainly have a tendency to increase this proportion, I should be sorry to see such a measure introduced, even if it were easily practicable, unless accompanied by some very strong and decisive limitations to the continued increase of the rates so equalized.

The other proposition of Mr. Curwen will, in like manner, be found to afford no security against the increase of pauperism. We know perfectly well that the funds of the friendly societies, as they are at present constituted, though managed by the contributors themselves, are seldom distributed with the economy necessary to their permanent efficiency; and in the national societies proposed, as a considerable part of the fund would be derived from the poor's rates, there is certainly reason to expect that every question which could be influenced by the contributors would be determined on principles still more indulgent and less economical.

On this account it may well be doubted whether it would ever be advisable to mix any public money, derived from assessments, with the subscriptions of the labouring classes. The probable result would be, that in the case of any failure in the funds of such societies, arising from erroneous calculations and too liberal allowances, it would be expected that the whole of the deficiency should be made up by the assessments. And any rules which might have been made to limit the amount applied in this way would probably be but a feeble barrier against claims founded on a plan brought forward by the higher classes of society.

Another strong objection to this sort of union of parochial and private contributions is, that from the first the members of such societies could not justly feel themselves independent. If one half or one third of the fund were to be subscribed from the parish, they would stand upon a very different footing from the members of the present benefit-clubs. While so considerable a part of the allowances to which they might be entitled in sickness or in age would really come from the poor's rates, they would be apt to consider the plan as what, in many respects, it really would be – only a different mode of raising the rates. If the system were to become general, the contributions of the labouring classes would have nearly the effects of a tax on labour, and such a tax has been generally considered as more unfavourable to industry and production than most other taxes.

The best part of Mr. Curwen's plan is that which proposes to give a credit to each contributor in proportion to the amount of his contributions, and to make his allowance in sickness, and his annuity in old age, dependent upon this amount; but this object could easily be accomplished without the objectionable accompaniments. It is also very properly observed, that 'want of employment must furnish no claims on the society; for, if this excuse were to be admitted, it would most probably be attended with the most pernicious consequences'. Yet it is at the same time rather rashly intimated, that employment must be found for all who are able to work; and, in another place, it is observed that timely assistance would be afforded by these societies, without degradation, on all temporary occasions of suspended labour.

On the whole, when it is considered that a large and probably increasing amount of poor's rates would be subscribed to these societies; that on this account their members could hardly be considered as independent of parish assistance; and that the usual poor's rates would still remain to be applied as they are now, without any proposed limitations, there is little hope that Mr. Curwen's plan would be successful in diminishing the whole amount of the rates and the proportion of dependent poor.

There are two errors respecting the management of the poor, into which the public seem inclined to fall at the present moment. The first is a disposition to attach too much importance to the effects of subscriptions from the poor themselves, without sufficient attention to the mode in which they are distributed. But the mode of distribution is much the more important point of the two; and if this be radically bad, it is of little consequence in what manner the subscriptions are raised, whether from the poor themselves or from any other quarter. If the labouring classes were universally to contribute what might at first appear a very ample proportion of their earnings, for their own support in sickness and in old age, when out of work, and when the family consisted of more than two children, it is quite certain that the funds would become deficient. Such a mode of distribution implies a power of supporting a rapidly increasing and unlimited population on a limited territory, and must therefore terminate in aggravated poverty. Our present friendly societies or benefit-clubs aim at only limited objects, which are susceptible of calculation; yet many have failed, and many more it is understood are likely to fail from the insufficiency of their funds. If any society were to attempt to give much more extensive assistance to its members; if it were to endeavour to imitate what is partially effected by the poor-laws, or to accomplish those objects which Condorcet thought were within the power of proper calculations; the failure of its funds, however large at first, and from whatever sources derived, would be absolutely inevitable. In short, it cannot be too often or too strongly impressed upon the public, especially when any question for the improvement of the condition of the poor is in agitation, that no application of knowledge and ingenuity to this subject, no efforts either of the poor or of the rich, or both, in the form of contributions, or in any other way, can possibly place the labouring classes of society in such a state as to enable them to marry generally at the same age in an old and fully-peopled country as they may do with perfect safety and advantage in a new one.

The other error towards which the public seems to incline at present is that of laying too much stress upon the *employment* of the poor. It seems to be thought that one of the principal causes of the failure of our present system is the not having properly executed that part of the 43d of Elizabeth which enjoins the purchase of materials to set the poor to work. It is certainly desirable, on many accounts, to employ the poor when it is practicable, though it will always be extremely difficult to make people work actively who are without the usual and most natural motives to such exertions; and a system of coercion involves the necessity of placing great power in the hands of persons very likely to abuse it. Still, however, it is probable that the poor might be employed more than they have hitherto been, in a way to be advantageous to their habits and morals, without being prejudicial in other respects. But we should fall into the grossest error if we were to imagine that any essential part of the evils of the poor-laws, or of the difficulties under which we are at present labouring, has arisen from not employing the poor; or if we were to suppose that any possible scheme for giving work to all who are out of employment can ever in any degree apply to the source of these evils and difficulties, so as to prevent their recurrence. In no conceivable case can the forced employment of the poor, though managed in the most judicious manner, have any direct tendency to proportion more accurately the supply of labour to the natural demand for it. And without great care and caution it is obvious that it may have a pernicious effect of an opposite kind. When, for instance, from deficient demand or deficient capital, labour has a strong tendency to fall, if we keep it up to its usual price by creating an artificial demand by public subscriptions or advances from the government, we evidently prevent the population of the country from adjusting itself gradually to its diminished resources, and act much in the same manner as those who would prevent the price of corn from rising in a scarcity, which must necessarily terminate in increased distress.

Without then meaning to object to all plans for employing the poor, some of which, at certain times and with proper restrictions, may be useful as temporary measures, it is of great importance, in order to prevent ineffectual efforts and continued disappointments, to be fully aware that the permanent remedy which we are seeking cannot possibly come from this quarter.

It may indeed be affirmed with the most perfect confidence that there is only one class of causes from which any approaches towards a remedy can be rationally expected; and that consists of whatever has a tendency to increase the prudence and foresight of the labouring classes. This is the touchstone to which every plan proposed for the improvement of the condition of the poor should be applied. If the plan be such as to co-operate with the lessons of

Nature and Providence, and to encourage and promote habits of prudence and foresight, essential and permanent benefit may be expected from it: if it has no tendency of this kind, it may possibly still be good as a temporary measure, and on other accounts, but we may be quite certain that it does not apply to the source of the specific evil for which we are seeking a remedy.

Of all the plans which have yet been proposed for the assistance of the labouring classes, the saving-banks, as far as they go, appear to me much the best, and the most likely, if they should become general, to effect a permanent improvement in the condition of the lower classes of society.[3] By giving to each individual the full and entire benefit of his own industry and prudence, they are calculated greatly to strengthen the lessons of Nature and Providence; and a young man, who had been saving from fourteen or fifteen, with a view to marriage at four or five and twenty, or perhaps much earlier, would probably be induced to wait two or three years longer if the times were unfavourable; if corn were high; if wages were low; or if the sum he had saved had been found by experience not to be sufficient to furnish a tolerable security against want. A habit of saving a portion of present earnings for future contingencies can scarcely be supposed to exist without general habits of prudence and foresight; and if the opportunity furnished by provident banks to individuals, of reaping the full benefit of saving, should render the practice general, it might rationally be expected that, under the varying resources of the country, the population would be adjusted to the actual demand for labour, at the expense of less pain and less poverty; and the remedy thus appears, so far as it goes, to apply to the very root of the evil.

The great object of saving-banks, however, is to prevent want and dependence by enabling the poor to provide against contingencies themselves. And in a natural state of society, such institutions, with the aid of private charity well directed, would probably be all the means necessary to produce the best practicable effects. In the present state of things in this

---

[3] [Savings Banks (or Parish Banks, as they were sometimes called) date only from the beginning of the nineteenth century. They must not be confused with the old Friendly Societies or Provident Associations, whose members subscribed their weekly pennies specifically for sickness, unemployment, or funeral benefits, and whose funds were often spent on what was politely termed 'entertainment', since they usually met in ale-houses. Savings Banks, in the words of the *Edinburgh Review* for June 1815, were organised by 'benevolent persons who take an interest in their humble neighbours'; their object was 'to open to the lower orders a place of deposit for their small savings, with the allowance of a reasonable monthly interest, and with full liberty of withdrawing their money at any time, either in whole or in part – an accommodation which it is impracticable for the ordinary banks to furnish'. There were two fundamental principles: the managers or trustees (often clergymen) were not to be paid for their services, and all funds were to be invested in government stock. Malthus himself is listed as a 'manager' of one such bank in London in 1816: see Patricia James, *Population Malthus* (Routledge and Kegan Paul, 1979), pp. 222–3.]

country the case is essentially different. With so very large a body of poor habitually dependent upon public funds, the institutions of saving-banks cannot be considered in the light of substitutes for the poor's rates. The problem how to support those who are in want in such a manner as not continually to increase the proportion which they bear to the whole society will still remain to be solved. But if any plan should be adopted either of gradually abolishing or gradually reducing and fixing the amount of the poor's rates, saving-banks would essentially assist it; at the same time that they would receive a most powerful aid in return.

In the actual state of things, they have been established at a period likely to be particularly unfavourable to them – a period of very general distress, and of the most extensive parochial assistance; and the success which has attended them, even under these disadvantages, seems clearly to show, that in a period of prosperity and good wages, combined with a prospect of diminished parochial assistance, they might spread very extensively, and have a considerable effect on the general habits of the people.[4]

With a view to give them greater encouragement at the present moment, an act has been passed allowing persons to receive parish assistance at the discretion of the justices, although they may have funds of their own under a certain amount in a saving-bank.[5] But this is probably a short-sighted policy. It is sacrificing the principle for which saving-banks are established, to obtain an advantage which, on this very account, will be comparatively of little value. We wish to teach the labouring classes to rely more upon their own exertions and resources, as the only way of really improving their condition; yet we reward their saving by making them still dependent upon that very species of assistance which it is our object that they should avoid. The progress of saving-banks under such a regulation will be but an equivocal and uncertain symptom of good; whereas without such a regulation every step would tell, every fresh deposition would prove the growth of a desire to become independent of parish assistance; and both the great extension of the friendly societies, and the success of the saving-banks in proportion to the time they have been established, clearly show that much progress might be expected in these institutions under favourable circumstances, without resorting to a measure which is evidently calculated to sacrifice the end to the means.

With regard to the plans which have been talked of for reducing and limiting the poor's rates, they are certainly of a kind to apply to the root of the evil; but they would be obviously unjust without a formal retraction of the

---

[4] [In 1826 (Vol. II, p. 409) this was altered to:
  ... the general habits of a people.
[5] [See ROSE, GEORGE, in the Alphabetical List.]

*right* of the poor to support; and for many years they would unquestionably be much more harsh in their operation than the plan of abolition which I have ventured to propose in a preceding chapter. At the same time, if it be thought that this country cannot entirely get rid of a system which has been so long interwoven in its frame, a limitation of the amount of the poor's rates, or rather of their proportion to the wealth and population of the country, which would be more rational and just, accompanied with a very full and fair notice of the nature of the change to be made, might be productive of essential benefit, and do much towards improving the habits and happiness of the poor.

# CHAPTER XIII

## *Of the necessity of general principles on this subject*

It has been observed by Hume that, of all sciences, there is none where first appearances are more deceitful than in politics.[1] The remark is undoubtedly very just, and is most peculiarly applicable to that department of the science which relates to the modes of improving the condition of the lower classes of society.

We are continually hearing declamations against theory and theorists, by men who pride themselves upon the distinction of being practical. It must be acknowledged that bad theories are very bad things, and the authors of them useless and sometimes pernicious members of society. But these advocates of practice do not seem to be aware that they themselves very often come under this description, and that a great part of them may be classed among the most mischievous theorists of their time. When a man faithfully relates any facts which have come within the scope of his own observation, however confined it may have been, he undoubtedly adds to the sum of general knowledge, and confers a benefit on society. But when, from this confined experience, from the management of his own little farm, or the details of the workhouse in his neighbourhood, he draws a general inference, as is very frequently the case,[2] he then at once erects himself into a theorist; and is the more dangerous because, experience being the only just foundation for theory, people are often caught merely by the sound of the word, and do not stop to make the distinction between that partial experience which, on such subjects, is no foundation whatever for a just theory, and that general experience on which alone a just theory can be founded.

There are perhaps few subjects on which human ingenuity has been more exerted than the endeavour to ameliorate the condition of the poor; and there is certainly no subject in which it has so completely failed. The question between the theorist who calls himself practical, and the genuine theorist, is, whether this should prompt us to look into all the holes and corners of workhouses, and content ourselves with mulcting the parish officers for their waste of cheese-parings and candle-ends, and with distributing more soups

---

[1] Essay xi. vol. i. p. 431. 8vo.     [2] [In 1817 (Vol. II, p. 282) the word *very* was excised.]

and potatoes; or to recur to general principles, which show us at once the cause of the failure, and prove that the system has been from the beginning radically erroneous. There is no subject to which general principles have been so seldom applied; and yet, in the whole compass of human knowledge, I doubt if there be one in which it is so dangerous to lose sight of them; because the partial and immediate effects of a particular mode of giving assistance are so often directly opposite to the general and permanent effects.

It has been observed in particular districts, where cottagers are possessed of small pieces of land, and are in the habit of keeping cows, that, during the late scarcities some of them were able to support themselves without parish assistance, and others with comparatively little.[3]

According to the partial view in which this subject has been always contemplated, a general inference has been drawn from such instances that, if we could place all our labourers in a similar situation, they would all be equally comfortable, and equally independent of the parish. This is an inference, however, that by no means follows. The advantage which cottagers who at present keep cows enjoy, arises in a great measure from its being peculiar, and would be destroyed if it were made general.[4]

A farmer or gentleman living in a grazing country[5] has, we will suppose, a certain number of cottages on his farm. Being a liberal man, and liking to see all the people about him comfortable, he may join a piece of land to his cottages[6] sufficient to keep one or two cows, and give, besides, high wages. His labourers will of course live in plenty, and be able to rear up large families; but a grazing farm requires few hands; and though the master may choose to pay those that he employs well, he will not probably wish to have more labourers on his farm than his work requires.[7] He does not therefore build more houses; and the children of the labourers whom he employs must evidently emigrate and settle in other countries. While such a system continues peculiar to certain families, or certain districts, no great inconveniences arise from it to the community in general;[8] and it cannot be doubted

---

[3] See an Inquiry into the State of Cottagers in the Counties of Lincoln and Rutland by Robert Gourlay. Annals of Agriculture, vol. xxxvii. p. 514.

[4] [In 1806 (Vol. II, p. 467) *destroyed* was modified to 'considerably diminished'.

[5] [In 1806 (Vol. II, p. 467) the words *living in a grazing country* were omitted.]

[6] [In 1817 (Vol. III, p. 284) this was altered to:

    ... he may join a piece of land to each cottage sufficient to keep one or two cows ...

[7] [In 1806 (Vol. II, p. 467) this was changed:

    ... large families; but his farm may not require many hands; and though he may choose to pay those which he employs well, he will not probably wish to have more labourers on his land than his work requires.

[8] [In 1806 (Vol. II, p. 467) this sentence was altered:

    ... or certain districts, the emigrants would easily be able to find work in other places; and it cannot be doubted ...

that the individual labourers employed on these farms are in an enviable situation, and such as we might naturally wish was the lot of all our labourers. But it is perfectly clear that such a system could not, in the nature of things, possess the same advantages if it were made general, because there would then be no countries to which the children could emigrate with any prospect of finding work. Population would evidently increase beyond the demand of towns and manufactories, and universal poverty must necessarily ensue.[9]

It should be observed also, that one of the reasons why the labourers who at present keep cows are so comfortable is that they are able to make a considerable profit of the milk which they do not use themselves; an advantage which would evidently be very much diminished if the system were universal. And though they were certainly able to struggle through the late scarcities with less assistance than their neighbours, as might naturally be expected, from their having other resources besides the article which in those individual years was scarce; yet if the system were universal, there can be no reason assigned why they would not be subject to suffer as much from a scarcity of grass and a mortality among cows,[10] as our common labourers do now from a scarcity of wheat. We should be extremely cautious therefore of trusting to such appearances, and of drawing a general inference from this kind of partial experience.

The main principle, on which the Society for Increasing the Comforts and Bettering the Condition of the Poor, professes to proceed, is excellent. To give effect to that masterspring of industry, the desire of bettering our condition,[11] is the true mode of improving the state of the lower classes; and we may safely agree with Mr. Bernard, in one of his able prefaces, that whatever encourages and promotes habits of industry, prudence, foresight, virtue, and cleanliness, among the poor, is beneficial to them and to the country; and whatever removes or diminishes the incitements to any of these qualities, is detrimental to the state and pernicious to the individual.[12]

Mr. Bernard indeed, himself, seems in general to be fully aware of the

---

[9] [In 1806 (Vol. II, p. 468) these two sentences were modified:
   ... no countries to which the children could emigrate with the same prospect of finding work. Population would evidently increase ... and the price of labour would universally fall.
[10] [In 1806 (Vol. II, p. 469) Malthus added a footnote here:
   At present the loss of a cow, which must now and then happen, is generally remedied by a petition and subscription; and as the event is considered as a most serious misfortune to a labourer, these petitions are for the most part attended to; but if the cow system were universal, losses would occur so frequently that they could not possibly be repaired in the same way, and families would be continually dropping from comparative plenty into want.
[11] Preface to vol. ii of the Reports.
[12] Preface to vol. iii of the Reports.
   [Mr Bernard became Sir Thomas Bernard on the death of his brother in 1810, and Malthus refers to him by his title in the editions of 1817 and 1826.]

difficulties which the Society has to contend with in the accomplishment of its object. But still it appears to be in some danger of falling into the error before alluded to, of drawing general inferences from insufficient experience. Without adverting to the plans respecting cheaper foods and parish shops, recommended by individuals, the beneficial effects of which depend entirely upon their being peculiar to certain families or certain parishes, and would be lost if they were general, by lowering the wages of labour; I shall only notice one observation of a more comprehensive nature, which occurs in the preface to the second volume of the Reports. It is there remarked, that the experience of the Society seemed to warrant the conclusion that the best mode of relieving the poor was by assisting them at their own homes, and placing out their children as soon as possible in different employments, apprenticeships, &c. I really believe that this is the best, and it is certainly the most agreeable mode in which occasional and discriminate assistance can be given. But it is evident that it must be done with caution, and cannot be adopted as a general principle and made the foundation of universal practice. It is open exactly to the same objection as the cow system, in pasture countries,[13] which has just been noticed, and that part of the act of the 43d of Elizabeth which directs the overseers to employ and provide for the children of the poor. A particular parish where all the children, as soon as they were of a proper age, were taken from their parents and placed out in proper situations, might be very comfortable; but if the system were general, and the poor saw that all their children would be thus provided for, every employment would presently be overstocked with hands, and the consequence need not be again repeated.

Nothing can be more clear than that it is within the power of money, and of the exertions of the rich, adequately to relieve a particular family, a particular parish, and even a particular district. But it will be equally clear, if we reflect a moment on the subject, that it is totally out of their power to relieve the whole country in the same way; at least without providing a regular vent for the overflowing numbers in emigration, or without the prevalence of a particular virtue among the poor, which the distribution of this assistance tends obviously to discourage.

Even industry itself is, in this respect, not very different from money. A man who possesses a certain portion of it, above what is usually possessed by his neighbours, will, in the actual state of things, be almost sure of a competent livelihood; but if all his neighbours were to become at once as industrious as himself, the absolute portion of industry which he before possessed would no longer be a security against want. Hume fell into a very

---

13 [In 1806 (Vol. II, p. 471) the words *in pasture countries* were omitted.]

great error[14] when he asserted that 'almost all the moral, as well as natural evils of human life, arise from idleness'; and for the cure of these ills required only that the whole species should possess naturally an equal diligence with that which many individuals are able to attain by habit and reflection.[15] It is evident that this given degree of industry possessed by the whole species, if not combined with another virtue of which he takes no notice, would totally fail of rescuing society from want and misery, and would scarcely remove a single moral or physical evil of all those to which he alludes.

I am aware of an objection which will, with great appearance of justice, be urged against the general tenour[16] of these reasonings. It will be said that to argue thus is at once to object to every mode of assisting the poor, as it is impossible, in the nature of things, to assist people individually without altering their relative situation in society, and proportionally depressing others; and that as those who have families are the persons naturally most subject to distress, and as we are certainly not called upon to assist those who do not want our aid, we must necessarily, if we act at all, relieve those who have children, and thus encourage marriage and population.

I have already observed, however, and I here repeat it again, that the general principles on these subjects ought not to be pushed too far, though they should always be kept in view; and that many cases may occur in which the good resulting from the relief of the present distress may more than overbalance the evil to be apprehended from the remote consequence.

All relief in instances of distress, not arising from idle and improvident habits, clearly comes under this description; and in general it may be observed, that it is only that kind of systematic and certain relief,[17] on which the poor can confidently depend, whatever may be their conduct, that violates general principles, in such a manner as to make it clear that the general consequence is worse than the particular evil.

Independently of this discriminate and occasional assistance, the beneficial effects of which I have fully allowed in a preceding chapter, I have before endeavoured to show that much might be expected from a better and more general system of education. Everything that can be done in this way has indeed a very peculiar value; because education is one of those advantages which not only all may share without interfering with each other, but the raising of one person may actually contribute to the raising of others. If, for instance, a man by education acquires that decent kind of pride, and those juster habits of thinking, which will prevent him from burdening society with

---

[14] [In 1817 (Vol. III, p. 290) the word *very* was excised.]
[15] Dialogues on Natural Religion, Part xi. p. 212.
[16] [In 1807 (Vol. II, p. 397) *tenour* was replaced by 'scope'.]
[17] [In 1806 (Vol. II, p. 473) Malthus italicised the words *systematic* and *certain*.]

a family of children which he cannot support, his conduct, as far as an individual instance can go, tends evidently to improve the condition of his fellow labourers; and a contrary conduct from ignorance would tend as evidently to depress it.

I cannot help thinking also, that something might be done towards bettering the situation of the poor by a general improvement of their cottages, if care were taken, at the same time, not to make them so large as to allow of two families settling in them; and not to increase their number faster than the demand for labour required. Perhaps[18] one of the most salutary and least pernicious checks to the frequency of early marriages in this country is the difficulty of procuring a cottage, and the laudable habits which prompt a labourer rather to defer his marriage some years, in the expectation of a vacancy, than to content himself with a wretched mud cabin, like those in Ireland.[19]

Even the cow system, upon a more confined plan, might not be open to objection. With any view of making it a substitute for the Poor Laws, and of giving labourers a right to demand land and cows in proportion to their families; or of taking the common people from the consumption of wheat, and feeding them on milk and potatoes; it appears to me, I confess, truly preposterous: but if it were so ordered as merely to provide a comfortable situation for the better and more industrious class of labourers,[20] and to supply, at the same time, a very important want among the poor in general, that of milk for their children, I think that it would be extremely beneficial, and might be made a very powerful incitement to habits of industry, economy, and prudence. With this view, however, it is evident that only a certain portion of the labourers in each parish could be embraced in the plan; that good conduct, and not mere distress, should have the most valid claim to preference; that too much attention should not be paid to the number of children; and that, universally, those who had saved money enough for the purchase of a cow should be preferred to those who required to be furnished with one by the parish.[21]

---

18 [In 1806 (Vol. II, p. 475) the word *Perhaps* was excised.]

19 Perhaps, however, this is not often left to his choice, on account of the fear which every parish has of increasing its poor. There are many ways by which our poor laws operate in counteracting their first obvious tendency to increase population, and this is one of them. I have little doubt that it is almost exclusively owing to these counteracting causes that we have been able to persevere in this system so long, and that the condition of the poor has not been so much injured by it as might have been expected.

20 [In 1817 (Vol. III, p. 295) the words *class of* were omitted.]

21 The act of Elizabeth which prohibited the building of cottages, unless four acres of land were annexed to them, is probably impracticable in a manufacturing country like England; but upon this principle, certainly the greatest part of the poor might possess land; because the

[22]●To facilitate the saving of small sums of money for this purpose, and encourage young labourers to economize their earnings with a view to a provision for marriage, it might be extremely useful to have country banks, where the smallest sums would be received, and a fair interest paid for them. At present the few labourers who save a little money are often greatly at a loss to know what to do with it; and under such circumstances we cannot be much surprised that it should sometimes be ill employed, and last but a short time. It would probably be essential to the success of any plan of this kind that the labourer should be able to draw out his money whenever he wanted it, and have the most perfect liberty of disposing of it in every respect as he pleased. Though we may regret that money so hardly earned should sometimes be spent to little purpose; yet it seems to be a case in which we have no right to interfere; nor if we had, would it, in a general view, be advantageous; because the knowledge of possessing this liberty would be of more use in encouraging the practice of saving than any restriction of it in preventing the misuse of money so saved.●[22]

One should undoubtedly be extremely unwilling not to make as much use as possible of that known stimulus to industry and economy, the desire of, and the attachment to, property: but it should be recollected that the good effects of this stimulus show themselves principally when this property is to be procured or preserved by personal exertions; and that they are by no means so general under other circumstances. If any idle man with a family could demand and obtain a cow and some land, I should expect to see both very often neglected.

It has been observed that those cottagers who keep cows are more industrious and more regular in their conduct than those who do not. This is probably true, and what might naturally be expected; but the inference that the way to make all people industrious is to give them cows, may by no means be quite so certain. Most of those who keep cows at present have purchased them with the fruits of their own industry. It is therefore more just to say that their industry has given them a cow, than that a cow has given them their industry; though I would by no means be understood to imply that the sudden possession of property never generates industrious habits.

The practical good effects which have been already experienced, from cottagers keeping cows,[23] arise in fact from the system being nearly such as

---

difficulty of procuring such cottages would always operate as a powerful check to their increase. The effect of such a plan would be very different from that of Mr. Young.

[22] [This paragraph was omitted in 1817 (Vol. III, p. 295) because the subject had been dealt with in the previous chapter, which was added in that year.]

[23] Inquiry into the State of Cottagers in the Counties of Lincoln and Rutland, by Robert Gourlay. Annals of Agriculture, vol. xxxvii. p. 514.

the confined plan which I have mentioned. In the districts where cottagers of this description most abound, they do not bear a very large proportion to the population of the whole parish: they consist in general of the better sort of labourers, who have been able to purchase their own cows; and the peculiar comforts of their situation arise more from the relative than the positive advantages which they possess.[24]

From observing, therefore, their industry and comforts, we should be very cautious of inferring that we could give the same industry and comforts to all the lower classes of people by giving them the same possessions. There is nothing that has given rise to such a cloud of errors as a confusion between relative and positive, and between cause and effect.

It may be said, however, that any plan of generally improving the cottages of the poor, or of enabling more of them to keep cows, would evidently give them the power of rearing a greater number of children, and, by thus encouraging population, violate the principles which I have endeavoured to establish. But if I have been successful in making the reader comprehend the principal bent of this work, he will be aware that the precise reason why I think that more children ought not to be born than the country can support, is, that the greatest possible number of those that are born may be supported. We cannot, in the nature of things, assist the poor, in any way, without enabling them to rear up to manhood a greater number of their children. But this is, of all other things, the most desirable, both with regard to individuals and the public. Every loss of a child from the consequences of poverty must evidently be preceded and accompanied by great misery to individuals; and in a public view, every child that dies under ten years of age is a loss to the nation of all that had been expended in its subsistence till that period. Consequently, in every point of view, a decrease of mortality at all ages is what we ought to aim at. We cannot however effect this object without first crowding the population, in some degree, by making more children grow up to manhood; but we shall do no harm in this respect if, at the same time, we can impress these children with the idea that, to possess the same advantages as their parents, they must defer marriage till they have a fair prospect of being able to maintain a family. And it must be candidly confessed that if we cannot do this all our former efforts will have been thrown away. It is not in the nature of things that any permanent and general improvement in the condition of the poor can be effected without an increase in the preventive check: and unless this take place, either with or without our efforts, everything that is done for the poor must be temporary and partial: a

---

[24] [In 1826 (Vol. II, p. 423) this was altered to:
    ... the peculiar comforts of their situation arise as much from the relative as the positive advantages which they possess.

diminution of mortality at present will be balanced by an increased mortality in future; and the improvement of their condition in one place will proportionally depress it in another. This is a truth so important, and so little understood, that it can scarcely be too often insisted on. [25] ● The generality of charitable people, and of the encouragers of marriage, are not in the smallest degree aware of the real effects of what they do. ● [25]

Dr. Paley, in a chapter on population, provision, &c. in his Moral Philosophy, observes that the condition most favourable to the population of a country, and at the same time to its general happiness, is 'that of a laborious frugal people ministering to the demands of an opulent, luxurious nation'. [26] Such a form of society has not, it must be confessed, an inviting aspect. Nothing but the conviction of its being absolutely necessary could reconcile us to the idea of ten millions of people condemned to incessant toil, and to the privation of everything but absolute necessaries, in order to minister to the excessive luxuries of the other million. But the fact is, that such a form of society is by no means necessary. It is by no means necessary that the rich should be excessively luxurious, in order to support the manufactures of a country, or that the poor should be deprived of all luxuries in order to make them sufficiently numerous. The best, and in every point of view the most advantageous manufactures in this country, are those which are consumed by the great body of the people. The manufactures which are confined exclusively to the rich are not only trivial on account of the comparative smallness of their quantity; but are further liable to the great disadvantage of producing much occasional misery among those employed in them, from changes of fashion. It is the spread[27] of luxury, therefore, among the mass of the people, and not an excess of it in a few, that seems to be the most advantageous, both with regard to national wealth and national happiness; and what Dr. Paley considers as the true evil and proper danger of luxury, I should be disposed to consider as its true good and peculiar advantage. If, indeed, it be allowed that in every society, not in the state of a new colony some powerful check to population must prevail; and if it be observed that a taste for the comforts and conveniences of life will prevent people from marrying under the

---

[25] [In 1807 (Vol. II, p. 405) this sentence was excised.]

[26] Vol. ii. c. xi. p. 359. From a passage in Dr. Paley's late work on Natural Theology, I am inclined to think that subsequent reflection has induced him to modify some of his former ideas on the subject of population. He has stated most justly, (chap. xxv. p. 539) that mankind will in every country breed up to a certain point of distress. If this be allowed, that country will evidently be the happiest where the degree of distress at this point is the least, and consequently, if the spread[(a)] of luxury, by producing the check sooner, tend to diminish this degree of distress, it is certainly desirable.

[(a)] [In 1817 (Vol. III, p. 301) *spread* was changed to 'diffusion'.

[27] [In 1817 (Vol. III, p. 302) *spread* was changed to 'diffusion'.

certainty of being deprived of these advantages; it must be allowed that we can hardly expect to find any check to marriage so little prejudicial to the happiness and virtue of society as the general prevalence of such a taste; and consequently that the spread of luxury[28] in this sense of the term is particularly desirable; and one of the best means of raising that standard of wretchedness, alluded to in the eighth chapter[29] of this book.

It has been generally found that the middle parts of society are most favourable to virtuous and industrious habits, and to the growth of all kinds of talents. But it is evident that all cannot be in the middle. Superior and inferior parts are, in the nature of things, absolutely necessary; and not only necessary, but strikingly beneficial. If no man could hope to rise or fear to fall in society; if industry did not bring with it its reward, and indolence its punishment; we could not expect to see that animated activity in bettering our condition which now forms the master-spring of public prosperity. But in contemplating the different states of Europe, we observe a very considerable difference in the relative proportions of the superior, the middle, and the inferior parts; and from the effect of these differences, it seems probable that our best-grounded expectations of an increase in the happiness of the mass of human society are founded in the prospect of an increase in the relative proportions of the middle parts. And if the lower classes of people had acquired the habit of proportioning the supplies of labour to a stationary or even decreasing demand, without an increase of misery and mortality, as at present; we might even venture to indulge a hope that at some future period the processes for abridging human labour, the progress of which has of late years been so rapid, might ultimately supply all the wants of the most wealthy society with less personal labour than at present; and if they did not diminish the severity of individual exertion, might, at least, diminish the number of those employed in severe toil. If the lowest classes of society were thus diminished, and the middle classes increased, each labourer might indulge a more rational hope of rising by diligence and exertion into a better

---

28 In a note to the tenth chapter of the last book, I have mentioned the point at which, alone, it is probable that luxury becomes really prejudicial to a country. But this point does not depend upon the spread of luxury, as diminishing the frequency of marriage among the poor, but upon the proportion which those employed in preparing or procuring luxuries bears to the funds which are to support them.

[In 1817 (Vol. III, pp. 302–3) *the spread of luxury* was altered to 'the extension of luxury', and the footnote was omitted. It refers to Malthus's long note 30 of chapter xi of Book III in this edition (Vol. I, pp. 430–32). This was the chapter 'Of Bounties on the Exportation of Corn', which was one of the four chapters re-written and expanded into six in 1817.]

29 [In 1817 (Vol. III, p. 303) this was changed to 'alluded to in a former chapter'. It is chapter ix of Book IV in this edition, 'Of the modes of correcting the prevailing opinions on the Subject of Population'. In the last two paragraphs of this chapter (Vol. II, p. 155) Malthus stressed the desirability of an increased demand for the conveniences and comforts of life.]

station; the rewards of industry and virtue would be increased in number; human society[30] would appear to consist of fewer blanks and more prizes; and the sum of social happiness would be evidently augmented.

To indulge, however, in any distant views of this kind, unaccompanied by the evils usually attendant on a stationary or decreasing demand for labour, we must suppose the general prevalence of such prudential habits among the poor as would prevent them from marrying when the actual price of labour, joined to what they might have saved in their single state, would not give them the prospect of being able to support a wife and six children[31] without assistance. And in every point of view[32] such a degree of prudential restraint would be extremely beneficial; and would produce a very striking amelioration in the condition of the lower classes of people.

It may be said, perhaps, that even this degree of prudence might not always avail, as when a man marries he cannot tell what number of children he shall have, and many have more than six. This is certainly true; and in this case I do not think that any evil would result from making a certain allowance to every child above this number; not with a view of rewarding a man for his large family, but merely of relieving him from a species of distress which it would be unreasonable in us to expect that he should calculate upon. And with this view, the relief should be merely such as to place him exactly in the same situation as if he had had six children. Montesquieu disapproves of an edict of Lewis the fourteenth, which gave certain pensions to those who had ten and twelve children, as being of no use in encouraging population.[33] For the very reason that he disapproves of it, I should think that some law of the kind might be adopted without danger, and might relieve particular individuals from a very pressing and unlooked-for distress, without operating in any respect as an encouragement to marriage.

If, at some future period, any approach should be made towards the more general prevalence of prudential habits with respect to marriage among the poor, from which alone any permanent and general improvement of their condition can arise, I do not think that the narrowest politician need be alarmed at it, from the fear of its occasioning such an advance in the price of labour as will enable our commercial competitors to undersell us in foreign markets. There are four circumstances that might be expected to accompany it, which would probably either prevent, or fully counterbalance, any effect of this kind. These are, 1st, The more equable and lower price of provisions, from the demand being less frequently above the supply. 2dly, The removal of

---

[30] [In 1806 (Vol. II, p. 485) this was amended to 'the lottery of human society'.
[31] [In 1807 (Vol. II, p. 410) this was changed to 'five or six children'.
[32] [In 1807 (Vol. II, p. 410) *in every point of view* was changed to 'undoubtedly'.
[33] Esprit des Loix, liv. xxiii. c. xxvii.

that heavy burden on agriculture, and that great addition to the present wages of labour, the poor's rates. 3dly, The national saving of a great part of that sum which is expended without return, in the support of those children who die prematurely from the consequences of poverty. And, lastly, The more general prevalence of economical and industrious habits, particularly among unmarried men, which prevent that indolence, drunkenness, and waste of labour, which at present are too frequently a consequence of high wages.

# CHAPTER XIV

## *Of our rational expectations respecting the future improvement of Society*

In taking a general and concluding view of our rational expectations respecting the mitigations of the evils arising from the principle of population, it may be observed that though the increase of population in a geometrical ratio be incontrovertible, and the period of doubling, when unchecked, has been uniformly stated in this work rather below than above the truth; yet there are some natural consequences of the progress of society and civilization which necessarily repress its full effects. There are, more particularly, great towns and manufactures, in which we can scarcely hope, and certainly not expect, to see any very material change. It is undoubtedly our duty, and in every point of view highly desirable, to make towns and manufacturing employments as little injurious as possible to the duration of human life; but, after all our efforts, it is probable that they will always remain less healthy than country situations and country employments; and consequently, operating as positive checks, will diminish in some degree the necessity of the preventive check.

In every old state it is observed that a considerable number of grown-up people remain for a time unmarried. The duty of practising the common and acknowledged rules of morality during this period has never been controverted in theory, however it may have been opposed in practice. This branch of the duty of moral restraint has scarcely been touched by the reasonings of this work. It rests on the same foundation as before, neither stronger nor weaker. And knowing how incompletely this duty has hitherto been fulfilled, it would certainly be visionary to expect any very material change for the better in future.[1]

The part which has been affected by the reasonings of this work is not, therefore, that which relates to our conduct during the period of celibacy, but to the duty of extending this period till we have a prospect of being able to maintain our children. And it is by no means visionary to indulge a hope of some favourable change in this respect; because it is found by experience that

---

[1] [In 1817 (Vol. III, p. 309) this was changed to:
... visionary to expect that in future it would be completely fulfilled.

the prevalence of this kind of prudential restraint is extremely different in different countries, and in the same countries at different periods.

It cannot be doubted that throughout Europe in general, and most particularly in the northern states, a decided change has taken place in the operation of prudential restraint since the prevalence of those warlike and enterprising habits which destroyed so many people. In later times the gradual diminution and almost total extinction of the plagues which so frequently visited Europe, in the seventeenth and the beginning of the eighteenth centuries, produced a change of the same kind. And in this country it is not to be doubted that the proportion of marriages has become smaller since the improvement of our towns, the less frequent returns of epidemics, and the adoption of habits of greater cleanliness. During the late scarcities, it appears that the number of marriages diminished;[2] and the same motives which prevented many people from marrying during such a period would operate precisely in the same way if, in future, the additional number of children reared to manhood from the introduction of the cow-pox were to be such as to crowd all employments, lower the price of labour, and make it more difficult to support a family.

Universally, the practice of mankind on the subject of marriage has been much superior to their theories; and however frequent may have been the declamations on the duty of entering into this state, and the advantage of early unions to prevent vice, each individual has practically found it necessary to consider of the means of supporting a family before he ventured to take so important a step. That great *vis medicatrix reipublicæ*,[3] the desire of bettering our condition, and the fear of making it worse, has been constantly in action, and has been constantly directing people into the right road in spite of all the declamations which tended to lead them aside. Owing to this powerful spring of health in every state, which is nothing more than an inference from the general course of the laws of nature, irresistibly forced on each man's attention, the prudential check to marriage has increased in Europe; and it cannot be unreasonable to conclude that it will still make further advances. If this take place, without any marked and decided increase of a vicious intercourse with the sex, the happiness of society will evidently be promoted by it; and with regard to the danger of such increase, it is consolatory to remark that those countries in Europe where marriages are the least frequent[4] are by

---

[2] [In 1817 (Vol. III, p. 311) Malthus added his usual footnote:
1800 and 1801.

[3] [This might be freely translated as: 'That great and wholesome force in the life of a nation, the desire of bettering our condition ...]

[4] [In 1817 (Vol. III, p. 312) this was amended to:
... where marriages are the latest or least frequent are by no means ...

no means particularly distinguished by vices of this kind. It has appeared that Norway, Switzerland, England, and Scotland, are above all the rest in the prevalence of the preventive check; and though I do not mean to insist particularly on the virtuous habits of these countries, yet I think that no person would select them as the countries most marked for profligacy of manners. Indeed, from the little that I know of the continent, I should have been inclined to select them as most distinguished for contrary habits, and as rather above than below their neighbours in the chastity of their women, and consequently in the virtuous habits of their men. Experience therefore seems to teach us that it is possible for moral and physical causes to counteract the effects that might at first be expected from an increase of the preventive check;[5] but allowing all the weight to these effects which is in any degree probable, it may be safely asserted that the diminution of the vices arising from indigence would fully counterbalance them; and that all the advantages of diminished mortality and superior comforts, which would certainly result from an increase of the preventive check, may be placed entirely on the side of the gains to the cause of happiness and virtue.

It is less the object of the present work to propose new plans of improving society, than to inculcate the necessity of resting contented with that mode of improvement which is dictated by the course of nature,[6] and of not obstructing the advances which would otherwise be made in this way.

It would be undoubtedly highly advantageous that all our positive institutions, and the whole tenour of our conduct to the poor, should be such as actively to co-operate with that lesson of prudence inculcated by the common course of human events; and if we take upon ourselves, sometimes, to mitigate the natural punishments of imprudence, that we could balance it by increasing the rewards of an opposite conduct. But much would be done, if merely the institutions which directly tend to encourage marriage were gradually changed, and we ceased to circulate opinions and inculcate doctrines which positively counteract the lessons of nature.

The limited good, which it is sometimes in our power to effect, is often lost by attempting too much, and by making the adoption of some particular plan essentially necessary even to a partial degree of success. In the practical application of the reasonings of this work, I hope that I have avoided this error. I wish to press on the recollection of the reader that, though I may have given some new views of old facts, and may have indulged in the contem-

---

[5] [In 1806 (Vol. II, p. 493) Malthus changed this to:
... an increase of the check to marriage; ...

[6] [In 1826 (Vol. II, p. 435) this was altered to:
... that mode of improvement, which already has in part been acted upon, as dictated by the course of nature ...

plation of a considerable degree of *possible* improvement, that I might not absolutely shut out that prime cheerer, hope;[7] yet in my expectations of probable improvement, and in suggesting the means of accomplishing it, I have been very cautious. The gradual abolition of the poor laws has already often been proposed, in consequence of the practical evils which have been found to flow from them, and the danger of their becoming a weight absolutely intolerable on the landed property of the kingdom. The establishment of a more extensive system of national education, has neither the advantage of novelty with some, nor its disadvantage with others, to recommend it. The practical good effects of education have long been experienced in Scotland; and almost every person, who has been placed in a situation to judge, has given his testimony, that education appears to have a considerable effect in the prevention of crimes,[8] and the promotion of industry, morality, and regular conduct. Yet these are the only plans which have been offered; and though the adoption of them in the modes suggested, would very powerfully contribute to forward the object of this work, and better the condition of the poor; yet if nothing be done in this way, I shall not absolutely despair of some partial good effects from the general tenour of the reasoning.[9]

If the principles which I have endeavoured to establish be false, I most sincerely hope to see them completely refuted; but if they be true, the subject is so important, and interests the question of human happiness so nearly, that it is impossible that they should not in time be more fully known and more generally circulated, whether any particular efforts be made for the purpose or not.

Among the higher and middle classes of society, the effect of this knowledge would,[10] I hope, be to direct without relaxing their efforts in bettering the condition of the poor; to show them what they can and what they cannot do; and that, although much may be done by advice and instruction, by encouraging habits of prudence and cleanliness, by occasional and discriminate charity,[11] and by any mode of bettering the present

---

[7] [In 1817 (Vol. III, p. 315) the word *absolutely* was omitted.]

[8] Mr. Howard found fewer prisoners in Switzerland and Scotland, than in other countries, which he attributed to a more regular education among the lower classes of the Swiss and the Scotch. During the number of years which the late Mr. Fielding presided at Bow-street, only six Scotchmen were brought before him. He used to say that of the persons committed, the greater part were Irish. Preface to vol. iii of the Reports of the Society for Bettering the Condition of the Poor, p. 32.

[9] [In 1817 (Vol. III, p. 316) this was changed to:
    ... not absolutely despair of some partial good resulting from the general effects of the reasoning.

[10] [In 1817 (Vol. III, p. 317) the word *would* was replaced by 'will'.]

[11] [In 1807 (Vol. II, p. 421) the words *occasional and* were expunged.]

condition of the poor which is followed by an increase of the preventive check; yet that, without this last effect, all the former efforts would be futile; and that, in any old and well-peopled state, to assist the poor in such a manner as to enable them to marry as early as they please, and rear up large families, is a physical impossibility. This knowledge, by tending to prevent the rich from destroying the good effects of their own exertions, and wasting their efforts in a direction where success is unattainable, would confine their attention to the proper objects, and thus enable them to do more good.

Among the poor themselves, its effects would be still more important. That the principal and most permanent cause of poverty has little or no relation[12] to forms of government, or the unequal division of property; and that, as the rich do not in reality possess the power of finding employment and maintenance for the poor, the poor cannot, in the nature of things, possess the right to demand them,[13] are important truths flowing from the principle of population, which, when properly explained, would by no means be above the most ordinary comprehensions. And it is evident that every man in the lower classes of society, who became acquainted with these truths, would be disposed to bear the distresses in which he might be involved with more patience; would feel less discontent and irritation at the government and the higher classes of society on account of his poverty; would be on all occasions less disposed to insubordination and turbulence; and if he received assistance, either from any public institution or from the hand of private charity, he would receive it with more thankfulness, and more justly appreciate its value.

If these truths were by degrees more generally known (which in the course of time does not seem to be improbable, from the natural effects of the mutual interchange of opinions) the lower classes of people, as a body, would become more peaceable and orderly; would be less inclined to tumultuous proceedings in seasons of scarcity, and would at all times be less influenced by inflammatory and seditious publications, from knowing how little the price of labour, and the means of supporting a family, depend upon a revolution. The mere knowledge of these truths, even if they did not operate sufficiently to produce any marked change in the prudential habits of the poor, with regard to marriage, would still have a most beneficial effect on their conduct in a political light; and undoubtedly, one of the most valuable of these effects would be the power that would result to the higher

---

[12] [In 1806 (Vol. ii, p. 498) this was altered to:

... little or no direct relation to forms of government, ...

[13] [In 1817 (Vol. iii, p. 318) the words *direct*, *power*, and *right* in this passage were all italicised.]

and middle classes of society of gradually improving their governments[14] without the apprehension of those revolutionary excesses, the fear of which, at present, threatens to deprive Europe even of that degree of liberty which she had before experienced to be practicable, and the salutary effects of which she had long enjoyed.

From a review of the state of society in former periods, compared with the present, I should certainly say that the evils resulting from the principle of population have rather diminished than increased, even under the disadvantage of an almost total ignorance of the real cause. And if we can indulge the hope that this ignorance will be gradually dissipated, it does not seem unreasonable to expect that they will be still further diminished. The increase of absolute population, which will of course take place, will evidently tend but little to weaken this expectation, as everything depends upon the relative proportion between population and food, and not on the absolute number of people. In the former part of this work, it appeared that the countries which possessed the fewest people often suffered the most from the effects of the principle of population; and it can scarcely be doubted that, taking Europe throughout, fewer famines, and fewer diseases arising from want have prevailed in the last century than in those which preceded it.

On the whole, therefore, though our future prospects respecting the mitigation of the evils arising from the principle of population may not be so bright as we could wish, yet they are far from being entirely disheartening, and by no means preclude that gradual and progressive improvement in human society, which, before the late wild speculations on this subject, was the object of rational expectation. To the laws of property and marriage, and to the apparently narrow principle of self-love,[15] which prompts each individual to exert himself in bettering his condition, we are indebted for all the noblest exertions of human genius, for everything that distinguishes the civilized from the savage state. A strict inquiry into the principle of population leads us strongly to the conclusion[16] that we shall never be able to throw down the ladder by which we have risen to this eminence; but it by no

---

[14] I cannot believe that the removal of all unjust grounds of discontent against constituted authorities would render the people torpid and indifferent to advantages which are really attainable. The blessings of civil liberty are so great that they surely cannot need the aid of false colouring to make them desirable. I should be sorry to think that the lower classes of people could never be animated to assert their rights but by means of such illusory promises as will generally make the remedy of resistance much worse than the disease that it was intended to cure.

[15] [In 1826 (Vol. II, p. 441) this was changed to 'self-interest'.

[16] [In 1806 (Vol. II, p. 501) Malthus amended this:

A strict inquiry into the principle of population obliges us to conclude that we shall never ...

means proves that we may not rise higher by the same means. The structure of society, in its great features, will probably always remain unchanged. We have every reason to believe that it will always consist of a class of proprietors and a class of labourers; but the condition of each, and the proportion which they bear to each other, may be so altered as greatly to improve the harmony and beauty of the whole. It would indeed be a melancholy reflection that, while the views of physical science are daily enlarging, so as scarcely to be bounded by the most distant horizon, the science of moral and political philosophy should be confined within such narrow limits, or at best be so feeble in its influence, as to be unable to counteract the increasing obstacles to human happiness arising from the progress of population.[17] But however formidable these obstacles may have appeared in some parts of this work, it is hoped that the general result of the inquiry is such as not to make us give up the cause of[18] the improvement of human society in despair. The partial good which seems to be attainable is worthy of all our exertions; is sufficient to direct our efforts and animate our prospects. And although we cannot expect that the virtue and happiness of mankind will keep pace with the brilliant career of physical discovery yet; if we are not wanting to ourselves, we may confidently indulge the hope that, to no unimportant extent, they will be influenced by its progress and will partake in its success.

---

[17] [In 1806 (Vol. II, p. 502) this was altered to:
    ... unable to counteract the obstacles to human happiness arising from a single cause.
[18] [In 1806 (Vol. II, p. 502) the words *the cause of* were omitted.]

# APPENDIX, 1806

[In 1806 (Vol. II, p. 505) this was headed simply 'Appendix'. A quarto version was published separately, for the convenience of those who possessed the edition of 1803, so that it could be bound in with the original work. This quarto version was entitled 'Reply to the Chief Objections which have been urged against the Essay on the Principle of Population, published in an Appendix to the Third Edition'.]

In the preface to the last[1] edition of this Essay, I expressed a hope that the detailed manner in which I had treated the subject and pursued it to its consequences, though it might open the doors to many objections, and expose me to much severity of criticism, might be subservient to the important end of bringing a subject so nearly connected with the happiness of society into more general notice. Conformably to the same views I should always have felt willing to enter into the discussion of any serious objections that were made to my principles or conclusions, to abandon those which appeared to be false, and to throw further lights, if I could, on those which appeared to be true. But though the work has excited a degree of public attention much greater than I could[2] have presumed to expect, yet very little has been written to controvert it; and of that little, the greatest part is so full of illiberal declamation, and so entirely destitute of argument, as to be evidently beneath notice. What I have to say therefore at present, will be directed rather more to the objections which have been urged in conversation, than to those which have appeared in print. My object is to correct some of the misrepresentations which have gone abroad respecting two or three of the most important points of the Essay; and I should feel greatly obliged to those who have not had leisure to read the whole work, if they would cast their eyes over the few following pages, that they may not, from the partial and incorrect statements which they have heard, mistake the import of some of my opinions, and attribute to me others which I have never held.

---

[1] [In 1807 (Vol. II, p. 429) *last* was changed to 'second'.
[2] [In 1826 (Vol. II, p. 443) *could* was altered to 'should'.

The first grand objection that has been made to my principles is that they contradict the original command of the Creator, to increase and multiply and replenish the earth. But those who have urged this objection have certainly either not read the work, or have directed their attention solely to a few detached passages, and have been unable to seize the bent and spirit of the whole. I am fully of opinion, that it is the duty of man to obey this command of his Creator, nor is there in my recollection a single passage in the work which, taken with the context, can to any reader of intelligence warrant the contrary inference.

Every express command given to man by his Creator is given in subordination to those great and uniform laws of nature which he had previously established; and we are forbidden both by reason and religion to expect that these laws will be changed in order to enable us to execute more readily any particular precept. It is undoubtedly true that, if man were enabled miraculously to live without food, the earth would be very rapidly replenished; but as we have not the slightest ground of hope that such a miracle will be worked for this purpose, it becomes our positive duty as reasonable creatures, and with a view of executing the commands of our Creator, to inquire into the laws which he has established for the multiplication of the species. And when we find, not only from the speculative contemplation of these laws, but from the far more powerful and imperious suggestions of our senses, that man cannot live without food, it is a folly exactly of the same *kind* to attempt to obey the will of our Creator by increasing population without reference to the means of its support, as to attempt to obtain an abundant crop of corn by sowing it on the wayside and in hedges, where it cannot receive its proper nourishment. Which is it, I would ask, that best seconds the benevolent intentions of the Creator in covering the earth with esculent vegetables, he who with care and foresight duly ploughs and prepares a piece of ground, and sows no more seed than he expects will grow up to maturity, or he who scatters a profusion of seed indifferently over the land, without reference to the soil on which it falls, or any previous preparation for its reception?

It is an utter misconception of my argument to infer that I am an enemy to population. I am only an enemy to vice and misery, and consequently to that unfavourable proportion between population and food which produces these evils. But this unfavourable proportion has no necessary connection with the quantity of absolute population which a country may contain. On the contrary, it is more frequently found in countries which are very thinly peopled than in those which are populous.

The bent of my argument on the subject of population may be illustrated by the instance of a pasture farm. If a young grazier were told to stock his land well, as on his stock would depend his profits, and the ultimate success of his undertaking, he would certainly have been told nothing but what was strictly true. And he would have to accuse himself, not his advisers, if in pursuance of these instructions he were to push the breeding of his cattle till they became lean and half-starved. His instructor, when he talked of the advantages of a large stock, meant undoubtedly stock in proper condition, and not such a stock as, though it might be numerically greater, was in value much less. The expression of stocking a farm well does not refer to particular numbers, but merely to that proportion which is best adapted to the farm, whether it be a poor or a rich one, whether it will carry fifty head of cattle or five hundred. It is undoubtedly extremely desirable that it should carry the greater number, and every effort should be made to effect this object; but surely that farmer could not be considered as an enemy to a large quantity of stock, who should insist upon the folly and impropriety of attempting to breed such a quantity, before the land was put into a condition to bear it.

The arguments which I have used respecting the increase of population are exactly of the same nature as these just mentioned. I believe that it is the intention of the Creator that the earth should be replenished;[3] but certainly with a healthy, virtuous, and happy population, not an unhealthy, vicious, and miserable one. And if in endeavouring to obey the command to increase and multiply, we people it only with beings of this latter description, and suffer accordingly, we have no right to impeach the justice of the command, but our irrational mode of executing it.

In the desirableness of a great and efficient population, I do not differ from the warmest advocates of increase. I am perfectly ready to acknowledge with the writers of old, that it is not extent of territory but extent of population that measures the power of states. It is only as to the mode of obtaining a vigorous and efficient population that I differ from them; and in thus differing I conceive myself entirely borne out by experience, that great test of all human speculations.

It appears from the undoubted testimony of registers, that a large proportion of marriages and births is by no means necessarily connected with a rapid increase of population, but is often found in countries where it is either stationary or increasing very slowly. The population of such countries is not only comparatively inefficient from the general poverty and misery of the inhabitants, but invariably contains a much larger proportion of persons in those stages of life in which they are unable to contribute their share to the resources or the defence of the state.

This is most strikingly illustrated in an instance which I have quoted from M. Muret, in a chapter on Switzerland, where it appeared that, in proportion

---

[3] This opinion I have expressed, page 491 of the 4to. edit. [And Vol. ii, p. 93 of this edition.]

to the same population, the Lyonois produced 16 births, the Pays de Vaud 11, and a particular parish in the Alps only 8; but that at the age of 20 these three very different numbers were all reduced to the same.[4] In the Lyonois nearly half of the population was under the age of puberty, in the Pays de Vaud one third, and in the parish of the Alps only one fourth. The inference from such facts is unavoidable, and of the highest importance to society.

The power of a country to increase its resources or defend its possessions must depend principally upon its efficient population, upon that part of the population which is of an age to be employed effectually in agriculture, commerce, or war; but it appears with an evidence little short of demonstration, that in a country, the resources of which do not naturally call for a larger proportion of births, such an increase, so far from tending to increase this efficient population, would tend materially to diminish it. It would undoubtedly at first increase the number of souls in proportion to the means of subsistence, and consequently[5] cruelly increase the pressure of want; but the number of persons rising annually to the age of puberty might not be so great as before, a larger part of the produce would be distributed without return to children who would never reach manhood; and the additional population, instead of giving additional strength to the country, would essentially lessen this strength, and operate as a constant obstacle to the creation of new resources.

We are a little dazzled at present by the population and power of France, and it is known that she has always had a large proportion of births: but if any reliance can be placed on what are considered as the best authorities on this subject, it is quite certain, that the advantages which she enjoys do not arise from any thing peculiar in the structure of her population; but solely from the great absolute quantity of it, derived from her immense extent of fertile territory.

[6]●The effective population in this country, compared with the whole, is considerably greater than in France; and England not only can, but does, employ a larger proportion of her population in augmenting and defending her resources than her great rival.●[6] According to the *Statistique générale et*

---

[4] Page 271, 4to. edit. [And Vol. I, pp. 218–19 of this edition.]

[5] [In 1826 (Vol. II, p. 446) *consequently* was changed to 'therefore'.

[6] [In 1807 (Vol. II, p. 436) Malthus excised this sentence, and began the paragraph as follows:
    Necker, speaking of the population of France, says that it is so composed, that a million of individuals present neither the same force in war, nor the same capacity for labour, as an equal number in a country where the people are less oppressed and fewer die in infancy.[(a)] And the view which Arthur Young has given of the state of the lower classes of the people at the time he travelled in France, which was just at the commencement of the revolution, leads directly to the same conclusion. According to the *Statistique générale et particulière* . . .

[(a)] Necker sur les Finances, Tom. i, ch. ix, p. 263, 12mo.

*particulière de la France* lately published, the proportion of the population under twenty is almost $\frac{9}{20}$; in England it is probably not much more than $\frac{7}{20}$.[7] Consequently, out of a population of ten millions, England would have a million more of persons above twenty than France, and would at least have three or four hundred thousand more males of a military age.[8] If our population were of the same description as that of France, it must be increased numerically by more than a million and a half in order to enable us to produce from England and Wales the same number of persons above the age of twenty as at present; and if we had only an increase of a million, our efficient strength in agriculture, commerce, and war, would be in the most decided manner diminished, while at the same time the distresses of the lower classes would be dreadfully increased. Can any rational man say that

---

[7] [In 1807 (Vol. II, pp. 436–7) a long footnote was added here:

I do not mention these numbers here, as vouching in any degree for their accuracy, but merely for the sake of illustrating the subject. [(a)] •Unfortunately there are no data respecting the classifications of the population of different countries according to age on which any reliance can be placed with safety.• [(a)] I have reason to think that those which are given in the *Statistique Générale* were not taken from actual enumerations, and the proportion of the population under 20 mentioned in the text, for England, is entirely conjectural and certainly too small. [(b)] Of this however we may be quite sure, that when two countries, from the proportion of their births to deaths, increase nearly at the same rate, the one in which the births and deaths bear the greatest proportion to the whole population will have the smallest comparative number of persons above the age of puberty. That England and Scotland have, in every million of people which they contain, more individuals fit for labour, than France, the data we have are sufficient to determine; but in what degree this difference exists cannot be ascertained, without better information than we at present possess. On account of the more rapid increase of population in England than in France before the revolution, England ought, *cæteris paribus*, to have had the largest proportion of births, yet in France the proportion was $\frac{1}{25}$ or $\frac{1}{26}$, and in England only $\frac{1}{30}$.

The proportion of persons capable of bearing arms has been sometimes calculated at one fourth, and sometimes at one fifth, of the whole population of a country. The reader will be aware of the prodigious difference between the two estimates, supposing them to be applicable to two different countries. In the one case, a population of 20 millions would yield five millions of effective men; and in the other case, the same population would only yield 4 millions. We cannot surely doubt which of the two kinds of population would be of the most valuable description both with regard to actual strength, and the creation of fresh resources. Probably, however, there are no two countries in Europe in which the difference in this respect is so great as that between $\frac{1}{4}$ and $\frac{1}{5}$.

[(a)] [In 1826 (Vol. II, p. 447) this sentence was omitted.]

[(b)] [At the same time, Malthus altered the sentence which followed it:

... illustrating the subject. I have reason to think that the proportion given in the *Statistique Générale* was not taken from actual enumerations, and that mentioned in the text for England is conjectural, and probably too small. Of this, however, we may be quite sure ...

[8] [In 1807 (Vol. II, p. 437) Malthus changed this to:

... France, and would upon this supposition have at least three or four hundred thousand more males of a military age.

an additional population of this description would be desirable, either in a moral or political view? And yet this is the kind of population which invariably results from direct encouragements to marriage, or from that want of personal respectability which is occasioned by ignorance and despotism.

It may perhaps be true that France fills her armies with greater facility and less interruption to the usual labours of her inhabitants than England; and it must be acknowledged that poverty and want of employment are powerful aids to a recruiting serjeant; but it would not be a very humane project, to keep our people always in want for the sake of enlisting them cheaper, nor would it be a very politic project, to diminish our wealth and strength with the same economical view. We cannot attain incompatible objects; if we possess the advantage of being able to keep nearly all our people constantly employed either in agriculture or commerce, we cannot expect to retain the opposite advantage of their being always at leisure, and willing to enlist for a very small sum.[9] But we may rest perfectly assured that, while we have the efficient population, we shall never want men to fill our armies if we propose to them adequate motives.

In many parts of the Essay I have dwelt much on the advantage of rearing the requisite population of any country from the smallest number of births. I have stated expressly that a decrease of mortality at all ages is what we ought chiefly to aim at; and as the best criterion of happiness and good government, instead of the largeness of the proportion of births, which was the usual mode of judging, I have proposed the smallness of the proportion dying under the age of puberty. Conscious that I had never intentionally deviated from these principles, I might well be rather surprised to hear that I had been considered by some as an enemy to the introduction of the vaccine inoculation, which is calculated to attain the very end which I have uniformly considered as so desirable. I have indeed intimated what I still continue most firmly to believe, that if the resources of the country would not permanently admit of a greatly accelerated rate of increase in the population (and whether they would or not, must certainly depend upon other causes besides the number of lives saved by the vaccine inoculation),[10] one of two things would happen, either an increased mortality of some other diseases, or a diminution in the proportion of births. But I have expressed my conviction that the latter

---

[9] This subject is strikingly illustrated in Lord Selkirk's lucid and masterly observations 'On the Present State of the Highlands, and on the Causes and Probable Consequences of Emigration', to which I can with confidence refer the reader.

[10] It should be remarked, however, that a young person saved from death is more likely to contribute to the creation of fresh resources than another birth. It is a great loss of labour and food to begin over again. And universally it is true that, under similar circumstances, that article will come the cheapest to market which is accompanied by fewest failures. [See JENNER, EDWARD, in the Alphabetical List and p. 298 in this volume.]

effect would take place; and therefore, consistently with the opinions which I have always maintained, I ought to be, and am, one of the warmest friends to the introduction of the cow-pox. In making every exertion which I think likely to be effectual, to increase the comforts and diminish the mortality among the poor, I act in the most exact conformity to my principles. Whether those are equally consistent who profess to have the same object in view, and yet measure the happiness of nations by the large proportion of marriages and births, is a point which they would do well to consider.

It has been said by some that the natural checks to population will always be sufficient to keep it within bounds, without resorting to any other aids; and one ingenious writer has remarked that I have not deduced a single original fact from real observations to prove the inefficiency of the checks which already prevail.[11] These remarks are correctly true, and are truisms exactly of the same kind as the assertion that man cannot live without food. For undoubtedly, as long as this continues to be a law of his nature, what are here called the natural checks cannot possibly fail of being effectual. Besides the curious truism that these assertions involve, they proceed upon the very strange supposition that the *ultimate* object of my work is to check population, as if anything could be more desirable than the most rapid increase of population unaccompanied by vice and misery. But of course my ultimate object is to diminish vice and misery, and any checks to population which may have been suggested are solely as means to accomplish this end. To a rational being, the prudential check to population ought to be considered as equally natural with the check from poverty and premature mortality, which these gentlemen seem to think so entirely sufficient and satisfactory; and it will readily occur to the intelligent reader, that one class of checks may be substituted for another, not only without essentially diminishing the population of a country, but even under a constantly progressive increase of it.[12]

On the possibility of increasing very considerably the effective population of this country, I have expressed myself in some parts of my work more sanguinely, perhaps, than experience would warrant. I have said that in the course of some centuries it might contain two or three times as many inhabitants as at present, and yet every person be both better fed and better clothed.[13] And in the comparison of the increase of population and food at the beginning of the Essay, that the argument might not seem to depend

---

[11] I should like much to know what description of facts this gentleman had in view when he made this observation. If I could have found one of the kind which seems here to be alluded to, it would indeed have been truly original.

[12] Both Norway and Switzerland, where the preventive check prevails the most, are increasing with some rapidity in their population; and in proportion to their means of subsistence, they can produce more males of a military age than any other country of Europe.

[13] P. 512, 4to edit. [And Vol. II, p. 111 of this edition.]

upon a difference of opinion respecting facts, I have allowed the produce of the earth to be unlimited, which is certainly going too far. It is not a little curious therefore, that it should still continue to be urged against me as an argument, that this country might contain two or three times as many inhabitants; and it is still more curious, that some persons, who have allowed the different ratios of increase on which all my principal conclusions are founded, have still asserted that no difficulty or distress could arise from population, till the productions of the earth could not be further increased. I doubt whether a stronger instance could readily be produced of the total absence of the power of reasoning than this assertion, after such a concession, affords. It involves a greater absurdity than the saying that because a farm can, by proper management, be made to carry an additional stock of four head of cattle every year, that therefore no difficulty or inconvenience would arise if an additional forty were placed in it yearly.

The power of the earth to produce subsistence is certainly not unlimited, but it is strictly speaking indefinite; that is, its limits are not defined, and the time will probably never arrive when we shall be able to say, that no farther labour or ingenuity of man could make further additions to it. But the power of obtaining an additional quantity of food from the earth by proper management, and in a certain time, has the most remote relation imaginable to the power of keeping pace with an unrestricted increase of population. The knowledge and industry which would enable the natives of New Holland[14] to make the best use of the natural resources of their country must, without an absolute miracle, come to them gradually and slowly; and even then, as it has amply appeared, would be perfectly ineffectual as to the grand object; but the passions which prompt to the increase of population are always in full vigour, and are ready to produce their full effect even in a state of the most helpless ignorance and barbarism. It will be readily allowed, that the reason why New Holland, in proportion to its natural powers, is not so populous as China, is the want of those human institutions which protect property and encourage industry; but the misery and vice which prevail almost equally in both countries, from the tendency of population to increase faster than the means of subsistence, form a distinct consideration, and arise from a distinct cause. They arise from the incomplete discipline of the human passions; and no person with the slightest knowledge of mankind has ever had the hardihood to affirm that human institutions could completely discipline all the human passions. But I have already treated this subject so fully in the course of the work, that I am ashamed to add any thing further here.

---

[14] [It is strange that Malthus never substituted 'Australia' for *New Holland*].

The next grand objection which has been urged against me, is my denial of the *right* of the poor to support.

Those who would maintain this objection, with any degree of consistency, are bound to show that the different ratios of increase with respect to population and food, which I attempted to establish at the beginning of the Essay, are fundamentally erroneous; since on the supposition of their being true, the conclusion is inevitable. If it appear, as it must appear on these ratios being allowed, that it is not possible for the industry of man to produce sufficient food[15] for all that would be born, if every person were to marry at the time when he was first prompted to it by inclination, it follows irresistibly that all cannot have a *right* to support. Let us for a moment suppose an equal division of property in any country. If, under these circumstances, one half of the society were by prudential habits so to regulate their increase that it exactly kept pace with their increasing cultivation, it is evident that they would always remain as at first. If the other half, during the same time, married at the age of puberty, when they would probably feel most inclined to it, it is evident that they would soon become wretchedly poor. But upon what plea of justice or equity could this second half of the society claim a right, in virtue of their poverty, to any of the possessions of the first half? This poverty had arisen entirely from their own ignorance or imprudence; and it would be perfectly clear, from the manner in which it had come upon them, that if their plea were admitted, and they were not suffered to feel the particular evils resulting from their conduct, the whole society would shortly be involved in the same degree of wretchedness. Any voluntary and temporary assistance which might be given as a measure of charity by the richer members of the society to the others, while they were learning to make a better use of the lessons of nature, would be quite a distinct consideration, and without doubt most properly applied; but nothing like a claim of *right* to support can possibly be maintained till we deny the premises; till we affirm that the American increase of population is a miracle, and does not arise from the greater facility of obtaining the means of subsistence.[16]

---

[15] [In 1826 (Vol. II, p. 452) there was an insertion here:

... to produce on a limited territory sufficient food ...

[16] It has been said that I have written a quarto volume to prove that population increases in a geometrical, and food in an arithmetical ratio; but this is not quite true. The first of these propositions I considered as proved the moment that the American increase was related, and the second proposition as soon as it was enunciated. The chief object of my work was to inquire what effects these laws, which I considered as established in the first six pages, had produced, and were likely to produce, on society: a subject not very readily exhausted. The principal fault of my details is that they are not sufficiently particular; but this was a fault which it was not in my power to remedy. It would be a most curious, and to every philosophical mind a most interesting piece of information, to know the exact share of the

In fact, whatever we may say in our declamations on this subject, almost the whole of our *conduct* is founded on the non-existence of this right. If the poor had really a claim of *right* to support, I do not think that any man could justify his wearing broadcloth, or eating as much meat as he likes for dinner, and those who assert this right, and yet are rolling in their carriages, living every day luxuriously, and keeping even their horses on food of which their fellow creatures are in want, must be allowed to act with the greatest inconsistency. Taking an individual instance without reference to consequences, it appears to me that Mr. Godwin's argument is irresistible. Can it be pretended for a moment that a part of the mutton which I expect to eat today would not be much more beneficially employed on some hard-working labourer who has not perhaps tasted animal food for the last week, or on some poor family who cannot command sufficient food of any kind fully to satisfy the cravings of appetite?[17] If these instances were not of a nature to multiply in proportion as such wants were indiscriminately gratified, the gratification of them, as it would be practicable, would be highly beneficial; and in this case I should not have the smallest hesitation in most fully allowing the right. But as it appears clearly both from theory and experience, that if the claim were allowed it would soon increase beyond the *possibility* of satisfying it, and that the practical attempt to do so, would involve the human race in the most wretched and universal poverty, it follows necessarily that our conduct, which denies the right, is more suited to the present state of our being, than our declamations which allow it.

The great author of nature,[18] indeed, with that wisdom which is apparent in all his works, has not left this conclusion to the cold and speculative consideration of general consequences. By making the passion of self-love beyond comparison stronger than the passion of benevolence, he has at once impelled us to that line of conduct which is essential to the preservation of the human race. If all that might be born could be adequately supplied, we cannot doubt that he would have made the desire of giving to others as ardent as that of supplying ourselves. But since, under the present constitution of things, this is not so, he has enjoined every man to pursue as his primary object his own safety and happiness, and the safety and happiness of those immediately connected with him; and it is highly instructive to observe that, in proportion as the sphere contracts, and the power of giving effectual assistance increases, the desire increases at the same time. In the case of children, who have certainly a claim of *right* to the support and protection of

---

full power of increase which each existing check prevents; but at present I see no mode of obtaining such information.

[17] [In 1817 (Vol. III, p. 345) *appetite* was changed to 'hunger'.

[18] [In 1817 (Vol. III, p. 345) 'Author' was spelt with a capital A.]

their parents, we generally find parental affection nearly as strong as self-love; and except in a few anomalous cases, the last morsel will be divided into equal shares.

By this wise provision the most ignorant are led to promote the general happiness, an end which they would have totally failed to attain if the moving principle of their conduct had been benevolence.[19] Benevolence indeed, as the great and constant source of action, would require the most perfect knowledge of causes and effects, and therefore can only be the attribute of the Deity. In a being so short-sighted as man, it would lead into the grossest errors, and soon transform the fair and cultivated soil of civilized society into a dreary scene of want and confusion.

But though benevolence cannot in the present state of our being be the great moving principle of human actions, yet, as the kind corrector of the evils arising from the other stronger passion, it is essential to human happiness; it is the balm and consolation and grace of human life, the source of our noblest efforts in the cause of virtue, and of our purest and most refined pleasures. Conformably to that system of general laws, according to which the Supreme Being appears with very few exceptions to act, a passion so strong and general as self-love could not prevail without producing much partial evil; and to prevent this passion from degenerating into the odious vice of selfishness,[20] to make us sympathise in the pains and pleasures of our fellow-creatures, and feel the same *kind* of interest in their happiness and misery as in our own, though diminished in degree, to prompt us often to put ourselves in their place, that we may understand their wants, acknowledge their rights, and do them good as we have opportunity; and to remind us continually, that even the passion which urges us to procure plenty for ourselves was not implanted in us for our own exclusive advantage, but as the means of procuring the greatest plenty for all; these appear to be the objects and offices of benevolence. In every situation of life there is ample room for the exercise of this virtue; and as each individual rises in society, as he advances in knowledge and excellence, as his power of benefiting others[21] becomes greater, and the necessary attention to his own wants less, it will naturally come in for an increasing share among his constant motives of

---

[19] In saying this let me not be supposed to give the slightest sanction to the system of morals inculcated in the *Fable of the Bees*, a system which I consider as absolutely false, and directly contrary to the just definition of virtue. The great art of Dr. Mandeville consisted in misnomers.

[20] It seems proper to make a decided distinction between self-love and selfishness, between that passion which under proper regulations is the source of all honourable industry, and of all the necessaries and conveniences of life, and the same passion pushed to excess, when it becomes useless and disgusting, and consequently vicious.

[21] [In 1817 (Vol. III, p. 348) Malthus changed *benefiting others* to 'doing good to others'.

action. In situations of high trust and influence it ought to have a very large share, and in all public institutions be the great moving principle. Though we have often reason to fear that our benevolence may not take the most beneficial direction, we need never apprehend that there will be too much of it in society. The foundations of that passion on which our preservation depends are fixed so deeply in our nature, that no reasonings or addresses to our feelings can essentially disturb it. It is just therefore, and proper, that all the positive precepts should be on the side of the weaker impulse; and we may safely endeavour to increase and extend its influence as much as we are able, if at the same time we are constantly on the watch to prevent the evil which may arise from its misapplication.

The law which in this country entitles the poor to relief is undoubtedly different from a full acknowledgment of the natural right; and from this difference and the many counteracting causes that arise from the mode of its execution, it will not of course be attended with the same consequences. But still it is an approximation to a full acknowledgment, and as such appears to produce much evil, both with regard to the habits and the temper of the poor. I have in consequence ventured to suggest a plan of gradual abolition, which, as might be expected, has not met with universal approbation. I can readily understand any objections that may be made to it, on the plea that the right having been once acknowledged in this country, the revocation of it might at first excite discontents; and should therefore most fully concur in the propriety of proceeding with the greatest caution, and of using all possible means of preventing any sudden shock to the opinions of the poor. But I have never been able to comprehend the grounds of the further assertion which I have sometimes heard made, that if the poor were really convinced that they had no claim of right to relief, they would in general be more inclined to be discontented and seditious. On these occasions the only way I have of judging is to put myself in imagination in the place of the poor man, and consider how I should feel in his situation. If I were told that the rich by the laws of nature and the laws of the land were bound to support me, I could not, in the first place, feel much obligation for such support; and in the next place, if I were given any food of an inferior kind, and could not see the absolute necessity of the change, which would probably be the case, I should think that I had good reason to complain. I should feel that the laws had been violated to my injury, and that I had been unjustly deprived of my right. Under these circumstances, though I might be deterred by the fear of an armed force from committing any overt acts of resistance, yet I should consider myself as perfectly justified in so doing, if this fear were removed; and the injury which I believed that I had suffered might produce the most unfavourable effects on my general dispositions towards the higher classes of society. I cannot indeed conceive anything more irritating to the human feelings, than to experience that degree of distress which, in spite of all our poor laws and benevolence, is not unfrequently felt in this country; and yet to believe that these sufferings were not brought upon me either by my own faults, or by the operation of those general laws which, like the tempest, the blight, or the pestilence, are continually falling hard on particular individuals, while others entirely escape, but were occasioned solely by the avarice and injustice of the higher classes of society.

On the contrary, if I firmly believed that by the laws of nature, which are the laws of God, I had no claim of *right* to support I should, in the first place, feel myself more strongly bound to a life of industry and frugality; but if want, notwithstanding, came upon me, I should consider it in the light of sickness, as an evil incidental to my present state of being, and which, if I could not avoid, it was my duty to bear with fortitude and resignation. I should know from past experience, that the best title I could have to the assistance of the benevolent would be, the not having brought myself into distress by my own idleness or extravagance. What I received would have the best effect on my feelings towards the higher classes. Even if it were much inferior to what I had been accustomed to, it would still, instead of an injury, be an obligation; and conscious that I had no claim of *right*, nothing but the fear of absolute famine, which would overcome all other considerations, could morally justify resistance.[22]

I cannot help believing that if the poor in this country were convinced that they had no claim of *right* to support; and yet in scarcities and all cases of urgent distress were liberally relieved, which I think they would be, the bond which unites the rich with the poor would be drawn much closer that at present, and the lower classes of society, as they would have less real reason for irritation and discontent, would be much less subject to these uneasy sensations.

Among those who have objected to my declaration that the poor have no claim of *right* to support is Mr. Young, who, with a harshness not quite becoming a candid inquirer after truth, has called my proposal for the gradual abolition of the poor laws a horrible plan, and asserted that the execution of it would be a most iniquitous proceeding. Let this plan however be compared for a moment with that which he himself and others have proposed, of fixing the sum of the poor's rates, which on no account is to be increased. Under such a law, if the distresses of the poor were to be aggravated tenfold, either by the increase of numbers or the recurrence of a scarcity, the same sum would invariably be appropriated to their relief. If the

---

[22] [In 1817 (Vol. III, p. 352) this sentence was altered:
 ... no claim of *right*, nothing but the dread of absolute famine, which might overcome all other considerations, could palliate the guilt of resistance.

statute which gives the poor a right to support were to remain unexpunged, we should add to the cruelty of starving them the extreme injustice of still *professing* to relieve them. If this statute were expunged or altered, we should virtually deny the right of the poor to support, and only retain the absurdity of saying that they had a right to a certain sum; an absurdity on which Mr. Young justly comments with much severity in the case of France.[23] In both cases the hardships which they would suffer would be much more severe, and would come upon them in a much more unprepared state, than upon the plan proposed in the Essay.

According to this plan all that are already married, and even all that are engaged to marry during the course of the year, and all their children, would be relieved as usual; and only those who marry subsequently, and who of course may be supposed to have made better provision for contingencies, would be out of the pale of relief.

Any plan for the abolition of the poor laws must presuppose a general acknowledgment that they are essentially wrong, and that it is necessary to tread back our steps. With this acknowledgment, whatever objections may be made to my plan, in the too frequently short-sighted views of policy, I have no fear of comparing it with any other that has yet been advanced, in point of justice and humanity; and of course the terms iniquitous and horrible 'pass by me like the idle wind which I regard not'.[24]

Mr. Young it would appear has now given up this plan. He has pleaded for the privilege of being inconsistent, and has given such reasons for it that I am disposed to acquiesce in them, provided he confines the exercise of this privilege to different publications, in the interval between which he may have collected new facts; but I still think it not quite allowable in the same publication; and yet it appears that in the very paper in which he has so

---

[23] The National Assembly of France, though they disapproved of the English poor laws, still adopted their principle, and declared that the poor had a right to pecuniary assistance; that the Assembly ought to consider such a provision as one of its first and most sacred duties; and that with this view, an expense ought to be incurred to the amount of 50 millions a year. Mr. Young justly observes, that he does not comprehend how it is possible to regard the expenditure of 50 millions a sacred duty, and not extend that 50 to 100 if necessity should demand it, the 100 to 200, the 200 to 300, and so on in the same miserable progression which has taken place in England. Travels in France, c. xv. p. 439.
[See COMITÉ DE MENDICITÉ in the Alphabetical List.]

I should be the last man to quote Mr. Young against himself, if I thought he had left the path of error for the path of truth, as such kind of inconsistency I hold to be highly praiseworthy. But thinking, on the contrary, that he has left truth for error, it is surely justifiable to remind him of his former opinions. We may recall to a vicious man his former virtuous conduct, though it would be useless and indelicate to remind a virtuous man of the vices which he had relinquished.

[24] [See SHAKESPEARE (6) in the Alphabetical List.]

severely condemned my scheme, the same arguments which he has used to reprobate it are applicable with equal force against his own proposal, as he has there explained it.[25]

He allows that his plan can only provide for a certain amount of families, and has nothing to do with the increase from them;[26] but in allowing this, he allows that it does not reach the grand difficulty attending a provision for the poor. In this most essential point, after reprobating me for saying that the poor have no claim of *right* to support, he is compelled to adopt the very same conclusion, and to own that 'it might be prudent to consider the misery to which the progressive population might be subject, when there was not a sufficient demand for them in towns and manufactures, as an evil which it was absolutely and physically impossible to prevent'. Now the sole reason why I say that the poor have no claim of *right* to support is the physical impossibility of relieving this progressive population. Mr. Young expressly acknowledges this physical impossibility; yet with an inconsistency scarcely credible still declaims against my declaration.

The power which the society may possess of relieving a certain portion of the poor is a consideration perfectly distinct from the general question; and I am quite sure I have never said that it is not our duty to do all the good that is practicable. But this limited power of assisting individuals cannot possibly establish a general right. If the poor have really a natural right to support, and if our present laws be only a confirmation of this right, it ought certainly to extend unimpaired to all who are in distress, to the increase from the cottagers as well as to the cottagers themselves; and it would be a palpable injustice in the society to adopt Mr. Young's plan, and purchase from the present generation the disfranchisement of their posterity.

Mr. Young objects very strongly to that passage of the Essay,[27] in which I observe that a man who plunges himself into poverty and dependence, by marrying without any prospect of being able to maintain his family, has more reason to accuse himself than the price of labour, the parish, the avarice of the rich, the institutions of society, and the dispensations of Providence; except in as far as he has been deceived by those who ought to have instructed him. In answer to this, Mr. Young says, that the poor fellow is justified in every one of these complaints, that of Providence alone excepted; and that seeing other cottagers living comfortably with three or four acres of land, he has cause to accuse institutions which deny him that

---

[25] [In 1817 (Vol. III, p. 355) Malthus changed *as he has there explained it* to:
... his own proposal as there explained.
[26] Annals of Agriculture, No. 239, p. 219.
[27] Book iv. c. iii. p. 506, 4to. edit. [Vol. II, p. 106 of this edition.]

which the rich could well spare, and which would give him all he wants.[28] I would beg Mr. Young for a moment to consider how the matter would stand, if his own plan were completely executed. After all the commons had been divided as he has proposed, if a labourer had more than one son, in what respect would this son be in a different situation from the man that I have supposed?[29] Mr. Young cannot possibly mean to say, that if he had the very natural desire of marrying at twenty, he would still have a right to complain that the society did not give him a house and three or four acres of land. He has indeed expressly denied this absurd consequence, though in so doing he has directly contradicted the declaration just quoted.[30] The progressive population, he says, would, according to his system, be cut off from the influence of the poor laws, and the encouragement to marry would remain exactly in that proportion less than at present. Under these circumstances, without land, without the prospect of parish relief, and with the price of labour only sufficient to maintain two children, can Mr. Young seriously think that the poor man, if he be really aware of his situation, does not do wrong in marrying, and ought not to accuse himself for following what Mr. Young calls the dictates of God, of nature, and of revelation? Mr. Young cannot be unaware of the wretchedness that must inevitably follow a marriage under such circumstances. His plan makes no provision whatever for altering these circumstances. He must therefore totally disregard all the misery arising from excessive poverty, or if he allows that these supernumerary members must necessarily wait, either till a cottage with land becomes vacant in the country, or that by emigrating to towns they can find the means of providing for a family, all the declamation which he has urged with such pomp against deferring marriage in my system, would be equally applicable in his own. In fact, if Mr. Young's plan really attained the object which it professes to have in view, that of bettering the condition of the poor, and did not defeat its intent by encouraging a too rapid multiplication, and consequently lowering the price of labour, it cannot be doubted that not only the supernumerary members just mentioned, but all the labouring poor, must wait longer before they could marry than they do at present.

The following proposition may be said to be capable of mathematical demonstration. In a country, the resources of which will not permanently admit of an increase of population more rapid than the existing rate, no improvement in the condition of the people which would tend to diminish mortality could *possibly* take place without being accompanied by a smaller

---

[28] Annals of Agriculture, No. 239, p. 226.
[29] In 1807 (Vol. II, p. 458) this was amended to:
    ... in what respect would the second or third be in a different situation ...?
[30] Annals of Agriculture, No. 239, p. 214.

proportion of births, supposing of course no particular increase of emigration.[31] To a person who has considered the subject, there is no proposition in Euclid which brings home to the mind a stronger conviction than this, and there is no truth so invariably confirmed by all the registers of births, deaths, and marriages that have ever been collected. In this country it has appeared that, according to the returns of the population act, the proportion of births to deaths is about 4 to 3.[32] This proportion with a mortality of 1 in 40,[33] would double the population in 83 years and a half; and as we cannot suppose that the country could admit of more than a quadrupled population in the next hundred and sixty-six years, we may safely say that its resources will not allow of a permanent rate of increse greater than that which is taking place at present.[34] But if this be granted, it follows as a direct conclusion that if Mr. Young's plan, or any other, really succeeded in bettering the condition of the poor, and enabling them to rear more of their children, the vacancies in cottages in proportion to the number of expectants would happen slower than at present and the age of marriage must inevitably be later. [35]●Those, therefore, who propose plans for bettering the condition of the poor, and yet at the same time reprobate later or fewer marriages, are guilty of the most puerile inconsistency; and I cannot but be perfectly astonished that Mr. Young, who once understood the subject, should have indulged himself in such a poor declamation about passions, profligacy, burning, and ravens. It is in fact a silly, not to say impious, declamation against the laws of nature and the dispensations of Providence.●[35]

With regard to the expression of later marriages, it should always be

---

[31] With regard to the resource of emigration, I refer the reader to the 4th chapter, Book iii. of the Essay. Nothing is more easy than to say, that three fourths of the habitable globe are yet unpeopled but it is by no means so easy to fill these parts with flourishing colonies. The peculiar circumstances which have caused the spirit of emigration in the Highlands, so clearly explained in the able work of Lord Selkirk before referred to, are not of constant recurrence; nor is it by any means to be wished that they should be so. And yet without some such circumstances, people are by no means very ready to leave their native soil, and will bear much distress at home, rather than venture on these distant regions. I am of opinion that it is both the duty and interest of government to facilitate emigration; but it would surely be unjust to oblige people to leave their country and kindred against their inclinations.

[32] [In 1817 (Vol. III, p. 360) Malthus inserted a footnote here:
    The returns of 1801.
    [In 1826 (Vol. II, p. 461) he omitted the footnote and amended the text instead:
    ... it has appeared that according to the returns of the Population Act in 1801, the proportion of births to deaths was about 4 to 3.

[33] Table iii. p. 238, 4to. edit. [And Vol. I, pp. 191–3 of this edition.]

[34] [In 1826 (Vol. II, p. 461) this was altered to:
    ... a permanent rate of increase greater than that which was then taking place.

[35] [In 1817 (Vol. III, p. 361) this passage was expunged.]

recollected that it refers to no particular age, but is entirely comparative. The marriages in England are later than in France, the natural consequence of that prudence and respectability generated by a better government; and can we doubt that good has been the result? The marriages in this country now are later than they were before the revolution, and I feel firmly persuaded that the increased healthiness observed of late years could not possibly have taken place without this accompanying circumstance.[36] Two or three years in the average age of marriage, by lengthening each generation, and tending, in a small degree, both to diminish the prolificness of marriages, and the number of born living to be married, may make a considerable difference in the rate of increase, and be adequate to allow for a considerably diminished mortality. But I would on no account talk of any limits whatever. The only plain and intelligible measure with regard to marriage is the having a fair prospect of being able to maintain a family. If the possession of one of Mr. Young's cottages would give the labourer this prospect, he would be quite right to marry; but if it did not, or if he could only obtain a rented house without land, and the wages of labour were only sufficient to maintain two children, does Mr. Young, who cuts him off from the influence of the poor laws, presume to say that he would still be right in marrying?[37]

Mr. Young has asserted that I have made perfect chastity in the single state absolutely necessary to the success of my plan; but this surely is a misrepresentation. Perfect virtue is indeed absolutely necessary[38] to enable man to avoid *all* the moral and physical evils which depend upon his own conduct; but whoever expected perfect virtue upon earth? I have said what I conceive to be strictly true, that it is our duty to defer marriage till we can feed our children, and that it is also our duty not to indulge ourselves in vicious gratifications; but I have never said that I expected either, much less both, of these duties to be completely fulfilled. In this, and a number of other cases, it may happen, that the violation of one of two duties will enable a man to perform the other with greater facility; but if they be really both duties, and both practicable, no power *on earth* can absolve a man from the guilt of violating either. This can only be done by that God who can weigh the crime against the temptation, and will temper justice with mercy. The moralist is still bound to inculcate the practice of both duties, and each individual must

---

[36] [In 1826 (Vol. II, p. 462) Malthus added a footnote here:

(1825) It appears from the three returns of the Population Act, in 1801, 1811, and 1821, that the proportion of marriages has been diminishing with the increasing health of the country, notwithstanding the augmented rate of increase in the population.

[37] The lowest prospect with which a man can be justified in marrying seems to be the power, when in health, of earning such wages as, at the average price of corn, will maintain the average number of living children to a marriage.

[38] [In 1817 (Vol. III, p. 363) the word *absolutely* was excised.]

be left to act under the temptations to which he is exposed as his conscience shall dictate. Whatever I may have said in drawing a picture *professedly* visionary, for the sake of illustration, in the practical application of my principles I have taken man as he is, with all his imperfections on his head. And thus viewing him, and knowing that some checks to the population must exist, I have not the slightest hesitation in saying that the prudential check to marriage is better than premature mortality. And in this decision I feel myself completely justified by experience.

In every instance that can be traced, in which an improved government has given to its subjects a greater degree of foresight, industry, and personal dignity, these effects, under similar circumstances of increase, have invariably been accompanied by a diminished proportion of marriages. This is a proof that an increase of moral worth in the general character is not at least *incompatible* with an increase of temptations with respect to one particular vice; and the instances of Norway, Switzerland, England and Scotland, adduced in the last chapter of this Essay, show that, in comparing different countries together, a small proportion of marriages and births does not necessarily imply the greater prevalence even of this particular vice. This is surely quite enough for the legislator. He cannot estimate with tolerable accuracy the degree in which chastity in the single state prevails. His general conclusions must be founded on general results, and these are clearly in his favour.

To much of Mr. Young's plan, as he has at present explained it, I should by no means object. The peculiar evil which I apprehended from it, that of taking the poor from the consumption of wheat, and feeding them on milk and potatoes might certainly be avoided by a limitation of the number of cottages; and I entirely agree with him in thinking that we should not be deterred from making 500 000 families more comfortable, because we cannot extend the same relief to all the rest. I have indeed myself ventured to recommend a general improvement of cottages, and even the cow system on a limited scale; and perhaps, with proper precautions, a certain portion of land might be given to a considerable body of the labouring classes.

If the law which entitles the poor to support were to be repealed, I should most highly approve of any plan which would tend to render such repeal more palatable on its first promulgation; and in this view, some kind of compact with the poor might be very desirable. A plan of letting land to labourers, under certain conditions, has lately been tried in the parish of Long Newnton in Gloucestershire; and the result, with a general proposal founded on it, has been submitted to the public by Mr. Estcourt. The present success has been very striking; but in this, and every other case of the kind, we should always bear in mind that no experiment respecting a provision for the poor can be said to be complete till succeeding generations have arisen.[39] I doubt if there ever has been an instance of anything like a liberal institution for the poor which did not succeed on its first establishment, however it might have failed afterwards. But this consideration should by no means deter us from making such experiments, when present good is to be obtained by them, and a future overbalance of evil not justly to be apprehended. It should only make us less rash in drawing our inferences.

With regard to the general question of the advantages to the lower classes of possessing land, it should be recollected that such possessions are by no means a novelty. Formerly this system prevailed in almost every country with which we are acquainted, and prevails at present in many countries where the peasants are far from being remarkable for their comforts, but are, on the contrary, very poor, and particularly subject to scarcities. With respect to this latter evil, indeed, it is quite obvious that a peasantry which depends principally on its possessions in land must be more exposed to it than one which depends on the general wages of labour. When a year of deficient crops occurs in a country of any extent and diversity of soil, it is always partial, and some districts are more affected than others. But when a bad crop of grass, corn, or potatoes, or a mortality among cattle, falls on a poor man, whose principal dependence is on two or three acres of land, he is in the most deplorable and helpless situation. He is comparatively without money to purchase supplies, and is not for a moment to be compared with the man who depends on the wages of labour, and who will of course be able to purchase that portion of the general crop, whatever it may be, to which his relative situation in the society entitles him. In Sweden, where the farmers' labourers are paid principally in land, and often keep two or three cows, it is not uncommon for the peasants of one district to be almost starving, while their neighbours at a little distance are living in comparative plenty. It will be found indeed generally that, in almost all the countries which are particularly subject to scarcities and famines, either the farms are very small, or the labourers are paid principally in land. China, Indostan, and the former state of the Highlands of Scotland furnish some proofs among many others of the truth of this observation; and in reference to the small properties of France, Mr. Young himself in his tour particularly notices the distress arising from the least failure of the crops; and observes that such a deficiency

---

[39] In any plan, particularly of a distribution of land, as a compensation for the relief given by the poor laws, the succeeding generations would form the grand difficulty. All others would be perfectly trivial in comparison. For a time everything might go on very smoothly, and the rates be much diminished; but afterwards they would either increase again as rapidly as before, or the scheme would be exposed to all the same objections which have been made to mine, without the same justice and consistency to palliate them.

as in England passes almost without notice, in France is attended with dreadful calamities.[40]

Should any plan therefore of assisting the poor by land be adopted in this country, it would be absolutely essential to its ultimate success to prevent them from making it their principal dependence. And this might probably be done by attending strictly to the two following rules. Not to let the divisions of land be so great as to interrupt the cottager essentially in his usual labours; and always to stop in the further distribution of land and cottages when the price of labour, independent of any assistance from land, would not at the average price of corn maintain three, or at least two children. Could the matter be so ordered that the labourer, in working for others, should still continue to earn the same real command over the necessaries of life that he did before, a very great accession of comfort and happiness might accrue to the poor from the possession of land, without any evil that I can foresee at present. But if these points were not attended to, I should certainly fear an approximation to the state of the poor in France, Sweden, and Ireland; nor do I think that any of the partial experiments that have yet taken place afford the slightest presumption to the contrary. The result of these experiments is indeed exactly such as one should have expected. Who could ever have doubted that if, without lowering the price of labour, or taking the labourer off from his usual occupations, you could give him the produce of one or two acres of land and the benefit of a cow, you would decidedly raise his condition? But it by no means follows that he would retain this advantage if the system were so extended as to make the land his principal dependence, to lower the price of labour and, in the language of Mr. Young, to take the poor from the consumption of wheat and feed them on milk and potatoes. It does not appear to me so marvellous as it does to Mr. Young that the very same system, which in Lincolnshire and Rutlandshire may produce now the most comfortable peasantry in the British dominions should,[41] in the end, if extended without proper precautions, assimilate the condition of the labourers of this country to that of the lower classes of the Irish.

It is generally dangerous and impolitic in a government to take upon itself to regulate the supply of any commodity in request, and probably the supply of labourers forms no exception to the general rule. I would on no account therefore propose a positive law to regulate their increase; but as any assistance which the society might give them cannot, in the nature of things, be unlimited, the line may fairly be drawn where we please; and with

---

[40] Travels in France, vol. i. c. xii. p. 409. That country will probably be the least liable to scarcities, in which agriculture is carried on as the most flourishing *manufacture* of the state.

[41] [See also GOURLAY, ROBERT, in the Alphabetical List.]

regard to the increase from this point, everything would be left as before to individual exertion and individual speculation.

If any plan of this kind were adopted by the government, I cannot help thinking that it might be made the means of giving the best kind of encouragement and reward to those who are employed in our defence. If the period of enlisting were only for a limited time, and at the expiration of that time every person who had conducted himself well was entitled to a house and a small portion of land, if a country labourer, and to a tenement in a town and a small pension, if an artificer, all inalienable, a very strong motive would be held out to young men, not only to enter into the service of their country, but to behave well in that service; and in a short time there would be such a martial population at home, as the unfortunate state of Europe seems in a most peculiar manner to require. As it is only limited assistance that the society can possibly give, it seems in every respect fair and proper that, in regulating this limit, some important end should be attained.

If the poor laws be allowed to remain exactly in their present state, we ought at least to be aware to what cause it is owing that their effects have not been more pernicious than they are observed to be, that we may not complain of, or alter those parts, without which we should really not have the power of continuing them. The law which obliges each parish to maintain its own poor is open to many objections. It keeps the overseers and church-wardens continually on the watch to prevent new comers, and constantly in a state of dispute with other parishes. It thus prevents the free circulation of labour from place to place, and renders its price very unequal in different parts of the kingdom. It disposes all landlords rather to pull down than to build cottages on their estates; and this scarcity of habitations in the country, by driving more to the towns than would otherwise have gone, gives a relative discouragement to agriculture, and a relative encouragement to manufactures. These, it must be allowed, are no inconsiderable evils; but if the cause which occasions them were removed, evils of much greater magnitude would follow. I agree with Mr. Young in thinking that there is scarcely a parish in the kingdom where, if more cottages were built, and let at any tolerably moderate rents, they would not be immediately filled with new couples. I even agree with him in thinking that, in some places, this want of habitations operates too strongly in preventing marriage. But I have not the least doubt that, considered generally, its operation in the present state of things is most beneficial; and that it is almost exclusively owing to this cause that we have been able so long to continue the poor laws. If any man could build a hovel by the roadside, or on the neighbouring waste, without molestation, and yet were secure that he and his family would always be supplied with work and food by the parish, if they were not readily to be obtained elsewhere, I do not believe that it would be long before the physical impossibility of executing the letter of the poor laws would appear. It is of importance, therefore, to be aware that it is not because this or any other society has really the power of employing and supporting all that might be born, that we have been able to continue the present system; but because by the indirect operation of this system, not adverted to at the time of its establishment, and frequently reprobated since, the number of births is always very greatly limited, and thus reduced within the pale of possible support.

The obvious tendency of the poor laws is certainly to encourage marriage; but a closer attention to all their indirect as well as direct effects, may make it a matter of doubt how far they really do this.[42] They clearly tend, in their general operation, to discourage sobriety and economy, to encourage idleness and the desertion of children, and to put virtue and vice more on a level than they otherwise would be; but I will not presume to say positively that they tend to encourage population.[43] It is certain that the proportion of births in this country compared with others in similar circumstances is very small: but this was to be expected from the superiority of the government, the more respectable state of the people, and the more general spread[44] of a taste for cleanliness and conveniences. And it will readily occur to the reader that, owing to these causes, combined with the twofold operation of the poor laws, it must be extremely difficult to ascertain, with any degree of precision, what has been their effect on population.[45]

The only argument of a general nature against the Essay which strikes me as having any considerable force is the following. It is against the application of its principles, not the principles themselves, and has not, that I know of, been yet advanced in its present form. It may be said that, according to my

---

[42] [In 1817 (Vol. III, p. 373) *how far* was replaced by:
  ... to what extent ...
[43] [In 1817 (Vol. III, p. 373) this was altered to:
  ... but I will not presume to say positively that they greatly encourage population.
[44] [In 1817 (Vol. III, p. 374) *spread* was changed to 'diffusion'.
[45] [In 1807 (Vol. II, p. 473) Malthus added a footnote here:
  The most favourable light, in which the poor laws can possibly be placed, is to say, that under all the circumstances, with which they have been accompanied, they do not encourage marriage;[(a)] and undoubtedly the returns of the Population Act seem to warrant the assertion. Should this be true, many of the objections which have been urged in the Essay against the poor laws will of course be removed; but I wish to press on the attention of the reader, that they will in that case be removed in strict conformity to the general principles of the work, and in a manner to confirm, rather than to invalidate,[(b)] the main positions which it has attempted to establish.
  [In 1817 (Vol. III, p. 374 n.) Malthus made two significant alterations to this footnote, one near the beginning and one at the end:
  (a) ... the poor laws ... do not much encourage marriage;
  (b) ... in a manner to confirm, not to invalidate, the main positions ...

own reasonings and the facts stated in my work, it appears that the diminished proportion of births, which I consider as absolutely necessary to the permanent improvement of the condition of the poor, invariably follows an improved government, and the greater degree of personal respectability which it gives to the lower classes of society. Consequently, allowing the desirableness of the end, it is not necessary, in order to obtain it, to risk the promulgation of any new opinions which may alarm the prejudices of the poor, and the effect of which we cannot with certainty foresee; but we have only to proceed in improving our civil polity, conferring the benefits of education upon all, and removing every obstacle to the general extension of all those privileges and advantages which may be enjoyed in common, and we may be quite sure that the effect to which I look forward, and which can alone render these advantages permanent, will follow.

I acknowledge the truth and force of this argument, and have only to observe, in answer to it, that it is difficult to conceive that we should not proceed with more celerity and certainty towards the end in view, if the principal causes which tend to promote or retard it were generally known. In particular, I cannot help looking forward to a very decided improvement in the habits and temper of the lower classes, when their real situation has been clearly explained to them; and if this were done gradually and cautiously, and accompanied with proper moral and religious instructions, I should not expect any danger from it. I am always unwilling to believe that the general dissemination of truth is prejudicial. Cases of the kind are undoubtedly conceivable, but they should be admitted with very great caution. If the general presumption in favour of the advantage of truth were once essentially shaken, all ardour in its cause would share the same fate, and the interests of knowledge and virtue most decidedly suffer. It is besides a species of arrogance not lightly to be encouraged, for any man to suppose that he has penetrated further into the laws of nature than the great Author of them intended, further than is consistent with the good of mankind.

Under these impressions I have freely given my opinions to the public. In the truth of the general principles of the Essay I confess that I feel such a confidence that, till something has been advanced against them very different indeed from anything that has hitherto appeared, I cannot help considering them as incontrovertible. With regard to the application of these principles the case is certainly different; and as dangers of opposite kinds are to be guarded against, the subject will of course admit of much latitude of opinion. At all events, however, it must be allowed that, whatever may be our determination respecting the advantages or disadvantages of endeavouring to circulate the truths on this subject among the poor, it must be highly advantageous that they should be known to all those who have it in their power to influence the laws and institutions of society. That the body of an army should not in all cases know the particulars of their situation may possibly be desirable; but that the leaders should be in the same state of ignorance will hardly, I think, be contended.

If it be really true, that without a diminished proportion of births[46] we cannot attain any *permanent* improvement in the health and happiness of the mass of the pople, and secure that description of population which, by containing a larger share of adults, is best calculated to create fresh resources, and consequently to encourage a continued increase of efficient population; it is surely of the highest importance that this should be known, that if we take no steps directly to promote this effect, we should not at least,[47] under the influence of the former prejudices on this subject, endeav-our to counteract it.[48] And if it be thought inadvisable to abolish the poor laws, it cannot be doubted that a knowledge of those general principles, which render them inefficient in their humane intentions, might be applied

---

[46] It should always be recollected that a diminished *proportion* of births may take place under a constant annual increase of the absolute number. This is, in fact, exactly what has happened in England and Scotland during the last forty years.
[This figure was never altered, although by 1826 another twenty years had elapsed.]
[47] [In 1817 (Vol. III, p. 378) the words *at least* were omitted.]
[48] We should be aware that a scarcity of men, owing either to great losses, or to some particular and unusual demand, is liable to happen in every country; and in no respect invalidates the general principle that has been advanced. Whatever may be the tendency to increase, it is quite clear that an extraordinary supply of men cannot be produced either in six months, or six years; but even with a view to a more than usual supply, causes which tend to diminish mortality are not only more certain but more rapid in their effects than direct encourage-ments to marriage. An increase of births may, and often does, take place, without the ultimate accomplishment of our object; but supposing the births to remain the same, it is impossible for a diminished mortality not to be accompanied by an increase of effective population.

We are very apt to be deceived on this subject by the almost constant demand for labour which prevails in every prosperous country; but we should consider that in countries which can but just keep up their population, as the price of labour must be sufficient to rear a family of a certain number, a single man would[(a)] have a superfluity, and labour would be in constant demand at the price of the subsistence of an individual. It cannot be doubted that in this country we could soon employ double the number of labourers if we could have them at our own price; because supply will produce demand as well as demand supply. The present great extension of the cotton trade did not originate in an extraordinary increase of demand, at the former prices, but it an increased supply at a much cheaper rate, which of course immediately produced an extended demand. As we cannot, however, obtain men at sixpence a day by improvements in machinery, we must submit to the necessary conditions of their rearing; and there is no man, who has the slightest feeling for the happiness of the most numerous class of society, or has even just views of policy on the subject, who would not rather choose that the requisite population should be obtained by such a price of labour, combined with such habits, as would occasion a very small mortality, than from a great proportion of births, of which comparatively few would reach manhood.
[(a)] [In 1817 (Vol. III, p. 378) *would* was changed to 'will'.]

so far to modify them and regulate their execution, as to remove many of the evils with which they are accompanied, and make them less objectionable.

There is only one subject more which I shall notice, and that is rather a matter of feeling than of argument. Many persons, whose understandings are not of that description that they can regulate their belief or disbelief by their likes or dislikes, have professed their perfect conviction of the truth of the general principles contained in the Essay; but, at the same time, have lamented this conviction, as throwing a darker shade over our views of human nature, and tending particularly to narrow our prospects of future improvement. In these feelings I cannot agree with them. If, from a review of the past, I could not only believe that a fundamental and very extraordinary improvement in human society was possible, but feel a firm confidence that it would take place, I should undoubtedly be grieved to find that I had overlooked some cause, the operation of which would at once blast my hopes. But if the contemplation of the past history of mankind, from which alone we can judge of the future, renders it almost impossible to feel such a confidence, I confess, that I had much rather believe that some real and deeply-seated difficulty existed, the constant struggle with which was calculated to rouse the natural inactivity of man, to call forth his faculties, and invigorate and improve his mind; a species of difficulty which it must be allowed is most eminently and peculiarly suited to a state of probation; than that nearly all the evils of life might with the most perfect facility be removed, but for the perverseness and wickedness of those who influence human institutions.[49]

A person who held this latter opinion must necessarily live in a constant state of irritation and disappointment. The ardent expectations, with which he might begin life, would soon receive the most cruel check. The regular progress of society, under the most favourable circumstances, would to him appear slow and unsatisfactory; but instead even of this regular progress, his eye would be more frequently presented with retrograde movements and the most disheartening reverses. The changes to which he had looked forward with delight would be found big with new and unlooked-for evils, and the

---

[49] The misery and vice arising from the pressure of the population too hard against the limits of subsistence, and the misery and vice arising from promiscuous intercourse, may be considered as the Scylla and Charybdis of human life. That it is possible for each individual to steer clear of both these rocks is certainly true, and a truth which I have endeavoured strongly to maintain; but that these rocks do not form a difficulty independent of human institutions, no person with any knowledge of the subject can venture to assert.

[Malthus has forgotten his classical studies here. According to legend, Scylla was either a rock or a monster, but Charybdis was indubitably a whirlpool; they were on opposite sides of the narrow Straits of Messina. Ships that tried to avoid the one were liable to be destroyed by the other, and Odysseus' passage of these Straits is described in the twelfth book of Homer's Odyssey.]

characters on which he had reposed the most confidence would be seen frequently deserting his favourite cause, either from the lessons of experience or the temptation of power. In this state of constant disappointment, he would be but too apt to attribute everything to the worst motives; he would be inclined to give up the cause of improvement in despair; and judging of the whole from a part, nothing but a peculiar goodness of heart and amiableness of disposition could preserve him from that sickly and disgusting misanthropy which is but too frequently the end of such characters.

On the contrary, a person who held the other opinion, as he would set out with more moderate expectations, would of course be less liable to disappointment. A comparison of the best with the worst states of society, and the obvious inference from analogy, that the best were capable of further improvement, would constantly present to his mind a prospect sufficiently animating to warrant his most persevering exertions. But aware of the difficulties with which the subject was surrounded, knowing how often in the attempt to attain one object some other other had been lost, and that though society had made rapid advances in some directions, it had been comparatively stationary in others, he would be constantly prepared for failures. These failures, instead of creating despair, would only create knowledge; instead of checking his ardour, would only[50] give it a wiser and more successful direction; and having founded his opinion of mankind on broad and general grounds, the disappointment of any particular views would not change this opinion; but even in declining age he would probably be found believing as firmly in the reality and general prevalence of virtue, as in the existence and frequency of vice; and to the last, looking forward with a just confidence to those improvements in society, which the history of the past, in spite of all the reverses with which it is accompanied, seems clearly to warrant.

It may be true that if ignorance is bliss, 'tis folly to be wise; but if ignorance be not bliss, as in the present instance; if all false views of society must not only impede decidedly the progress of improvement, but necessarily terminate in the most bitter disappointments to the individuals who form them; I shall always think that the feelings and prospects of those who make the justest estimates of our future expectations are the most consolatory; and that the characters of this description are happier themselves, at the same time that they are beyond comparison more likely to contribute to the improvement and happiness of society.[51]

---

[50] [In 1817 (Vol. III, p. 382) the word *only* was omitted.]

[51] While the last sheet of this Appendix was printing, I heard with some surprise that an argument had been drawn from the Principle of Population in favour of the the slave trade. As the just conclusion from that principle appears to me to be exactly the contrary, I cannot help saying a few words on the subject.

If the only argument against the slave trade had been that, from the mortality it occasioned, it was likely to unpeople Africa or extinguish the human race, some comfort with regard to these fears might, indeed, be drawn from the Principle of Population; but as the necessity of the abolition has never, that I know of, been urged on the ground of these apprehensions, a reference to the laws which regulate the increase of the human species was certainly most unwise in the friends of the slave trade.

The abolition of the slave trade is defended principally by the two following arguments:

1st. That the trade to the coast of Africa for slaves, together with their subsequent treatment in the West Indies, is productive of so much human misery, that its continuance is disgraceful to us as men and as Christians.

2d. That the culture of the West-India islands could go on with equal advantage, and much greater security, if no further importation of slaves were to take place.

With regard to the first argument it appears, in the Essay on the Principle of Population, that so great is the tendency of mankind to increase, that nothing but some physical or moral check operating in an *excessive* and *unusual* degree, can permanently keep the population of a country below the average means of subsistence. In the West India islands a constant recruit of labouring negroes is necessary; and consequently the immediate checks to population must operate with *excessive* and *unusual* force. All the checks to population were found resolvable into moral restraint, vice, and misery. In a state of slavery moral restraint cannot have much influence; nor in any state will it ever continue permanently to diminish the population. The whole effect, therefore, is to be attributed to the *excessive* and *unusual* action of vice and misery; and a reference to the facts contained in the Essay incontrovertibly proves that the condition of the slaves in the West Indies, taken altogether, is most wretched, and that the representations of the friends of the abolition cannot easily be exaggerated.

It will be said that the principal reason why the slaves in the West Indies constantly diminish is that the sexes are not in equal numbers, a considerable majority of males being always imported; but this very circumstance decides at once on the cruelty of their situation, and must necessarily be one powerful cause of their degraded moral condition.

It may be said also, that many towns do not keep up their numbers, and yet the same objection is not made to them on that account. But the cases will admit of no comparison. If, for the sake of better society or higher wages, people are willing to expose themselves to a less pure air, and greater temptations to vice, no hardship is suffered that can reasonably be complained of. The superior mortality of towns falls principally upon children, and is scarcely noticed by people of mature age. The sexes are in equal numbers, and every man after a few years of industry may look forward to the happiness of domestic life. If during the time that he is thus waiting, he acquires various[a] habits which indispose him to marriage, he has nobody to blame except himself. But with the negroes the case is totally different. The unequal number of the sexes shuts out at once the majority of them from all chance of domestic happiness. They have no hope of this kind to sweeten their toils, and animate their exertion; but are necesarily condemned either to unceasing privation, or to the most vicious excesses; and thus shut out from every cheering prospect, we cannot be surprised that they are in general ready to welcome that death which so many meet with in the prime of life.

The second argument is no less powerfully supported by the Principle of Population than the first. It appears, from a very general survey of different countries, that under every form of government, however unjust and tyrannical, in every climate of the known world, however apparently unfavourable to health, it has been found that population, with the sole exception above alluded to, has been able to keep itself up to the level of the means of subsistence. Consequently, if by the abolition of the trade to Africa, the slaves in the West Indies were placed only in a *tolerable* situation, if their civil condition and moral habits were only made to *approach* to those which prevail among the mass of the human race in the worst-governed countries of the world, it is contrary to the general laws of nature to suppose

[a] [In 1807 (Vol. II, p. 483) *various* was changed to 'vicious'.

that they would not be able, by procreation, fully to supply the effective demand for labour; and it is difficult to conceive that a population so raised would not be in every point of view preferable to that which exists at present.

It is perfectly clear, therefore, that a consideration of the laws which govern the increase and decrease of the human species tends to strengthen, in the most powerful manner, all the arguments in favour of the abolition.

With regard to the state of society among the African nations, it will readily occur to the reader that, in describing it, the question of the slave trade was foreign to my purpose; and I might naturally fear that if I entered upon it I should be led into too long a digression. But certainly all the facts which I have mentioned, and which are taken principally from Park, if they do not absolutely *prove* that the wars in Africa are excited and aggravated by the traffic on the coast, tend powerfully to confirm the *supposition*. The state of Africa, as I have described it, is exactly such as we should expect in a country where the capture of men was considered as a more advantageous employment than agriculture or manufactures. Of the state of these nations some hundred years ago it must be confessed that we have little knowledge that we can depend upon: but allowing that the regular plundering excursions, which Park describes, are of the most ancient date; yet it is impossible to suppose that any circumstance which, like the European traffic, must give additional value to the plunder thus acquired, would not powerfully aggravate them, and effectually prevent all progress towards a happier order of things. As long as the nations of Europe continue barbarous enough to purchase slaves in Africa, we may be quite sure that Africa will continue barbarous enough to supply them.

[The rumour that Malthus approved of the slave trade was probably due to a malicious article by William Cobbett (1763–1835) in his *Political Register* for 16 February 1805. It was headed 'Jamaica Complaints', and in an oblique reference to homosexuality Cobbett wrote:

But, as to the Africans, it is not pretended. I believe, that the constant fresh supply is rendered necessary by the destructiveness of the climate, so much as by the effects of *celibacy*, and other circumstances therewith connected. And, is this an *evil*? A question not to be settled without a discussion, into which, I should think, that even Mr Wilberforce would not be inclined to enter, at least not very minutely. If he were, however, it might be quite sufficient to refer him to the profound work of Mr Malthus, who has not scrupled to recommend *checks to population*, as conducive to the *good* of mankind.

Eleven months later, on 18 January 1806, Cobbett quoted Malthus's quotation from Mungo Park (q.v. in the Alphabetical List) about the Africans voluntarily selling their children into slavery when food was short. (See Vol. 1, pp. 88–9). This could well have been 'While the last sheet of this Appendix was printing'.

Just over a year after that, Malthus went up to London from Hertford, to the House of Commons, when the chief debate on the abolition of the slave trade took place on 23 February 1807. He was able 'to see Mr Wilberforce before he went into the house, and to furnish him with data to rescue my character from the imputation of being a friend to the slave trade'. (See Patricia James, *Population Malthus*, Cambridge University Press, 1979, p. 125). In the editions of the *Essay* of 1817 and 1826 Malthus inserted '(1807)' at the beginning of this note 51, after 'While the last sheet of this Appendix was printing ...' The date is presumably incorrect, and one must assume that Malthus jotted it down absent-mindedly, while he was recalling the year of this meeting with Wilberforce and the passing of the Act.]

# APPENDIX, 1817

Since the publication of the last edition of this Essay in 1807, two Works have appeared, the avowed objects of which are directly to oppose its principles and conclusions. These are *the Principles of Population and Production*, by Mr. Weyland; and *an Inquiry into the Principle of Population*, by Mr. James Grahame.

I would willingly leave the question, as it at present stands, to the judgment of the public, without any attempt on my part to influence it further by a more particular reply; but as I professed my readiness to enter into the discussion of any serious objections to my principles and conclusions, which were brought forward in a spirit of candour and truth; and as one at least of the publications above mentioned may be so characterized, and the other is by no means deficient in personal respect, I am induced shortly to notice them.

I should not, however, have thought it necessary to advert to Mr. Grahame's publication, which is a slight work without any very distinct object in view, if it did not afford some strange specimens of misrepresentation, which it may be useful to point out.

Mr. Grahame in his second chapter, speaking of the tendency exhibited by the law of human increase to a redundance of population, observes that some philosophers have considered this tendency as a mark of the foresight of nature, which has thus provided a ready supply for the waste of life occasioned by human vices and passions; while 'others, of whom Mr. Malthus is the leader, regard the vices and follies of human nature, and their various products, famine, disease and war, as *benevolent remedies* by which nature has enabled human beings to correct the disorders that would arise from that redundance of population which the unrestrained operation of her laws would create'.[1]

These are the opinions imputed to me and the philosophers with whom I am associated. If the imputation were just, we have certainly on many accounts great reason to be ashamed of ourselves. For what are we made to say? In the first place, we are stated to assert that *famine*[2] is a benevolent

---

[1] P. 100.    [2] [In 1826 (Vol. ii, p. 477) the word *famine* was not italicised.]

remedy for *want of food*, as redundance of population admits of no other interpretation than that of a people ill supplied with the means of subsistence, and consequently the benevolent remedy of famine here noticed can only apply to the disorders arising from scarcity of food.

Secondly, we are said to affirm that nature enables human beings by means of diseases to correct the disorders that would arise from a redundance of population – that is, that mankind willingly and purposely create diseases, with a view to prevent those diseases which are the necessary consequence of a redundant population, and are not worse or more mortal than the means of prevention.

And thirdly, it is imputed to us generally, that we consider the vices and follies of mankind as benevolent remedies for the disorders arising from a redundant population; and it follows as a matter of course that these vices ought to be encouraged rather than reprobated.

It would not be easy to compress in so small a compass a greater quantity of absurdity, inconsistency, and unfounded assertion.

The two first imputations may perhaps be peculiar to Mr. Grahame; and protection from them may be found in their gross absurdity and inconsistency. With regard to the third, it must be allowed that it has not the merit of novelty. Although it is scarcely less absurd than the two others, and has been shown to be an opinion not to be inferred from any part of it, it has been continually repeated in various quarters for fourteen years, and now appears in the pages of Mr. Grahame. For the last time I will now notice it; and should it still continue to be brought forward, I think I may be fairly excused from paying the slightest further attention either to the imputation itself, or to those who advance it.

If I had merely stated that the tendency of the human race to increase faster than the means of subsistence was kept to a level with these means by some or other of the forms of vice and misery, and that these evils were absolutely unavoidable, and incapable of being diminished by any human efforts; still I could not with any semblance of justice be accused of considering vice and misery as the remedies of these evils, instead of the very evils themselves. As well nearly might I be open to Mr. Grahame's imputations of considering the famine and disease necessarily arising from a scarcity of food as a benevolent remedy for the evils which this scarcity occasions.

But I have not so stated the proposition. I have not considered the evils of vice and misery arising from a redundant population as unavoidable, and incapable of being diminished. On the contrary, I have pointed out a mode by which these evils may be removed or mitigated by removing or mitigating their cause. I have endeavoured to show that this may be done consistently with human virtue and happiness. I have never considered any possible increase of population as an evil, except as far as it might increase the proportion of vice and misery. Vice and misery, and these alone, are the evils which it has been my great object to contend against. I have expressly proposed moral restraint as their rational and proper remedy; and whether the remedy be good or bad, adequate or inadequate, the proposal itself, and the stress which I have laid upon it, is an incontrovertible proof that I never can have considered vice and misery as themselves remedies.

But not only does the general tenour of my work, and the specific object of the latter part of it, clearly show that I do not consider vice and misery as remedies; but particular passages in various parts of it are so distinct on the subject, as not to admit of being misunderstood but by the most perverse blindness.[3]

It is therefore quite inconceivable that any writer with the slightest pretension to respectability should venture to bring forward such imputations; and it must be allowed to show either such a degree of ignorance, or such a total want of candour, as utterly to disqualify him for the discussion of such subjects.

But Mr. Grahame's misrepresentations are not confined to the passage above referred to. In his Introduction he observes that, in order to check a redundant population, the evils of which I consider as much nearer than Mr. Wallace, I 'recommend immediate recourse to human efforts, to the restraints prescribed by Condorcet, for the correction or mitigation of the evil'.[4] This is an assertion entirely without foundation. I have never adverted to the check suggested by Condorcet without the most marked disapprobation. Indeed I should always particularly reprobate any artificial and unnatural modes of checking population, both on account of their immorality and their tendency to remove a necessary stimulus to industry. If it were possible for each married couple to limit by a wish the number of their children, there is certainly reason to fear that the indolence of the human race would be very greatly increased; and that neither the population of individual countries, nor of the whole earth, would ever reach its natural and proper extent. But the restraints which I have recommended are quite of a different character. They are not only pointed out by reason and sanctioned by religion, but tend in the most marked manner to stimulate industry. It is not easy to conceive a more powerful encouragement to exertion and good conduct than the looking forward to marriage as a state peculiarly desirable; but only to be enjoyed in comfort by the acquisition of habits of industry,

---

[3] [In 1826 (Vol. ii, p. 478) the word *but* was excised, so that the sentence concluded:
... as not to admit of being misunderstood by the most perverse blindness.

[4] P. 18.

economy and prudence. And it is in this light that I have always wished to place it.[5]

In speaking of the poor-laws in this country, and of their tendency (particularly as they have been lately administered) to eradicate all remaining spirit of independence among our peasantry, I observe that 'hard as it may appear in individual instances, dependent poverty ought to be held disgraceful'; by which of course I only mean that such a proper degree of pride as will induce a labouring man to make great exertions, as in Scotland, in order to prevent himself or his nearest relations from falling upon the parish, is very desirable, with a view to the happiness of the lower classes of society. The interpretation which Mr. Grahame gives to this passage is that the rich 'are so to embitter the pressure of indigence by the stings of contumely, that men may be driven by their pride to prefer even the refuge of despair to the condition of dependence!!'[6] – a curious specimen of misrepresentation and exaggeration.

I have written a chapter expressly on the practical direction of our charity; and in detached passages elsewhere have paid a just tribute to the exalted virtue of benevolence. To those who have read these parts of my work, and have attended to the general tone and spirit of the whole, I willingly appeal, if they are but tolerably candid, against these charges of Mr. Grahame, which intimate that I would root out the virtues of charity and benevolence, without regard to the exaltation which they bestow on the moral dignity of our nature; and that in my view the 'rich are required only to harden their hearts against calamity, and to prevent the charitable visitings of their nature from keeping alive in them that virtue which is often the only moral link between them and their fellow-mortals'.[7] It is not indeed easy to suppose that Mr. Grahame can have read the chapter to which I allude, as both the letter and spirit of it contradict, in the most express and remarkable manner, the imputations conveyed in the above passages.

These are a few specimens of Mr. Grahame's misrepresentations, which might easily be multiplied; but on this subject I will only further remark that it shows no inconsiderable want of candour to continue attacking and dwelling upon passages which have ceased to form a part of the work controverted. And this Mr. Grahame has done in more instances than one,

---

[5] See vol. ii., p. 241, of 4th. edit.; p. 493 of the quarto edit.; and vol. III, of the present edition. In 1826 (Vol. II, p. 479) this note was amended:

See vol. ii. p. 241, of 4th edit.; p. 493 of the quarto edit.; vol. iii. p. 82 of the 5th edit. and vol. ii. p. 262 of this edition.

[In the present edition this passage in the chapter 'Of moral restraint' will be found on pp. 91–2 of Vol. II.]

[6] P. 236.      [7] Ibid.

although he could hardly fail to know that he was combating expressions and passages which I have seen reason to alter or expunge.

I really should not have thought it worth while to notice these misrepresentations of Mr. Grahame if, in spite of them, the style and tone of his publication had not appeared to me to be entitled to more respect than most of my opponents.

With regard to the substance and aim of Mr. Grahame's work, it seems to be intended to show that emigration is the remedy provided by nature for a redundant population; and that if this remedy cannot be adequately applied, there is no other that can be proposed which will not lead to consequences worse than the evil itself. These are two points which I have considered at length in the Essay; and it cannot be necessary to repeat any of the arguments here. Emigration, if it could be freely used, has been shown to be a resource which could not be of long duration. It cannot therefore under any circumstances be considered as an adequate remedy. The latter position is a matter of opinion, and may rationally be held by any person who sees reason to think it well founded. It appears to me, I confess, that experience most decidedly contradicts it; but to those who think otherwise, there is nothing more to be said, than that they are bound in consistency to acquiesce in the necessary consequences of their opinion. These consequences are that the poverty and wretchedness arising from a redundant population or, in other words, from very low wages and want of employment, are absolutely irremediable, and must be continually increasing as the population of the earth proceeds; and that all the efforts of legislative wisdom and private charity, though they may afford a wholesome and beneficial exercise of human virtue, and may occasionally alter the distribution and vary the pressure of human misery, can do absolutely nothing towards diminishing the general amount or checking the increasing weight of this pressure.

Mr. Weyland's work is of a much more elaborate description than that of Mr. Grahame. It has also a very definite object in view: and although, when he enters into the details of his subject, he is compelled entirely to agree with me respecting the checks which practically keep down population to the level of the means of subsistence, and has not in fact given a single reason for the slow progress of population, in the advanced stages of society, that does not clearly and incontrovertibly come under the heads of moral restraint, vice or misery; yet it must be allowed that he sets out with a bold and distinct denial of my premises, and finishes, as he ought to do from such a beginning, by drawing the most opposite conclusions.

After stating fairly my main propositions, and adverting to the conclusion which I have drawn from them, Mr. Weyland says: 'Granting the premises, it is indeed obvious that this conclusion is undeniable.'[8]

---

[8] Principles of Population and Production, p. 15.

I desire no other concession than this; and if my premises can be shown to rest on unsolid foundations, I will most readily give up the inferences I have drawn from them.

To determine the point here at issue it cannot be necessary for me to repeat the proofs of these premises derived both from theory and experience, which have already so fully been brought forward. It has been allowed that they have been stated with tolerable clearness; and it is known that many persons have considered them as unassailable, who still refuse to admit the consequences to which they appear to lead. All that can be required therefore on the present occasion is to examine the validity of the objections to these premises brought forward by Mr. Weyland.

Mr. Weyland observes, 'that the origin of what are conceived to be the mistakes and false reasonings, with respect to the principle of population, appears to be the assumption of a tendency to increase in the human species, the quickest that can be proved possible in any particular state of society, as that which is natural and theoretically possible in all; and the characterizing of every cause which tends to prevent such quickest possible rate as checks to the natural and spontaneous tendency of population to increase; but as checks evidently insufficient to stem the progress of an overwhelming torrent. This seems as eligible a mode of reasoning, as if one were to assume the height of the Irish giant as the natural standard of the stature of man, and to call every reason, which may be suggested as likely to prevent the generality of men from reaching it, checks to their growth.'[9]

Mr. Weyland has here most unhappily chosen his illustration, as it is in no respect applicable to the case. In order to illustrate the different rates at which population increases in different countries, by the different heights of men, the following comparison and inference would be much more to the purpose.

If in a particular country we observed that all the people had weights of different sizes upon their heads, and that invariably each individual was tall or short in proportion to the smallness or greatness of the pressure upon him; that every person was observed to grow when the weight he carried was either removed or diminished, and that the few among the whole people, who were exempted from this burden, were very decidedly taller than the rest; would it not be quite justifiable to infer that the weights which the people carried were the cause of their being in general so short; and that the height of those without weights might fairly be considered as the standard to which it might be expected that the great mass would arrive, if their growth were unrestricted?

---

[9] P. 17.

For what is it, in fact, which we really observe with regard to the different rates of increase in different countries? Do we not see that, in almost every state to which we can direct our attention, the natural tendency to increase is repressed by the difficulty which the mass of the people find in procuring an ample portion of the necessaries of life, which shows itself more immediately in some or other of the forms of moral restraint, vice and misery? Do we not see that invariably the rates of increase are fast or slow, according as the pressure of these checks is light or heavy; and that in consequence Spain increases at one rate, France at another, England at a third, Ireland at a fourth, parts of Russia at a fifth, parts of Spanish America at a sixth, and the United States of North America at a seventh? Do we not see that, whenever the resources of any country increase, so as to create a great demand for labour and give the lower classes of society a greater command over the necessaries of life, the population of such country, though it might before have been stationary or proceeding very slowly, begins immediately to make a start forwards? And do we not see that in those few countries, or districts of countries, where the pressure arising from the difficulty of procuring the necessaries and conveniences of life is almost entirely removed, and where in consequence the checks to early marriages are very few, and large families are maintained with perfect facility, the rate at which the population increases is always the greatest?

And when to these broad and glaring facts we add, that neither theory nor experience will justify us in believing, either that the passion between the sexes, or the natural prolificness of women, diminishes in the progress of society; when we further consider that the climate of the United States of America is not particularly healthy, and that the qualities which mainly distinguish it from other countries are its rapid production and distribution of the means of subsistence – is not the induction as legitimate and correct as possible, that the varying weight of the difficulties attending the maintenance of families, and the moral restraint, vice and misery which these difficulties necessarily generate, are the causes of the varying rates of increase observable in different countries; and that, so far from having any reason to consider the American rate of increase as peculiar, unnatural and gigantic, we are bound by every law of induction and analogy to conclude that there is scarcely a state in Europe where, if the marriages were as early, the means of maintaining large families as ample, and the employment of the labouring classes as healthy, the rate of increase would not be as rapid, and in some cases, I have no doubt, even more rapid, than in the United States of America?

Another of Mr. Weyland's curious illustrations is the following: He says that the *physical tendency* of a people in a commercial and manufacturing state to double their number in twenty-five years is 'as absolutely gone as the tendency of a bean to shoot up further into the air, after it has arrived at its full growth'; and that to assume such a *tendency* is to build a theory upon a mere shadow, 'which, when brought to the test, is directly at variance with experience of the fact; and as unsafe to act upon, as would be that of a general who should assume the force of a musket-shot to be double its actual range, and then should calculate upon the death of all his enemies as soon as he had drawn up his own men for battle within this line of assumed efficiency'.[10]

Now I am not in the least aware who it is that has assumed the *actual* range of the shot, or the actual progress of population in different countries, as very different from what it is observed to be; and therefore cannot see how the illustration, as brought forward by Mr. Weyland, applies, or how I can be said to resemble his miscalculating general. What I have really done is this (if he will allow me the use of his own metaphor): having observed that the range of musket-balls, projected from similar barrels and with the same quantity of powder of the same strength, was, under different circumstances, very different, I applied myself to consider what these circumstances were; and, having found that the range of each ball was greater or less in proportion to the smaller or greater number of the obstacles which it met with in its course, or the rarity or density of the medium through which it passed, I was led to infer that the variety of range observed was owing to these obstacles; and I consequently thought it a more correct and legitimate conclusion, and one more consonant both to theory and experience, to say that the *natural tendency* to a range of a certain extent, or the force impressed upon the ball, was always the same, and the actual range, whether long or short, only altered by external resistance; than to conclude that the different distances to which the balls reached must proceed from some mysterious change in the *natural tendency* of each bullet at different times, although no observable difference could be noticed either in the barrel or the charge.

I leave Mr. Weyland to determine which would be the conclusion of the natural philosopher, who was observing the different velocities and ranges of projectiles passing through resisting media; and I do not see why the moral and political philosopher should proceed upon principles so totally opposite.

But the only arguments of Mr. Weyland against the *natural tendency* of the human race to increase faster than the means of subsistence are a few of these illustrations which he has so unhappily applied, together with the acknowledged fact, that countries under different circumstances and in different stages of their progress, do really increase at very different rates.

Without dwelling therefore longer on such illustrations, it may be observed, with regard to the fact of the different rates of increase in different

---

[10] P. 126.

countries, that as long as it is a law of our nature that man cannot live without food, these different rates are as absolutely and strictly *necessary* as the differences in the power of producing food in countries more or less exhausted; and that to infer from these different rates of increase, as they are actually found to take place, that 'population has a *natural tendency* to keep within the powers of the soil to afford it subsistence in every gradation through which society passes', is just as rational as to infer that every man has a *natural tendency* to remain in prison who is necessarily confined to it by four strong walls; or that the pine of the crowded Norwegian forest has no *natural* tendency to shoot out lateral branches, because there is no room for their growth. And yet this is Mr. Weyland's first and grand proposition, on which the whole of his work turns!!!!<sup>11</sup>

But though Mr. Weyland has not proved, or approached towards proving, that the *natural* tendency of population to increase is not unlimited; though he has not advanced a single reason to make it appear probable that a thousand millions would not be doubled in twenty-five years just as easily as a thousand, if moral restraint, vice and misery, were equally removed in both cases; yet there is one part of his argument which undoubtedly might, under certain circumstances, be true; and if true, though it would in no respect impeach the premises of the Essay, it would essentially affect some of its conclusions.

The argument may be stated shortly thus – that the natural division of labour arising from a very advanced state of society, particularly in countries where the land is rich, and great improvements have taken place in agriculture, might throw so large a portion of the people into towns, and engage so many in unhealthy occupations, that the immediate checks to population might be too powerful to be overcome even by an abundance of food.

It is admitted that this is a possible case; and, foreseeing this possibility, I provided for it in the terms in which the second proposition of the Essay was enunciated.

The only practical question then worth attending to, between me and Mr. Weyland, is whether cases of the kind above stated are to be considered in the light in which I have considered them in the Essay, as exceptions of very rare occurrence, or in the light in which Mr. Weyland has considered them, as a state of things naturally accompanying every stage in the progress of improvement. On either supposition, population would still be repressed by some or other of the forms of moral restraint, vice or misery; but the moral and political conclusions, in the actual state of almost all countries, would be

---

<sup>11</sup> [In 1826 (Vol. II, p. 485) Malthus reduced the number of exclamation marks here from three to one.]

essentially different. On the one supposition moral restraint would, except in a few cases of the rarest occurrence, be one of the most useful and necessary of virtues; and on the other, it would be one of the most useless and unnecessary.

This question can only be determined by an appeal to experience. Mr. Weyland is always ready to refer to the state of this country; and, in fact, may be said almost to have built his system upon the peculiar policy of a single state. But the reference in this case will entirely contradict his theory. He has brought forward some elaborate calculations to show the extreme difficulty with which the births of the country supply the demands of the towns and manufactories. In looking over them the reader, without other information, would be disposed to feel considerable alarm at the prospect of depopulation impending over the country; or at least he would be convinced that we were within a hair's breadth of that formidable point of *non-reproduction*, at which, according to Mr. Weyland, the population *naturally* comes to a full stop before the means of subsistence cease to be progressive.

These calculations were certainly as applicable twenty years ago as they are now; and indeed they are chiefly founded on observations which were made at a greater distance of time than the period here noticed. But what has happened since? In spite of the enlargement of all our towns; in spite of the most rapid increase of manufactories, and of the proportion of people employed in them; in spite of the most extraordinary and unusual demands for the army and navy; in short, in spite of a state of things which, according to Mr. Weyland's theory, ought to have brought us long since to the point of *non-reproduction*, the population of the country has advanced at a rate more rapid than was ever known at any period of its history. During the ten years from 1800 to 1811, as I have mentioned in a former part of this work, the population of this country (even after making an allowance for the presumed deficiency of the returns in the first enumeration) increased at a rate which would double its numbers in fifty-five years.

This fact appears to me at once a full and complete refutation of the doctrine that, as society advances, the increased indisposition to marriage and increased mortality in great towns and manufactories always overcome the principle of increase; and that, in the language of Mr. Weyland, 'population, so far from having an inconvenient tendency uniformly to press against the means of subsistence, becomes by degrees very slow in overtaking those means'.

With this acknowledged and glaring fact before him, and with the most striking evidences staring him in the face that, even during this period of rapid increase, thousands both in the country and in towns were prevented from marrying so early as they would have done, if they had possessed sufficient means of supporting a family independently of parish relief, it is quite inconceivable how a man of sense could bewilder himself in such a maze of futile calculations, and come to a conclusion so diametrically opposite to experience.

The fact already noticed, as it applies to the most advanced stage of society known in Europe, and proves incontrovertibly that the actual checks to population, even in the most improved countries, arise principally from an insufficiency of subsistence, and soon yield to increased resources, notwithstanding the increase of towns and manufactories, may I think fairly be considered as quite decisive of the question at issue.

But in treating of so general and extensive a subject as the Principle of Population, it would surely not be just to take our examples and illustrations only from a single state. And in looking at the other countries Mr. Weyland's doctrine on population is, if possible, still more completely contradicted. Where, I would ask, are the great towns and manufactories in Switzerland, Norway and Sweden, which are to act as *the graves of mankind*, and to prevent the possibility of a redundant population? In Sweden the proportion of the people living in the country is to those who live in towns as 13 to 1; in England this proportion is about 2 to 1; and yet England increases much faster than Sweden. How is this to be reconciled with the doctrine that the progress of civilization and improvement is always accompanied by a correspondent abatement in the natural tendency of population to increase? Norway, Sweden and Switzerland have not on the whole been ill governed; but where are the necessary 'anticipating alterations', which, according to Mr. Weyland, arise in every society as the powers of the soil diminish, and 'render so many persons unwilling to marry, and so many more, who do marry, incapable of reproducing their own numbers, and of replacing the deficiency in the remainder'?[12] What is it that in these countries indisposes people to marry, but the absolute hopelessness of being able to support their families? What is it that renders many more who do marry incapable of reproducing their own numbers, but the diseases generated by excessive poverty – by an insufficient supply of the necessaries of life? Can any man of reflection look at these and many of the other countries of Europe, and then venture to state that there is no moral reason for repressing the inclination to early marriages; when it cannot be denied that the alternative of not repressing it must necessarily and unavoidably be premature mortality from excessive poverty? And is it possible to know that in few or none of the countries of Europe the wages of labour, determined in the common way by the supply and the demand, can support in health large families; and yet assert that population does not press against the means of subsistence, and

---

[12] P. 124.

that 'the evils of a redundant population can never be necessarily felt by a country till it is actually peopled up to the full capacity of its resources'?[13]

Mr. Weyland really appears to have dictated his book with his eyes blindfolded and his ears stopped. I have a great respect for his character and intentions; but I must say that it has never been my fortune to meet with a theory so uniformly contradicted by experience. The very slightest glance at the different countries of Europe shows, with a force amounting to demonstration, that to all practical purposes the *natural tendency* of population to increase may be considered as a given quantity; and that the actual increase is regulated by the varying resources of each country for the employment and maintenance of labour, in whatever stage of its progress it may be, whether it is agricultural or manufacturing, whether it has few or many towns. Of course this actual increase, or the actual limits of population, must always be far short of the utmost powers of the earth to produce food; first, because we can never rationally suppose that the human skill and industry actually exerted are directed in the best *possible* manner towards the production of food; and secondly because, as I have stated more particularly in a former part of this work, the greatest production of food which the powers of the earth would admit cannot possibly take place under a system of private property. But this acknowledged truth obviously affects only the actual quantity of food and the actual number of people, and has not the most distant relation to the question respecting the *natural tendency* of population to increase beyond the powers of the earth to produce food for it.

The observations already made are sufficient to show that the four main propositions of Mr. Weyland, which depend upon the first, are quite unsupported by any appearances in the state of human society, as it is known to us in the countries with which we are acquainted. The last of these four propositions is the following: 'This tendency' (meaning the natural tendency of population to keep within the powers of the soil to afford it subsistence) 'will have its complete operation so as constantly to maintain the people in comfort and plenty in proportion as religion, morality, rational liberty and security of person and property approach the attainment of a perfect influence.'[14]

In the morality here noticed, moral or prudential restraint from marriage is not included: and so understood, I have no hesitation in saying that this proposition appears to me more directly to contradict the observed laws of nature than to assert that Norway might easily grow food for a thousand millions of inhabitants. I trust that I am disposed to attach as much importance to the effects of morality and religion on the happiness of society,

---

[13] P. 123.    [14] C. iii. p. 21.

even as Mr. Weyland; but among the moral duties I certainly include a restraint upon the inclination to an early marriage when there is no reasonable prospect of maintenance for a family; and unless this species of virtuous self-denial be included in morality, I am quite at issue with Mr. Weyland; and so distinctly deny his proposition as to say that no degree of religion and morality, no degree of rational liberty and security of person and property, can under the existing laws of nature place the lower classes of society in a state of comfort and plenty.

With regard to Mr. Weyland's fifth and last proposition;[15] I have already answered it in a note which I have added, in the present edition, to the last chapter of the third book,[16] and will only observe here that an illustration to show the precedence of population to food, which I believe was first brought forward by an anonymous writer, and appears so to have pleased Mr. Grahame as to induce him to repeat it twice, is one which I would willingly take to prove the very opposite doctrine to that which it was meant to support. The apprehension that an increasing population would starve[17] unless a previous increase of food were procured for it, has been ridiculed by comparing it with the apprehension that increasing numbers would be obliged to go naked unless a previous increase of clothes should precede their births. Now however well or ill-founded may be our apprehensions in the former case, they are certainly quite justifiable in the latter; at least society has always acted as if it thought so. In the course of the next twenty-four hours there will be about 800 children born in England and Wales; and I will venture to say that there are not ten out of the whole number, that come at the expected time, for whom clothes are not prepared before their births. It is said to be dangerous to meddle with edged tools which we do not know how to handle; and it is equally dangerous to meddle with illustrations which we do not know how to apply, and which may tend to prove exactly the reverse of what we wish.

On Mr. Weyland's theory it will not be necessary further to enlarge. With regard to the practical conclusions which he has drawn from it in our own country, they are such as might be expected from the nature of the premises. If population, instead of having a tendency to press against the means of subsistence, becomes by degrees very slow in overtaking them, Mr. Weyland's inference, that we ought to encourage the increase of the labouring

---

[15] C. iii. p. 22.

[16] P. 245, et seq.

[In 1826 (Vol. II, p. 490) this was corrected to 'Vol. iii. p. 46, et seq.' with reference to the fifth edition of 1817, although the text remained unaltered. In the present edition this note will be found on pp. 445–6 of Vol. I.]

[17] This I have never said; I have only said that their condition would be deteriorated, which is strictly true.

classes by abundant parochial assistance to families, might perhaps be maintained. But if his premises be entirely wrong, while his conclusions are still acted upon, the consequence must be that universal system of unnecessary pauperism and dependence which we now so much deplore.[18] Already above one-fourth of the population of England and Wales are regularly dependent upon parish relief;[19] and if the system which Mr. Weyland recommends, and which has been so generally adopted in the midland counties, should extend itself over the whole kingdom, there is really no saying to what height the level of pauperism may rise. While the system[20] of making an allowance from the parish for every child above two is confined to the labourers in agriculture, whom Mr. Weyland considers as the breeders of the country, it is essentially unjust, as it lowers without compensation the wages of the manufacturer and artificer: and when it shall become just by including the whole of the working classes, what a dreadful picture does it present! What a scene of equality, indolence, rags and dependence, among one-half or three-fourths of the society! Under such a system to expect any essential benefit from *saving banks* or any other institutions to promote industry and economy is perfectly preposterous. When the wages of labour are reduced to the level to which this system tends, there will be neither power nor motive to save.

Mr. Weyland strangely attributes much of the wealth and prosperity of England to the cheap population which it raises by means of the poor-laws; and seems to think that, if labour had been allowed to settle at its natural rate, and all workmen had been paid in proportion to their skill and industry, whether with or without families, we should never have attained that commercial and manufacturing ascendancy by which we have been so eminently distinguished.

A practical refutation of so ill-founded an opinion may be seen in the state of Scotland, which in proportion to its natural resources has certainly increased in agriculture, manufactures and commerce, during the last fifty years, still more rapidly than England, although it may fairly be said to have been essentially without poor-laws.

It is not easy to determine what is the price of labour most favourable to the progress of wealth. It is certainly conceivable that it may be too high for the prosperity of foreign commerce. But I believe it is much more frequently

---

[18] [In 1826 (Vol. II, p. 491) this was altered:
  ... still acted upon, the consequence must be a constantly increasing amount of unnecessary pauperism and dependence. ...

[19] [In 1826 (Vol. II, p. 491) this sentence was changed:
  Already above one-fourth of the population of England and Wales have been dependent upon parish relief; and if the system ...

[20] [In 1826 (Vol. II, p. 491) *the system* was changed to 'the practice'.

too low; and I doubt if there has ever been an instance in any country of very great prosperity in foreign commerce, where the working classes have not had good money wages. It is impossible to sell very largely without being able to buy very largely; and no country can buy very largely in which the working classes are not in such a state as to be able to purchase foreign commodities.

But nothing tends to place the lower classes of society in this state so much as a demand for labour which is allowed to take its natural course, and which therefore pays the unmarried man and the man with a family at the same rate; and consequently gives at once to a very large mass of the working classes the power of purchasing foreign articles of consumption, and of paying taxes on luxuries to no inconsiderable extent. While, on the other hand, nothing would tend so effectively to destroy the power of the working classes of society to purchase either home manufactures or foreign articles of consumption, or to pay taxes on luxuries, as the practice of doling out to each member of a family an allowance, in the shape of wages and parish relief combined, just sufficient, or only a very little more than to furnish them with the mere food necessary for their maintenance.

To show that, in looking forward to such an increased operation of prudential restraint as would greatly improve the condition of the poor, it is not necessary to suppose extravagant and impossible wages, as Mr. Weyland seems to think, I will refer to the proposition of a practical man on the subject of the price of labour; and certainly much would be done, if this proposition could be realized, though it must be effected in a very different way from that which he has proposed.

It has been recommended by Mr. Arthur Young so to adjust the wages of day-labour as to make them at all times equivalent to the purchase of a peck of wheat. This quantity, he says, was earned by country labourers during a considerable period of the last century, when the poor-rates were low, and not granted to assist in the maintenance of those who were able to work. And he goes on to observe that 'as the labourer would (in this case) receive 70 bushels of wheat for 47 weeks' labour, exclusive of five weeks for harvest; and as a family of six persons consumes in a year no more than 48 bushels; it is clear that such wages of labour would cut off every pretence of parochial assistance; and of necessity the conclusion would follow, that all right to it in men thus paid should be annihilated for ever'.[21]

An adjustment of this kind, either enforced by law, or used as a guide in the distribution of parish assistance, as suggested by Mr. Young, would be open to insuperable objections. At particular times it might be the means of

---

[21] Annals of Agriculture, No. 270, p. 91, note.

converting a dearth into a famine. And in its general operation, and supposing no change of habits among the labouring classes, it would be tantamount to saying that, under all circumstances, whether the affairs of the country were prosperous or adverse; whether its resources in land were still great, or nearly exhausted; the population ought to increase exactly at the same rate – a conclusion which involves an impossibility.

If, however, this adjustment, instead of being enforced by law, were produced by the increasing operation of the prudential check to marriage, the effect would be totally different, and in the highest degree beneficial to society. A gradual change in the habits of the labouring classes would then effect the necessary retardation in the rate of increase, and would proportion the supply of labour to the effective demand, as society continued to advance, not only without the pressure of a diminishing quantity of food, but under the enjoyment of an increased quantity of conveniences and comforts; and in the progress of cultivation and wealth the condition of the lower classes of society would be in a state of constant improvement.

A peck of wheat a day cannot be considered in any light as excessive wages. In the early periods of cultivation, indeed, when corn is low in exchangeable value, much more is frequently earned; but in such a country as England, where the price of corn, compared with manufactures and foreign commodities, is high, it would do much towards placing the great mass of the labouring classes in a state of comparative comfort and independence; and it would be extremely desirable, with a view to the virtue and happiness of human society, that no land should be taken into cultivation that could not pay the labourers employed upon it to this amount.

With these wages as the average minimum, all those who were unmarried, or, being married, had small families, would be extremely well off; while those who had large families, though they would unquestionably be subjected sometimes to a severe pressure, would in general be able, by the sacrifice of conveniences and comforts, to support themselves without parish assistance. And not only would the amount and distribution of the wages of labour greatly increase the stimulus to industry and economy throughout all the working classes of the society, and place the great body of them in a very superior situation, but it would furnish them with the means of making an effectual demand for a great amount of foreign commodities and domestic manufactures, and thus, at the same time that it would promote individual and general happiness, would advance the mercantile and manufacturing prosperity of the country.[22]

---

[22] The merchants and manufacturers who so loudly clamour for cheap corn and low money wages, think only of selling their commodities abroad, and often forget that they have to find a market for their returns at home, which they can never do to any great extent, when the

Mr. Weyland, however, finds it utterly impossible to reconcile the necessity of moral restraint either with the nature of man, or the plain dictates of religion on the subject of marriage. Whether the check to population, which he would substitute for it, is more consistent with the nature of a rational being, the precepts of revelation, and the benevolence of the Deity, must be left to the judgment of the reader. This check, it is already known, is no other than the unhealthiness and mortality of towns and manufactories.[23] And though I have never felt any difficulty in reconciling to the goodness of the Deity the necessity of practising the virtue of moral restraint in a state allowed to be a state of discipline and trial; yet I confess that I could make no attempt to reason on the subject, if I were obliged to believe, with Mr. Weyland, that a large proportion of the human race was doomed by the inscrutable ordinations of Providence to a premature death in large towns.

If indeed such peculiar unhealthiness and mortality were the proper and natural check to the progress of population in the advanced stages of society, we should justly have reason to apprehend that, by improving the healthiness of our towns and manufactories, as we have done in England during the last twenty years, we might really defeat the designs of Providence. And though I have too much respect for Mr. Weyland to suppose that he would deprecate all attempts to diminish the mortality of towns, and render manufactories less destructive to the health of the children employed in them; yet certainly his principles lead to this conclusion, since his theory has been completely destroyed by those laudable efforts which have made the mortality of England – a country abounding in towns and manufactories, less than the mortality of Sweden – a country in a state almost purely agricultural.

It was my object in the two chapters on *Moral Restraint*, and its *Effects on Society*, to show that the evils arising from the principle of population were exactly of the same nature as the evils arising from the excessive or irregular gratification of the human passions in general; and that from the existence of these evils we had no more reason to conclude that the principle of increase was too strong for the purpose intended by the Creator, than to infer, from the existence of the vices arising from the human passions, that these passions required diminution or extinction, instead of regulation and direction.

---

money wages of the working classes, and monied incomes in general, are low. (a) ●One of the principal causes of this check which foreign commerce has experienced during the last two or three years, has been the great diminution of the home market for foreign produce. ●(a)

(a) [In 1826 (Vol. II, p. 494) this sentence was omitted.]

23 With regard to the indisposition to marriage in towns, I do not believe that it is greater than in the country, except as far as it arises from the greater expense of maintaining a family, and the greater facility of illicit intercourse.

If this view of the subject be allowed to be correct, it will naturally follow that, notwithstanding the acknowledged evils occasioned by the principle of population, the advantages derived from it under the present constitution of things may very greatly overbalance them.

A slight sketch of the nature of these advantages, as far as the main object of the Essay would allow, was given in the two chapters to which I have alluded; but the subject has lately been pursued with considerable ability in the Work of Mr. Sumner on the Records of the Creation; and I am happy to refer to it as containing a masterly development and completion of views of which only an intimation could be given in the Essay.

I fully agree with Mr. Sumner as to the beneficial effects which result from the principle of population, and feel entirely convinced that the natural tendency of the human race, to increase faster than the possible increase of the means of subsistence, could not be either destroyed, or essentially diminished, without diminishing that hope of rising and fear of falling in society, so necessary to the improvement of the human faculties and the advancement of human happiness. But with this conviction on my mind, I feel no wish to alter the view which I have given of the evils arising from the principle of population. These evils do not lose their name or nature because they are overbalanced by good: and to consider them in a different light on this account, and cease to call them evils, would be as irrational as the objecting to call the irregular indulgences of passion vicious, and to affirm that they lead to misery, because our passions are the main sources of human virtue and happiness.

I have always considered the principle of population as a law peculiarly suited to a state of discipline and trial. Indeed I believe that, in the whole range of the laws of nature with which we are acquainted, not one can be pointed out which in so remarkable a manner tends to strengthen and confirm this scriptural view of the state of man on earth. And as each individual has the power of avoiding the evil consequences to himself and society resulting from the principle of population by the practice of a virtue clearly dictated to him by the light of nature, and sanctioned by revealed religion, it must be allowed that the ways of God to man with regard to this great law of nature are completely vindicated.

I have, therefore, certainly felt surprise as well as regret that no inconsiderable part of the objections which have been made to the principles and conclusions of the Essay on Population has come from persons for whose moral and religious character I have so high a respect, that it would have been particularly gratifying to me to obtain their approbation and sanction. This effect has been attributed to some expressions used in the course of the work which have been thought too harsh, and not sufficiently indulgent to the weaknesses of human nature and the feelings of Christian charity.

## Appendix, 1817

It is probable that, having found the bow bent too much one way, I was induced to bend it too much the other, in order to make it straight. But I shall always be quite ready to blot out any part of the work which is considered by a competent tribunal as having a tendency to prevent the bow from becoming finally straight, and to impede the progress of truth. In deference to this tribunal I have already expunged the passages which have been most objected to, and I have made some few further corrections of the same kind in the present edition. By these alterations I hope and believe that the work has been improved without impairing its principles. But I still trust that whether it is read with or without these alterations, every reader of candour must acknowledge that the practical design uppermost in the mind of the writer, with whatever want of judgment it may have been executed, is to improve the condition and increase the happiness of the lower classes of society.

# NOTE, 1825

Since the last edition of this work was published an answer from Mr. Godwin has appeared, but the character of it both as to matter and manner is such that I am quite sure every candid and competent inquirer after truth will agree with me in thinking that it does not require a reply. To return abusive declamation in kind would be as unedifying to the reader as it would be disagreeable to me, and to argue seriously with one who denies the most glaring and best attested facts respecting the progress of America, Ireland, England, and other states,[1] and brings forward Sweden, one of the most barren and worst supplied countries of Europe, as a specimen of what would be the natural increase of population under the greatest abundance of food, would evidently be quite vain with regard to the writer himself, and must be totally uncalled for by any of his readers whose authority could avail in the establishment of truth.

---

[1] See article *Population* in the Supplement to the 'Encyclopædia Britannica'.
[This anonymous article was written by Malthus himself.]

# ALPHABETICAL LIST OF AUTHORITIES QUOTED OR CITED BY MALTHUS IN HIS *ESSAY ON THE PRINCIPLE OF POPULATION*

This list is arranged according to the names of the people responsible for the works to which Malthus refers, whether or not their authorship was known to him, with the following 12 exceptions:

1   *Analyse des Procès-Verbaux des Conseils Généraux de Département.*
2   *Asiatic Researches.*
3   *Book of Common Prayer* (1662).
4   *Bullion Report.*
5   Bureau des Longitudes.
6   Comité de Mendicité.
7   Corn Laws.
8   *Lettres Édifiantes et Curieuses.*
9   *Revue Encyclopédique.*
10   *Richesse de la Hollande*, which is attributed by respectable books of reference to three different authors.
11   *Statistique Générale et Particulière de la France.*
12   *The Tatlers.*

Apart from these works, the names of authors not given by Malthus are entered in the relevant footnotes. For those who may not be reading the *Essay* straight through in this edition, Malthus's own references have also been entered alphabetically in the list: thus, 'BIBLIOTHÈQUE BRITANNIQUE, *see under* Barton, William'.

To avoid tedious repetition, the editor only mentions in these notes such quotations in Malthus's *Essay* as seem to require amplification or comment. Those seeking all Malthus's references to a particular author may find them in the index.

Assistance with individual references is acknowledged in the relevant notes, but the editor's gratitude to all the librarians who have helped in this work is, as always, far beyond the customary formal expressions of it. Special thanks are due to the staff of the Bodleian Library; the British Library; the Cambridge University Library; the Chipping Norton Branch of the Oxfordshire County Libraries; the Goldsmiths' Library of the University of London; Lady Margaret Hall, Oxford; the London Library, and the Malthus Library at Jesus College, Cambridge.

ABUL GHAZI, is Malthus's version of this author's name, catalogued in the British Library as Husain (Abu al-Ghazi) Baikara, Sultan of Khorasan, who lived from 1605 to 1663.

It seems likely that Malthus made careful notes from borrowed books (his page references are all correct) without copying the separate titles of the two volumes. The work was *A General History of the Turks, Moguls, and Tartars, vulgarly called Tartars, together with a Description of the Countries they inhabit,* 2 vols. octavo, London 1730. The first volume was entitled *The Genealogical History of the Tartars, translated from the Tartar Manuscript written in the Mogul Language by Abu'l Ghâzi Bahâder, Khan of Khowârazm.*

Vol. II was basically the work of the anonymous French translator of Vol. I; the English 'Editor' made 'several Improvements and Additions', and entitled the second volume: *An Account of the Present State of the Northern Asia Relating to the Natural History of Grand Tartary and Siberia: and the Manners, Customs, Trade, Laws, Religion and Polity of the different People inhabiting the same, together with Some Observations concerning China, India, Persia, Arabia, Turky [sic.] and Great Russia, The Whole compiled out of the Notes belonging to the foregoing History, and digested into Method by the Translator.*

Malthus's quotation from Vol. II, p. 390 (Bk I, ch. vii, n. 7) should perhaps be given in its context: 'It may be said in general of all the *Mohammedan Tartars*, that they live purely by robbing and preying on their Neighbours, as well in Peace as in War, wherein they differ much from the Callmaks and Mungals; who, though *Pagans*, live quietly on the Produce of their Flocks, and do no harm to any one except they first do harm to them.'

AESOP (*c*.600–560 B.C.), was said to have been born in Phrygia, today part of the north-west of Turkey. He became a slave in a number of Athenian households, and delighted his employers' families with his moral fables about animals, such as 'The Dog in the Manger', 'The Fox and the Sour Grapes', and so on. It is now known that many of the stories attributed to Aesop were current in Egypt several centuries earlier, but 'Aesop's Fables', as such, were absorbed into the proverbial and literary heritage of European children. Socrates, awaiting his death in prison in 399 B.C., amused himself by putting some of these fables into verse.

Aesop's fables were among the very first books to be printed in German and Italian towards the end of the fifteenth century, were 'compylit in Scottis meter' by Robert Henryson (*c*.1430–*c*.1506) and used extensively for Latin exercises: the philosopher John Locke (1632–1704) arranged an interlinear translation. Within living memory Aesop's fables were regarded as an aid to proficiency in the French language, through the rhyming verses of Jean de la Fontaine (1621–1695) and Malthus himself might well have been made to learn some of them by heart.

The fable to which Malthus alludes in Bk IV, ch. iii, n. 13, is that of 'The Race between the Hare and the Tortoise'. The hare was so sure of winning that, while the tortoise plodded along the course, he ostentatiously lay down for a nap; he awoke too late to overtake the tortoise as it trudged past the winning-post.

AGRICULTURE, ANNALS OF, *see under* Gourlay, Robert, and Young, Arthur.

AGRICULTURE, BOARD OF, *see under* Mann, Theodore Augustus.

AIKIN, JOHN, M.D. (1747–1822), personally known to Malthus, belonged to a prominent Unitarian family. His father was John Aikin, D.D., Principal of the Dissenting Academy at Warrington; his sister Anna Letitia Barbauld and his daughter Lucy (who continued the friendship with Malthus) were both respected writers in their day; his sons Arthur and Charles were educational pioneers, especially in popularising the study of geology and chemistry.

Malthus's quotation is from *A Description of the Country from thirty to forty Miles round Manchester*, 'The Materials arranged and the Work composed by J. Aikin MD'. It was a quarto of 624 pages, with 73 engravings, published in London in 1795; the subscribers included William Bray, the father-in-law of Malthus's youngest sister. The long passage quoted by Malthus is part of the 'description' of the parish of Eccles.

ANALYSE DES PROCÈS-VERBAUX DES CONSEILS GÉNÉRAUX DE DEPARTEMENT (Analysis of the written reports of the General Councils of the Departments). This volume of over 800 quarto pages does, as Malthus says, give a detailed account of France in the year VIII – 22 September 1799 to 21 September 1800. Some of the Prefects who reported were patently trying to curry favour with the new government, but most of their 'Observations or specific requests' were pitifully candid: they illustrate the effects not only of ten years of war and civil war, but also the outcome of drastic revolution. What strikes the modern reader is not only the decay of roads and bridges, the dilapidation of prisons and hospitals, but also the bewilderment of ordinary people who could not accept the Republican Calendar and the abolition of Sunday. Students today might be more impressed than Malthus was by the 25 Departments appealing desperately for higher rewards for the destruction of wolves, and no less than 75 emphasised the urgent need for more stud-farms for the breeding of horses.

The book gives the findings of what is called the Session of the year IX, published in the year X in Paris at the Printing Press of the Republic. There had been a sketchy volume the previous year, but no more such reports were produced. The massive *Analysis* was presented formally to the 'Citizen Consuls' – of whom Napoleon was the First of the Three – by Chaptal, the Minister of the Interior; it is quite possible that Malthus had met him in Paris when he was there in 1802 with his family party. Jean-Antoine-Claude Chaptal (1756–1832) was a great practical chemist with a flair for administration; George Washington had tried to entice him to the United States, but he refused to leave his own country, even during the Terror. He became Minister of the Interior at the beginning of 1801 and, following this survey, did much to set France on her feet again.

Malthus was assuredly right in assuming that Chaptal's volume was not intended for general circulation. The copy sent for the editor's use to the library at Chipping Norton had all its pages uncut, and the writer on Chaptal in the *Dictionnaire Biographique Française* had obviously never seen one.

Article 1, on Population, is the first section of Chapter VII, which is headed simply 'Administration', and covers a variety of topics (in 29 Articles) ranging from postal services and boundary disputes to religious freedom. With regard to population, Malthus has taken his figures from p. 807 of the 'Récapitulation Générale'. On pp. 832–3 of the 'Table générale par ordre des Matières', which is arranged in subjects like an index, the figures are as follows:

| | |
|---|---|
| Increasing population ... | 17 Departments |
| Decreasing population ... | 44 Departments |
| Stationary population ... | 14 Departments |
| Total | 75 |

In fact, 78 Departments reported on 'Population' (pp. 650–64) but the three omitted from the 'General Table of Subjects' were too vague to be categorised. Malthus's reference to the 'general prosperity diffused among the people' is from the report of the Department of Ariège in the foothills of the Pyrenees; this report also attributes population growth to the good morals of the mountain people and the healthy air they breathed.

Chapter II of the *Analysis* is devoted to Agriculture (Chapter I is concerned with taxation) and here again Malthus obtains his figures from the 'General Recapitulation'. As before, this differs from the subject index, which in turn differs from the actual reports, but the variations are slight. Where Malthus does not perhaps give a true picture is over the clearances – *les défrichements:* there is universal condemnation of the clearance of forests, not only because they led to a long-term dearth of wood, but also because of the damage done through soil erosion on hillsides. Article II on clearance and drainage overlaps with Article XIV on forests, and also with Article IX of Chapter VII on common pastures; here again there is almost unanimous indignation that this rough grazing land should be turned over to cultivation.

Malthus's quotations from three separate departmental reports may be amplified. He abbreviated the statement of the Department of Aude; the complete sentence might be translated: 'The great extent of the waste land brought under cultivation has not increased the yield of our harvests; for the most part the soil is poor and infertile, and the additional labour needed to work it is beyond the capacity of the number of hands which can be employed in agriculture; thus it follows that the total labour force on the land has become less productive.' The Council of Seine-Inférieure who decided that it was more profitable to cultivate less, and cultivate well, was referring specifically to the clearing of woodland. With regard to the sharing out of common land in the Vosges, the Prefect reported that public opinion was equally divided between those who approved and those who disliked the policy: then follows the sentence which Malthus quotes.

It is perhaps worth remarking that the Protestant Malthus was concerned chiefly with the lack of money for the 'hospitals and charitable establishments'. Many General Councils were more concerned with the lack of staff, and there are constant appeals to 'Recall the Sisters of Charity'. Chaptal followed this advice, and also set up the first national college for the training of midwives. On the whole, Malthus would have approved of Chaptal's point of view: on pp. vii–viii of his introduction he advocated private benevolence rather than recourse to public authority; it was the government's duty to maintain law and order, but the disposal of an individual's capital and labour should be left to his own self-interest.

(The editor is greatly indebted for the loan of this work to the Bibliothèque Nationale in Paris, the International Lending Section of the British Library at Boston Spa, the Oxfordshire County Libraries, and their Branch Library at Chipping Norton.)

ANDERSON, JAMES, LL.D., F.R.S., etc. (1739–1808), was an extremely prolific writer on agriculture and kindred subjects. He farmed at Monkshill in Aberdeenshire, where he raised a large family, before moving to Edinburgh in 1783; in 1797 he moved again, to Isleworth, then in the country to the south-west of London. In 1777 he wrote a pamphlet called *An Inquiry into the Nature of the Corn Laws, with a View to the Corn Bill proposed for Scotland*, which anticipates the differential theory of rent later associated with Malthus and Ricardo.

The work quoted by Malthus is *A Calm Investigation of the Circumstances that have led to the present Scarcity of Grain in Britain; Suggesting the Means of alleviating the Evil, and of preventing the Recurrence of such a Calamity in future* (London, 1801). A copy of this is in the Malthus Library at Jesus College, Cambridge, inscribed 'Dr Malthus from the Author'. Anderson had presumably read and disagreed with the anonymous 1798 *Essay on Population*, for he harks back to the good old days of Sir Robert Walpole: 'A man was not then ashamed of a moderate competency, and therefore married, and lived in quiet in the bosom of a contented family. No man now could think of such a thing. Marriage must be postponed till he has obtained a *fortune*.' (p. 11, n.)' James Anderson believed that: 'The earth is an indulgent mother to all her children, ever ready to yield her stores in abundance to all those who know properly how to draw them from her' (p. 5), and that the country 'could support, without foreign aid, a population beyond anything that there is the smallest probability it can ever be made to attain . . . for no one can set bounds to the discoveries of man, nor to the capabilities of nature when assisted by art'. (pp. 35, 36).

ANDERSON, WILLIAM, was surgeon's mate on board Captain Cook's ship, the Resolution, on his second voyage of discovery, 1772–75. On Cook's third voyage, Anderson combined the study of native vocabularies with that of flora and fauna. He died of consumption on 3 August 1778; his name was given to Anderson's Island, first sighted on that day, and also to the genus *Andersonia*.

(*See also* Cook, James.)

ANNALS OF AGRICULTURE, *see under* Gourlay, Robert, and Young, Arthur.

ARISTOTLE (384–322 B.C.), Greek philosopher, a pupil of Plato (q.v.); he was the son of a physician in Macedonia, and in 335 B.C. he set up his own school near Athens. He and his followers were known as the Peripatetics, because they held their discussions walking up and down the shady paths which surrounded the Lyceum, a gymnasium outside the city. He wrote on ethics, logic, political theory and zoology, and became the tutor of Alexander the Great.

Malthus's summary of Aristotle's views is extremely fair, except that he does not quote Aristotle's dictum that no deformed child should ever be allowed to live. When parents had an excessive number of children, Aristotle preferred abortion to exposure: 'Let abortion be procured before sense and life have begun; what may or may not be lawfully done in these cases depends on the question of life and sensation.' (Jowett's translation, *Politica*, Bk VII. 16.)

*See also* Gillies, John.

ASIATIC RESEARCHES. This was the name given to the published papers of the Asiatick Society of Bengal, founded in 1784 by Warren Hastings, with Sir William Jones (q.v.) as the first President. The full title of these volumes is *Asiatick Researches and*

*Transactions of the Society instituted in Bengal for enquiring into the History and Antiquities, the Arts, Sciences, and Literature of Asia.* They were printed by the Honourable East India Company's Press in Calcutta, and sold in London by P. Elmsly.

All three of Malthus's page references to the *Asiatic Researches* are incorrect, and the editor can find no explanation of this.

The account of the Andaman Islanders (Bk I, ch. iii, n. 4) is on pp. 389–90 of Vol. IV (1795) and not p. 401 as stated by Malthus. It is in Article XXVII, by Lieut. R. H. Colebrooke, brother of H. T. Colebrooke (q.v.), who described this race of men as 'the least civilized perhaps in the world; being nearer to a state of nature than any people we read of . . . In the morning they rub their skins with mud, or wallow in it like buffaloes, to prevent the annoyance of insects.' Yet they were clever at shooting fish with their bows and arrows.

With regard to India (Bk I, ch. xi, n. 27), the page reference should be 340–2 of Vol. IV. The 'engagement' of 1789 is printed in full, and is an excellent example of how the East India Company tried to govern their subjects according to local beliefs: anyone who killed a female was 'to suffer in the *nerk*, or hell, called *Kat Shootul*, for as many years as there are hairs on that female's body', and afterwards to be born again as a leper. The author of this paper was Sir John Shore, who succeeded Jones as President in 1794. John Shore (1751–1834), later Baron Teignmouth, was one of the most noteworthy Evangelicals among the Company's Civil Servants.

The article about the Nayrs is the first in Vol. v (1798) 'by Jonathan Duncan, Esq.'. He was at that time the Governor of Bombay, a post he held for 16 years, until his death in 1811 at the age of 55. Duncan's facts are taken from a book in 'the Arabick Language', said to be by Zeirreddien Mukhdom, an Egyptian subject of the Turkish Empire, who travelled to Malabar in about 1580, with the idea of helping the natives against the Portuguese. The relevant pages are 12 and 13, although Duncan has a footnote running on to p. 14 to the effect that the Nayr women north of the Cotta river 'are said to be prohibited from having more than one male connection at a time'.

BARTON, WILLIAM, was a well-known Pennsylvania lawyer; his father, the Rev. Thomas Barton, was an episcopalian rector interested in botany and mineralogy, and his distinguished family background may be traced in the Dictionary of American Biography.

William Barton wrote a paper for the American Philosophical Society at Philadelphia, entitled *Observations on the Probabilities of the Duration of Human Life, and the Progress of Population, in the United States of America*, which was presented on 18 March 1791. In 1793 this paper was duly published in Vol. III of the *Transactions of the American Philosophical Society*, but there is no evidence that Malthus ever read it in the original.

Malthus came to Barton's work, in so far as he paid any attention to it, through the *Bibliothèque Britannique*: this might be described as a cross between a modern 'digest' and a journal which uses book reviews as spring-boards for essays very distantly related to the work cited at the head of the article. The *Bibliothèque Britannique* contained extracts from ordinary periodicals and the transactions of Societies and Academies, not only from Great Britain, but also 'd'Asie, d'Afrique et d'Amerique', all edited in Geneva by 'a society of men of letters'. It appeared quarterly.

Thus a summary of Barton's paper, with extracts, was printed in two parts in Vol. IV of the series on *Sciences et Arts*, published in 1797. These articles occupy pp. 34–58 and pp. 304–30. Under the general heading 'Arithmétique Politique' the title of Barton's paper is given in full, with the information that it is taken from the third volume of the Philadelphia *Transactions*. Yet when Malthus refers to 'the author of a valuable paper in the Bibliothèque Britannique' (Bk II, ch. iv(a), n. 12), he does not mean Barton at all; he is praising 'O', an anonymous man of letters, who wrote the note on pp. 38–9 in the first person, having the figures for Geneva beside him, 'sous la main'. The same applies to the reference in Bk II, ch. vii, n. 11; pp. 327–30 in the *Bibliothèque Britannique* consist solely of an Appendix by 'O' giving statistics for Geneva. In fact, throughout both articles, O's principal concern is to publish his own views on the population of Switzerland.

(The editor is grateful for help with this note from the American Philosophical Society in Philadelphia and the Schweizerische Landesbibliothek in Berne.)

BENNELONG, *see under* Collins, David.

BERKELEY, GEORGE (1685–1753), was one of the greatest of British philosophers. He is best known for his theory of ideas, which Dr Johnson claimed to have refuted by kicking a stone, thereby showing – he believed – that the stone was an 'object', and not an 'idea', either in his own mind or in God's. From 1734 until his death Berkeley was the Anglican Bishop of Cloyne, and took a great interest in the unhappy state of Ireland.

Malthus's allusion in Bk III, ch. C, is to *The Querist*, a series of questions (with no answers) which was published in parts in 1735, 1736 and 1737, and which Berkeley rearranged, with alterations, in 1750. Two examples will illustrate the tone of the work:

Q. 19. Whether the bulk of our Irish natives are not kept from thriving, by that Cynical content in dirt and beggary, which they possess to a degree beyond any other people in Christendom?

Q. 20. Whether the creating of wants be not the likeliest way to produce industry in a people? and whether, if our peasants were accustomed to eat beef and wear shoes, they would not be more industrious?

Malthus's reference is to

Q. 134. Whether, if there was a wall of brass a thousand cubits high, round this kingdom, our natives might not, nevertheless, live cleanly and comfortably, till the land, and reap the fruits of it?

This was followed by

Q. 135. What should hinder us from exerting ourselves, using our hands and brains, doing something or other, man, woman and child, like the other inhabitants of God's earth?

Berkeley's last query was no. 595: 'Whose fault is it if poor Ireland still continueth poor?'

BERNARD, SIR THOMAS (1750–1818), spent his boyhood in North America, where his father was a colonial Governor, first of New Jersey, and then of Massachusetts Bay. In 1780 Thomas was called to the English Bar, but retired from practice after marrying an heiress. Having no children, he devoted all his resources to various works of philanthropy, and in 1796 founded the Society for Bettering the Condition and Increasing the Comforts of the Poor; his most famous colleague was William Wilberforce. The President was Shute Barrington, Bishop of Durham, and what

Malthus calls Bernard's 'able prefaces' to the Society's Reports (Bk IV, ch. xiii, nn. 4, 5) were in fact Introductory Letters to the Lord Bishop of Durham.

Malthus's quotation (Bk IV, ch. viii, n. 1) from Vol. III of the *Reports*, published in 1802, is taken from the following passage on pp. 20–1: 'Twenty shillings in the pound may be levied throughout the Kingdom (and more than that is now raised in some manufacturing parishes), without the object being attained, of providing a comfortless and hopeless maintenance for a forlorn and depressed body of poor. The national debt, with all its magnitude of terror, is of little moment, when compared with the increase of the poor rates. In that instance, what is received from one subject, is paid, in a greater part, to another; so that it amounts to little more than a rent-charge, from one class of individuals to another. But the poor's rate is the barometer, which marks, *in all the apparent sun-shine of prosperity*, the progress of internal weakness and debility; ... as our commerce encircles the terraqueous globe, it [the poor's rate] increases with a fecundity most astonishing; it grows with our growth and augments with our strength; its root, according to our present system, being laid in the *vital source* of our existence and prosperity.'

BERNE, Mémoires de la Société economique de, *see under* Muret, Jean-Louis.

'BESCHREIBUNG VON BERN', *see under* Heinzmann, Johann Georg.

BIBLIOTHÈQUE BRITANNIQUE, *see under* Barton, William.

BIRKBECK, MORRIS (1764–1825), came of Quaker stock from Westmorland, where successful dealing in wool enabled the family to make loans to their neighbours, and so gradually to emerge as general merchants and bankers. Morris's father bought 1600 acres at Wanborough, in Surrey, where he himself farmed until he emigrated to America in 1817; he held 'advanced' views, and was drowned while swimming his horse across the river Wabash in Illinois, on his way home from a visit to Robert Owen (q.v.) at New Harmony.

Malthus's reference (Bk II, ch. ix, n. 8) with his characteristic mis-spelling of the author's name, is to Birkbeck's *Notes on a Journey through France from Dieppe through Paris and Lyons, to the Pyrenees, and back through Toulouse, in July, August and September 1814, describing the Habits of the People and the Agriculture of the Country.* (3rd edn, with Appendix, London 1815.) Birkbeck was predisposed to find things in republican France not only better than they had been before the revolution, but also better than they were in monarchical England: 'The labouring class here is certainly much higher on the social scale than with us. Every opportunity of collecting information on this subject confirms my first impression, that there are few really poor people in France. In England, a poor man and a labourer are synonymous terms: we speak familiarly of *the poor*, meaning the labouring class: not so here.' (p. 22.)

With regard to actual wages, Malthus's reference to Birkbeck's p. 13, about a farm near Rouen, is echoed on p. 53 when he is at Montpellier: 'The general wages of labourers in husbandry 20d per day, which is equal to 3s 4d with us, as every article of expenditure is somewhat below half the price.'

BOARD OF AGRICULTURE, *see under* Mann, Theodore Augustus.

BOOK OF COMMON PRAYER, the Prayer Book of the Church of England, was first issued in 1662, after 'the late unhappy confusions' of the Civil War and Cromwell's Protectorate, and then the 'happy restoration' of Charles II in 1660. Malthus would have taken this book completely for granted; there was a furore when an attempt was made to revise it in 1928; it is still beloved of elderly Anglicans, although now largely superseded by modern versions.

1. *Banns* is the word still in use for the notification of an Anglican marriage; according to the rubric of 1662, they must be read in the parish churches of both parties (if they do not live in the same parish) 'on three several Sundays' in the course of Morning or Evening Service, immediately after the Second Lesson. The announcement was followed by the words: 'If any of you know cause, or just impediment, why these two persons should not be joined together in holy matrimony, ye are to declare it.'

2. In Bk IV, ch. viii, n. 23, Malthus is thinking of the second of the Ten Commandments in the words he would have learned by heart as a child, in the Anglican Catechism:

Thou shalt not make to thyself any graven image, nor the likeness of any thing that is in heaven above, or in the earth beneath, or in the water under the earth. Thou shalt not bow down to them, nor worship them. For I the Lord thy God am a jealous God, and visit the sins of the fathers upon the children unto the third and fourth generation of them that hate me, and shew mercy unto thousands in them that love me and keep my commandments.

This sentiment is expressed four times in the Old Testament; in Malthus's Bible, that authorised by James II in 1611, the word used in each instance is *iniquity*; the divines who compiled the Prayer Book Catechism presumably thought that *sins* was an easier word for children, and thus Malthus (and countless other Anglicans) have remembered what is, strictly speaking, a mis-quotation.

BOUGAINVILLE, LOUIS-ANTOINE DE (1729–1811), was an able soldier; after a brief period at the French Embassy in London, he went to North America as A.D.C. to Montcalm. Wolfe's victory in Canada and Clive's in India inspired the French to look elsewhere for colonies; Bougainville actually took possession of the Malvinas, now the Falkland Islands. They were ceded to Spain for a handsome indemnity, which provided the money for Bougainville's voyage around the world.

It is perhaps surprising that Malthus only makes one passing reference to Bougainville, in Bk I, ch. v, n. 25. Bougainville's account of his *Voyage autour du Monde, par la Frégate du Roi La Boudeuse, et la Flute l'Etoile; en 1766, 1767, 1768 & 1769*, was published in Paris, in one quarto volume, in 1771; there is a copy in the Malthus Library at Jesus College, Cambridge.

Since Bougainville was an active supporter of the independence of the United States, was imprisoned during the Terror, released on the fall of Robespierre, and honoured by Napoleon, Malthus would have known his name from boyhood and read of him in contemporary newspapers. The genus *Bougainvillaea* is called after him.

BRIDGE, THE REV. BEWICK, B.D., F.R.S. (1767–1833), the author of a number of text-books, was a colleague of Malthus at the East India College, being a Professor of

Mathematics and Natural Philosophy from 1805 to 1816, when he retired for the sake of his health, and became vicar of Cherry Hinton, near Cambridge.

Malthus's reference to Bridge's *Elements of Algebra* (Bk II, ch. xi, n. 7) is probably to the first edition of 1810, of which it has been impossible to find a copy: this is often the case with early works expressly published 'For Schools and Young Persons'. In the fifth edition (London 1821) this formula, rather differently set out, is given on pp. 219–20, followed by $4\frac{1}{2}$ pages of examples and questions.

'Example 1' is identical to Question 16 of an examination paper set by Bridge for his pupils at the East India College in 1808: 'Suppose the population of Great Britain in the year 1800 to have been ten millions; that $\frac{1}{40}$th part *die* annually; that the births are to the deaths as 40:30; and that no emigration takes place during the present century; what will be the state of its population in the year 1900?'

The answer given in the book, but not of course on the examination paper, is 22 930 000.

BROUGHAM, HENRY (1778–1868), later Lord Brougham and Vaux, was a Scots Whig lawyer of the *Edinburgh Review* circle; he came to London in 1805, and was on friendly terms with Malthus. In 1810 Brougham became a member of parliament, and eventually a somewhat flamboyant Lord Chancellor in 1830. His legal and political career was probably not as important as his far less publicised work for education.

At this period England had but two universities, whereas Scotland had four. It was a letter to *The Times* from another Scot, the poet Thomas Campbell (1777–1844) – who also knew Malthus – that gave the final successful impetus to the establishment of a university in London, secular and non-resident, a complete break with the 'monastic' traditions of Oxford and Cambridge. Under the chairmanship of Brougham, University College was launched on a joint-stock basis in 1826, and the first lectures were given in 1828. From the beginning, emphasis was laid on the teaching of particular subjects, as distinct from the time-honoured practice of expounding the works of such writers as Aristotle, Euclid, or Newton. Brougham followed Scottish and continental models, especially those of Germany, stressing scientific research and the advancement of learning, as well as the professors' duty of passing on to their students the inheritance of accepted knowledge.

King's College, London, was founded by Anglicans in 1831, with Malthus's lifelong friend, the Rev. William Otter (1768–1840) as the first Principal. In 1836 the two colleges were federated, and empowered to confer degrees in arts, law and medicine.

What Malthus calls 'the Mechanics Institution' (Bk IV, ch. ix, n. 10) was in fact the London Mechanics' Institution, which Brougham helped to establish in 1823. George Birkbeck, M.D. (1776–1841) was the first President; as a very young man, he had founded a similar institution in Glasgow, where he was concerned to find that intelligent artisans had no idea of the scientific principles which lay behind their work.

In the year 1825, Brougham's *Practical Observations upon the Education of the People* went into no less than 20 editions, and there were over a hundred mechanics' institutes by the end of 1826. The movement was then hit by the current financial and industrial crisis, but revived later. Also in 1825, Brougham founded the Society for the Diffusion of Useful Knowledge, for the publication of cheap and informative works; in addition to this, the Society provided a central forum for the Mechanics' Institutes, with facilities for the bulk purchase of apparatus and the exchange of books. *A Manual for Mechanics' Institutions* published by the Society in London in 1839 gives 'Outlines of Lectures' in four subjects:

1. Politics and Political Economy.
2. Mechanics.
3. Hydrostatics.
4. Optics.

BRUCE, JAMES (1730–1794), of Kinnaird, but educated at Harrow, the son of a wine merchant; after a restless, wandering youth he became British Consul at Algiers in 1763. Like many others, he was obsessed with the idea of tracing the Nile to its source, and he did indeed 'find' where the Blue Nile began. In 1790, from his retirement in Scotland, he published in Edinburgh in five huge quarto volumes his *Travels to Discover the Source of the Nile in the Years 1768, 1769, 1770, 1771, 1772 and 1773*.

Malthus obviously shared in the general scepticism which greeted this work, and might perhaps have ignored it, had he not received a letter from his friend E. D. Clarke, from Aboukir Bay, dated 9 September 1801. Clarke wrote: 'You are to give full credit to Bruce', and listed a number of people who had confirmed this traveller's accounts of the Christian Ethiopians' astonishing habits.

Malthus's reference in Bk I, ch. iv, n. 5, to p. 559 of Bruce's second volume, should perhaps be amplified: Bruce does indeed describe the Shangalla as people who 'live sparingly under a blazing sun', but he attributes their lack of passion to their lack of clothes: 'No one can doubt, but that the constant habit of seeing people of all ages naked at all times, in the ordinary transactions and necessities of life, must greatly check unchaste propensities.' (p. 558.)

With regard to Bruce's attitude towards the proportion of male and female births, and therefore towards polygamy, Malthus is not quite fair (Bk I, ch. viii, *passim*). In his first volume, pp. 280–8, Bruce maintains that the birth of more males than females 'to make up for the havock occasioned by war, murder, drunkenness, and all species of violence to which women are not subject', is a baseless supposition, and concludes: 'The reasons, then, against polygamy, which subsist in England, do not by any means subsist in Arabia; and that being the case, it would be unworthy of the wisdom of God, and an unevenness in his ways, which we shall never see, to subject two nations, under such different circumstances, absolutely to the same observances.'

BUFFON, GEORGES-LOUIS LECLERC, COMTE DE (1707–1788), from a highly cultivated Burgundian family. In the course of his youthful travels he was noteworthy for studying in Rome not antiquities but insects. In 1740 he became *Intendant du Jardin du Roi*, which meant that he could spend four months of the year in Paris and eight working in the seclusion of his native Montbard.

In 1749 Buffon published the first three volumes of his great *Histoire Naturelle, Théorie de la Terre et l'Histoire de l'Homme*. In 1751 the theologians of the

Sorbonne denounced him as a heretic, for stating that the earth was created 60 000 years ago; Buffon's manuscripts show that he believed the earth to be almost three million years old.

Buffon, with the help of collaborators, went on to complete 31 volumes in all, with lengthy *Histories* of Quadrupeds, Birds, and Minerals; he dealt with such problems as the unity of the human race and the mutability of species, as well as with practical advice on animal husbandry. He had to rely on other travellers for information about distant peoples, and he apparently believed that the inhabitants of Formosa had tails likes foxes. The *Natural History of Man* was divided into four sections: Infancy, Puberty, Manhood, and Old Age and Death, and it is in this last that he has the table to which Malthus refers in the quarto (Bk II, ch. iv(a), n. 10 and ch. viii, n. 25).

William Smellie (1740–1795) the Scottish printer, naturalist and antiquary, published an edited and abbreviated English translation of the *Natural History*, with Buffon's 'approbation and encouragement'. It first appeared, in Edinburgh, in 1781, in nine octavo volumes; the third edition was published in 1791. Smellie's version of the passage quoted by Malthus in Bk I, ch. viii, n. 6, is as follows:

Though the Guiney Negroes enjoy good health and have vigorous constitutions, they seldom reach old age. A Negroe of 50 years is a very old man. Their premature commerce with the women is, perhaps, the cause of the brevity of their lives. Their children, when very young, are allowed to commit every species of debauchery; and nothing is so rare among these people as to find a girl who can remember the time when she ceased to be a virgin.

BULLION REPORT (1810). Malthus's references to the Appendix to the Bullion Report (Bk II, ch. E, nn. 6 and 7) were omitted from the Everyman Edition of the *Essay*; they are both correct.

In two articles in the *Edinburgh Review*, in 1811, Malthus himself had taken part in the general debate on the depreciation of the paper currency since 1797. In that year there was a rush for gold, following an unfounded rumour of a French invasion, and the Bank of England had been released from its legal obligation to honour all its notes in specie on demand. A Select Committee of the House of Commons, under the chairmanship of Francis Horner – a close friend of Malthus – was set up on 19 February 1810 to enquire into the high price of gold bullion; its Report, together with Minutes of Evidence and Accounts, were ordered to be printed on 8 June. (Parliamentary Papers, Session 23 January–21 June 1810, Vol. III.)

The Report itself runs from pp. 1–33, the Minutes of Evidence from pp. 35–151, and the Appendix of Accounts from pp. 153–232. Why Spanish corn prices figure in such a report is obvious if one studies the tables immediately before and after those quoted by Malthus. Tables 23–8 are concerned with Mexico, Chile and Peru, the imports of gold and silver into Spain, and the total amount of these metals extracted from Spanish and Portuguese America; tables 29–32 concern the prices of wheat and barley in five Spanish districts, from 1675 to 1804; table 33 gives an 'Estimate of the Quantities of Gold and Silver, added annually to the Commerce of Europe, from 1790 to 1802'.

Malthus takes only the more spectacular variations in the price of wheat to illustrate his point, and ignores barley, which in general was worth about half the price of wheat.

A note on p. 183 of the Appendix to the Bullion Report states that 'The *fanega* used in this and the following accounts is that of Castille, and 100 fanegas Castellanes make 152 English bushels.' The English bushel (which was not standardised until 1792) is a measure of capacity, not weight, and is equal to 4 pecks, 8 gallons, or 36.368 litres.

This note further explains that 'the *real vellon* is a money of account, and one is equal to $\frac{1}{20}$th of a dollar'. It is important to remember in this connection that the United States dollar did not come into use until 1794, and that it was based on the Spanish dollar, the most familiar coin in North as well as South America.

BUREAU DES LONGITUDES. This *Annuaire* is still published. The Bureau was set up in 1795, by the National Convention, to provide basic astronomical information, tide-tables and so on, of the kind found in almanacs, for the whole of the French Republic. But since many astronomers were also interested in demography, like Halley in England, Nicander in Sweden (q.v.) and Quetelet in Belgium – the last two personally known to Malthus – it did not seem strange at the time that those responsible for calculating the phases of the moon for each year's calendar should also be responsible for tabulating population statistics, and publishing the mathematical conclusions they drew from the data available.

There is extant a letter from Malthus to a book-seller, dated 18 January 1825, in which he asks among other things for 'the last *Annuaire* par Le Bureau des Longitudes, a small 18°. My last is for 1823. The one for 1824 is probably come out.'

(The editor is indebted for a photocopy from a recent *Annuaire* to the Librarian of the Institut Français du Royaume-Uni in London.)

'BURKE'S AMERICA' was published anonymously in 1757, and went into a number of editions; Malthus's page references fit the third, 'with improvements', published in London in two volumes in 1760. The work is usually attributed to William Burke (d.1798), an unpopular Whig politician, but is assumed to have been written in collaboration with his famous cousin Edmund (1729–1797), the statesman and orator.

The book, entitled *An Account of the European Settlements in America*, is in six parts. Vol. I contains the first four: A Short History of the Discovery of that Part of the World; The Manners and Customs of the original Inhabitants; Of the Spanish Settlements; Of the Portuguese. Part V deals with the French, Dutch and Danish, Part VI with the English. In the Preface the anonymous author wrote that 'The affairs of America have lately engaged a great deal of the public attention. Before the present war [that between Britain on the one hand, and France and Spain on the other, 1756–63] there were but a very few who made the history of that quarter of the world any part of their study; though the matter is certainly very curious in itself, and extremely interesting to us as a trading people.'

Malthus's reference in Bk I, ch. iv, n. 4 omits a statement that might be significant; the full text of the relevant passage on p. 187 of Vol. I is: 'Their marriages are not fruitful, seldom producing above two or three children, but they are brought forth with less pain than our women suffer upon such occasions, and with little consequent weakness. Probably the severe life that both sexes lead is not favourable to procreation.'

BÜSCHING, ANTON FRIEDRICH (1724–1793), was a Lutheran pastor and pedagogue who wrote more than a hundred works on a great variety of subjects. He was quoted by Süssmilch and William Tooke (qq.v.) because of his *Neue Erdbeschreibung* – A New Description of the World – of which the first part, dealing with Europe, appeared in 1754.

In his new 'political–statistical' geography Büsching did not neglect 'names and places' and physical features, but he also included a mass of information about manufactures and commerce, forms of government, revenue and taxation, population, men under arms, and even the number of fighting ships and field artillery which each nation was alleged to possess. Many of his figures were incorrect, and were inevitably soon out of date, but Büsching in his day was highly regarded, and much of his work was translated into French.

CAESAR, GAIUS JULIUS (*c.*100–44 B.C.), one of the world's greatest soldiers and statesmen. His account of his conquest of Gaul, written in simple Latin, was usually the first classical text to be read by British children, both before and after Malthus's time, as well as being a source-book for historians of the Roman Republic.

Malthus's reference in Bk I, ch. vi, nn. 34 and 35, is to the following passage (Bohn's translation, London 1879, pp. 151–2):

They do not pay much attention to agriculture, and a large portion of their food consists in milk, cheese, and flesh; nor has any one a fixed quantity of land or his own individual limits; but the magistrates and the leading men each year apportion to the tribes and families, who have united together, as much land as, and in the place in which, they think proper, and the year after compel them to remove elsewhere. For this enactment [*ejus rei*] they advance many reasons – lest seduced by long-continued custom, they may exchange their ardour in the waging of war for agriculture; lest they may be anxious to acquire extensive estates, and the more powerful drive the weaker from their possessions; lest they construct their houses with too great a desire to avoid cold and heat; lest the desire of wealth spring up, from which cause divisions and discords arise; and that they may keep the common people in a contented state of mind, when each sees his own means placed on an equality with those of the most powerful.

CANZLER, JOHANN GEORG (1740–1809), was secretary of the Elector of Saxony's legation in Stockholm from 1768 to 1775; on his return to Dresden he wrote his *Mémoires pour servir à la Connoissance des Affaires politiques et économiques du Royaume de Suède, jusqu'à la fin de la 1775:me année*. It is typical of the period that this work about Sweden, by a German, was written in French, and published in 1776 *à Londres et se trouve à Dresde chez George Conrad Walther*.* The book is rather small to be designated a quarto, and only the author's initials are given, J.G.C., which possibly accounts for

---

* *Notes to Assist in Understanding the Political and Economic Conditions of the Kingdom of Sweden up to the End of the Year 1775.* The work could be obtained in Dresden at Walther's bookshop.

Malthus's mis-spelling of the name; he might only have heard it by word of mouth when he was in Stockholm in 1799. Sweden is extremely important in the history of demography, as there was the equivalent of a census from 1749 onwards.

Malthus's reference (Bk II, ch. ii, n. 4) to Canzler's p. 187 is not quite accurate, as Canzler wrote that the proportion of town to country dwellers was 1:13 in 1760, with the implication that things might have changed in the past 15 years. On p. 195 he states categorically: 'On a de tout tems observé, qu'en général la *Population* d'un Pays n'est considerable, qu'*à proportion de l'Agriculture*, parceque c'est du dégré général de *Subsistance*, que dépend le nombre des habitans.'*

CATHERINE II, called the Great (1729–1796). She was born a princess of Anhalt-Zerbst, and in 1745 married Peter III of Russia, whose murder she is believed to have arranged in 1762, when she was crowned Empress. She achieved much in the extension and civilisation of her dominions, largely with the aid of immigrants from Western Europe, who were mostly of German origin. Her *Instructions Addressed to the Commission for Framing a New Code of Laws* became a popular publication, in both French and German. The editor has been unable to trace that quoted by Malthus (in the quarto only, Bk II, ch. iv(a), n. 5) but his reference may easily be found in the French version in the Bodleian Library (Amsterdam 1775) which originally belonged to the Minerva Rooms in Cork.

Section 253 of Chapter VII draws attention to the need for a greater population in Russia, of which vast stretches of land are uncultivated; section 254, which Malthus quotes, about the death-rate of the peasants' children, goes on to consider what faults of diet, way of life, or education are responsible for destroying the hope of the Empire.

CATTEAU-CALLEVILLE, JEAN-PIERRE-GUILLAUME (d.1819), came from a French protestant family; they had become refugees in Brandenburg after Louis XIV (in 1685) had revoked Henry IV's famous Edict of Nantes, which in 1598 had given protection to the Huguenots. In 1783 Jean-Pierre Catteau, as he then was, became chaplain to the French protestant community in Stockholm; after the Revolution of 1789 had granted religious freedom, he was able to settle in France and devote himself to his writing, based on his extensive travels in Scandinavia and Northern Europe.

Catteau's *Tableau des États Danois, Envisagés sous les rapports du Mécanisme Social*,** was published in Paris in 'An X – 1802' in three octavo volumes. Chapter VIII of Vol. II concerns 'Population', followed by one on 'Industrie Productive'. Catteau provides definite figures for Denmark, Norway, and the Duchies of Schleswig and Holstein, with estimates in the text for Denmark's outlying islands and colonial possessions. The listed births and deaths are on p. 95, the marriages on p. 96; the proportions may be found on p. 108.

---

* 'It has always been observed that the population of a country, in general, is great only in proportion to its agriculture, because the number of its inhabitants depends on the amount of its subsistence.'

** *Report on the Danish Dominions, considered in connection with the Structure of Society.*

Malthus took only the figures for Norway for 1795–99 inclusive, and the editor is unable to agree with his arithmetic over the births:

| | |
|---|---|
| 1795 | 27 249 |
| 1796 | 26 844 |
| 1797 | 28 154 |
| 1798 | 28 010 |
| 1799 | 28 540 |
| Total | 138 797 |

(The editor is indebted for this note to the Royal Library in Copenhagen and to the kind offices of the Press and Cultural Attaché of the Royal Danish Embassy in London.)

CHARDIN, SIR JOHN (1643–1712), was the son of a wealthy French protestant jeweller; his account of his travels and adventures in pursuit of his trade in Persia and India was praised by Montesquieu, Gibbon, and Sir William Jones (qq.v.). Owing to increased religious persecution in his own country, he settled in England in 1681, where he was knighted by Charles II and made a Fellow of the Royal Society.

The first volume of Chardin's *Journal du Voyage* appeared simultaneously in French and English in 1686, dedicated to James II, and many subsequent editions and extracts were published. Malthus's reference (Bk I, ch. vii, n. 17) is to the account of 'Sir John Chardin's Travels into Persia', published in a *Collection of Voyages* compiled by John Harris, D.D. (q.v.). In this folio, all the nouns were printed with capital letters, as in German, but Malthus in his quotation followed the practice of his own period, using capital letters for proper names only.

CHARLEVOIX, PIERRE FRANÇOIS XAVIER (1682–1761), was a Jesuit who taught at the Collège in Paris, where Voltaire was among his pupils, and became Professor of Grammar at the Collège de Quebec in 1705. In 1719 he was sent on what was virtually a project of exploration, to find a western route across America and the Pacific, to reach the Jesuit missions in South-East Asia. He wrote much, after his return to France, including an account of the establishment of Christianity in Japan.

The work cited by Malthus (Bk I, ch. iv) is Charlevoix's *Histoire Générale de la Nouvelle France, avec le Journal historique d'un Voyage dans l'Amerique Septentrionnale*, a three-volume quarto published in Paris in 1744. On pp. 303–4 of Tom. III, to which Malthus refers, Charlevoix mentions homosexuality as one of the vices which limit the growth of population. In Malthus's England *buggerie*, as it was legally designated, was a capital offence, and unmentionable in explicit terms in such a work as the *Essay on Population*. See also the final footnote to the 1806 Appendix.

'COLEBROOKE, SIR GEORGE'.

COLEBROOKE, HENRY THOMAS (1765–1837), a notable Sanskrit scholar, was in fact the son of Sir George Colebrooke, to whom Malthus wrongly attributes the anonymous *Remarks on the Present State of the Husbandry and Commerce of Bengal*, a quarto printed in Calcutta in 1795. In 1804 an amended octavo edition, equally anonymous, was also published in Calcutta, under the title *Remarks on the Husbandry and Internal*

*Commerce of Bengal.* Sir George Colebrooke, a wealthy banker, M.P. for Arundel and a Director of the East India Company, had obtained a post for his son Henry in the Company's Civil Service. Henry, however, was utterly averse to the Company's monopoly of Indian trade; he sent copies of his original *Remarks* home to his father, who showed them to Pitt and Dundas; they disapproved, and Henry was considered lucky to be allowed to remain in the Service.

Malthus's reference (Bk III, ch. E, n. 2) is to p. 103, not p. 108, of the edition of 1804. The relevant text is: 'The price of corn, which, in Bengal, fluctuates much more than in Europe, has a considerable influence on the value of most other articles, though it cannot regulate the price of all. When the demand is limited to few persons, as it is under a commercial monopoly, the purchaser is enabled to fix his own price.' Note 4 reads: 'Without famine or scarcity, we have known corn four times dearer at the first hand in one year, than in the preceding'.

Henry Thomas Colebrooke returned to England after 32 years absence in 1815, some two years before this chapter of *Population* was first published, but there is no evidence that he (or anyone else) noticed that Malthus had confused him with his father.

COLLINS, DAVID (1756–1810), was Irish-born, but educated at Exeter Grammar School, and became a captain in the Royal Marines. He went to Australia in 1787 with Governor Arthur Phillip, to found the first convict settlement, which they did at Port Jackson, now part of Sydney. In 1796 he returned to England, and published in 1798 (London, Cadell & Davies) *An Account of the English Colony in New South Wales*, by David Collins Esquire, Late Judge Advocate and Secretary of the Colony. The main account of the Aborigines is in the Appendix, published in 1802. Collins went back to Australia as Governor of Tasmania, then called Van Diemen's Land, where he founded the city of Hobart.

Malthus in Bk I, ch. iii, perhaps makes the lot of the 'hungry savage' sound worse than it was. On p. 550 Collins describes the Aborigines' tree-climbing: 'By this method they ascend very quick, always cutting [steps] with the right hand and clinging with the left, resting the whole weight of the body on the ball of either foot.' Such ingenuity, skill and speed do not suggest a very poor physical condition.

Bennilong (*c.*1764–1813) is not described as 'a native', because his name would have been familiar to English readers. Governor Phillip ordered his capture in 1789, as he wished to learn from him about the Aborigines' language and customs; he brought him to England in 1792 where, suitably attired, he was presented to George III. Collins has a delightful engraving of Bennilong in his court dress on p. 439. On his return to Australia, the poor man found he could associate happily with neither whites nor blacks, and took to drink. Even so, Bennelong (as he is spelt in the *Australian Dictionary of Biography*) has the eastern point of Sydney Cove named after him.

COLQUHOUN, PATRICK (1745–1820), a merchant in the cotton trade who, after a youthful failure in Virginia, became so successful in Glasgow that he was elected Lord Provost in 1782, and founded the Glasgow Chamber of Commerce. He moved to London in 1789, where he became well known as a magistrate and pamphleteer, advocating amongst other things a Board of Education and a national poor-rate uniformly assessed.

Colquhoun's *Treatise on the Police of the Metropolis*, first published anonymously in 1795, ran into a number of editions. 'Police' in this context means policy with regard to order and welfare: there was no police force in the modern sense, only 'watchmen', as in Shakespeare's time, controlled by innumerable petty authorities.

Malthus's references in Bk IV, ch. iv, may be supplemented by a quotation from pp. 355–6 of the *Treatise* (6th edn, London 1800, the first with the author's name): Colquhoun wrote of the children,

Familiarized in infancy to the Pawnbrokers' shop, and to other even less reputable means of obtaining temporary subsistence, they too soon become adept in falsehood and deceit. Imperious necessity has given an early spring to their ingenuity. They are generally full of resource, which good pursuits might render them good and valuable members of the Community; but unhappily their minds have acquired a wrong bias, and they are reared insensibly in the walks of vice, without knowing, in many instances, that they are at all engaged in evil pursuits.

Mr Colquhoun's 'plan', as set out on pp. 373–7, was extremely comprehensive and humane, as well as economical; it involved the registration of 'distressed individuals', and the provision of 'Work-rooms in various central and convenient situations in the Metropolis, where persons destitute of employment may receive a temporary subsistence for labour'. He believed that 'information and facts of the greatest importance, to the best interests of Society, would spring from this source'.

COMITÉ DE MENDICITÉ. This was set up by the French National Assembly in 1790, when it was believed in some circles that France would become a constitutional monarchy on the English model. The Church having been deprived of its land and wealth, there was an obvious need to find other ways of performing the traditional charitable work of the religious, and the National Assembly publicly declared that they would consider the care of the poor as one of their primary duties.

The *Comité pour l'extinction de la Mendicité* produced five reports, and Malthus's quotation is from p. 7 of the fourth (Bk IV, ch. viii, n. 2). After describing the English poor-rate, the Committee remarked: 'Mais cet example est un grand et important leçon pour nous: car, indépendamment des vices qu'elle [la taxe des pauvres] nous présente, et d'une dépense monstrueuse, et d'un encouragement necessaire à la fainéantise, elle nous découvre la plaie politique d'Angleterre la plus dévorante, qu'il est egalement dangereux pour sa tranquillité et son bonheur de détruire ou de laisser subsister.'*

Malthus may have read this for himself, but it is possible that he transcribed it from p. 438 of Vol. 1 of Arthur Young's *Travels in France*. The chairman of the Comité de Mendicité was the Duc de Liancourt, known by then as M. de la Rochefoucauld Liancourt; Arthur Young (q.v.) had met his sons when they visited England with

---

* But this example is a harsh and important lesson for us. The poor-rate, apart from its obvious defects, the enormous expense and the inevitable encouragement of idleness, exposes England's most destructive political disease; it is equally dangerous to her good order and prosperity to abolish it or to allow it to continue.

their tutor, to study agriculture and political economy, as well as the English language.

COMMONS, HOUSE OF. *See under* Bullion Report and Corn Laws.

CONDORCET, JEAN-ANTOINE-NICHOLAS CARITAT, MARQUIS DE (1743–1794), was so distinguished as a mathematician and philosopher that he became Secretary of the Académie Française at the age of 30. In 1791 he was a member of the National Assembly, also the Jacobin Club, but quarrelled with Robespierre and wrote in hiding his *Sketch for a Historical View of the Progress of the Human Mind*. He was caught and imprisoned; it is generally believed that he was allowed to commit suicide. His book was published posthumously in Paris almost at once, in 1794, followed by a second edition in 1795, the year in which Joseph Johnson brought out the first English translation. In both languages it was a best-seller in Britain, and the name at least would have been familiar to most of Malthus's readers.

Malthus's account of Condorcet's thinking in Bk III, ch. i, would not be regarded as altogether fair today. It is possible that Malthus did not fully appreciate Condorcet's reference to contraception: he argued that men's duty to potential beings was to give them happiness, not merely a brief existence, and also to consider the welfare of society and their own families, so as not to cumber the world with useless and miserable people (see pp. 188–9 of June Barraclough's translation, Weidenfeld & Nicolson, 1955).

COOK, JAMES (1728–1779), was the son of an agricultural labourer in Yorkshire. He started his career as an ordinary seaman, and initially attracted attention by his skill as a marine surveyor in the St Lawrence river, during the war against the French, in 1759. His three famous voyages need to be distinguished:

1. That made in the *Endeavour*, from 1768 to 1771, at the instance of the Royal Society, to observe the transit of the planet Venus across the sun; this was done off Tahiti (Malthus's Otaheite) on 3 June 1769, after a voyage round Cape Horn. On the return voyage, Cook charted the coast of New Zealand and all the east coast of what is now Australia (Malthus's New Holland) which Cook called New South Wales, because he thought it resembled the northern shore of the Bristol Channel. On this voyage Sir Joseph Banks named and delighted in Botany Bay. They sailed back to England by way of what is now Indonesia and the Cape of Good Hope.

This expedition, to which Malthus refers as Cook's First Voyage, is described in the second and third volumes of compilation by John Hawkesworth: *An Account of the Voyages undertaken by the Order of His Present Majesty for making Discoveries in the Southern Hemisphere by Commodore Byron, Captains Wallis, Carteret and Cook, in the Dolphin, Swallow, and Endeavour, Drawn up from the Journals which were kept by the several Commanders ...*, etc. Hawkesworth was a humble aspirant to literary honours, and died in 1773 when his three quarto volumes were published in London.

2. Cook, now promoted from Lieutenant to Commander, sailed in the *Resolution*, accompanied by the *Adventure*, for further exploration of the Pacific; this time he went eastwards round the Cape of Good Hope and skirted Antarctica, trying to find a 'great southern continent'. The voyage lasted from July 1772 to July 1775, and in the

course of it Cook again dropped anchor off New Zealand and Tahiti, as well as discovering and charting more Pacific islands.

3. As Captain Cook, he volunteered to explore the North Pacific in search of a 'passage' round the northern coast of America, again in the *Resolution*, accompanied by the *Discovery*. They left Plymouth in July 1776, rounded the Cape of Good Hope, and touched at Van Diemen's Land, now Tasmania, which was not then recognised as an island; they visited New Zealand a third time, and discovered the Sandwich Islands en route for the north-west coast of America. Driven back by ice, Cook sailed south, and was killed on 14 February 1779 in a skirmish with some natives of Hawaii. It is perhaps relevant to note that his widow outlived Malthus, dying in 1835 at the age of ninety-three.

Innumerable accounts of Cook's voyages were published, in Scotland and Ireland as well as England, some of them in parts, to be collected over many months. Malthus's copy of Hawkesworth's *Voyages* is a bibliographical mystery, no three-volume edition having been found in which Vol. III starts at p. 1, and corresponds with Malthus's pagination. For Cook's second voyage Malthus used the two-volume edition published in London in 1777, and for the third a three-volume version published in 1784.

Malthus in Bk I, ch. iii, omits the comment made on the lives of the wretched inhabitants of Tierra del Fuego on p. 59 of Vol. II of Hawkesworth's *Voyages*:

Upon the whole, these people appeared to be the most destitute and forlorn, as well as the most stupid, of all human beings . . . destitute of every convenience that is furnished by the rudest art, having no implement even to dress their food: yet they were content. They seem to have no wish for any thing more than they possessed . . . How much they may be gainers by an exemption from the care, labour, and solicitude, which arise from a perpetual and unsuccessful effort to gratify that infinite variety of desires which the refinements of artificial life have produced among us, is not very easy to determine; possibly this may counterbalance all the real disadvantages of their situation in comparison with ours, and make the scales by which good and evil are distributed to man hang even between us.

In Bk I, ch. v, n. 12, Malthus shows that the word 'clam' was not yet in polite general use in England to describe various bivalve shellfish (it is not in Dr Johnson's Dictionary) although it goes back to the sixteenth century in Scotland. Thus Malthus lists clams with yams as a 'vegetable production'. In Vol. III of Hawkesworth's *Voyages*, however (p. 441 of the 1773 quarto), Cook reports 'shell-fish in great variety, particularly clams, cockles, and oysters', and on the following page makes it clear that, apart from coconuts, the New Zealanders' only vegetable food was fern-root, yams, and potatoes.

It is possible that Malthus exaggerated the oscillations in the population of Tahiti (Bk I, ch. v, n. 39). On pp. 182–3 of Vol. I of the Second Voyage (London 1777) Cook notes that Otaheite in September 1773 was ill supplied with hogs and fowls as compared with 1767 and 1768; at the time he believed the scarcity was caused by visiting seamen carrying them off, or to wars between the two kings. When he returned in May 1774 (p. 346) he was astonished at the improved houses and canoes, after only eight months, which he attributed to the iron tools the islanders had acquired from European ships. He continued: 'The number of hogs was another thing that excited our wonder. Probably they were not so scarce, when we were here before, as we imagined, and, not chusing to part with them, they had conveyed them out of our sight.'

The same might have been true of the scarcity of women on Easter Island. Cook wrote: 'They either have but few females among them, or else many were restrained from making their appearance during our stay; for though we saw nothing to believe that the men were of a jealous disposition, or the women afraid to appear in public, something of this kind was probably the case.' (March 1774, p. 289 of Vol. I of James Cook's *A Voyage towards the South Pole and Round the World performed in His Majesty's Ships the Resolution and Adventure in the Years 1772, 1773, 1774 and 1775.*)

CORN LAWS: 1. House of Commons, July 1814. In Bk III, ch. D, n. 3 Malthus is quoting the Minutes of Evidence from the *Report of the House of Commons Select Committee on Petitions relating to the Corn Laws of this Kingdom.* These petitions, apart from actual rioting, were the only way in which ordinary people without votes could protest against high prices (or anything else) to an unreformed Parliament.

The witness quoted by Malthus was called on 5 July 1814, a Mr Peter Giles of London, who had been a corn factor between 30 and 40 years, but was 'not engaged in any pursuit of agriculture himself'. England, Spain and Portugal were the chief importers of Polish wheat; often it was sent to England first, and stored 'under bond and lock', to be re-exported to the best market.

Malthus did not copy out Mr Giles' statement quite accurately, for according to the Minutes he said: 'When the crops are unfavourable in one part of Europe, it generally happens that they are so more or less in another.'

CORN LAWS: 2. House of Lords, Report dated 25 July 1815. In Bk III, ch. E, n. 15, the Report cited is that of the Lords' Committee appointed to 'enquire into the State of the Growth, the Commerce, and the Consumption of Grain, and all Laws relating thereto'.

The Examinations of Witnesses were classified thus:
1. Comparative Quality and Value of Foreign and Homegrown Grain.
2. State of the Agriculture of the United Kingdom.
3. Connection betwixt the Price of Grain and the Wages of Labour.
4. Profits acquired by the Miller.
5. Comparative Advantage of conveying Wheat and Flour by Sea.

Malthus's reference is to the evidence of Patrick Milne, Esq., M.P., a landed proprietor in Scotland, who also had large concerns as a manufacturer in Aberdeen, in cotton and linen. The significant passage begins on p. 50:

Supposing there are in any one parish 100 labourers, who are able to do the work of that parish; if provisions rise, those labourers will do double work; of course, there being only a certain demand for labour, the [price of] labour falls: if provisions on the contrary fall, those labourers do much less work, probably not one half; you must therefore go into other parishes and seek more labourers; this makes a demand for labour, and labour rises. I have always observed that the price of labour was governed by the demand and supply, like every other commodity, and not by the price of grain; the price of grain has certainly some effect upon the price of labour, and so has the price of shoes, and the price of cloth; but it does not appear to me that the price of labour is governed entirely by it. This reasoning applies to Scotland, where in most instances we have no poors rates; in England the reasoning must be very different.

Mr Milne also remarked that often a workman 'does too much work, and works beyond his strength, when grain is very high; at other times he is idle, when grain is low'.

CREUXIUS, FRANCISCUS (1596–1666), whom Malthus cites in Bk I, ch. iv, n. 26, had not in fact observed the American Indians for himself. He was François Ducreux, a Jesuit, who compiled Greek and Latin grammars, taught rhetoric, and wrote a life of St Francis de Sales. His *Historiae Canadiensis seu Novae Franciae,** dedicated to Louis XIV, is a beautiful quarto illustrated with engravings, published in Paris in 1664. He put it together mainly from the reports of Jesuit missionaries; apart from a description of the country, the book is full of adventure stories, with a pull-out mounted on fine linen of priests and converts being horrifically martyred. Ducreux recorded that in addition to the usual heavy domestic tasks, carrying water and firewood, the Indian women also repaired the canoes.

CROME, AUGUST FRIEDRICH WILHELM (1753–1833), was the third of the 20 children of a Lutheran pastor, educated at the University of Halle, acted as a tutor in noble families, and then became Professor of Statistics and Public Finance and Administration (Kameralwissenschaft) at the University of Giessen. He was later somewhat unhappily involved in Napoleonic politics.

Crome published 30 works in all. *Ueber die Grösse und Bevölkerung der sämtlichen europaischen Staaten*** (Leipzig 1785) is correctly quoted by Malthus, and the page references are accurate. In this case, as in that of the '*Beschreibung von Bern*', (*see under* Heinzmann) it seems likely that Malthus had some help with the German text from an educated person, which he does not appear to have had with Süssmilch (q.v.).

CRUMPE, SAMUEL, M.D. (1766–1796), was an Irish physician educated in Edinburgh who lived in the city of Limerick. He published *An Inquiry into the Nature and Properties of Opium* (London 1793) which was translated into German. The work quoted by Malthus in Bk IV, ch. xi, n. 18, which won a prize medal from the Royal Irish Academy, was entitled *An Essay on the best Means of providing Employment for the People of Ireland* (Dublin 1793, 2nd edn, London 1795). This was translated into both French and German.

It is difficult to be specific about what Malthus calls Dr Crumpe's 'project', since his suggestions range from 'a proper and universal system of education' and the abolition of tithes to a tax on 'the materials of ebriety'; this should be high enough 'to render the gratification of the desire extremely difficult to the lower and laborious class'. Crumpe believed that the greatest cause of Ireland's poverty was a lack of capital to initiate improvements in agriculture and manufactures; to this end he urged a bounty on the export of corn, to encourage good farming, and the formation of societies to distribute among the poor what he designated '*small* premiums' of such things as seed, ploughs, and horse-shoes.

---

* *History of Canada or New France.*
** *On the Greatness and Population of all the Countries in Europe.*

CURRIE, JAMES, M.D. (1756–1805), was born in Scotland; after his efforts to establish himself in Virginia were terminated by the American War of Independence, he settled as a physician in Liverpool; here he became president of the Philosophical and Literary Society, of which Malthus's life-long Cambridge friend William Smyth was also a member, and he sent to Wilberforce in London first-hand information about slave-ships. His principal medical work was concerned with the cold-water treatment of fevers, and he was one of the first regular users of a clinical thermometer. Malthus visited him in Bath in 1804.

Currie only met Robert Burns once, in 1792, but undertook the editing of the poet's collected works for the benefit of his widow and children. This was first published in London in 1800, in four octavo volumes. Malthus's reference to it (Bk IV, ch. ii, nn. 5 and 7) is to Currie's 'Prefatory Remarks on the Character and Condition of the Scottish Peasantry' which preceded his memoir of Burns' life. In Appendix No. I, Note B (Vol. I, pp. 353–4) Currie wrote:

The principle of population acts in no country to the full extent of its power: marriage is every where retarded beyond the period pointed out by nature, by the difficulty of supporting a family; and this obstacle is greatest in long-settled communities. The emigration of a part of a people facilitates the marriage of the rest, by producing a relative increase in the means of subsistence ... The subject has been well investigated by Sir James Steuart [q.v.] whose principles have been expanded and farther illustrated in a late truly-philosophical *Essay on Population*.

It seems more than likely that Currie knew who had written the anonymous *Essay* of 1798.

CURWEN, JOHN CHRISTIAN, M.P. (1756–1828), of Workington Hall, Cumberland, published a hotch-potch of 364 pages entitled *Hints on the Economy of Feeding Stock and Bettering the Condition of the Poor* (London 1808). In this he gave instructions on the steaming of potatoes as a substitute for hay in the feeding of working horses, and supplying cheap milk for the poor by feeding cattle with kale, kohlrabi, swedes, turnips and cabbages; on p. 345 he made a complimentary reference to 'Mr Malthus's valuable work'.

'Mr Curwen's plan' to which Malthus refers in Bk IV, ch. xii, was outlined in two speeches in the House of Commons, on 28 May 1816 and 21 February 1817, reprinted in *The Pamphleteer*, Vols. VIII and X. Curwen described his own private scheme in the Workington and Harrington Collieries, where the men had sixpence a week compulsorily deducted from their wages to form a benefit fund; this, with contributions from the proprietors, had reached £20 000 in 30 years. His national plan was based on parochial committees, who would administer the funds contributed by 'capital and land', as well as by the labouring classes, and also by compulsory deductions from the pay of men serving in the army or navy. He thought one proper use of these funds would be the purchase of 'settlements' in other parishes, for working men who had 'emigrated' to districts where they could find better employment.

Curwen was in full agreement with Malthus about 'the degraded state of pauperism', where 'Every sense of shame is lost sight of, and with it all consideration beyond the present moment'.

DAVENANT, CHARLES (1656–1714), combined miscellaneous pamphleteering with membership of the House of Commons, and held office as Commissioner of the Excise from 1678 to 1689. He lost this post on the accession of William and Mary, but under Queen Anne he acted as secretary to the Commissioners appointed to treat for the Parliamentary Union with Scotland. He is best known as one of the pioneers of 'Political Arithmetick', the precursor of statistics and political economy.

In the paragraphs added in 1806 to chapter x of Book II, there is only a passing reference to Davenant's estimate of the number of houses in England in 1690; it is quite likely that Malthus derived the information from a secondary source. Mr John Harrison has traced the actual figure of 1 319 215 to pp. 76–7 of Davenant's *Essay upon Ways and Means of Supplying the War*, published in 1695: see the bibliography in the Pickering *Works of Malthus* (1986). In 1698 Davenant was more cautious: in his anonymous *Discourses on the Publick Revenues and the Trade of England* he merely stated that: 'There are in England about 1 300 000 houses'. (p. 177.) Presumably Davenant, unlike Malthus, thought that he had previously erred on the side of excess.

DE BROSSES, CHARLES (1709–1777), was educated by Jesuits, and became conseiller in the Parlement of his native Dijon in 1730; he was twice exiled, but was the first President of the Parlement of Burgundy when it was re-established in 1775. He travelled in Italy for a year, 1739–40, but never left Europe.

In 1756 de Brosses published his *Histoire des Navigations aux Terres australes, où se trouvent, concernant l'Australie, quantité des suggestions dont les Anglais firent leur profit*. The work was anonymous, and Malthus might never have known by whom it was compiled.

The two volumes form a popular collection of travellers' tales. They are arranged in three parts: En Magellanie, En Australasie, and En Polynesie; the first begins with the voyage of Amerigo Vespucci in 1501.

*See also* Legobien, Charles, and 'Roggewein', Jakob.

DEFOE, DANIEL (*c.*1660–1731), was the son of a prosperous butcher named Foe. He changed his name to de Foe when he was about 40, and his pamphlet *Giving Alms No Charity* appeared under this name in November 1704. Defoe was an adventurous turncoat in politics, with experience of poverty, pillory and prison before he embarked on his successful novels, of which *Robinson Crusoe* and *Moll Flanders* are the best known.

*Giving Alms No Charity* was provoked by Sir Humphry Mackworth, M.P. for Cardiganshire (see the D.N.B.) who published as a pamphlet his *Bill for the better Relief, Imployment, and Settlement of the Poor*. Malthus quotes Defoe at second-hand, from Sir Frederick Morton Eden's *State of the Poor* (q.v.); the phrases 'address to parliament' and 'speaking' are perhaps misleading to modern readers: Defoe was never an M.P., but the pamphlet was directed *at* parliament (Bk III, ch. vi, n. 11).

DE LESSEPS, JEAN-BAPTISTE BARTHÉLEMY (1766–1834), was the son of a French consular agent, who worked mainly in Hamburg and St Petersburg; he took the opportunity of learning most European languages, and at the age of 17 was French consul at Cronstadt. His final posting before his death was as consul general in Lisbon.

The adventure of his life was when he accompanied the explorer La Pérouse (q.v.) on his voyage to find the 'passage' from the Pacific Ocean round the north-west coast of America, through the Bering Sea, which Captain Cook (q.v.) had failed to discover. After two years, de Lesseps was sent home overland with Pérouse's reports; he was delayed in Kamchatka for three months by bad weather, then travelled across Siberia under terrible conditions.

De Lesseps reached France in the autumn of 1788, and his account of his journey was published in 1790, in two volumes, in French and English. Joseph Johnson, who was to become Malthus's publisher, was responsible for the English version, which Malthus used in Bk I, ch. ix, nn. 1–5. It was entitled *Travels in Kamtschatka during the years 1787 and 1788, translated from the French of M. de Lesseps, Consul of France, and Interpreter to the Count de La Pérouse, now engaged in a voyage round the world, by command of His Most Christian Majesty* [Louis XVI].

Malthus's paragraph about small-pox could be misleading; de Lesseps wrote:

The small pox, whose ravages I have already mentioned, appears not to be natural to the country, nor is it very common. Since the invasion of the Russians, and the frequent emigrations that succeeded it, this epidemical disease has only made its appearance in 1767 and 1768. It was then brought into the country by a Russian vessel ... a sailor ... communicated this cruel malady to the poor Kamtschadales, which carried off three fourths of them. As it has not appeared since, it is supposed that these people are not subject to it.

DE MANDELSLOE, JOHANN ALBERT (1615–1644), was born of a good family in the Duchy of Mecklenburg, according to John Harris (q.v.) and 'received from Nature an happy and inquisitive Genius'. He was 'a Scholar and a Gentleman', but he 'kept in Mind the Design of the Improvement of Trade' when his patron, the Duke of Holstein, sent him with an embassy to Persia in 1638, 'in order to promote a Project he had formed, of establishing an East-India Company in his Dominions'.

The Shah offered de Mandelsloe what Michaud calls 'une pension considérable', but he left the court and travelled on, through India and Ceylon, returning to Europe round the Cape of Good Hope. He died of small-pox in Paris, and his friend Oléarius published his letters and journals posthumously; there were many subsequent versions, including that in Harris's *Voyages*.

Johann de Mandelsloe did not pretend to have visited Formosa, and distinguished carefully between what he saw for himself and the stories of other travellers, about which he was properly sceptical. Malthus's reference (Bk I, ch. v, n. 60) is to the second part of Harris's extracts from de Mandelsloe's writings: 'Observations on the Commerce of the Portugeze, English and Dutch at that time'.

The mis-spelling of de Mandelsloe's name as *de Mandesloe* began with the quarto, and was repeated in all subsequent editions.

DESCARTES, RENÉ (1596–1650), was the most famous of 'modern' as distinct from the Greek classical philosophers; he was also a pioneer of analytical geometry and the founder of optics as a branch of science. Descartes's preliminary philosophical exercise, of doubting all the evidence of his senses, is by no means despised by physical scientists today. Had Malthus read Leibniz (1646–1716) he might well have effected a compromise between rationalism and empiricism by distinguishing 'truths of reason' from 'truths of fact'; as it happened, Malthus probably only knew of Leibniz as one of the antagonists of Newton (q.v.).

Throughout the eighteenth century, Leibniz was the hero of German philosophers, just as the French supported the views of Descartes and the British those of Newton. The principal disputes were between the Cartesians and the Newtonians, and Malthus would have been familiar with them from the works of Voltaire (1694–1778). Voltaire made enemies in his own country by plunging into the controversy on Newton's behalf, after his three years' residence in England; a copy of his *Lettres écrites de Londres*, published in 1734, is in the Malthus Library at Jesus College, Cambridge.

For a note by a professional philosopher, see Antony Flew's edition of the 1798 *Essay*, pp. 278–9 (Pelican 1970).

DE WITT, JAN (1625–1672), was the son of a famous Burgomaster of Dordrecht, and became Pensionary of his native town – that is to say, its representative in the States-General of Holland, opposed to the House of Orange. The Stadholder, William II (who had married the eldest daughter of Charles I of England) died in 1650, leaving a posthumous son; thus de Witt was able to become Grand Pensionary of the United Provinces, and for 20 years governed the affairs of his country, including wars against England under both Cromwell and Charles II. He was finally defeated by Louis XIV of France, and William III restored as Stadholder. Jan de Witt and his brother Cornelis were literally torn to pieces by a crowd at the Hague; the young William, later King of England, made no attempt to save them.

*'t Intrest van Holland* was first published in Amsterdam in 1662, without de Witt's knowledge, according to an English translation published in London in 1702: *The True Interest and Political Maxims of the Republick of Holland and West-Friesland* 'Written by John de Witt and other Great Men in Holland, Publish'd by Authority of the States'. On p. xxvi of the Preface one reads that 'the matters treated in this Book have been carefully weighed and considered since the Year 1662'.

This 1702 edition is in one volume of 492 pages, but divided into three Parts, the chapters in each Part being numbered separately. Chapter IX of Part I (pp. 37–44) is headed: 'That the Inhabitants of Holland, being in a State of Freedom, are by a common Interest wonderfully linked together; which is also shew'd by a rough Calculation of the Number of Inhabitants, and by what Means they subsist.' This must be what Malthus means in Bk III, ch. B, n. 10, by 'vol. i p. 9'.

On p. 41 de Witt writes: 'I shall give a guess as by vulgar Report, that the whole Number, without excluding any Inhabitants whatsoever, may amount to two millions and four hundred thousand People.' After a list of occupations and the numbers maintained thereby, he concludes (pp. 42–3): 'And tho this Calculation, whether consider'd as to the Number of Inhabitants, or their proportionable means of Subsistence, is very rough and uncertain; yet I suppose it to be evident, that the eighth part of the Inhabitants of Holland could not be supplied with Necessaries out of its own product, if their Gain otherwise did not afford them all other necessaries.'

(The editor is indebted for this reference to Mrs Jill Richardson, of the War Memorial Library, Jesus College, and to Mr John Harrison of the Cambridge University Library.)

DIONYSIUS OF HALICARNASSUS, where he was born between 60 and 55 B.C.; he is known to have lived for some time after A.D. 7. He wrote a history of Rome in Greek, of which the traditional English title is *Roman Antiquities*, although a better translation might be *Early History and Ancient Lore of Rome*.

Romulus, son of the god Mars, suckled by a she-wolf, was the mythical founder of Rome, allegedly in 753 B.C. The Loeb translation of the passage to which Malthus refers, describing the means by which Romulus made the city large and populous, is as follows:

In the first place, he obliged the inhabitants to bring up all their male children and the first-born of the females, and forbade them to destroy any children under three years of age unless they were maimed or monstrous from their very birth. These he did not forbid their parents to expose, provided they first showed them to their five nearest neighbours and these also approved. Against those who disobeyed this law he fixed various penalties, including the confiscation of half their property. (P. 355 of the 1937 edition, translated by Ernest Cary.)

DIROM, ALEXANDER, lived at Muiresk in Scotland. In 1787, shortly before his death, he wrote *An Inquiry into the Corn Laws and the Corn Trade of Great Britain, and their Influence on the Prosperity of the Kingdom*; his son, a soldier (see the D.N.B.) found this among his deceased father's papers when he returned from the East Indies in 1792, and it was published in Edinburgh in 1796, with a dedication to Henry Dundas.

On pp. vii-viii of his Preface, Alexander Dirom the younger wrote of his father's work: 'His statements, founded upon *facts*, tend to prove, that abundance of grain at home, and at a moderate price, cannot be obtained by *importation* from abroad, and can only be secured by giving such liberal encouragement to *exportation*, as may render agriculture, or the raising of corn, the favourite object of industry in the kingdom.'

Such sentiments would have appealed to Malthus, who quoted Dirom in Bk III (ch. xi, n. 2) of both the quarto and the 1806 editions of *Population*. By 1807 he obviously believed that the figures given by James Anderson and Adam Smith (qq.v.) were more reliable.

D'IVERNOIS, SIR FRANCIS (1757–1842), the son of a Genevese clock-maker; he studied law and became involved in politics. In 1782 he published his *Tableau Historique et Politique des Révolutions de Genève*,* which led to his having to flee to Ireland, to join a sizeable colony of exiles from Geneva in Waterford. Thereafter he became something between a spy and a negotiator, in Sweden, Germany and Russia, under the protection of George III, who knighted him. At the Congress of Vienna, he

---

* *An Account of the History and Policies of the Revolutions in Geneva.*

was awarded £10 000 on resigning his British pension of £200 a year; then he returned to Geneva and became a Conseiller d'État.

The *Tableau Historique et Politique des Pertes que la Révolution et la Guerre ont causées au Peuple français, dans sa population, son agriculture, ses colonies, ses manufactures et son commerce* ...* was published in London in 1799. French and English versions appeared simultaneously, but Malthus obviously preferred the French. The work would now be described as propaganda, for it was written deliberately to contradict a statement of the French Directory, made on 19 June 1797, to the effect that 'Les ressources de la République sont entières.'** Sir Francis takes some 500 pages to disprove this, stressing the military and economic weakness of the enemy, and the disaffected misery of the civilian population. Rather inconsistently, he concludes with a passionate appeal to the northern Protestant nations not to remain passive spectators of the struggle, for if they do, the regicide government of France will be sure of its prey, devouring the weaklings one at a time, like the companions of Ulysses.

In spite of Malthus's criticisms, Sir Francis became 'un fanatique des théories de Malthus et presque toutes ses publications de vieillesse sont des défenses du malthusianisme sous la forme la plus intransigeante'.*** (Otto Karmin, *Sir Francis d'Ivernois*, Geneva 1920, p. 622.)

DRUMMOND, HENRY (1786–1860), founded in 1825 the Chair of Political Economy at Oxford which still bears his name. He was a wealthy and eccentric banker, a Tory member of parliament, and he also built a large and ornate Holy Catholic Apostolic Church, for the evangelist Edward Irving, near the Malthus family home at Albury in Surrey.

The first Drummond Professor was Nassau Senior (1790–1864) who held the chair from 1825 to 1830. He delivered *Two Lectures on Population* in 1828, and published with them, in 1831, the letters he had exchanged with Malthus on the subject. The two men knew each other quite well, and met at the Political Economy Club (limited to 30 members) which was founded in 1821.

DUHALDE, JEAN-BAPTISTE (1674–1743), a priest who became a Jesuit in 1708, the year Legobien died (q.v.) and who was entrusted with the task of continuing the *Lettres Édifiantes et Curieuses* (q.v.). He was responsible for collecting and arranging Sections IX–XXVI. In addition, Duhalde's own separate work on China, compiled from the records of successive missionaries, was published in Paris in 1735: *Description géographique, historique, chronologique, politique et physique de l'Empire de la Chine et de la Tartaire chinoise.*

The first edition of Richard Brookes's English translation, published in London in

---

* *A Historical Account, with the Political Implications, of the Losses which Revolution and War have inflicted upon the French People, in their population, agriculture, colonial possessions, manufactures and commerce.*

** 'The resources of the Republic are unaffected' [i.e., as great as they were before].

*** 'a fanatical adherent to the theories of Malthus, and almost all the publications of his old age were defences of Malthusianism in its most uncompromising form'.

four octavo volumes in 1736, had an even more comprehensive title: *The General History of China, containing a Geographical, Historical, Chronological, Political and Physical Description of the Empire of China, Chinese-Tartary, Corea and Thibet, including an Exact and Particular Account of their Customs, Manners, Ceremonies, Religion, Arts and Sciences.* As late as 1838 this work was described in *The Biographical Treasury* (2nd edn, London) as 'the best account ever published of that immense empire'.

The editor has not been able to see a copy of the two-volume folio edition used by Malthus, but his references are quite easy to check in the four-volume edition. Malthus quotes many passages almost verbatim, often without inverted commas; with regard to the exposure of babies, he omits Duhalde's account of the Catechists who were instructed to 'walk out every Morning to baptize a Multitude of dying Children', and the Christian women who were allowed by 'the Infidel Midwives' to baptize the female infants in the 'Bason of Water' in which they were drowned, so that 'by this Means these unhappy Victims to the Indigence of their Parents find eternal Life in the same Water that deprives them of a short and transient Being'. (4-vol. octavo edn of 1736, Vol. II, pp. 126–7.)

DUPONT, PIERRE-SAMUEL, Député de Nemours (1739–1817), was the son of a clock-maker with court connections; he turned to political economy after trying to be a protestant pastor, army officer, doctor and actor. He wrote an anonymous pro-agricultural pamphlet, which led to his becoming acquainted with Quesnay, Mirabeau, Turgot (whose works he later edited) and Vergennes. He was imprisoned during the Terror, and fled to America with the idea of setting up an agricultural colony; he found this too bleak, so turned to industry instead, and joined his son Éleuthère who was profitably manufacturing gunpowder. In 1803 Dupont returned to Paris and became a successful business man, but was forced to flee to the United States again on Napoleon's escape from Elba; he died there in 1817. His widow, a highly cultivated woman, probably met Malthus in Paris in 1820; he lent her a copy of his *Principles of Political Economy*, and she wrote of him to Sismondi as 'notre bon Malthus'.

The work quoted by Malthus in Bk III, ch. xi, n. 15, is *Physiocratie ou Constitution Naturelle du Gouvernement le plus avantageux au genre humain*: 'Recueil publié par Du Pont, des Sociétés Royales d'Agriculture de Soissons & d'Orléans, et Correspondant de la Société d'Émulation de Londres.' It was published in Leyden in 1768, and the British Library copy is bound in one octavo volume; it could, however, easily have been split into two, the first dealing with Quesnay's *Tableau Économique*, the second (to which Malthus refers) being *Maximes Générales du Gouvernement Économique d'un Royaume Agricole*.

Malthus must have had in mind Maxims XVIII, XIX and XX (pp. 116–17, pp. 162–4 for the Notes thereon) in which Dupont maintains that abundance without commercial value does not constitute wealth: high prices and scarcity lead to misery, but high prices and plenty lead to opulence. The higher the price of corn, the higher the wages of the common people – whose pay 's'établit assez naturellement' according to the price of grain – so that they had more money for other commodities. Dupont stressed the importance of the masses, as consumers, and as producers of the revenue of the state: poor peasants, poor kingdom.

Malthus's text here, in 1806, is the same as in 1803, and there is no obvious reason why this footnote should have been omitted from the 1806 edition, unless he wished completely to dissociate himself from the physiocrats.

DURAND, FRANÇOIS-JACQUES (1727–1816), was a pastor in Berne; in 1785 he became Professor of both Statistics and Ecclesiastical History at the Academy of Lausanne; in addition, in 1791, he was made Professor of Moral Philosophy.

The full title of the work quoted by Malthus in Bk II, ch. vii, n. 40, is *Statistique Élémentaire ou Essai sur l'État géographique, physique et politique de la Suisse*; it is described as *Ouvrage consacré à l'instruction de la jeunesse.*\* There are four octavo volumes, published in Lausanne 1795–96. The passage quoted begins: 'Depuis 1583 jusqu'en 1654, le Conseil Souverain de la République admit dans la bourgeoisie de Berne quatre cent quatre-vingt-sept familles, dont plusieurs n'ont pas joui longtems de ce privilège.'\*\* Malthus has throughout changed Durand's figures to Arabic numerals.

There is a copy of this work in the Malthus Library at Jesus College, Cambridge, and it seems likely that he bought it on his tour of Switzerland in 1802.

EDEN, SIR FREDERICK MORTON (1766–1809), the eldest son of a baronet who was at one time Governor of the Colony of Maryland; he was educated at Christ Church, Oxford, and became one of the founders of the Globe Insurance Company. He was so impressed by the suffering caused by the high price of food in 1794–95 that he conducted what would now be called a survey at his own expense. Eden not only sent a questionnaire to clergymen, but also employed to obtain information 'a remarkably faithful and intelligent person, who has spent more than a year in travelling from place to place'.

This resulted in the publication in London in 1797, in three quarto volumes, of his classic *The State of the Poor*; 'or an History of the Labouring Classes in England from the Conquest to the present period; in which are particularly considered their domestic economy with respect to diet, dress, fuel and habitation; and the various plans which, from time to time, have been proposed and adopted for the relief of the poor, &c'.

When plans for the first British census were being discussed in Parliament, Eden published *An Estimate of the Number of Inhabitants in Great Britain and Ireland* (London 1800). At that time many people were opposed to the whole idea (see in the Bible the 21st chapter of the First Book of Chronicles) and Eden pointed out that the proposed Enumeration under the Population Act 'would itself, alone, furnish no proof whether our population was progressive, retrograde, or stationary'. Malthus naturally included Eden's estimate of the ratio of deaths to total population among those of other recognised authorities.

---

\* *Elementary Statistics or an Essay on the geographical, physical and political state of Switzerland.* A work dedicated to the instruction of youth.

\*\* 'Between 1583 and 1654 the Sovereign Council of the Republic admitted four hundred and eighty-seven families as burghers of Berne, of whom many did not enjoy this privilege for very long.'

ELLIS, HENRY (1721–1806), an eccentric character who joined a perilous expedition at his own expense, and published in London in 1748 *A Voyage to Hudson's Bay by the Dobbs Galley* [180 tons] *and the California* [150 tons] *in the Years 1746 and 1747 for Discovering a North-West Passage.* The book was popular as an adventure story, and also because it gave an account of the Eskimo people, then almost unknown.

Malthus (Bk I, ch. iv, n. 76) does not give the conclusion of the story to which he refers. On pp. 196–7 Ellis wrote of the starving couple who ate two of their children on a journey:

On their Arrival at the Factory, the distracted Indian, whose Heart overflowed with Grief, told this melancholy Affair to the English Governor, with all its affecting Circumstances, which was received with a loud Laugh. The poor Savage, with a look of Amazement, said in his broken English, *This is no Laughing Talk!* and so went his Way, highly edified, no Doubt, with these Christian Morals.

Ellis then goes on to mention

a very strange Maxim of Policy which prevails much amongst them; and which is, that of suffering, or rather obliging their Women to procure frequent Abortions, by the Use of a certain Herb common in that Country, and not unknown here; that they may in some Measure be eased of that heavy Burthen they feel, in providing for a helpless Family.

ENCYCLOPAEDIA BRITANNICA, SUPPLEMENT of 1824, *see under* William Jacob for Prussia, John Ramsay McCulloch for Corn Laws, Joshua Milne for Mortality, and Dugald Stewart for the Preliminary Dissertation.

ESTCOURT, THOMAS GRIMSTON (1748–1818), educated at St John's College, Oxford, and M.P. for Cricklade 1790–1806. He should not be confused with his better known kinsman, Thomas Grimston Bucknall Estcourt (1775–1853) of Corpus Christi College, Oxford, who was M.P. for Devizes 1805–26, and then for the University 1826–47. Both men came from a family established since 1330 at Long Newnton, near Tetbury, on the borders of Gloucestershire and Wiltshire.

In 1804 the Board of Agriculture printed for T. G. Estcourt *An Account of an Effort to better the Condition of the Poor in a Country Village (Long Newnton) and some Regulations suggested, by which the same might be extended to other parishes of a similar description.* The cottagers were allowed to rent small parcels of land at £1. 12s an acre; the land was to be forfeited if it were not properly cultivated, or if the tenant received parish relief, other than purely medical. The scheme greatly decreased the poor-rate in the village, but did not impress Robert Gourlay (q.v.):

I have repeatedly been at Long Newton [sic], seen Mr Estcourt's provision for the poor, and inquired into his plan. . . . Its continuance rests with Mr Estcourt's will and pleasure. Mr Estcourt can deprive his poor tenants of the ridges now let to them; on which they grow a little grain, beans, potatoes and so forth. The poor must be made *independent* of all caprice: they must have something which they can call their own. They must have the power of loco-motion; they must have the chance of acquiring a freehold – an opportunity of rising from out the mud in which they are now stuck. (*General Introduction to a Statistical Account of Upper Canada, compiled with a View to a Grand System of Emigration, in connection with a Reform of the Poor Laws.* London 1822, pp. clxix–xx.)

ETON, WILLIAM, describes himself on the title-page of his major work as 'many years resident in Turkey and Russia'. Malthus quotes almost verbatim from *A Survey of the Turkish Empire*, 'In which are considered i. Its government, ... history, ... and population. ii. The state of the provinces ... iii. The cause of the decline of Turkey ... iv. The British Commerce with Turkey, etc.' All Malthus's references are to the second edition of 1799, the first having appeared a year earlier, both published in London by Cadell & Davies.

There is a point of interest with regard to Malthus's views on the functions of government and the free market of grain in Bk I, ch. x, n. 19. He quotes exactly Eton's five principal causes of depopulation, except in the case of famine. Eton's text reads:

4thly Famine, owing to the want of precaution in the government, when a crop of corn fails, and to the avarice and villainy of the pashas, who generally endeavour to profit by this dreadful calamity.

This was very much the point of view of British rioters during the scarcity of 1800, against which Malthus had written his pamphlet on *The Cause of the Present High Price of Provisions* in the November of that year.

In Bk III, ch. lv, n. 9 Malthus gives no reference, but the passage can be found on pp. 327–8:

When I was in quarantine at the Russian frontier, in September 1778, there passed 75 000 Christians, obliged by the Russians to emigrate from the Crimea (35 769 males). The Armenian women, who came from Kaffa, were more beautiful, and, I think, approached nearer that perfect form which the Grecians have left us in their statues, than the women of Tino. These people were sent to inhabit the country abandoned by the Nogai Tatars [*sic*]

... and so on, as quoted by Malthus, only without inverted commas. The colony from Italy was planted in 1783.

EULER, LEONHARD (1707–1783), was born in Basle, and a pupil at the University there of Jean Bernoulli; some account in English of the work of both master and pupil may be found in Isaac Todhunter's *History of the Mathematical Theory of Probability* (London, 1865). Euler studied Latin, Cartesian and Newtonian philosophy, theology and oriental languages; but mathematics was his forte, and, as was not uncommon at the time, he applied it to both astronomy and demography. He died in St Petersburg, where he had gone at the invitation of the Empress Catherine (q.v.) to teach mathematics at the Academy.

In both the original and revised versions of his chapter on the fruitfulness of marriages, Malthus expressly states that he took Euler's tables from Süssmilch (q.v.).

FELIX, MARCUS MINUCIUS, a Father of the Church, was a Roman lawyer of the third century, who was converted to Christianity and wrote a dialogue in its defence called *Octavius*. The protagonists were Octavius, a Christian; Caecilius, a Heathen – who is afterwards converted by this conversation – with Minicius as their common friend chosen to moderate between the two disputants.

The passage quoted by Malthus in Bk I, ch. XIV, n. 8, is in reply to the allegation that Christians were initiated into the mysteries of their religion by drinking the blood of a murdered baby. After denying this, Minicius accuses the heathens in their turn:

And indeed I observe that you expose your new-born children to be devoured by wild beasts and birds, or that you miserably strangle them. There are women who, by using potions, extinguish the first principles of man in their very bowels, and thus, even before they bring forth, commit parricide.

This English translation is by Sir David Dalrymple (Lord Hailes) which was published in Edinburgh in 1781, and reprinted by Macmillan and Bell (Cambridge and London) in 1854.

FIELDING, HENRY (1707–1754), an Etonian contemporary of the elder Pitt, who later became famous as one of the originators of the English novel, *Tom Jones* being his best-known work. He was always short of money, so his old school-fellow Lord Lyttleton obtained for him the post of magistrate at Westminster, in 1748, and the Duke of Bedford provided him with a house in Bow Street. Fielding was so successful in 'improving the good order of the Metropolis' that he was unanimously elected chairman of the Quarter Sessions. In 1751 he published his *Enquiry into the Causes of the late Increase in Robbers*; he opposed public executions, which made a hero of the criminal, and stressed alcohol and gambling, as well as poverty, as factors leading to violent crime.

Fielding's *Proposal for Making an Effectual Provision for the Poor* (1753) was dedicated to the prime minister Henry Pelham, and slipped into oblivion when both he and Pelham died in the following year. In this 90 pp. tract Fielding pointed out that the sufferings of the poor are less observed than their misdeeds: 'They starve and freeze and rot among themselves, but they beg, steal and rob among their betters.' He proposed that a Country House, for over 5000 inmates, should be set up for the London poor, near the village of Acton; the scheme would be self-supporting, through the Labours of the Industrious, who were to rise at 4 a.m. – lights out at 9 p.m.

FRANKLIN, BENJAMIN (1706–1790), scientist and statesman, who helped draft the American Declaration of Independence, and was the first ambassador to France of the United States. He was the fifteenth of 17 children born to a tallow-chandler, who had emigrated from England to Massachusetts.

The 'Miscellany' of Franklin's works quoted by Malthus was published by Joseph Johnson in 1779. The relevant essay was entitled 'Observations concerning the Increase of Mankind, Peopling of Countries, &c.'. In it the gist of Malthus's principle of population was set out in less than 11 octavo pages; it had been written in Pennsylvania in 1751, and first published in Boston in 1755 as a 'political tract'.

From 1757 to 1762, and again from 1764 to 1775, Franklin was in England as agent for the colony of Pennsylvania. He was made an honorary doctor of the Universities of St Andrews, Edinburgh and Oxford, as well as a Fellow of the Royal Society – this last largely in recognition of his work on electricity and his invention of the lightning conductor. Thus it was no doubt natural for Malthus to refer to Franklin, in his Preface to the quarto, as 'among our own writers', especially as others he mentioned had written in Greek or French. Malthus does, however, correct Franklin's English grammar: Franklin wrote: 'Was the face of the earth vacant of other plants . . .' which Malthus amended to 'Were . . .' (Bk I, ch. i, n. 2.)

In his chapter on Emigration (Bk III, ch. iv, n. 10) Malthus cites 'Extracts of a Letter of R.J. Esq; of London, to Benjamin Franklin, Esq; at Philadelphia'; this was printed by Johnson immediately after Franklin's 'Observations concerning the Increase of Mankind'. Malthus quotes R.J. on this issue almost verbatim (p. 23) except for his final sentence: 'And it is particularly observable that none of the *English* colonies became in any way considerable, till the necessary manners were born and grew up in the country, excepting those to which singular circumstances at home forced manners fit for the forming of a new state.' Presumably R.J. was thinking of those disciplined communities, such as the Quakers, who had suffered from religious persecution in Europe.

GARNIER, GERMAIN (1754–1821), was secretary to Madame Adélaïde, Louis XVI's aunt, and was known as a wit and light versifier. He fled to Switzerland in 1792 but returned three years later, held office under Napoleon, welcomed the restoration of the monarchy, and was made a peer of France. He translated Lady Mary Wortley Montagu and Anne Radcliffe, but his most famous work was his translation of Adam Smith's *Wealth of Nations*, published in Paris in 1802 – 'An x' – in five octavo volumes. It seems likely that Malthus bought a set when he and a party of relations took advantage of the Peace of Amiens to travel in France and Switzerland; he met Garnier in Paris in 1820.

*Recherches sur la Nature et les Causes de la Richesse des Nations, Traduction nouvelle, avec des notes et observations*, begins with 127 pages of preliminary matter by Garnier, and Vol. v contains 444 pages of his notes, together with comparative tables of British and French weights and measures, and so on, with both the 'ancient' and the new metric system for France.

Malthus's reference in Bk II, ch. viii, n. 11, is a summary of a three-page dissertation of Garnier's on what the revolutionary wars ('la guerre dernière') had cost the population of France. He thought that the loss during the eight years of war had been greatly exaggerated. Garnier maintained that the men called up had left in the country districts an excess of food, which would have encouraged the growth of the population; thus the only damage to the state was the substitution of children for those past adolescence, a disadvantage which would fade away in the course of a few years. This long note was on Part I of Chapter I of Book v of the *Wealth of Nations*, 'Of the Expence of Defence'.

GELLIUS, AULUS (*c*.A.D. 123–165), was a Roman official during the reigns of the emperors Trajan and Marcus Aurelius. Malthus's reference (Bk I, ch. xiv, n. 11) is to his miscellany *Noctes Atticae*, a sort of commonplace book for the diversion of himself and his children, written during the many long winter nights which he spent *en poste* in Attica.

An English translation of *Attic Nights* by the Rev. William Beloe was published in

1795; the passage from the speech of Metellus Numidicus also appears in English in Gibbon's *Decline and Fall of the Roman Empire* (n. 64 of Chap. VI). Both these versions are quite different from Malthus's, who obviously made his own translation. A two-volume Latin edition published in Leipsig in 1762 is in the Malthus Library at Jesus College, Cambridge.

GIBBON, EDWARD (1737–1794), whose *Decline and Fall of the Roman Empire* is possibly the most famous history in the English language, regarded himself as the Lepidus in the triumvirate of British historians, the other two being Hume and Robertson (qq.v.). Gibbon's first quarto volume appeared in 1776, containing chapters 1–16; chapters 17–38, in vols. II and III, were published in 1781, including 'General Observations on the Fall of the Roman Empire in the West'. In 1783 Gibbon retired to Lausanne to complete the work, the last three volumes appearing in 1788.

It is known, from a letter to his father, that Malthus read the earlier volumes while he was at Cambridge: he wrote of Gibbon: 'He is a very entertaining writer in my opinion; his style is sometimes really sublime, everywhere interesting and agreeable, though perhaps it may in general be called rather too florid for history.'

Malthus transcribes Gibbon almost verbatim, with or without quotation marks, in chapters VI and VII of Book I. In ch. VII, n. 2, he omits a fine Gibbonesque phrase; the passage reads in the original: 'It was proposed, not in the hour of victory and passion, but in calm and deliberate council, to exterminate all the inhabitants ...'

There is in the Malthus Library at Jesus College, Cambridge, a set of the octavo 12-volume edition published between 1783 and 1790.

GILLIES, JOHN, LL.D. (1747–1836), was a classical scholar, a Scot who migrated to England, chiefly known for his *History of Greece*, published in 1783. The work to which Malthus refers in Bk I, ch. XIII, nn. 7–11 is in two quarto volumes which appeared in 1797: *Aristotle's Ethics and Politics, comprising his practical philosophy, translated from the Greek. Illustrated by Introductions and Notes; the Critical History of his Life; and a new analysis of his speculative works by John Gillies* ... Dr Gillies thought that 'modern economists', not excepting Hume and Smith, Montesquieu and Machiavelli, should have acknowledged their debt to Aristotle.

Malthus's use of Gillies's work is significant. There is at Jesus College, Cambridge, a bound volume of manuscript speeches and essays, neatly transcribed and signed by their authors. This contains one by Malthus dated 1787; it is a 'declamation' in Latin on a quotation from Horace's *Satires* (2, 4, 91): 'As a translator you will give just as much pleasure.' Horace had lamented the way he was flogged by his schoolmaster for trifling mistakes with classical Greek accents; Malthus sympathised with the young Roman, and expressed in appropriate rhetorical prose his own anger that so much of a boy's life should be embittered by what was, for him, a completely unprofitable study; good translations of Greek and Latin authors would enable the fountains of true learning and wisdom to flow freely, for the benefit of everyone, and so on.

Gillies's *Aristotle* was published too late for the schoolboy Malthus, but it aroused a controversy which must have interested him. A Mr Thomas Taylor, replying in 1804 to Gillies's own defence of his work, poured scorn upon his 'endeavour to benefit the lowest order of the human race by disseminating among them truths of a nature so arduous and sublime, that they can only be understood by the highest class of our species'.

(The editor is indebted to the Master and Council of Jesus College, Cambridge, for permission to cite Malthus's unpublished dissertation, and to Mrs Phyllida Upstone for translating it.)

GOBIEN, *see under* Legobien, Charles.

GODWIN, WILLIAM (1756–1836), began his career as a dissenting minister, then became known as a prolific writer of every form of literature except verse; his name was constantly before the public for half a century, after he had ceased to style himself 'reverend' in 1785. He is today also remembered as the husband of Mary Wollstone-craft, who published her *Vindication of the Rights of Woman* in 1792; the father of her daughter, another Mary, who became the wife of Shelley and the author of *Frankenstein*; and the step-father of Clare Clairmont, the mother of Byron's illegiti-mate daughter Allegra.

Less dramatically, Godwin was acquainted with most of the writers of his day who held liberal views. Although he had a reputation for financial incompetence and 'sponging' on his friends, men of standing and probity helped him all his life, and a sinecure bestowed upon him by Lord Grey's Whig government enabled the old philosophical anarchist to die in comfort as a pensioner of the establishment.

Malthus, in the Preface to the anonymous 1798 version of the *Essay on Population*, states that it owed its origin 'to a conversation with a friend, on the subject of Mr Godwin's Essay, on avarice and profusion, in his Enquirer. The discussion started the general question of the future improvement of society; and the Author at first sat down with an intention of merely stating his thoughts to his friend, upon paper, in a clearer manner than he thought he could do in conversation.'

*The Enquirer* is a collection of miscellaneous essays published in 1797; the relevance of that on 'Avarice and Profusion' to the argument which Malthus had with his 'friend' – his romantically eccentric father – is not very apparent to the modern reader. It seems probable that the discussion rapidly shifted to Godwin's major two-volume philosophical work, *An Enquiry concerning Political Justice and its Influence on Morals and Happiness*; there were three editions, in 1793, 1796, and 1798, which last runs to over a thousand pages. Malthus quoted from both the first and third editions when writing the 1798 *Essay on Population*; his title-page states explicitly that the author is concerned with the *Principle of Population as it affects the Future Improvement of Society, with Remarks on the Speculations of Mr Godwin, M. Condorcet, and other Writers*.

When Malthus put together the great quarto, he 'quarried' many passages from the first *Essay*, especially at the beginning of Bk III, in the first two chapters 'Of Systems of Equality', the second being devoted entirely to Godwin. In 1803, 1806, and 1807 ch. iii of Bk III was also concerned with Godwin: it was an answer to Godwin's pamphlet (published in 1801) entitled *Thoughts Occasioned by the Perusal of Dr Parr's Spital Sermon, being a Reply to the Attacks of Dr Parr, Mr Mackintosh [qq.v.] the Author of an Essay on Population, and Others*. That Godwin's egalitarian and utopian ideals should be attacked on all sides, especially after the reign of terror in

France, is hardly suprising; yet Godwin wrote in his *Reply* that he approached the anonymous author of the *Essay on Population* 'with a sentiment of unfeigned approbation and respect ... For myself, I cannot refuse to take some pride, in so far as by my writings I gave the occasion, and furnished an incentive, to the producing so valuable a treatise ... Let it be recollected, that I admit the ratios of the author to their full extent, and that I do not attempt in the slightest degree to vitiate the great foundations of his theory.' (pp. 55–6, 61.)

It should be remembered that through their common publisher, Joseph Johnson, Malthus and Godwin had exchanged letters as early as August 1798, and dined together at his house on at least one occasion, in May 1805.

Then in 1817, when Malthus made his most thorough revision of the great quarto, he cut out altogether the chapter relating to Godwin's *Reply* of 1801, and replaced it with one headed simply 'Of Systems of Equality (continued)'. In this chapter Malthus was mainly concerned with a newcomer to the reforming scene, Robert Owen (q.v.). Godwin was obviously hurt by this substitution, and in 1820 he published *Of Population. An Inquiry concerning the Power of Increase in the Numbers of Mankind: being an Answer to Mr Malthus's Essay on that Subject.* A copy was sent to Malthus 'From the Author'.

In this work Godwin entirely repudiated his former opinions, maintaining that populations did not in fact increase very rapidly; if they did, more food could easily be produced; in any case, most of the earth was still uninhabited. It is a pathetic book of some 600 pages, bitter and repetitive, but it was quoted in the House of Commons during the debate on a Poor Relief Bill.

Malthus's friend Francis Jeffrey (1773–1850), the editor of the *Edinburgh Review*, had been much embarrassed by Malthus's attitude towards the Corn Laws, and his disagreements with the Ricardian school. After the death of Francis Horner in 1817, the *Review*'s principal writer on economic affairs was J. R. McCulloch (q.v.) and Jeffrey felt it better to ignore Malthus's *Principles of Political Economy* altogether rather than allow it to be reviewed by his adversary. He therefore welcomed the opportunity to ask Malthus to write an article on Godwin's *Of Population*. This, although it appeared anonymously, as was the custom, in the issue for July 1821, was generally known to be Malthus's work, and Godwin was hurt yet again; he wrote about it to their common friend, Sir James Mackintosh.

Hence Malthus's extremely brief addendum to the *Appendix* was all that he considered necessary, by way of a rejoinder to Godwin, in the 1826 edition of the *Essay on Population*.

GOURLAY, ROBERT, was a man of many grievances, as may be learned from his *General Introduction to a Statistical Account of Upper Canada compiled with a View to a Grand System of Emigration, in connection with a Reform of the Poor Laws* (London 1822). On page xxx he states that he was born to an inheritance of considerable landed estates, but that his fair hopes of an independent fortune were sunk in 1815, when he was 37, with a wife and five children. He emigrated to Canada, where he failed to make good and was, according to himself, wrongfully imprisoned, returning to Britain in December 1819.

Gourlay would appear, however, to have a real grievance against Arthur Young (q.v.) and was hurt by Malthus citing him (Bk IV, ch. xiii, n. 3) in 'that edition of his Essay on Population which attracted such general notice'. As a young man, 'having time and money at command', Gourlay was sent by Arthur Young to Rutland and Lincoln, 'where the practice prevailed of letting the poor have land and cows'; he was to show how labourers' families with a patch of garden and a cow were less likely to apply for poor relief than those without. Poor Gourlay wished to relinquish the undertaking, 'being ashamed of plodding about merely to prove a truism'.

Arthur Young completely misrepresented Gourlay in the *Annals of Agriculture*, who felt justified in defending himself:

Mr Malthus has very properly pointed out the insufficiency of Mr Young's proposal as a general remedy for the evil of poor laws; and, besides this, it is palpably impracticable, as a scheme that could be legally enforced throughout. The quantity of land required to keep a cow varies, according to soil and situation, from one to twenty acres, or more. In some parts of the country adapted to pasturage, the practice could easily be adopted . . . In other parts it is very different . . .

Gourlay wrote that much as he admired him in many respects, he had felt obliged to drop Mr Young's acquaintance. (*op. cit.* pp. lxxxiii–lxxxix.)

*See also* Estcourt, Thomas Grimston.

GRAHAME, JAMES (?1791–1861), possibly a Scot from Lanarkshire who came to Cambridge from the University of Glasgow in 1811, first as a pensioner of St John's and then as a fellow-commoner of St Catherine's, 'afterwards a writer'.

What Malthus called James Grahame's 'slight work' was *An Inquiry into the Principle of Population including an Exposition of the Causes and the Advantages of a Tendency to Exuberance of Numbers in Society, a Defence of Poor Laws, etc.* (Edinburgh 1816). It is understandable that Malthus should have taken some five octavo pages of the *Appendix* added in 1817 to deny Grahame's misrepresentations, and in particular to feel annoyed at Grahame's references to passages which Malthus had 'seen reason to alter or expunge'. These passages included the famous paragraph about the unwelcome intruders at nature's mighty feast (Bk IV, ch. vi, n. 10) and the heartless sentences about abandoned children (Bk IV, ch. viii, nn. 15–17); these were omitted and modified respectively in 1806. With regard to the abandoned children, Grahame actually quotes the quarto version while giving the 1806 reference, which does suggest extreme carelessness, if not actual malice.

This book, however, is worth perusal. Grahame maintained that without the compulsory almsgiving embodied in the Poor Laws, 'the peaceable co-existence of wealth and poverty in the same community' would be impossible: 'Legislative provisions to this effect add as much to the comfort of the rich, and of all those who are most interested in the stability of the institutions of society, as they do to the happiness of the poor.' (pp. 207–8.) He had some good things to say about education. 'Knowledge multiplies the pleasures of life without increasing the expenses of living.' (p. 253.)

GRAUNT, JOHN, F.R.S. (1620–1674), was a respected draper and haberdasher and a member of the Common Council of the City of London; he was brought up a puritan but became a Roman Catholic, and was among those (wrongly) rumoured to be responsible for the great fire of London of 1666. The work for which Charles II recommended him to the Royal Society was published in 1662 and much reprinted and quoted: the short title was *Natural and Political Observations on the Bills of Mortality*.

These 'bills' were in fact registers of the causes of death in London parishes. Each parish clerk was supposed to take a list every Tuesday night to the Clerk of the Common Hall, who made up the general account on Wednesday and had it printed on Thursday; the annual subscription was four shillings. The scheme had been instituted towards the end of the reign of Elizabeth I, in an effort to ascertain the number of deaths from plague in 1592. After 1603, another bad plague year, an attempt was made to keep regular records, but since the London Bills of Mortality were printed on loose sheets, and no one was responsible for their binding or storing, many were 'irrecoverably lost'.

Apart from this, the bills were incomplete and unreliable. The causes of death were reported by parish 'searchers', 'ancient matrons sworn to their office', according to Graunt, who were called in by the sexton to inspect a corpse before the funeral; in most cases they 'could only bring back such an account as the family and friends of the deceased would be pleased to give'. Three of the causes of death listed were Teeth, Lethargy, and Planet-struck. Graunt himself noted that deaths from the French pox were returned as 'sores and ulcers', 'from whence I concluded, that only hated persons, and such, whose very noses were eaten off, were reported by the searchers to have died of this too frequent malady'.

The passage quoted by Malthus (Bk II, ch. x, n. 34) cited by Dr Short (q.v.) occurs in paragraph 8 of Graunt's Chapter v, and reads in the original: 'I say it followeth, that let the mortality be what it will, the city repairs its loss of inhabitants within two years.'

GROSIER, ABBÉ JEAN-BAPTISTE-GABRIEL-ALEXANDRE (1743–1823), left the Society of Jesus to become a man of letters; he edited *L'Année Littéraire* and the *Journal de Littérature, des Sciences, et des Arts*, in which he defended church and monarchy against the attacks of Voltaire.

Grosier's initial work on the history of China was to reduce to order an indigenous compilation, translated into French, with immense notes, by the 'venerable missionary' Father Joseph de Mailla (1670–1748); he had sent it back to France in 1737, 11 years before his death in Peking. Grosier duly produced 12 quarto volumes of de Mailla's work, the *Great Annals of China*; then, in 1785, he added a thirteenth, written entirely by himself, which proved to be the most popular.

The two-volume English translation of Grosier's *China*, used by Malthus, was first published in London in 1788 and reprinted in 1795. The full title was *A General Description of China, containing the Topography of the Fifteen Provinces which compose this Vast Empire, that of Tartary, and the Isles, and other Tributary Countries*. According to Grosier, the sale of 'a kind of spiritous liquor called *rack*' was nowhere forbidden, although the distillation of it was; officers shut their eyes if the owner of a still-house slipped into their hands a few pieces of silver.

HANWAY, JONAS (1712–1786), was 12 years with British traders in Lisbon before joining the Russia Company in 1743; he made an adventurous journey from St

Petersburg to Persia, of which he wrote an account of his return to London in 1750. He was not a successful merchant; but his bachelor state, an appointment as one of the Commissioners for Victualling His Majesty's Navy, together with a legacy from a distant relative, enabled him to devote most of his life to active, practical philanthropy, chiefly with the Foundling Hospital and the Marine Society. He was strongly in favour of increasing the population, to 'make our natural strength in Men correspond with our artificial Power in Riches, and both with the Grandeur and Extent of the British Empire'.

Hanway's propagandist works were innumerable, but there is in the Malthus Library at Jesus College, Cambridge, a copy of his *Letters on the Importance of the Rising Generation of the Labouring Part of our Fellow-subjects*, in two octavo volumes (London 1767). In this work Hanway writes 'An account of the miserable state of the infant parish poor', which is relevant to Malthus's passing reference in Bk III, ch. vi, n. 9.

These two volumes give a moving impression of eighteenth-century Christian altruism, with 'Public Love' as essential to the constitution of a free nation (Vol. I, p. iii). 'The preservation of the Poor is the first lesson in political arithmetic.' (Vol. I, p. 16.) 'How barbarity of any kind ever came to be extended to *infants*, will be as wonderful in *our* annals ... as the folly and ambition of that prince who made war with the Messiah in his infant state of life, in contempt of the decrees of Heaven.' (Vol. I, pp. 175–6.) 'If you gain a feast or pecuniary emolument by the death of a child, whose life you took no care to preserve, so far you *eat* the child. Rather forego a hundred scenes of jollity, than offer up the life of a child to Ceres, Bacchus, or Venus.' (Vol. II, p. 33.)

HARRIS, JOHN, D.D., F.R.S. (*c.*1666–1719), is described in the *Dictionary of National Biography* as culpably improvident and generally in distress, in spite of much ecclesiastical preferment. He worked as a literary hack for London booksellers, and produced in 1705 his *Navigantium atque Itinerantium Bibliotheca, or A compleat Collection of Voyages and Travels, consisting of above Four Hundred of the most authentick Writers* in two huge folio volumes.

Malthus's references fit an edition published in 1744, revised and enlarged by John Campbell (1708–75) another miscellaneous writer, who knew Dr Johnson. In his quotations, Malthus has dropped the capital letters which were used in the original work for all common nouns; the enormous pages are divided into columns of small print, clearly intended for a popular readership who wanted their money's worth.

The travellers' tales which Malthus took from Harris were those of Sir John Chardin, Johann Albert de Mandelsloe, and Guillaume de Rubruquis (qq.v.).

HAYGARTH, JOHN, M.D. (1740–1827), was a physician in Chester from 1767 to 1798, when he moved to Bath. His principal medical work was concerned with the isolation and treatment of 'contagious fevers', but he also helped to set up savings banks in Bath, and it is quite possible that he was personally known to Malthus.

The references in Bk IV, ch. v, nn. 11 and 12, are to *A Sketch of a Plan to exterminate the Casual Small-pox from Great Britain and to introduce general Inoculation*, published by Joseph Johnson in 1793, in two octavo volumes, but with continuous pagination; there are ten 'correspondents', including Dr John Aikin and Dr James Currie (qq.v.).

quoted or cited by Malthus

Dr Haygarth thought that if small-pox could be eradicated, Great Britain would become proportionally as populous as Holland. He believed that small-pox was the chief cause of mortality among young children, and that

Britain is in a rapid state of improvement. Such an increase of youth of both sexes could not be a hindrance but a help to her prosperity. The fear of numerous families deters men of high and middle rank from marriages; but, to these, inoculation already exerts its utmost mischief, in preserving their children from destruction by the small-pox. (*op. cit.* pp. 147–8.)

HEBERDEN, WILLIAM, the younger, M.D., F.R.S. (1767–1845), was at St John's College, Cambridge, and like Malthus graduated in 1788. He studied medicine at Oxford, and was well known in his day as one of the physicians who attended George III and other members of the royal family.

The work quoted by Malthus is *Observations on the Increase and Decrease of Different Diseases and particularly the Plague* (London 1801). It is a quarto-sized pamphlet of just over a hundred pages, written for the medical profession.

In commenting on the increased number of deaths from 'consumptions, gout, lunacy and palsy', Dr Heberden referred to the patron of the first Apothecary Malthus, Dr Thomas Sydenham (1624–89): as the discerning Sydenham had observed, 'acute diseases come from God, but chronical diseases originate with ourselves'. Heberden went on:

Indeed we cannot doubt, that idleness and intemperance, with their long train of vices; that covetousness and anxiety, the necessary attendants upon commerce; and manufactories, which supply the materials for it, – must all in their several ways be injurious to health. And it is not improbable that they may very largely have contributed to swell out the number of deaths under each of the diseases in question. (*op. cit.* p. 45.)

HEINZMANN, JOHANN GEORG (1757–1802), a native of Ulm who set up in Berne as a bookseller and publisher; he produced what the *Dictionnaire Historique et Biographique de la Suisse* describes as 'vastes ouvrages de compilation', such as a history of eighteenth-century painting, and also started a newspaper which became the *Neue Berner Zeitung*. When Malthus and his family party were in Berne in September 1802 they were probably attracted to Heinzmann's shop by his many 'manuels de tourisme', and there Malthus presumably saw what he called '*Beschreibung von Bern*'.

The first volume of *Beschreibung der Stadt und Republik Bern* (Description of the City and Republic of Bern) was published in 1794. The second, in 1796, is said to contain 'various important corrections and additions to the first part', and the section on Population begins by drawing the reader's attention to pp. 9–11 of the first volume. Malthus's references in Bk II, ch. vii, nn. 41 and 51 are correct. Even though he quotes only statistics, he must have had some help with the German he was unable to read for himself.

(The editor is indebted for this reference to the Schweizerische Landesbibliothek in Berne.)

HENNEPIN, LOUIS (c.1640–c.1705), a Franciscan missionary who travelled about Europe, and was at one time attached to a regiment at Maastricht, tending the sick

293

and injured, before spending some 11 years in North America from 1676 to 1687; for eight months he was a prisoner of the Sioux, but was well treated because of his medical skill. He wrote two books about his adventures, both extremely popular.

The work cited by Malthus (Bk I, ch. iv, nn. 7 and 82) is *Description de la Louisiane, nouvellement découverte au Sud'Oüest de la Nouvelle France par Ordre du Roy, Avec la Carte du Pays: Les Moeurs et la Manière de Vivre des Sauvages** (Paris 1683). Although bound in one volume, this is virtually two books, separately paginated; the running head of the first part (312 pp.) is 'Description de la Louisiane', and the second is 'Les Moeurs des Sauvages' (107 pp.). Malthus's page references are both correct, but the fact that he did not give the full title of the work made it difficult to identify: the editor is indebted to Mr John Harrison of Cambridge University Library.

Hennepin was much concerned with the sexual morality of the American 'Indians'. He wrote on p. 37 of 'Les Moeurs des Sauvages' of a French immigrant whose husband had gone off on an expedition, and who was told by 'les femmes Sauvages ... "tu n'as point d'esprit, prend pour le present un autre homme, et quand le tien sera revenu, tu laisseras celuy-la."'** Hennepin comments: 'Cette grande inconstance & changement des femmes, est une grande opposition aux maximes du Christianisme, que nous voulions donner aux Sauvages, & un des obstacles plus considerables à la Foy.'*** He goes on to talk of polygamy in some regions, where men might have ten or eleven wives.

HERMANN, BENEDIKT FRANZ JOHANN (1755–1815), was born in Styria and studied mineralogy in Vienna, one of the many German-speaking learned men whom Catherine the Great (q.v.) encouraged to come to Russia. He directed ironworks, supervised the school of mining, and in 1803 set up the first press for printing books in Siberia, which was also the first-ever to print in Russian. The Transactions of the Imperial Academy of Sciences of St Petersburg are in Latin or French, the latter predominating towards the end of the eighteenth century, while instructions to the book-binder, with regard to the insertion of plates, etc., are given in German.

Tomus IV of the *Nova Acta Academiae Scientiarum Imperialis Petropolitanae* was published in 1789. Hermann's paper was read on 22 June 1786. It begins on p. 59, and is entitled 'Mémoire sur les naissances, mariages et morts dans quelques provinces et villes de la Russie'. In his introductory remarks Hermann praised Peter I's Ordinance of 1722 which required the clergy to report births and deaths every four months, thus providing him with figures for calculating the number of his subjects.

In the table showing the ratio of deaths to inhabitants (pp. 84–5 of *Nova Acta*,

---

\* *Description of Louisiana, recently discovered towards the South-West of New France, by Command of the King, with a Map of the Territory: The Customs of the Savages and their Way of Life.*

\*\* ... was told by 'the female Savages ... "you haven't any sense, take another man for the time being; you can give him up when your own comes back."

\*\*\* 'This widespread faithlessness and changing of partners, on the part of the women, is the prime source of resistance to the precepts of Christianity which we are seeking to give to these Savages, and one of the most serious impediments to [their conversion to] the Faith.'

Vol. IV) Malthus has for no apparent reason omitted six of Hermann's fractions. Thus:

|                              | Dies annually              |
| ---------------------------- | -------------------------- |
| District of Moscow ...       | 1 in 74$\frac{2}{3}$       |
| Tver ...                     | 1 in 75$\frac{3}{4}$       |
| Resan ...                    | 1 in 50$\frac{7}{9}$       |
| Veronesch ...                | 1 in 79$\frac{6}{11}$      |
| Archbishopric of Vologda ... | 1 in 65$\frac{2}{5}$       |
| Town of Tobolsk ...          | 1 in 32$\frac{3}{5}$       |

HISTOIRE DES NAVIGATIONS AUX TERRES AUSTRALES, *see under* de Brosses, Charles.

HOWARD, JOHN (?1726–1790), was so renowned for his work in prisons that Malthus needed to give no particular reference, and his name is commemorated in the Howard League for Penal Reform founded in 1866. In the summer of 1781 Howard investigated conditions in Danish, Swedish and Russian prisons; he met the Swedish astronomer and statistician Wargentin (q.v.) who was, like Howard himself, a friend and correspondent of Richard Price (q.v.).

HOWLETT, JOHN, B.D. (1731–1804), was an Essex country parson; he was much concerned with the controversy as to whether the population of Britain had increased or decreased during the eighteenth century. Richard Price (q.v.) believed that numbers were falling, and in the *Essay* of 1798 Malthus himself wrote:

Judging simply from this controversy, I think one should say, that Dr Price's point is nearer being proved than Mr Howlett's. Truth, probably, lies between the two statements, but this supposition makes the increase of population, since the revolution [of 1688], to have been very slow, in comparison with the increase of wealth. (pp. 314–15.)

By the time Malthus came to write the second version of the *Essay* the census of 1801, imperfect though it was, had shown that the population of England and Wales was very much greater than had been expected, and that it must in fact have been increasing very rapidly in recent years. Thus Malthus's passing reference to Howlett in Bk III, ch. vi, is concerned not with the depopulating effects of enclosure acts, but with Howlett's 118-page pamphlet on the poor, published in 1788. The title was *The Insufficiency of the Causes to which the Increase of our Poor and of the Poor's Rates have been commonly ascribed; the True One stated; with an Enquiry into the Mortality of Country Houses of Industry*, etc.

According to Howlett, the 'great and real Cause of the increased Proportion of our Poor, as well as of the increased Expense of maintaining them, is that the Price of Labour [during the past 40 years] has not advanced so much as the Price of Provisions'. Yet the rents of houses and land 'are increased eight or ten millions; the wealth of our farmers and tradesmen is augmented in similar proportion; that of our merchants and manufacturers in a degree infinitely greater'. Thus he felt that to complain 'of the burdensomeness of our Poor', whose labour had provided all this abundance, was 'something peculiarly ungenerous'. (*op. cit.* pp. 53, 75.)

With regard to the pauper children, Howlett deplored Thomas Gilbert's Act of 1782, which permitted several parishes to form Unions for the provision of larger poor-houses. The assumed reduction of expense was 'a mere trifling consideration' compared with the 'influence of these institutions upon the lives, the health and strength of the Poor'. After giving statistics of the burials in several country parishes, Howlett goes on:

> If these houses annually *kill* such a number of children, we may be sure they proportionably impair the health and weaken the constitution of those whose lives are spared. Thus, while they diminish the parish expenses for the *present*, by the slaughter of some of the *Poor*, they will greatly augment them for the *future*, by furnishing a succession of weak, infirm creatures ... consequently very early prepared for a return to a parochial workhouse. (*op. cit.* pp. 83, 86, 102, 104.)

HUMBOLDT, ALEXANDER, BARON VON (1769–1859), was declared to be, with the exception of Napoleon, the most famous man in Europe, and he came to London with the triumphant allied sovereigns in 1814. Thus it was unnecessary for Malthus, writing in 1817, to make more than a passing reference to him.

Humboldt studied at the Mining Academy of Freiburg, met Volta and Pictet, and followed up some of Galvani's experiments. He intended to travel to Egypt, but by chance went to Madrid, where the patronage of the prime minister set him off on his voyage to Spanish America, and his work on the current off the west coast which bears his name. He worked in Paris on the material he had collected (60 000 specimens) from 1808 to 1827, when he returned to his native Berlin.

What interested Malthus was Humboldt's classic, *Essai Politique sur le Royaume de la Nouvelle Espagne*, published first in Paris in two quarto volumes in 1808, and again in 1811 in five octavo volumes. This latter was quoted at some length by Malthus in his *Principles of Political Economy* (1820) for Humboldt's views on the demoralising effects of the easily cultivated banana and maize coincided with his own on the deplorable Irish potato. In 1820 (p. 382) he almost repeated a phrase he used in 1817 when he wrote of the man whose indolence 'may make him prefer the luxury of doing little or nothing, to the luxury of possessing conveniences and comforts'. In the *Principles* Malthus gave a detailed reference to Humboldt's octavo edition: Tom. III, livre IV, ch. IX, p. 28.

HUME, DAVID (1711–1776), was an outstanding Scots philosopher, historian, and political economist; when Malthus was three weeks old, Hume visited his father's house, with Rousseau, who was looking for a cottage in Surrey.

Hume's *Discourses* were widely read and discussed; Malthus referred to that on 'the Populousness of Antient Nations' in the 1798 *Essay* (pp. 57–9), and clearly regarded it as a work which his readers would know about. In writing the quarto on *Population*, Malthus used two separate editions of Hume's collected essays. In Bk I, ch. v, n. 22, and Bk IV, ch. xiii, n. 1, he quotes from the two-volume octavo edition of 1764; in Bk I, ch. xiii and xiv, his references are to the quarto edition of 1768. All the page numbers are given accurately, and the inference must be that Malthus worked on his 'much enlarged' *Essay* in different places, making use of such books as were available to him at different times between 1798 and 1803.

With regard to infanticide, it is interesting to compare Hume's language with Malthus's. Hume wrote, in his Essay xi, 'Of the Populousness of Antient Nations':

The barbarous practice of the antients might render those times more populous. By removing the terrors of too numerous a family, it would engage many people in marriage; and such is the force of natural affection, that very few, in comparison, would have resolution enough, when it came to the push, to carry into execution their former intentions.

Malthus returns to this same page in Bk iv, with his remark on the deceitfulness of first appearances in politics. Hume's point is that foundling hospitals 'seem favourable to the increase of numbers', but probably have just the opposite effect, since so many of the abandoned infants die from the lack of individual attention. According to Hume: 'To kill one's own child is shocking to nature, and must therefore be pretty unusual; but to turn over the care of him upon others is very tempting to the natural indolence of mankind.'

Malthus gives no reference for Hume's *Euthanasia*. It occurs in Essay vi, 'Whether the British Government inclines more to Absolute Monarchy or to a Republic'. Hume concluded the Essay, "'Tis well known that every government must come to a period, and that death is unavoidable to the political as well as to the animal body. But as one kind of death may be preferable to another . . .' the question was whether it be more desirable for the British constitution to terminate in a popular government or an absolute monarchy. Hume harked back to Cromwell, to the inevitable violence that follows political upheavals, so that in the end we

find repose in absolute monarchy, which it would have been happier for us to have established peaceably from the beginning. Absolute monarchy, therefore, is the easiest death, the true *Euthanasia* of the British constitution.

Thus, if we have reason to be more jealous of monarchy, because the danger is more imminent from that quarter; we have also reason to be more jealous· of popular government, because that danger is more terrible. This may teach us a lesson of moderation in all our political controversies.

In Bk iv, ch. xiii, n. 15, Malthus cites Hume's *Dialogues concerning Natural Religion*, first published posthumously by his nephew in 1779. Were humanity only exempt from the vice or infirmity of idleness, Hume maintained that

the perfect cultivation of land, the improvement of arts and manufactures, the exact execution of every office and duty, immediately follow; and men at once may fully reach that state of society, which is so imperfectly attained by the best-regulated government. . . . It is hard, that being placed in a world so full of wants and necessities, where almost every being or element is either our foe, or refuses its assistance – we should also have our own temper to struggle with, and should be deprived of that faculty which can alone fence against these multiplied evils.

*See also* Paley, William and Wallace, Robert.

JACOB, WILLIAM (?1762–1851), was a merchant, a traveller, a Tory member of parliament from 1808 to 1812, and a prolific writer on agriculture and political economy. Ricardo and Malthus thought he was 'very deficient in scientific knowledge' after he had published two pamphlets on the Corn Laws in 1814 and 1815. Jacob became a Fellow of the Royal Society in 1807, but his name is not among those who supported Malthus's successful application in 1818.

In 1820 Jacob published *A View of the Agriculture, Manufactures, Statistics and State of Society in Germany and parts of Holland and France; taken during a journey in 1819*: this certainly qualified him for his article on Prussia in the *Supplement* to the *Encyclopaedia Britannica*.

JENNER, EDWARD, M.D. (1749–1823), is famous for his discovery of vaccination against small-pox; he observed that the milkmaids of his native Gloucestershire, exposed to cow-pox, did not catch small-pox, and showed that this virus actually conferred immunity against small-pox in human beings (Latin, *vacca*, a cow). Earlier in the eighteenth century some protection against small-pox was obtained by inoculation, which involved giving a healthy child an injection from an infected person, to produce a mild and localised form of the disease; this method was more dangerous and less effective than vaccination.

Dr Jenner's discovery was quickly appreciated – particularly by the Duke of York, as Commander-in-Chief of the army – and he was much commended for making his work public, when he could have amassed a fortune by confining it to his own private practice. He was granted £10 000 by parliament in 1802; in 1806, when Malthus was writing his first *Appendix*, Jenner again petitioned for parliamentary assistance, and received a grant of £20 000. Jenner was supported by Lord Henry Petty, with whom Malthus was personally acquainted.

JONES, SIR WILLIAM (1746–1794), was said to have known 13 languages thoroughly, and another 28 fairly well; oriental philology and literature had fascinated him from an early age. Owing to his widowed mother's poverty, he acted as tutor in the family of the Spencers of Althrop, while also keeping the requisite terms' residence at University College, Oxford. He took up the law for a livelihood, which led to his appointment in 1783 as judge of the high court at Calcutta.

Jones hoped to codify the laws of India, and translated into English from the original Sanskrit *The Institutes of Hindu Law or the Ordinances of Menu*. Menu, as Sir William explained in his Preface, was 'the first of created beings, and not the oldest only, but the holiest of legislators'.

For Bk I, ch. xi, Malthus used the six-volume quarto edition of *The Works of Sir William Jones*, published by his widow Anna Maria and his friend Lord Teignmouth in 1799.

*See also Asiatic Researches.*

JORNANDES, a Goth, was a Christian monk of the sixth century, who may possibly have been Bishop of Ravenna. His *History of the Goths, De Getarum sive Gothorum origine et rebus gestis*, known as *De rebus geticis*, was probably written in about the year 550.

Malthus's quotation in Bk I, ch. vi, n. 63, comes from the beginning of Jornandes' Chapter IV. It is believed that southern Europeans assumed Scanzia or Scandinavia to be an island because its inhabitants came pouring out of the north in ships. A French translation of *officina gentium ... vagina nationum* is 'la fabrique des nations ou bien le réservoir des peuples'. (*Collection des Auteurs Latins*, Paris 1878, p. 427.)

JUVENALIS, DECIMUS JUNIUS (*c.* A.D. 55–130), was a rancorously satirical Roman poet, sometimes regarded as the last of the classical Latin writers. Of his sixth *Satire*, quoted by Malthus in Bk I, ch. xiv, n. 8, Dryden wrote that it was 'a bitter Invective against the fair Sex', describing 'the Vices of an Age which was the most Infamous of any on Record'. Lust was the chief characteristic of these Roman ladies, who learned 'the Arts of Miscarrying and Barrenness'.

The lines after *lecto* in Malthus's footnote were omitted from school editions of Juvenal's *Satires* from 1860 onwards, although they may be found in the Penguin Classics, translated by Peter Green (1967).

Here is Dryden's translation, published in 1702, which Malthus might have seen:

> You seldom hear of the rich Mantle spread
> For the Babe born in the great Lady's Bed.
> Such is the Pow'r of Herbs; such Arts they use
> To make them barren, or their Fruit to lose.

A more literal translation of the last line would be 'To make them sterile, or to induce the slaughter of men within the womb'.

KAEMPFER, ENGELBERT, M.D. (1651–1716), was a native of Lemgo in Westphalia; after travelling in Russia and Persia, he took service with the Dutch East India Company, and spent some six years in south-east Asia. He ended his life quietly as physician to the little court of Lippe.

The posthumously published work cited by Malthus in Bk I, ch. xii, n. 53, was *The History of Japan* ... 'written in High-Dutch by Engelbertus Kaempfer, M.D., Physician to the Dutch Embassy to the Emperor's Court, and translated from his Original Manuscript, never before printed, by J. G. Scheuchzer, F.R.S., and a member of the College of Physicians, London'. (Two volumes bound in one folio, London 1727.)

Bk II, pp. 143–202, gives, as Malthus says, a grim account of rebellions, wars, arson, inundations and famine. According to Kaempfer, on 12 April 1638 thirty-seven thousand Christians were 'put to death on one day. This act of cruelty at once put an end to the rebellion, and a finishing stroke to the total abolition of the Christian Religion in Japan.' (p. 197.)

John Gaspar Scheuchzer (1702–29) called Scheutzer in the D.N.B., was a young doctor of promise, librarian to Sir Hans Sloane; he was able to translate the 'High-Dutch' – *Hoch-deutsch* – because he was born in Zürich, where he qualified.

KAMES, LORD; HENRY HOME (1696–1782), a Scottish judge – his title relates solely to his office as a lord of session – who was also a voluminous writer, on morality and natural religion as well as the law. Malthus might be forgiven for mis-spelling his name as 'Kaimes', since even the posthumous edition of his most notable work was published anonymously. This, cited by Malthus, was *Sketches of the History of Man*, 'considerably enlarged by the last additions and corrections of the author', in four octavo volumes (Edinburgh and London 1788).

In his Preface Kames wrote that his book was 'intended for those who, free from the corruption of opulence and the depression of bodily labour, are fond of useful knowledge'. Much of his 'knowledge' was speculation, and like Buffon (q.v.) whom he quotes, Kames may be regarded as a precursor of Darwin: he could not make up his mind whether all human beings were the offspring of a single pair, Adam and Eve, or whether the different and dark-skinned races were a completely separate creation.

Malthus's reference to Kames in Bk I, ch. iv, n. 99, is perhaps unfair; Kames believed that the North American Indians were forced to continue to exist as hunters because their climate was too cold for agriculture (*op. cit.*, Vol. I, p. 101). A few pages later (pp. 105–7) comes the passage cited by Malthus in Bk III, ch. xii, n. 2. Kames wrote:

A country where the inhabitants live chiefly by hunting, must be very thin of inhabitants, as 10 000 acres, or double that number, are no more than sufficient to maintain a single family. ... A tribe soon becomes too populous for the primitive state of hunting and fishing: it may easily become too populous for the shepherd-state; but it cannot easily become too populous for husbandry. In the two former states, food must decrease in quantity as consumers increase in number: but agriculture has the signal property of producing, by industry, food in proportion to the number of consumers.

KING, GREGORY (1648–1712), was a modest man whose gifts embraced genealogy and heraldry, including the emblazoning of armorial bearings, surveying and the making and engraving of maps, and what was called 'Political Arithmetick'. His contribution to this study is entitled *Natural and Political Observations and Conclusions upon the State and Condition of England, 1696*. It is a fascinating pamphlet, much used – with King's permission – by Charles Davenant (q.v.) but it was not published in full until 1804. King's work was then printed as an Appendix to his own *Estimate of the Comparative Strength of Great Britain* by George Chalmers (1742–1825) an antiquarian collector and compiler.

Thus Malthus could not have read the original *Observations and Conclusions* when he cited 'Mr King' on p. 125 of the *Essay* of 1798. The passing reference to Gregory King in Bk II, ch. x, which was added to the quarto version in 1806, gives no indication of further reading on Malthus's part; there, as in 1798, King's name is joined with that of Dr Thomas Short (q.v.). Malthus did, however, quote George Chalmers' *Estimate* in the *Principles of Political Economy* (1820), p. 318.

KRAFFT, WOLFGANG LUDWIG (1743–1814), also spelt Kraft, the son of a well-known mathematician of Tübingen in the Duchy of Württemberg, was Professor of Astronomy at the Academy of St Petersburg from 1767 until his death. He worked with Euler (q.v.) on his *Theoria motuum lunae nova methodo pertractata* (1772) but Krafft's contributions to the *Nova Acta* of the Academy, on the marriages births and deaths in St Petersburg, were written in French.

Malthus seems to have read only the fourth volume of the *Nova Acta* (see the note on Hermann) so he missed a paper by Krafft which was published in Vol. III in 1782; this was headed 'Essai sur les tables des mariages, des naissances et des morts de la Ville de St Pétersbourg dans la période de 17 ans depuis 1764 jusqu'à 1780' (pp. 3–66). The paper from which Malthus quotes in Bk II, ch. iii, n. 16, runs from pp. 174–208 of Vol. IV, and is entitled 'Suite du Mémoire sur les listes des mariages, des naissances et des morts à St Pétersbourg, contenant la période de 1781 jusqu'en

1785'. The date is given as 21 August 1788. For modern readers, a major point of interest is Krafft's preoccupation, like other writers of his period, with the number of years in which a population will double itself. Malthus does not give Krafft's fourth main cause of death (p. 184) which is simply *vieillesse* – old age.

LABILLARDIÈRE, JACQUES-JULIEN HOUTON DE (1755–1834), was both a botanist and an explorer, initially in Syria, who wrote the account of the expedition in search of La Pérouse (q.v.) begun in 1791 under the command of Admiral Bruny Dentrecasteaux. The editor has been unable to trace the English translation to which Malthus refers in Bk I, ch. v, n. 65. The description of the New Caledonians eating *stéatite* (soap-stone) may be found on p. 205 of Vol. II of the French edition published in 1800 in two quarto volumes. The title-page is worth quoting at length:

*Relation du Voyage à la Recherche de La Pérouse* fait par ordre de l'Assemblée Constituante, pendant les années 1791, 1792, et pendant la 1ᵉʳᵉ et la 2ᵈᵉ année de la République Française. Par le Gen. Labillardière, Correspondent de la ci-devant Academie des Sciences de Paris, membre de la Société d'Histoire Naturelle, et l'un des naturalistes de l'expédition. Paris, An. VIII de la République Française.

Labillardière noted that the soap-stone one of the islanders ate was very soft, greenish, and as large as two fists. Later the party saw others who eagerly ate the same substance; Labillardière observed that although it had no nourishing juice (*suc nourricier*) soap-stone was invaluable as a stomach-filler for people who often had to go without food for a long time.

Malthus's use of the word *steatite* in this connection is given as an example in the Oxford English Dictionary.

The editor cannot trace Malthus's authority for the statement that the inhabitants of New Caledonia ate spiders.

LAFITAU, JOSEPH-FRANÇOIS (c.1680–1740), was a native of Bordeaux who became a Jesuit missionary to the North American Indians.

Malthus's reference in Bk I, ch. iv, n. 4 is to his *Moeurs des Sauvages Amériquains comparées aux Moeurs des premiers Temps*, published in Paris in two quarto volumes in 1724. The customs of the barbarians of the Old World, with which he compares those of the indigenous Americans, are the practices described by a number of Greek and Latin authors. Like Burke and Robertson (q.v.) Lafitau took 'America' as a whole, with a map of the entire continent, north and south; there is a delightful engraved frontispiece of Adam and Eve and Jesus Christ, representing Truth. Unfortunately Lafitau was much concerned with theological disputes, especially those between the Jesuits and the Franciscans and, as Robertson remarks, the article on religion extends to 347 tedious pages.

LA PÉROUSE, JEAN-FRANÇOIS DE, COMTE DE GALAUP (1741–?1788), a sailor who was taken prisoner by the British when Hawke defeated the French fleet off Belle-Isle in 1759, and later fought against the British for the United States of America. He was sent by the French government on a voyage of exploration which was to include everything from the prospects of whaling in the South Atlantic to trading furs across the North Pacific.

Malthus's references in Bk I, ch. iv and ch. v, are to La Pérouse's own account of his voyage, which was brought back to Paris by Jean-Baptiste de Lesseps (q.v.) and published posthumously in 1797 in four volumes, after all hope of La Pérouse's return had been abandoned. The editor cannot explain why Malthus should have cited a quarto edition published in London in 1794. His quotations, however, are quite accurate, and may easily be found in Vol. II of a three-volume (octavo) English version published by Joseph Johnson in 1798; there was a second edition in 1799. The work was entitled *A Voyage Round the World in the Years 1785, 1786, 1787 and 1788* 'by J. F. G. de la Pérouse'.

In this connection it is relevant to remember that theories on the perfectibility of man without government were still linked to the concept of the noble savage. Before giving his account of the squalors of primitive life among the American Indians, in terms far more explicit than those used by Malthus, La Pérouse had written

In vain may philosophers exclaim against this picture. They write books in their closets, whilst I have been engaged in voyages during a course of thirty years. I have been a witness of the injustice and deceptions of these people, whom they have described to us as so good, because they are very near to a state of nature. (Johnson's 1798 edn, Vol. II, p. 132.)

LEGOBIEN, CHARLES (1653–1708), was a Jesuit from a Breton family who worked in Paris. He wrote much on the Jesuit missionaries in south-east Asia, the Emperor of China's edict in favour of Christianity, and the Chinese attitude towards Confucius and their dead ancestors.

He published in Paris in 1700 his *Histoires des Isles Marianes, nouvellement converties à la Religion Chréstienne; et de la mort glorieuse des premiers Missionaires qui y ont prêché la Foy.** By a strange coincidence the copy of this work in the Bodleian Library is the one which actually belonged to Charles de Brosses (q.v.) in whose *Histoire des Navigations aux Terres australes* Malthus read extracts from 'Père Gobien'. The Count de Brosses has cut Legobien's work and altered paragraphs, but Malthus's reference in Bk I, ch. v, n. 58, corresponds fairly well with pp. 59–62 of Legobien's original octavo edition.

What Malthus does not tell his readers is why Legobien thought so many young men on the Marianne Islands remained unmarried. According to him, married men had no authority over their wives, whose rule in the home was absolute; they could leave their husbands – taking their property and children with them – whenever they felt so inclined. If a wife were unfaithful, the husband might kill her lover, but not ill-treat her in any way: on the other hand, an injured wife could gather all the women of the village together, to steal or lay waste all the stores and crops of the erring husband: 'Cet empire des femmes dans le ménage est cause qu'une infinité de jeunes gens ne veulent pas se marier.'** (Vol. II of de Brosses's *Histoire*, pp. 505–7.)

* *History of the Mariane Islands, recently converted to the Christian Religion; and of the glorious death of the first Missionaries who preached the Faith there.*
** 'This supremacy of the women in their households is the reason why a multitude of young men do not wish to get married.'

See also *Lettres Édifiantes et Curieuses.*

LETTRES ÉDIFIANTES ET CURIEUSES, *écrites des Missions étrangères par quelques Missionaires de la Compagnie de Jésus.* This series of reports from Jesuit missionaries was first put together by Père Charles Legobien (q.v.) who published in 1702 a volume of *Lettres de quelques Missionaires de la Compagnie de Jésus, écrites de la Chine et des Indes Orientales.* This book was such a success that he began the publication in parts of the *Lettres Édifiantes et Curieuses*; he published eight before he died, and Duhalde (q.v.) carried on with numbers IX–XXVI.

The Society of Jesus was founded by St Ignatius Loyola (a Basque nobleman) and constituted a religious order in 1540 by Pope Paul III. In addition to the usual vows of poverty, chastity and obedience, the members promised to be entirely at the Pope's disposal all over the world; this involved the Society actively in the mission field and in the Counter-Reformation against Protestantism. In the eighteenth century, political considerations led to the Jesuits being expelled from Portugal, France and Spain, and the Order was suppressed in 1773. It was revived in 1814.

The suppression of the Society of Jesus does not seem to have affected the popularity of the *Lettres Édifiantes* as what a later generation would describe as 'thrillers'. Malthus used a duodecimo edition in 24 volumes, published in Paris in 1780–81, 'avec approbation et privilège du roi', which is now at Jesus College, Cambridge.

LE VAILLANT, FRANÇOIS (1753–1824), was born in Dutch Guiana (now Surinam) and wrote about parrots and other birds of the West Indies. His wealthy merchant family returned to Paris in 1777, and in 1780–85 he travelled in South Africa, being impelled to go there because 'c'étoit la terre encore vierge'.* In fact he was never very far from the Dutch at the Cape of Good Hope.

In Bk I, ch. iv, n. 6, Malthus refers to Le Vaillant's *Voyage dans l'Intérieur d'Afrique*, pp. 12–13 of tom. I. This should be tom. II of the two-volume edition published in Paris in 1790, with attractive engravings of naked Hottentots not looking in the least phlegmatic.

When he came to write specifically about Africa, Malthus used only Bruce, Park and Volney (qq.v.); it is impossible to tell whether this was a matter of deliberate choice, or simply due to the fact that other books about Africa, such as Le Vaillant's, were not available to him at the time he was writing ch. viii of Bk I.

LIVY, in Latin TITUS LIVIUS (*c.*59 B.C.–*c.*A.D. 17), was famous for his *History of Rome.* The first ten books cover the legendary arrival of Aeneas, after the fall of Troy, to about 290 B.C., when Rome had become the paramount power among the warring peoples of central Italy. Malthus's reference in Bk I, ch. xiv, n. 2, may be found on pp. 232–5 in Vol. II of the Loeb edition (trans. B. O. Foster 1924):

I doubt not that those who are surfeited with reading in all these books about endless wars waged with the Volsci will ask, as with great astonishment I did myself... where the so oft defeated Volsci and Aequi got their supply of soldiers. It is probable either that in the

---

* 'it was still virgin territory'.

intervals between wars successive generations sprang up – as happens nowadays in the levies of the Romans – which they used for their frequent renewals of war; or that it was not always the same tribes from which they enrolled their armies – though it was always the same nation which made war; or else that there was an innumerable multitude of freemen in those regions, which in our day scarce afford a scanty seed-plot for soldiers, and are only saved from becoming a waste desert by gangs of Roman slaves.

LORDS, HOUSE OF, *see under* Corn Laws.

LOWE, JOSEPH, an unknown gentleman who published in London in 1822 an octavo volume entitled *The Present State of England in regard to Agriculture, Trade and Finance; with a comparison of the prospects of England and France.* There was a second edition, very much revised, in 1823.

The quotation Malthus takes from Thomas Tooke (q.v.) is from Lowe's first edition – it only appears in Tooke's second edition – and is on p. 149. Later on, in this same first edition, Lowe rather contradicted himself; he disagreed with Malthus's principle of population, believing that 'subsistence is more easy of acquisition as society advances'; on p. 236 Lowe wrote:

From the great diversity of soil and climate in the cultivated portion of the globe, scarcity is never general: 'when famine was in other lands, in the land of Egypt there was bread.' If this apply to an age when civilization extended over hardly ten degrees of latitude, how much more does it hold at present ... Extended communication by water enables even distant countries to supply the deficiency of each other; while in the same territory improved methods of preserving corn, additional granaries, augmented capital, all concur to enable the inhabitants to keep over the surplus of one year as a provision for the possible failure of the next.

By 1823 Lowe must have realised that this was not enough to confound the 'anti-populationists', and on p. 243 of his second edition his emphasis is on the completely new sources of food – the extension of tillage along the shores of the Black Sea, and the vastly increased cultivation of the United States of America.

It is possible that Malthus copied out Tooke's quotation from Lowe without ever reading the original work himself.

McCULLOCH, JOHN RAMSAY (1789–1864), began his career as a lawyer's clerk, having left Edinburgh University without a degree in order to marry at the age of 22; he was the father of 12 children, of whom ten grew up and did well. He was Ricardo's principal disciple, and actively disliked Malthus. As a contributor to the *Scotsman* and the *Edinburgh Review* he wielded considerable influence, and published important works of his own, as well as an edition of the *Wealth of Nations* in 1828.

When Macvey Napier was looking for contributors to the *Supplement* to the *Encyclopaedia Britannica* (finally published in full in 1824) McCulloch was the obvious choice for the main article on 'Political Economy', as well as on 'Corn Laws and Trade'; it is this latter article which Malthus cites in his long footnote added in 1825 to Bk III, ch. E (n. 18).

The sentences quoted by Malthus come from Vol. III of the *Supplement*, p. 361, column 2:

No one instance of universal scarcity blackens the history of mankind; but it is constantly found, that when the crops of one country fail, plenty reigns in some other quarter.

A freedom of trade is alone wanted to guarantee a country like Britain, abounding in all the varied products of industry, in merchandise suited to the wants of every society, from the possibility of a scarcity. The nations of the earth are not condemned to throw the dice to determine which of them shall submit to famine. There is always an abundance of food in the world ...

In this article, McCulloch repeatedly criticised Malthus by name, especially for his chapter 'Of Systems of Agriculture and Commerce Combined' in Bk iii of the 1817 edition of *Population*; on p. 362 there is a marginal heading, 'Error of Mr Malthus on the subject of the Corn Laws'.

After Ricardo's death in September 1823 a group of his friends met, without Malthus, to arrange a series of lectures in his memory. Twenty-one lectures, two a week, were given by McCulloch in London, beginning in April 1824. The course was extremely successful, attended by celebrities from both the Whig and Tory parties; Malthus did not go, on account of his duties at the East India College. Later in the year, McCulloch was invited to give a similar course of lectures, thrice weekly, at the Liverpool Royal Institution: this had been founded in 1814 by a group of public-spirited businessmen, and other visiting lecturers included Thomas Campbell on Ancient and Modern Poetry, P. M. Roget on Physiology, and Antonio Panizzi on Italian Literature.

It says much for Malthus's enthusiasm for his subject that (in his n. 10 of ch. ix in Book iv) he could generously refer to two courses of lectures given by a man who was commonly regarded as his enemy.

MACHIAVELLI, NICCOLO (1469–1527), is perhaps better known for his *Prince*, regarded as a manual of power politics, than for his *History of Florence*, of which city he was a native, at the time of the convulsions caused by the banishment and return of the Medici family. Machiavelli maintained that it was the emperors' removal from Rome to Constantinople which so weakened the western division of the empire that it was left open to pillage by the barbarians of the north.

Malthus's translation of the first paragraph of Machiavelli's *History of Florence* (Bk i, ch. vi, n. 32) differs from that of Gibbon (q.v.) and cannot be traced. It is possible that it was provided by one of Malthus's sisters, or his cousin Jane Dalton, all known for their 'highly cultivated minds'.

MACKINTOSH, SIR JAMES (1765–1832), originally studied medicine, then turned to law and journalism, and wrote *Vindiciae Gallicae* (London 1791) in answer to Edmund Burke's *Reflections on the Revolution in France* published the year before. After the Terror, Mackintosh changed his mind, which led Charles Lamb to compare him to Judas Iscariot.

Mackintosh became more widely known for a course of 39 lectures on 'The Law of Nature and Nations', delivered to an audience of 150, including six peers and 12 members of parliament, in the Hall of Lincoln's Inn, from February to June 1799. It was at this period that Malthus and Mackintosh became acquainted. In 1803 Mackintosh was knighted on his appointment as Recorder of Bombay – then the principal judge of the Presidency – where he remained until 1812; he returned to England to become a conspicuous Whig member of parliament and, from 1818 to 1824, a colleague of Malthus on the staff of the East India College.

Mackintosh's 'attack' on Godwin (q.v.) in the published *Prospectus* of his lectures was all the more painful because the two men were close friends. Godwin felt he was being taunted personally when Mackintosh referred to 'such fanciful chimeras as a golden mountain or a perfect man'. Sir James and Lady Mackintosh, however, remained among Godwin's principal apologists and benefactors.

MALLET, PAUL HENRI (1730–1807), was a member of a distinguished family, originally from Rouen, who became citizens of Geneva in 1558. In 1752 he was appointed Professeur de Belles-Lettres françaises – Professor of French Literature – at the Academy of Copenhagen. As no one there was particularly interested in French, Mallet found that he had plenty of time to study the history and literature of the northern peoples, which were then but little known.

In 1755 Mallet published his *Introduction à l'Histoire de Dannemarc ou l'on traite de la Religion, des Loix, des Moeurs at des Usages des anciens Danois (Introduction to the History of Denmark, in which are considered the religion, the laws, the manners and customs of the Danes of earlier times)*. There were many editions. Malthus's page references fit one published in Geneva in six duodecimo volumes in 1763; the editor has been unable to find one published in 1766. One cannot but admire Malthus's translation of *des ravages et d'effroi* as 'desolation and terror'.

MANDEVILLE, BERNARD DE (1670–1733), was a native of Dordrecht in Holland, a doctor of medicine, who settled in England for unknown reasons, and in 1705 published his doggerel *The Grumbling Hive, or Knaves Turned Honest*. It was reprinted many times, later entitled *The Fable of the Bees, or Private Vices, Public Benefits*; Mandeville added much commentary in prose, which was referred to extensively by Adam Smith.

Despite Malthus's strictures in the 1806 *Appendix*, it is impossible not to enjoy the verses:

> Vast Numbers throng'd the fruitful Hive
> Yet those vast Numbers made 'em thrive;
> Millions endeavouring to supply
> Each other's Lust and Vanity ...

Mandeville castigates Church and State, Medicine and Law, then explains:

> Thus every Part was full of Vice,
> Yet the whole Mass a Paradise ...
> The worst of all the Multitude
> Did something for the Common Good ...
> Their darling Folly, Fickleness
> In Diet, Furniture and Dress,
> That strange ridic'lous Vice was made
> The very Wheel that turn'd the Trade ...
> For what was well done for a Time,
> In half a Year became a Crime ...
> Thus Vice nurs'd Ingenuity,
> Which joyn'd with Time and Industry
> Had carry'd Life's Conveniencies,

> Its real Pleasures, Comforts, Ease,
> To such a Height, the very Poor
> Liv'd better than the Rich before.

But the stupid bees grumbled, and prayed for *Honesty* (which seems to have included Frugality, as nobody contracted debts) and when their prayer was granted the whole fabric of society fell to pieces, the hive was overcome by their foes, and the survivors flew away to live miserably in a hollow tree.

MANN, THEODORE AUGUSTUS (1735–1809), was the son of a Yorkshire surveyor of roads and bridges; he ran away to France in 1754 and in 1756 became a Roman Catholic. Thereafter he led a life of travel, intense study, and prolific writing on a variety of scientific and historical subjects. In 1777 he was established in Brussels, then part of the Austrian Empire, as Minister for Public Instruction, and as the Abbé Mann he was a European literary celebrity, F.R.S., F.S.A. and so on.

The Board of Agriculture, an emergency war-time organisation, was set up by the Prime Minister, William Pitt the Younger, in 1793, with Arthur Young (q.v.) as Secretary.

The work to which Malthus refers in Bk III, ch. xii, n. 22, was published in 1797: *Communications to the Board of Agriculture; on subjects relative to the Husbandry and Internal Improvement of the Country.* Part IV was 'Foreign Communications' and the Abbé Mann wrote:

What is cultivated in the Campine, is owing to the religious houses established in it, especially to the two great abbeys of Tongerloo and Everbode. Their uninterrupted duration for five or six hundred years past, and their indefatigable industry, have conquered these barren harsh sands, and rendered many parts of them highly productive. The method they follow is simple and uniform; they never undertake to cultivate more of this barren soil at a time than they have sufficient manure for.

MEARES, JOHN (?1756–1809), left the Navy for the merchant service after the Peace of Paris in 1783, and formed a company in Calcutta for developing trade with north-west America; Nootka Sound was named after his ship, in which he brought back a cargo of furs to Canton. Two of his company's ships sent on a similar voyage were seized by the Spaniards, which caused a furore in England, and a fleet was assembled under Lord Howe; the Spanish government acceded to the British demands.

This publicity led to Meares publishing the work quoted by Malthus in Bk I, ch. iv and ch. xii. It was entitled *Voyages made in the Years 1788 and 1789 from China to the North West Coast of America; to which are prefixed an Introductory Narrative of a Voyage performed in 1786, from Bengal, in the Ship Nootka; Observations on the probable existence of a North West Passage, etc.* (London 1790, quarto).

Malthus's faint tinge of scepticism about the house in which eight hundred people lived (Bk I, ch. iv, n. 44) was possibly due to George Dixon's allegations that Meares had 'misrepresented a number of important Facts'. Dixon, a former petty-officer under Captain Cook, had explored in the same waters, and much of the subsequent pamphlet warfare between Meares and Dixon was concerned with the sobriety or otherwise of their respective crews.

MILL, JOHN STUART (1806–1873), moral and political philosopher, logician and economist, the son of Ricardo's friend and mentor James Mill, who educated him at home, and produced a prodigy of learning at the expense of a normal childhood. John followed his father as a clerk in the London office of the East India Company, and as a contributor to the *Westminster Review*, founded in 1824 as the organ of the 'philosophical radicals'. John also adopted his father's pro-Ricardo and anti-Malthus position with regard to political economy; in January 1825 John had published in the *Westminster* a witty criticism of Malthus's review in the *Quarterly* of McCulloch's article on 'Political Economy' in the *Supplement* to the *Encyclopaedia Britannica*.

The article on the Corn Laws to which Malthus refers in Bk III, ch. E, n. 18, appeared in April 1825, anonymously, as was the custom, just a month before John's nineteenth birthday; it was nominally concerned with a long pamphlet by an M.P. named Whitmore. It is enjoyable reading, castigating that 'idol called agriculture', and the doctrine that rich landlords are more conducive to the happiness of a community than cheap food. The passage quoted by Malthus may be found on p. 61 of Vol. IV of the *Collected Works of J. S. Mill* (University of Toronto Press and Routledge, Kegan, Paul, 1967).

On this same page the anonymous young John praises Thomas Tooke (q.v.): 'A small variation in the supply of such a commodity as corn produces a much more than proportional variation in price: a proposition which Mr Tooke, who has explained so many of the complicated phenomena of prices, has shown to be as conformable to observed facts as it is to sound reasoning.'

On p. 69 John writes that although Mr Ricardo, like Mr Whitmore, recommended a fixed duty on imported wheat of 10s. a quarter, he had advised 'as a measure of indulgence to the agriculturists ... that the duty be originally fixed at 20s. and lowered 1s. every year until reduced to 10. We shall be believed when we say, it is with the greatest hesitation we presume to differ from so great an authority, but ... we suspect that if the annual reduction proposed by Mr Ricardo were adopted, the anticipated fall of price ... might involve the producers in all the evils of a glut.'

MILNE, JOSHUA (1776–1851), was an actuary whose life tables, based on the bills of mortality for the city of Carlisle, were a great improvement on those of Richard Price for Northampton. In spite of his limited data, Milne's calculations were remarkably accurate, and his book is regarded as a landmark in actuarial science: *A Treatise on the Valuation of Annuities and Assurances on Lives and Survivorships; on the Construction of Tables of Mortality; and on the Probabilities and Expectations of Life* (2 vols., London 1815).

Milne was the obvious authority for Macvey Napier to approach for an article in the *Supplement* to the *Encyclopaedia Britannica*, on 'Mortality, Human, Law of', which may be found in Vol. V, pp. 543–59. The historical section is well worth reading. For example, Milne wrote:

85. It ought also to be observed, that most of the tables of mortality ... have been constructed from observations made upon the whole population of very large towns, such as London, Paris, Vienna and Stockholm; in each of which there are particular quarters inhabited only by the very lowest of the people, who, unfortunately, are also very numerous, badly clothed and fed, therefore exposed to serious injury from the

inclemencies of the weather; extremely ignorant and vicious, indulging in the abuse of spirituous liquors, and inattentive to cleanliness both in their persons and habitations; which last are crowded, badly ventilated, and surrounded with mud and the putrid remains of animals and vegetables. ...

86. It is, therefore, obvious, that in such places, the average mortality at every age must be considerably greater than that which prevails among the middling and higher classes of society even in such towns.

87. But the lives upon which leases, annuities, reversions, and assurances depend, are very seldom exposed to the influence of the causes of mortality mentioned in No. 85. Whence it follows, that a table of mortality on which those causes have had no great influence, is best adapted to the valuation of such interests.

And these kind of valuations are the most important purposes to which tables of mortality can be applied.

MILTON, JOHN (1608–1674), the poet who became a political writer and Latin Secretary to Cromwell's Council of State; on the Restoration of the Monarchy he returned to poverty and poetry with his epic *Paradise Lost*.

Malthus took it for granted his readers would recognise this quotation, which is from the last nine lines of the poem. Adam has been comforted by the Angel Michael, prophesying man's redemption through Christ; then he and Eve are driven out of the Garden:

> They looking back; all th'Eastern side beheld
> Of Paradise, so late their happy seat,
> Wav'd over by that flaming Brand, the Gate
> With dreadful Faces throng'd and fiery Arms:
> Some natural tears they dropp'd, but wip'd them soon;
> The World was all before them, where to choose
> Their place of rest, and Providence their guide:
> They hand in hand with wand'ring steps and slow,
> Through Eden took their solitary way.

MIRABEAU, VICTOR RIQUETTI, MARQUIS DE (1715–1789), of a Provençal family, originally from Naples: this *économiste* should not be confused with his two more dramatic sons, who were conspicuous during the French Revolution. The first three parts of *L'Ami des Hommes, ou Traité de la Population* were published anonymously in 1756; this is presumably why Malthus refers to 'the author of *L'Ami des Hommes*' in Bk III, ch. xii, n. 17, although it is possible that it was prudent not to mention the name of Mirabeau in an English book in 1803.

Malthus's reference may be found on p. 84 of Vol. VI of the 1761 Avignon edition of *L'Ami des Hommes*. The catalogues of major libraries contain many versions of Mirabeau's works, which changed in character as he came more and more under the influence of Quesnay and the Physiocrats, and this set is described as *nouvelle édition corrigée*. Malthus's quotation is from a section of separately numbered pages – *L'Ami des Hommes, suite de la VI Partie* – and is devoted to the 'Tableau Économique avec ses explications'. Malthus translates Mirabeau fairly literally – 'j'avois ... fondamentalement erré' – but omits Mirabeau's tribute to Quesnay as one more able than himself, who had confronted him with his mistake, and to whom he had been happy to listen.

MISSIONARY VOYAGE, *see under* Wilson, William.

MOHEAU. *Recherches et Considerations sur la Population de la France par M. Moheau.* This was published in Paris in 1778, Livre I consisting of 280 pages, Livre II of 157, bound together in one octavo volume.

The copy of this work in the Bodleian Library has a manuscript note: 'La plus grande partie de ce livre est attribuée à Antoine-Jean-Baptiste Auget, baron de Montyon.' According to the *Dictionnaire de la Noblesse* (1863) Antoine-Jean-Baptiste-Robert Auget, Seigneur de Boissy, Baron de Monthion, etc., was born in 1733, but there is no further information.

Malthus's passing reference to Moheau with Necker (q.v.) in Bk II, ch. viii, n. 19, suggests that he had never himself seen this attractive book. It is dedicated to Louis XVI, who came to the throne in 1774, and Moheau wrote with unintentional irony: 'Il est possible que, sous Louis XVI, la Nation prenne un caractère nouveau'; * he prayed that public affairs would be directed in the way most advantageous to the propagation and conservation of the human species.

MONTESQUIEU, CHARLES-LOUIS DE SECONDAT, BARON DE (1689–1755), was President of the *Parlement* of Bordeaux in 1716. In 1721 he published his *Lettres persanes*; in these he enjoyed himself criticising French institutions, through the eyes of imaginary visitors from Persia, who were supposed to have lived in Paris from 1711 to 1719. Montesquieu then gave up his civil offices in order to travel, and spent three years in England; on his return to France he retired to his country estates to write his *Considérations sur les Causes de la Grandeur des Romains, et de leur Décadence*, which was published in 1734. His greatest work, *De l'Esprit des Loix*, appeared in 1748.

In Bk I, ch. vi, n. 42, Malthus gives a page number but no edition for his reference to 'Grandeur et Décad. des Rom'. When quoting Montesquieu's other works, he merely gives a reference to either a *Lettre*, or to *livre* and *chapitre*, sometimes in Roman numerals, sometimes in Arabic. There were innumerable editions of all three of Montesquieu's classics, but the references are not difficult to trace.

Malthus's quotation from the *Lettres persanes* in Bk II, ch. v, n. 27, deserves amplification: Montesquieu compares the children lost to France, through the marriage of parents too young and too poor to care for them, with plants which will only grow successfully when they are well cultivated.

References to *De l'Esprit des Loix* are the most numerous. That in Bk I, ch. v, n. 60, is incorrect: it is in *chapitre* XVI of *livre* XXIII that Montesquieu describes the peculiar custom of the people of Formosa. In Bk II, ch. v, n. 28, Malthus's reference is also to *livre* XXIII, which is concerned with 'Des Loix dans le Rapport qu'elles ont avec le Nombre des Habitans'. Montesquieu believed that among emerging nations – *les peuples naissans* – large families were of practical use to their parents; exactly the opposite was true, once a State had been fully established. Hence the suggestions which Malthus found 'perfectly astonishing', but which were quite logical from Montesquieu's point of view, based on population and power politics: if prosperous

---

* 'It is possible that, under Louis XVI, the nation will assume a different character.'

married couples did not wish to be inconvenienced by children, it was up to the State to provide inducements to propagation. Montesquieu's objection to Louis XIV's edict of 1666, to which Malthus refers in Bk IV, ch. xiii, n. 33, was that it would merely be rewarding the exceptionally prolific; he thought that for the general encouragement of population the negative approach of the Roman *jus trium liberorum* was more satisfactory; this, in theory, debarred any man with less than three children from various offices and privileges.

MURET, JEAN-LOUIS (1715–1796), a pastor at Vevey, who was also Secretary of the town's Société Oeconomique, and published a *Lettre sur l'Agriculture Perfectionée*. The paper quoted by Malthus was the prize-winning essay in a competition organised by the Société Oeconomique of Berne, for the best account of the population of the Canton or of 'un district particulier'.

Muret's *Mémoire sur l'État de la Population dans le Pays de Vaud* may be found in the *Mémoires et Observations recueillies par la Société Oeconomique de Berne* (octavo, 1766) which also contains accounts of the Society's meetings during the previous year, and papers from English correspondents on agricultural improvements. The pages of Muret's article are numbered 1–130, the tables are numbered separately on pp. 1–127, which may account for some of Malthus's references in Bk II, ch. vii being incorrect. Malthus's translation of Muret's text is very accurate.

NECKER, JACQUES (1732–1804), was the son of the Professor of Civil Law at Geneva, and sent to a Paris banking house at the age of fifteen; here he acquired both wealth and reputation as a financier, but resigned from the Royal Treasury when his religion (he was a Calvinist) debarred him from admission to the Council.

Necker bought the barony of Copet, near Geneva, and wrote in exile his *De l'Administration des Finances de la France* (3 vols. octavo 1785). A copy of this edition is in the Malthus Library at Jesus College, Cambridge, with the book-plate of his son Henry; the pagination corresponds with Malthus's references, and it seems likely that this is the set he actually used. Malthus met Necker's daughter, Germaine de Staël, when she visited England in 1813.

Most of Malthus's references to Necker's Chapter IX, 'Sur la Population du Royaume', need no comment. In the passage cited in Bk IV, ch. v, n. 1, Necker goes on to say that the birth-rate in cities may be one for every 27–30 inhabitants, but he was fully aware that many of the inhabitants of towns were immigrants born else-where. The passage referred to in the 1806 *Appendix*, n. 6, elaborates on the dispro-portionate number of children who will die before they are three or four years old, because their parents are too poor to give them sufficient nourishment or medical care when they are ill; Necker seems to appreciate that food alone is not enough to keep little children alive.

NEWTON, SIR ISAAC (1642–1727), is usually regarded as one of the first scientists, in the modern specialised sense of the word. 'Newtonian physics' and his Laws of Gravitation were virtually undisputed until Einstein (1879–1955) published his *General Theory of Relativity* in 1913. Like Descartes (q.v.) with whom he disagreed, Newton wrote in Latin, and his *Philosophiae Naturalis Principia Mathematica*, first published in 1687, was a standard textbook for the undergraduate Malthus.

Alexander Pope (q.v.) composed for a tablet in the room in which Newton was born:

> Nature and all her works lay hid in night;
> God said, Let Newton be, – and all was light.

NICANDER, HENRIK (1744–1815), was a mathematician primarily interested in astronomy, on which he lectured at the University of Uppsala, but he also did statistical work on trade and agriculture. Euler and Condorcet (qq.v.) were among his correspondents. In 1784 he succeeded Wargentin (q.v.) as Secretary of the Royal Swedish Academy of Sciences in Stockholm; from this year, until 1803, he was responsible for the astronomical information in calendars and almanacs. In 1790 Nicander became Secretary to the Tabellkommission of Sweden and Finland, the first central statistical office in the world: this had been set up in 1756 to correlate the data which local pastors had been obliged to collect at five-yearly intervals from 1749 onwards.

Nicander's great work on Swedish and Finnish statistics from 1772 to 1795 was published in eight parts during 1799–1801 (the complete version appeared in 1802) so that he must have been immersed in it when Malthus met him in Stockholm in the late summer of 1799. It is unfortunate that this part of Malthus's Scandinavian journal is lost.

There is also the possibility that correspondence between Nicander and Malthus has been lost. Malthus quotes figures (Bk II, ch. ii, n. 41) from the 'Transactions of the Royal Academy of Sciences in Stockholm' for the year 1809; these may be found in Tom. xxx, Tab. B: *Medium af Döde och Lefvande i alla åldrar under Quinquennium 1801–05*. The relevant article, the first in the volume, was by Nicander, who provided a contribution on population statistics for each quarterly number of the Academy's journal. There is no evidence that Malthus received this from Nicander, but it seems quite likely.

(The editor is indebted for help with this note to Mrs Barbro Edwards of the Cultural Department of the Swedish Embassy in London, and to Dr Gustav Lundqvist of the Royal Swedish Academy of Sciences.)

*See also* Süssmilch, Johann Peter.

NIEBUHR, CARSTEN (1733–1815), was a student of mathematics at Hamburg and Göttingen, and went as geographer on an official Danish scientific expedition to Arabia in 1761. He was the sole survivor, returning to Copenhagen in 1767 after appalling adventures in what are now Egypt, Yemen, Iran and Turkey. Carsten Niebuhr must not be confused with his son Berthold Georg (1776–1831) the Roman historian, who was a student in Edinburgh in 1798–99, and travelled in Britain afterwards.

Malthus used an English translation of Niebuhr's *Travels in Arabia* (2 vols. octavo, Edinburgh 1792) and it is perhaps surprising that there is only one reference to it, that in Bk I, ch. vii, n. 30.

NOVA ACTA, *see under* Hermann, Benedikt Franz Johann and Krafft, Wolfgang Ludwig.

OBSERVATIONS ON THE RESULTS OF THE POPULATION ACTS, *see under* Rickman, John.

ODDY, JOSHUA JEPSON, unsuccessfully contested the borough of Stamford, in Lincolnshire, in 1809, as a reforming Whig. It was Stamford's first parliamentary contest since 1734, as the member since that date has always been the nominee of 'the noble house of Burghley', and invariably returned unopposed. Mr Oddy is described in an account of this shocking but hilarious election as 'a Russian merchant of some consequence, and an author of some estimation on subjects connected with political economy'.

The work quoted by Malthus in 1807 is a quarto of over 600 pages, published in London in 1805. The title is *European Commerce, shewing new and secure Channels of Trade with the Continent of Europe, detailing the produce, manufactures and commerce of Russia, Prussia, Sweden, Denmark and Germany … with a General View of the Trade, Produce and Manufactures of the United Kingdom of Great Britain and Ireland, and its unexplored and improvable resources of interior wealth, Illustrated with a Canal and River map of Europe.* In his Preface, Mr Oddy states that he is concerned with 'uniting individual gain and prosperity with public security and greatness'.

The passage to which Malthus refers begins on p. 510:

The effect of the French revolution with respect to the corn trade, in driving it from Holland, should be the introducing it into this country. … Let all foreign grain be allowed importation at all times … under the King's lock, upon the principle of an entrepôt; there let it lay the pleasure of the owner for a market.

This stored grain could be sold in England in times of scarcity, under the existing laws: 'And if the price advanced, under these circumstances, it would rise from an actual deficiency in the country. … For want of such stock, prices frequently rapidly advance here, and this advance is anticipated abroad; so that it costs us enormous prices unnecessarily created.'

Oddy goes on to describe how American grain ships touched at Cork or Falmouth 'to learn the state of the European markets', and foretold how they would compete with the Baltic countries in the corn trade, a remarkable prophecy from a man who could not possibly have envisaged the development of railways and steam-ships.

OWEN, ROBERT (1771–1858), was the son of a Welsh saddler, and became the master of cotton mills at New Lanark in Scotland, after learning the trade in London and Manchester. While Malthus was writing his substitute third chapter of Bk III in 1816, Robert Owen was at the height of his fame, with royal and noble visitors flocking to see his model factory, school, and workers' houses.

In 1817 Owen made a public declaration of atheism, which damaged his causes, and Malthus's publisher John Murray felt obliged to tell him privately that in the circumstances he could not publish his work. (The editor is grateful to John Murray for permission to cite this, from the letter-book of John Murray II.) Neither Malthus nor Murray, however, thought it necessary in 1826 to alter either the third chapter of Bk III, or ch. xii of Bk IV, in which Malthus referred again to Owen's utopian schemes. The unpublished diary of Fanny Mackintosh (now in Keele

University Library) reveals that Owen was the guest of the Principal of the East India College on 12 August 1821, and that Malthus and her father (Sir James Mackintosh, q.v.) had much talk with him.

It is possible that Malthus first met Owen when he made a northern tour in the summer of 1810, and noted in his pocket-book that at the cotton mill at Lanark: 'The hours of working are from 6 in the morning to 7 in the evening. A good school is established in the village, but the spinners cannot have much leisure to attend it, as after their day's work they will naturally want some recreation. Sunday is therefore the only day on which they can be expected to give much attention to reading.' (*The Travel Diaries of T. R. Malthus*, Cambridge University Press 1966, p. 223.)

Robert Owen began his campaign for reduced working hours for children in 1815, in a shilling pamphlet entitled *Observations on the Effect of the Manufacturing System*, 'with hints for the improvement of those parts of it which are most injurious to health and morals'. He wanted the hours of work to be reduced to 12 a day, six hours for children under 12 years old. No children should be employed in a factory until they were ten, and 'until they can read and write in a useful manner, understand the first four rules of arithmetic, and the girls be likewise competent to sew their common garments of clothing'. (p. 9.)

*A New View of Society* consisted of four Essays on the Formation of the Human Character. The first essay was written in 1812, but the first collected edition was published in 1816. Although Owen continued to speak of the 'lower orders', he also used the phrase 'working classes' in these essays, and urged the 'manufacturer for pecuniary profit', like himself, to devote as much care to his vital machines as to those of wood, brass or iron, and especially to 'the prevention of unnecessary friction'. (pp. 73–5.)

In *A New View of Society* Owen expressed the common opinion of the English Poor Laws: 'Can that system be right, which compels the industrous, temperate and comparatively virtuous, to support the ignorant, the idle, and the comparatively vicious?' (p. 142.) Basically he disagreed with the principle of population: Malthus is correct 'when he says that the population of the world is ever adapting itself to the quantity of food raised for its support; but he has not told us how much more food an intelligent and industrious people will create from the same soil, than will be produced by one ignorant and ill-governed. It is however as one, to infinity.' (p. 174.)

'Mr Owen's plan' to which Malthus refers in Bk IV, ch. 12, was derided by Cobbett as 'parallelograms of paupers'. The scheme was to set up self-sufficient villages of two to three hundred families, grouped round the public buildings in the centre, in which all labour was to be for the good of the community as a whole. In agriculture, the spade was to replace the plough; other suggestions were equally ridiculous, quite contrary to the common sense that Robert Owen had displayed earlier.

PAINE, THOMAS (1737–1809), was born at Thetford in Norfolk of Quaker stock, and therefore naturally anti-monarchist. Benjamin Franklin (q.v.) urged him to go to America to use his pen on behalf of the 'Colonists', and Paine's pamphlet *Common Sense* is believed to have accelerated the Declaration of Independence. He went on diplomatic and trade missions to France on behalf of the Americans, returning to England in 1787. Paine's *The Rights of Man* was published in two parts, the first in 1791 being the most notorious, as it was written in reply to Edmund Burke's *Reflections on the Revolution in France*, and defiantly dedicated to George Washington, the President of the United States. 'Part the Second, Combining Principle and Practice', appeared a year later.

Malthus's attitude to Paine in Bk IV, ch. vi, sounds strange to modern readers, for his 'rights' of free speech and free elections, on the principle of one man, one vote, in both central and local government, are taken for granted today in democratic countries: it should be remembered that this was the period of the unreformed House of Commons and closed municipal corporations.

A warrant was issued for Paine's arrest, and he was burned in effigy in Cambridge after he had fled to France. While he was in prison in Paris, for opposing the execution of 'Louis Capet', Paine wrote *The Age of Reason*, with much criticism of the Bible, and an outline of his own position as a deist; one of the theologians who answered him was Malthus's old tutor Gilbert Wakefield (1756–1801) who was himself a liberal Unitarian. Tom Paine spent the last seven years of his life in America, and died in New York.

PALEY, WILLIAM, D.D. (1743–1805), was a Fellow of Christ's College, Cambridge (and the tutor of Malthus's tutor, William Frend) until 1776, when he married and held various livings in the north-west of England.

Malthus has three references to Paley's *Principles of Moral and Political Philosophy*, which was first published in 1785. The first, in Bk IV, ch. ii, n. 14, shows clearly how both men were concerned with the greatest happiness of the greatest number; the sentence quoted by Malthus is the conclusion of Paley's chapter on 'The Will of God'.

The reference in Bk IV, ch. iii, n. 10, is to Paley's chapter 'Of Population and Provision; and of Agriculture and Commerce, as subservient thereto'. In this, Paley asserted that 'in comparing adjoining periods, in the same country, the collective happiness will be nearly in the exact proportion of the numbers, that is, twice the number of inhabitants will produce double the quantity of happiness'. Therefore, 'the decay of population is the greatest evil that a state can suffer; and the improvement of it the object which ought, in all countries, to be aimed at, in preference to every other political purpose whatsoever'. In pursuing this theme, Paley pointed out that 'habitual superfluities become real wants', and men would not marry and raise families if by doing so they had 'to reduce their mode of living'.

This argument leads on (Malthus's reference in Bk IV, ch. xiii, n. 26) to the somewhat uncongenial conclusion with regard to the 'true evil and proper danger of *luxury*'. Paley believed that the luxury of a few is favourable to trade and employment, and 'gives not only support, but existence, to multitudes of families': the too-great diffusion of luxury is inimical to population, because it discourages young men from marrying.

The last work Paley published before his death was *Natural Theology: or Evidences of the Existence and Attributes of the Deity collected from the Appearances of Nature* (London 1802). The passage quoted by Malthus in Bk IV, ch. i, n. 10, continues with a criticism of Hume's diatribe against idleness (q.v.): Paley wrote, apropos reason and self-government: 'It will be found, I believe, to be true, that in every community there is a large class of its members, whose idleness is the best quality about them, being the corrective of other bad ones ... nothing would be so dangerous as an incessant, universal, indefatigable activity.'

Malthus is very modest about Paley's altered views on population in Bk IV, ch. xiii, n. 26; Paley himself on p. 540 of *Natural Theology* has a footnote: 'See this subject stated in a late treatise upon population' – which was, of course, the anonymous 1798 *Essay*. Paley wrote in 1802: 'The order of generation proceeds by something like a geometrical progression. The increase of provision, under circumstances even the most advantageous, can only assume the form of an arithmetic series. Whence it follows, that the population will always overtake the provision, will pass beyond the line of plenty, and will continue to increase till checked by the difficulty of procuring subsistence. Such difficulty, therefore, along with its attendant circumstances, *must* be found in every old country; and these circumstances constitute what we call poverty, which, necessarily, imposes labour, servitude, restraint. It seems impossible to people a country with inhabitants who shall be all in easy circumstances. For suppose the thing to be done, there would be such marrying and giving in marriage amongst them, as would in a few years change the face of affairs entirely.'

PALLAS, PETER SIMON (1741–1811), born and died in Berlin, studied at Halle, Göttingen and Leyden; in 1777 he accepted an invitation from Catherine the Great to join 'the Committee for the Measurement and Topography of Russia', which involved extensive travel throughout the empire. He was rewarded with estates in the Crimea, where he was visited by Malthus's friend Edward Daniel Clarke.

The editor is greatly indebted to Dr Régis de Courten, of the Schweizerische Landesbibliothek, for finding that Malthus's *'Découvertes Russes'*, from which he quotes extensively in Bk I, chs. vii, ix and x, was in fact entitled *Histoire des Découvertes*. The title-page continues: 'faites par divers Savans Voyageurs, Dans plusieurs contrées de la Russie & de la Perse, relativement à l'Histoire civile & naturelle, à l'Économie rurale, au Commerce, &c'.* Rather surprisingly, Vols. III and IV appeared in 1781, published in Berne by the Nouvelle Société Typographique, while Vols. I and II were published by J. P. Heubach in Lausanne in 1784. The anonymous collection was put together by Jakob Samuel Wyttenbach (1748–1830) a notable pastor of Berne; he combined an active evangelical religious life with the study of natural history, geography, geology and folklore.

It seems extraordinary that Malthus should have correctly noted all the pages of the *Histoire des Découvertes*, in the three volumes he used, without taking the trouble to record the title, yet such is apparently the case.

Malthus's quotations from the *Histoire des Découvertes* are fairly literally translated, but in Bk I, ch. vii, n. 33 his translation of Pallas is perhaps misleading: Pallas wrote

---

* *Russian Discoveries; History of Discoveries* ... 'made by various well informed travellers in many lands of Russia and Persia, relating to their natural and political history, their rural economy, commerce, etc.'.

(Vol. III, p. 399) '... empêchent qu'aucun d'entr'eux veuille se mettre au service d'un autre'; '... prevents anyone from wishing to enter the service of others' would give the sense better than Malthus's version. Malthus occasionally bowdlerises, as in Bk I, ch. vii, n. 40: according to Pallas (Vol. III, p. 319): 'Les Kalmoucs sont non-seulement très-portés a l'amour, mais ils sont encore très prolifiques.'*

The five-volume quarto published in Paris in 1788, to which Malthus refers in Bk I, ch. ix, n. 6, is *Voyages de M[onsieur] P. S. Pallas, en différentes provinces de l'Empire de la Russie, et dans l'Asie septentrionale, traduits de l'Allemand par M. Gauthier de la Peyronie, Commis des Affaires Étrangères.*** Pallas is here described, among other things, as a Doctor of Medicine and a Fellow of the Royal Society of London.

Here again, Malthus is not always quite accurate, as in his quotation from Vol. IV, p. 60. What Pallas actually wrote was: 'On se fera facilement une idée de la puanteur, des vapeurs fétides, et de l'humidité qui règnent dans leurs Iourtens, lorsque l'on saura que les hommes, les femmes, les enfans, et les chiens font leurs besoins par-tout, et que personne n'a soin de les enlever.'***

PARENNIM, DOMINIQUE (1665–1741), was possibly the most outstanding of the French Jesuit missionaries in China, which accounts for Malthus mentioning him by name in Bk I, ch. xii, n. 45. He was sent to China in 1698, where he remained until he died in Pekin, highly regarded by the emperor and his predecessor, for whom Parennim had translated scientific works into Manchu; he also helped to prevent war between China and Russia, and drew up a treaty between the two empires.

PARK, MUNGO (1771–1806), qualified as a surgeon in Edinburgh, and then came south to seek his fortune. Through the influence of Sir Joseph Banks, he was appointed assistant medical officer on an East-Indiaman, and studied hitherto unknown plants and fishes in Sumatra. Banks then arranged for him to go on an expedition to discover the true course of the river Niger, 'under the direction and patronage of the African Association'. This was founded in 1788, and its aims may be summed up in Park's own words:

> If I should succeed in rendering the geography of Africa more familiar to my countrymen, and in opening to their ambition and industry new sources of wealth and new channels of commerce, I knew that I was in the hands of men of honour, who would not fail to bestow that remuneration which my successful services should appear to them to merit.

Mungo Park was away for three-and-a-half years of hardship and adventure, and the account of his *Travels in the Interior Districts of Africa ... in the years 1795, 1796 and 1797* (quarto, London 1799) went into three editions within a year. He disappeared

---

* 'The Kalmuks are not only much addicted to love-making, but they are also very prolific.'
** *The Travels of Mr P. S. Pallas in different provinces of the Russian Empire, and in northern Asia, translated from the German by Mr Gauthier de la Peyronie, of the Department of Foreign Affairs.*
*** 'One may easily imagine the stench, the putrid exhalations, and the prevailing dampness of their yourts, when one realises that the men, women, children and dogs do their business everywhere, and nobody troubles to clear it up.'

on a second expedition, and no definite account of his death reached Europe until 1812.

Malthus quotes Park almost verbatim; he assumes his readers will know that Dr John Laidley lived at Pisania, a British trading station on the Gambia river, and that Mungo Park stayed with him for five months to learn what he called the Mandingo language, and to get over his first bout of fever.

Malthus's life-long Cambridge friend, John Whishaw, was a director of the African Institution, founded to watch over the operation of the Act of 1807 which abolished the slave trade (but not slavery) in all British possessions. In 1814 Whishaw promised John Murray a life of Mungo Park, to be published with his journals, for the benefit of Park's widow and children; it was probably through this connection that Malthus himself became 'one of Mr Murray's authors'.

PARR, SAMUEL, D.D. (1747–1825), a distinguished Whig Latinist and pedagogue, who was well known to Malthus's friends, and whom Malthus himself met at the home of Sir James Mackinstosh (q.v.) in September 1821. The 'attack' of Dr Parr on William Godwin was delivered in a charity sermon which he preached on Easter Tuesday, 15 April 1800, before the Lord Mayor of London, the Court of Aldermen, and the Governors of the City hospitals; the published version of this *Spital Sermon* ran to 161 pages, and contained erudite notes more lengthy than the sermon itself.

Dr Parr's text was from St Paul: 'As we have therefore opportunity, let us do good to all men, especially unto them which are of the household of faith.' (Galatians, VI, 10, Bible of 1611.) Parr used this as a spring-board for commending the particular benevolence of the City charities, while he derided the doctrine of universal benevolence and the Godwinian view that moral actions were inspired by 'an ineffable ardour for the good of all'.

PAUL OF TARSUS, ST PAUL (*c.* 3 A.D.–*c.* 67 A.D.), was an educated Jew with Roman citizenship; he took part in the persecution of Christians until he was suddenly converted by a vision, on a journey to Damascus. St Paul is generally regarded as the founder of institutionalised Christianity, and his Epistles – his letters to the churches which he established on his missionary travels – form part of the New Testament of the Bible. He was put to death by the Roman Emperor Nero.

(1) Malthus's reference to St Paul's declarations respecting marriage (he made many) is most likely to be to the beginning of the seventh chapter of the first Epistle to the Corinthians. In Malthus's Bible, that of 1611, this reads

It is good for a man not to touch a woman. Nevertheless, to avoid fornication, let every man have his own wife, and let every woman have her own husband. . . . I would that all men were even as I myself. But every man hath his proper gift of God, one after this manner, and another after that. I say therefore to the unmarried and widows, It is good for them if they abide even as I. But if they cannot contain, let them marry: for it is better to marry than to burn.

(2) In Bk IV, ch. x, n. 12, Malthus refers to the third chapter of St Paul's second Epistle to the Thessalonians, from the eighth verse. Writing from Athens, Paul reminds the Christians of Thessaly:

Neither did we eat any man's bread for naught; but wrought with labour and travail night and day, that we might not be chargeable to any of you: not because we have not power, but to make ourselves in ensample unto you to follow us. For even when we were with you, this we commanded you, that if any would not work, neither should he eat. For we hear that there are some which walk among you disorderly, working not at all, but are busybodies. Now them that are such we command and exhort by our Lord Jesus Christ, that with quietness they work, and eat their own bread. But ye, brethren, be not weary in well doing. And if any man obey not our word by this epistle, note that man, and have no company with him, that he may be ashamed.

PAULUS DIACONUS (Paul the Deacon), also known as Paul of Friuli, born Paul Warnefried (*c.*720–90). He served the Duke of Benevento, whose wife was the daughter of the last Longobard king before Charlemagne conquered Lombardy in 774, and he died at the Benedictine monastery of Monte Cassino.

Paul's *History of the Longobards* was extremely popular in Europe in the sixteenth and seventeenth centuries. The following translation of Malthus's quotation in Bk I, ch. vi, n. 33 is taken from that of William Dudley Foulke (New York 1907). It covers the first three chapters of *De Gestis Longobardorum*, pp. 1–5.

The region of the north, in proportion as it is removed from the heat of the sun and is chilled with snow and frost, is so much more healthful to the bodies of men and fitted for the propagation of nations, just as, on the other hand, every southern region, the nearer it is to the heat of the sun, the more it abounds in diseases and is less fitted for the bringing up of the human race. ... And for the reason that it [the north] brings forth so many human beings that it can scarcely nourish them, there have frequently emigrated from it many nations that have indeed become the scourge of portions of Asia, but especially of the parts of Europe which lie next to it.

... Since, therefore, the peoples ... had grown to so great a multitude that they could not now dwell together, they divided their whole troop into three parts, as is said, and determined by lot which part of them had to forsake their country and seek new abodes.

Therefore the section to which fate had assigned the abandonment of their native soil and the search for foreign fields, after two leaders had been appointed over them, to wit: Ibor and Aio, who were brothers ['Germans'] in the bloom of youthful vigour and more eminent than the rest, said farewell to their own people as well as their country, and set out upon their way to seek for lands were they might dwell and establish their abodes.

Paul goes on: 'The mother of these leaders, Gambara by name, was a woman of the keenest ability and most prudent in counsel among her people, and they trusted not a little to her shrewdness in doubtful matters.'

PERCIVAL, THOMAS, M.D. (1740–1804), is said to have been the first pupil of the Dissenting Academy at Warrington, where Malthus was among the last. He studied in Edinburgh, where he became the friend of Robertson and Hume (qq.v.) and qualified in Leyden in 1765. From 1767 until his death he practised as a physician in Manchester; here he was a prominent advocate of factory legislation, municipal sanitation and public baths, and a founder member in 1781 of the Manchester Literary and Philosophical Society.

Malthus quotes at second-hand from Dr Price (q.v.) Percival's 'Observations on the State of Population in Manchester and other adjacent Places'; this may be found on pp. 1–67 of Vol. II of Thomas Percival's *Essays Medical, Philosophical and Experi-*

*mental* (Warrington 1788). Dr Percival also communicated the results of his work to the Royal Society. He arranged a survey, 'executed with great care', of the towns of Manchester and Salford in the summer of 1773, and then in 1774 he did the same for 31 other townships, excluding Manchester and Salford. He gave the numbers of houses, families, males and females, the married, widowers and widows, those under 15 and those above 50, male and female lodgers, and empty houses. In an 'Appendix to the Foregoing Observations' he brought his figures up to 1788.

PÉROUSE, *see under* La Pérouse.

PETTY, SIR WILLIAM (1623–1687), was the son of a clothier; he went to sea as a boy, and was abandoned in France by his shipmates, with a broken leg. Young Petty first gave English lessons, to make money, then studied at the Jesuit College at Caen; later he went on to Utrecht, Amsterdam, Leyden and Paris, where he met Hobbes. In 1649 he qualified in medicine at Oxford, and in 1652 became Physician-General to Cromwell's army in Ireland. Here he established his fame, by surveying the forfeited lands with which the Lord Protector rewarded his soldiers and money-lenders. Petty weathered the Restoration, got on well with Charles II and James II, was the friend of Aubrey, Evelyn and Pepys, and one of the foundation members of the Royal Society.

As with Davenant, Graunt and King (qq.v.) the statistical work of Petty (much of it collected and published posthumously) would have been sufficiently well known to Malthus's readers for him to have taken it for granted that no explanations were necessary. His reference in Bk I, ch. i, n. 10, fits an octavo edition of *Several Essays in Political Arithmetick* (London 1755) which is in the Malthus Library at Jesus College, Cambridge.

In justice to Petty, it should be stated that he believed London doubled itself in forty years, but the whole of England in three hundred and sixty years, and 'the periods of doubling the people are found to be in all degrees, from between ten to twelve hundred years'. His 'doubling table' began with the four couples from Noah's ark, in the year after the Flood, on the assumption that: 'Every teeming woman [aged 15 to 44] can bear a child once in two years.' He considered 'one acre sufficient to raise bread and drink-corn for every head, and two acres will furnish hay for every necessary horse'.

PEUCHET, JACQUES (1758–1830), is described as 'publiciste et littérateur français'; he gave up medicine for law, and before the French Revolution he worked on the *Dictionnaire Universel de Commerce*. Peuchet was briefly imprisoned as a pro-monarchy journalist, but by 1800 he was able to address his *Essai d'une Statistique Générale de la France* to the First Consul's Minister of the Interior, Chaptal.

Malthus's reference to this work in Bk II, ch. viii, might give the impression that Peuchet was concerned entirely with population: in fact his book (which he hoped would be useful to young people who planned to study political economy) is concerned with the territorial extent of France and her colonies, her vegetable, animal, mineral and aquatic products, and her industries, which he classifies according to whether they use vegetable, animal or mineral raw materials. Peuchet points out that information formerly supplied by parish priests and royal intendants must now be obtained from the prefects, sub-prefects and mayors.

In the supplementary chapter on France written in 1817, Malthus refers to Peuchet's *Statistique Elémentaire de la France* published in Paris in 1805; this was to show the application of the principles of the science of statistics to the wealth and power of the French Empire. The marriage laws described here, to which Malthus refers in Bk II, ch. ix, n. 5, were extremely complicated. In 1792 the lowest age for marriage had been fixed at 15 for males and 13 for females; those under 21 had to obtain the consent of their parents, but that of one parent was sufficient if the other were not available. Nine years later, the permission of both parents was necessary for males under 25 and females under 21; if this were not granted, a man had virtually to wait until he was 30 before he could get married. These 'Acts of Consent' had to be ratified by two notaries, or one notary and two witnesses, and there were severe penalties for civil officers who married couples of an age 'le plus avancé' if they had not been through this tedious procedure. The difficulties were greater when parents were dead, and those wishing to marry were ignorant of where the deaths had taken place, owing to the disturbed state of France. As might be expected, there was a marked increase in the number of 'mariages naturels' and illegitimate children. (*op. cit.* pp. 233–5).

PEW, RICHARD, M.D., published pamphlets on the National Debt and Taxation generally in 1803 and 1822, but the one in which Malthus read or heard the views of Dean Tucker (q.v.) must have been that printed in London in 1783: *Twenty Minutes Observations on a better Mode of Providing for the Poor; in which it is rendered probable that they may be effectually relieved, in a Manner more agreeable to the general Feelings of Mankind, at the same time that Two Millions Sterling, or more, may be annually saved to the Nation.* Pew here calls himself a 'Fellow of the Royal Society of Medicine, Edinburgh'.

In this shilling pamphlet of 28 pages Richard Pew described a 'club', which had been successfully functioning in Wellingborough, Northamptonshire, for 40 years. In 1783 there were 48 members, who each paid one shilling every four weeks; after they had subscribed for a year, men were entitled to six shillings a week during sickness, for six months, and three shillings a week thereafter; the corresponding rates for women were two shillings and one-and-sixpence, although they seem to have paid the same subscription. Every two or three years the club was able to distribute a bonus of a guinea to each of its members.

Mr Pew's plan was to extend this scheme on a parochial basis throughout the entire country, with compulsory contributions from all males of 18 upwards; females were to start contributing when they were 17. Thus 'the youthful, the vigorous, and the active, would insensibly become the supporters of the aged, the infirm, and the diseased', but Pew endearingly wrote on p. 26: 'Perhaps difficulties may occur in the execution, which I, in my zeal, may have overlooked.'

PLATO (*c.*427–348 B.C.), the Greek philosopher who was a pupil and admirer of Socrates, and who in *c.*386 B.C. began teaching in the *Academy*, which was an olive grove near Athens.

In Malthus's Europe, Greek books were commonly entitled and edited in Latin, which is why he refers in Bk I, ch. xiii, to Plato's *Laws* as *De Legibus*; his quotations from this work may most easily be found in Jowett's translation, pp. 306–9 of Vol. v, 3rd edn, 1892. According to Plato

If after all there be very great difficulty about the equal preservation of the 5040 houses, and there be an excess of citizens, owing to the too great love of those who live together, and we are at our wits' end, there is still the old device often mentioned by us of sending out a colony, which will part friends with us, and be composed of suitable persons. If, on the other hand, there comes a wave bearing a deluge of disease, or a plague of war, and the inhabitants become much fewer than the appointed number by reason of bereavement, we ought not to introduce citizens of spurious birth and education, if this can be avoided; but even God is said not to be able to fight against necessity.

The relevant passages in the dialogue about procreation, between Socrates and Glaucon, in Plato's *Republic*, are in Vol. III, pp. 314–17, of Jowett's translation. Malthus glosses over the full horror of the scheme, to breed the élite guardians of the state even more cold-bloodedly than a farmer breeds animals: the females were not to be allowed to suckle, or even to know their own children, in the communal 'pen or fold'. What Malthus does not make clear is that this system was to apply only to the ruling or warrior classes, whose qualifications Plato described in detail in *Lib*. III, not *Lib*. v. These chilling passages are in fact concerned only with the eugenics of Plato's austere aristocracy, and not with over-population as such; ordinary people were to live in family households in the usual way.

PLINY, SECUNDUS CAIUS (A.D. 23–79), sometimes called Pliny the Elder, to distinguish him from his nephew. He was born in Como, became a lawyer and orator in Rome, then served in the army in Germany and as a revenue officer in Spain; the Emperor Titus made him prefect of the fleet at Misenum, a port on the Bay of Naples, where he died from the poisonous fumes of the eruption of Mount Vesuvius.

Malthus's reference (Bk I, ch. xiv, n. 8) is to Pliny's *Historia Naturalis*; in modern works it would be given as Bk XXIX. xxvii. 85. This Book deals mainly with medicines extracted from animals, as distinct from those of botanical origin.

Malthus quotes only the last part of the last sentence of a passage which might be translated as follows:

Among the breeds of spiders is one the Greeks call a phalangion, which they distinguish by the name of 'wolf.' There is a third class of phalangion named the 'hairy spider,' with an extremely large head. When this is cut open, it is said that two little worms are found inside it; these, in a doe-skin bag, attached to women before sunrise, will ensure that they do not conceive. ... Their potency lasts for a year. Of all such precautions, it is proper that I should speak only of this one, since the fecundity of some women, [over-] full of children, requires such an indulgence.

(The editor is indebted for this reference to Mr John Harrison of the Cambridge University Library.)

PLUTARCH (*c*.A.D. 46–120), was a Greek writer patronised by the Roman Emperor Trajan, who made him governor of Illyria, and he is chiefly known for his 23 parallel *Lives* of comparable Greek and Romans.

Malthus's reference in Bk I, ch. xiv, n. 7, is to a collection of Plutarch's essays known by their Latin name, *Moralia*. *De Amore Prolis* literally means 'concerning the love of offspring', but there is no real translation of the Greek το φιλοδτοργον, which is a combination of sexual and domestic family tenderness. Plutarch himself in this unfinished fragment refers to the *ius trium liberorum*, the law of the Emperor Augustus which favoured men who begot three or more children: their rights of inheritance were enhanced, and they were given priority in holding offices or being assigned a province. It is difficult to see how this law could be relevant to the truly 'poor' mass of the people. Plutarch's essay concludes:

For when poor men do not rear their children, it is because they fear that if they are educated less well than is befitting, they will become servile and boorish and destitute of all the virtues; since they consider poverty the worst of evils, they cannot endure to let their children share it with them, as though it were a kind of disease, serious and grievous. (Translation of W. C. Helmbold, Loeb edition 1962, Vol. VI, p. 357.)

POPE, ALEXANDER (1688–1744), the poet and satirist, with whom Malthus took it for granted his readers would be familiar.

The quotation (Bk III, ch. i, n. 17) is from Pope's philosophical poem *An Essay on Man*: it was first published in 1732–34, in the form of four epistles to Henry St John Bolingbroke. The main thesis is that man's vision of the universe is too limited for him to comprehend the perfection of the divine plan which brought it into being. The fourth epistle concludes with the poet's thanks to his patron, who was his 'guide, philosopher and friend':

That urg'd by thee, I turn'd the tuneful art
From sounds to things, from fancy to the heart;
For Wit's false mirror held up Nature's light;
Shew'd erring Pride, WHATEVER IS, IS RIGHT . . .

Malthus quotes from the beginning of Epistle I, where Pope undertakes to 'vindicate the ways of God to Man':

Say first, of God above, or Man below,
What can we reason, but from what we know?
Of Man what see we, but his station here,
From which to reason, or to which refer?
Thro' worlds unnumber'd tho' the God be known,
'Tis ours to trace him only in our own.

POPULATION ABSTRACTS, *see under* Rickman, John.

PORTLAND, 3RD DUKE OF, William Henry Cavendish-Bentinck (1738–1808), twice Prime Minister, was Home Secretary 1794–1801 and therefore responsible for law and order. His letter to the Lord Lieutenant of the County of Oxfordshire (George Spencer, 4th Duke of Marlborough) is dated 29 September 1800, and begins with congratulating him on the suppression of bread riots in Witney; at this period the Lord Lieutenant was personally responsible for the County Militia, whose duties included dealing with public disturbances, since there was no civil police force.

The 'small pamphlet' to which Malthus refers in Bk III, ch. v, n. 5, was his own anonymous contribution to the current controversy over the high price of flour, 'by the Author of the Essay on the Principle of Population'. On p. 26 of this pamphlet Malthus quoted the Duke of Portland's letter as official confirmation of the fact that 'of late years, even in the best seasons, we have not grown corn sufficient for our own consumption'. The Duke of Portland, like Malthus, was concerned that the populace should understand that the high price of bread was due to actual scarcity, owing to a bad harvest, and not to profiteering by farmers and dealers.

From n. 6 of ch. vi of Bk IV it is apparent that Malthus had not always approved of the Duke of Portland. In his anxiety lest 'French principles' should spread to England, the Duke had abandoned the old Whig party and joined William Pitt; Pitt rewarded him with high office, the blue ribbon of the Order of the Garter, the lord-lieutenancy of Nottinghamshire for himself, and that of Middlesex for his eldest son. Edmund Burke (1729–97) was another defecting Whig, and received a civil list pension.

PREMARE, JOSEPH-HENRI (*c*.1670–*c*.1735), was a Jesuit from Normandy who died in Peking after working in China for some 35 years, learning to write fluently for his Chinese converts, in their own language, upon complicated aspects of theology. Malthus's reference in Bk I, ch. xii, n. 24, is to one of the three letters he contributed to the *Lettres Édifiantes et Curieuses* (q.v.).

PRÉVOST, PIERRE (1751–1839), was a native of Geneva, where he studied theology, law and medicine; he met Rousseau in Paris, and lectured on philosophy in Berlin at the request of Frederick the Great. He settled permanently in Geneva in 1784, as Professor of Philosophy and Physics, and translated Adam Smith and David Hume (qq.v.). In 1809 Prévost brought out a French translation of Malthus, *Essai sur le Principe de Population* (Paris and Geneva) in three octavo volumes. He and Malthus corresponded, and they had many acquaintances in common. It was as a friend of the author that in 1823 Prévost published an improved and enlarged translation of the *Essay*, in four volumes (also Paris and Geneva) based on Malthus's 'much revised' edition of 1817.

As was customary at the time, Pierre Prévost added considerable notes of his own to the original writer's work, and Malthus refers to two sets of these.

The first concerns Switzerland: in n. 43 (Bk II, ch. vii) which was added in 1826, Malthus refers to both editions of Prévost's *Essai*; in the edition of 1809, this Note A runs from pp. 59–63 of Tom. II; in what Malthus calls 'a later account in the last translation', that of 1823, the Note runs from pp. 59–66, and is dated 1821. The canton is Glaris, not *Glavis*, possibly a printer's error of 1826 which was repeated in subsequent editions.

With regard to France, Prévost makes extensive and detailed comments on the long footnote 32 of ch. viii of Bk. II; he points out some deficiencies in Malthus's summary of the *Analyse des Procès-Verbaux*, but thought that in general Malthus was right in his conclusions. In Bk II, ch. ix, n. 2, Malthus is, of course, referring to Prévost's first translation of 1809: in the translation of 1823 the relevant comments are in Tom. II, pp. 94–8.

PRICE, RICHARD, D.D. (1723–1791), was a learned non-conformist minister, extremely well known in his day for his dissertations on morals and providence, his democratic views (Congress invited him to emigrate to the United States), and his sermon *On the Love of our Country*, which inspired Burke's *Reflections on the Revolution in France*. His most lasting influence, however, was through a miscellaneous collection of essays which first appeared in 1771: ultimately the work's full title was *Observations on Reversionary Payments; on Schemes for providing Annuities for Widows, and for Persons in Old Age; on the Method of Calculating the Values of Assurances on Lives; and on the National Debt, also Essays on different Subjects in the Doctrine of Life-Annuities and Political Arithmetic; a Collection of New Tables, and a Postscript on the Population of the Kingdom.*

The census of 1801 showed conclusively that Price was wrong in assuming that the population of England had declined since 1688, owing to the Enclosure Acts driving people away from the wholesome countryside to die in vicious and unhealthy towns. Yet as late as 1875 a writer in *The Journal of the Institute of Actuaries* (Vol. XVIII, pp. 107–9) could lament bitterly that Price's Northampton Table had 'played such an important part in the life insurance transactions of this country, and is still used to such a considerable extent': Price had not appreciated that the small number of christenings in Northampton, as compared with burials, was due simply to a very high proportion of Baptists, whose practice of adult immersion meant that their infants did not figure in any register.

Malthus, when writing the 1798 *Essay*, used the posthumous fifth edition of Price's *Reversionary Payments*, which appeared in two octavo volumes in 1792. This is shown by a reference on p. 338 of the *Essay* to Price's 'Vol. 2, p. 243'; in fact, the reference is to p. 265, but by a strange chance the printer numbered just this one p. 243 by mistake, and Malthus copied the error.

While he was at work on the quarto, Malthus used the fourth edition of *Reversionary Payments*, also in two octavo volumes, which came out in 1783. By 1817 this was quite out of date, as in 1816 William Morgan had published a complete edition of all his Uncle Richard's works, in ten volumes, the texts unaltered, but arranged according to subject-matter. Malthus, however, did not amend his footnotes in the 1817 revision of the *Essay*, and he even quoted from his old 1783 *Reversionary Payments* – of which there is a copy in his library at Jesus College – in the *Edinburgh Review* for July 1821, when he contributed an article on *Of Population* by William Godwin (q.v.).

This gave Godwin's collaborator David Booth an opportunity for ridicule in *A Letter to the Rev. T. R. Malthus*, published in January 1823. Of Malthus's references to *Reversionary Payments* Booth wrote:

Your readers, if they wish to follow you, have to grope their way through a modern copy; and if they find your quotation at all, it is sure to be at a very distant page, and often in a different volume from that to which you refer. This was sufficiently tormenting to patient perusers of your larger work, but it was rather too mischievous to cite so often from the same antiquated copy, (without even mentioning the edition), when you were writing for the more volatile readers of a modern Review. (pp. 69–70.)

Malthus took this rebuke to heart, and quoted Morgan's edition in his article on Population in the 1824 *Supplement* to the *Encyclopaedia Britannica*, subsequently reprinted by Murray as *A Summary View of the Principle of Population* in 1830. But he clearly could not face the drudgery of altering all the footnotes when he came to prepare the 1826 edition of the *Essay*, which retains the original references to Richard Price's 1783 fourth edition of *Reversionary Payments*.

PRYME, GEORGE (1781–1868), was the first Professor of Political Economy at Cambridge, but he was not recognised as such until 1828, and the chair not properly established until 1863.

Pryme became a barrister in London after a brilliant academic record at Trinity College, but his health broke down and, rather surprisingly, he returned to Cambridge on medical advice. Here he had a successful career in law, and in local and national politics, becoming M.P. for the Borough of Cambridge in 1832.

The courses of lectures to which Malthus refers (Bk iv, ch. ix, n. 10) were begun by Pryme in 1816, with the grudging consent of the University authorities, who feared that the study of political economy would distract students from the regular curriculum. Pryme published nothing relevant to economics except what he called his *Syllabus*, which is not very informative; the concluding paragraph of his Preface is as follows:

These Lectures are intended to explain and demonstrate the principles of the Science to those who have not previously studied it. The Author however recommends the perusal of the first and second Books of Malthus's Essay on Population: not that he will suppose the possession of this knowledge; but because the short abstract of them, which forms a part of the second Lecture, must bring comparatively inadequate conviction to the minds of his hearers.

RAYNAL, GUILLAUME-THOMAS-FRANÇOIS (1713–1796), is hardly known today, but was ranked in his time with Voltaire, Montesquieu, and Rousseau. A Jesuit priest, he was expelled from St Sulpice for financial malpractices, so he renounced his vocation and became an habitué of the salons of great ladies, while at the same time denouncing the entire régime.

Raynal's major work was his *Histoire Philosophique et Politique des Établissemens et du Commerce des Européens dans les deux Indes*, concluding that the effects of the discovery of the New World on life in Europe was as much harmful as beneficial. It first appeared in 1770, in four octavo volumes, Raynal having mounted what would now be called a promotion campaign, and it was 'improved' through successive editions with a hotch-potch of pirated contributions. Raynal himself travelled no further than St Petersburg, where he was received by Catherine the Great. Malthus used Raynal's last edition, that of 1795, and judging from his quotations he must have searched through the ten volumes very thoroughly.

The reference in Bk iv, ch. vi, n. 11, is to Raynal's section on Taxes. He was against all taxation, except possibly a land-tax; he did admit that a citizen, to a certain extent, could adjust his expenditure so that he paid the minimum of indirect taxation: 'But if the tax be imposed on essential articles of food, it is the height of cruelty. Before any laws were made, man had the right to eat, to keep himself alive. Has he then lost this right, through the establishment of law in society? It is robbery, to sell to the people the fruits of the earth at an artificially enhanced price; it is an attack on the very basis of their existence to deprive them, through taxation, of the means of maintaining life ...' and so on.

*quoted or cited by Malthus*

REVUE ENCYCLOPÉDIQUE, was published quarterly in Paris from 1819 to 1833. The full title was *Revue Encyclopédique, ou Analyse Raisonnée des Productions les plus remarquables dans les Sciences, les Arts industriels, la Littérature et les Beaux-Arts; par une Réunion des Membres de l'Institut, et d'autres hommes de lettres.*

The fat octavo volumes appeared in January, April, July and October; the statistics which Malthus quotes are on pp. 853–54 of Vol. xxv, which is dated January 1825, and not March, as stated by Malthus. His figures are all copied accurately.

REYNIER, JEAN-LOUIS-ANTOINE (1762–1824), a Swiss naturalist, who was born and died in Lausanne, and a prolific miscellaneous writer as well as a practical farmer. He went to Egypt in 1798 with his younger brother, Jean-Louis-Ebenezer (1771–1814) who had been educated in Paris and became a general in the French army. Both brothers were renowned for their probity, and the elder held a number of official positions under the Bonapartes.

The full title of Reynier's 'valuable paper', to which Malthus refers in n. 55 at the end of ch. viii of Bk I, was *Considérations générales sur l'Agriculture de l'Egypte et sur les Améliorations dont elle est susceptible, et Observations sur le Palmier-dattier et sur sa Culture.* It was first published as a pamphlet of 124 pages, by Madame Huzard in Paris, with no date.

The *Mémoires sur l'Egypte* in four volumes, Paris 1800–03, were a collection of articles on all aspects of the life of the country, which Napoleon's campaign had in effect opened up for the first time to European scholars and scientists.

RICARDO, DAVID (1772–1823), Malthus's warm friend and rival economist, a Jewish stockbroker turned country landowner and member of parliament, whose *Principles of Political Economy and Taxation* first appeared in 1817.

'Mr Ricardo's recommendation' to which Malthus refers in Bk iii, ch. E, n. 18, was rejected in the House of Commons (by 25 votes to 218) on 9 May 1822. He had proposed a duty of 20s. a quarter on imported wheat, 'when the price shall rise above 70s., to lower 1s. a year for ten years, and then 10s. being the permanent duty, and 7s. the bounty afterwards'. Ricardo gave the reasons for his proposal in an extremely able speech (see *The Works and Correspondence of David Ricardo*, ed. Sraffa, Vol. v, pp. 177–85) and in a pamphlet entitled *On Protection to Agriculture* which had appeared on 18 April (*ibid.* Vol. iv, pp. 201–70).

Ricardo himself was deeply committed to complete free trade. His justification of protection for agriculture was based on the fact that producers of corn were subject to unavoidable taxes from which the producers of manufactured goods were exempt: the ecclesiastical tithe, an unfair proportion of the poors' rates, the agricultural horses tax, and so on. He estimated that these cost the farmer 10s. for every quarter of wheat which he grew. With regard to the 'bounty', which Ricardo called a drawback, and distinguished from a bounty proper, it was simply returning to the corn exporter the taxes he had already paid; this drawback 'he must have to place him in a fair state of competition in the foreign markets, not only with the foreign producer, but with his own countrymen who are producing other commodities'. (*op. cit.* Vol. iv, p. 243.)

RICHESSE DE LA HOLLANDE. This anonymous work was published in two octavo volumes: *La Richesse de la Hollande*. '*Ouvrage dans lequel on expose l'origine du Commerce et de la Puissance des Hollandois; l'accroissement successif de leur Commerce et de leur Navigation; les causes qui ont contribué à leurs progrès, celles qui tendent à les détruire; et les moyens qui peuvent servir à les relever. A Londres. Aux dépens de la Compagnie.* 1778'.*

The Company was the Dutch East India Company, granted a monopoly charter in 1602, which established its headquarters in Batavia (now Jakarta) in 1619.

The authorship of the book is attributed to Jacques Accarias de Sérionne (1706–92) a French lawyer who acted as secretary to Louis XV, who ennobled him; de Sérionne ironically bankrupted himself through paying too much for his appointment as a commissioner in bankruptcy, and had to leave France; he obtained a post in Holland under the Austrian Viceroy of the Netherlands. It is also attributed to his son, Jean-Jacques de Sérionne (1751–1842) who combined a miscellaneous literary output with a successful career in the French government service. A third attribution is to Elie Luzac (1723–96) who published a version in Dutch (Leyden 1780).

Malthus's citation (Bk III, ch. B, n. 11) is from a passage where the author comments on the very considerable wealth of the public treasury of the United Provinces, which would be astonishing from such a small territory, with only about two million inhabitants, were it not for the fact that the principal source of the government's revenue was the taxes imposed on the nation's prosperous commerce.

RICKMAN, JOHN (1771–1840), was the son of a clergyman, educated at Oxford, whose career as an outstanding civil servant began when, in 1796, he wrote an essay on the method and advantages of taking a census of the population. He was for this reason 'taken up' by Charles Abbot (later Speaker of the House of Commons, and Lord Colchester) who secured for him a number of official appointments, all of which Rickman filled with efficiency.

Rickman was responsible for organising and reporting on the censuses of 1801, 1811, 1821, and 1831, for each of which he received a fee of 500 guineas. There was no official anonymity, and it was natural for Malthus to refer to 'Mr Rickman's tables', since his signature was on all the printed documents, with the note, 'Appointed by His Majesty's most Honourable Privy Council to digest and reduce into Order the above Abstract', or '... the Parish Register Returns', as the case might be.

It is important to remember that the early British censuses were in two parts. The Act of 1800 was 'for taking an Account of the Population of Great Britain, and of the Increase or Diminution thereof'. Thus there was, firstly, the Enumeration, when the clergy (and later, the Overseers of the Poor) had to visit every house in their parishes; they had to record the number of inmates, most of whom would have been illiterate,

* *The Wealth of Holland.* 'A work in which is expounded the origins of the Commerce and Power of the Dutch; the progressive development of their Trade and Shipping; the causes which have contributed to their advance, and those which tend towards their overthrow; and the means by which they might be revived. London. Published at the Company's expense. 1778.'

their sexes (ages not until 1821), and whether their income was from Agriculture; Trade, Manufactures, or Handicraft; or neither. Secondly, the clergy had to complete returns of the baptisms, marriages and burials in their parish registers. In 1801 they had to produce them for each of the years 1700, 1710, 1720 and so on, up to 1780, after which they had to make returns for each year, with two columns for the sexes of those christened or buried. In 1811 they had merely to make returns for ten years, from 1801 to 1810.

Rickman's Parish Register Abstract interested Malthus far more than the Enumeration Abstract. This preoccupation led to his making a serious mistake in the dates of the censuses, which was pointed out in David Booth's *Letter to the Rev. T. R. Malthus* (London 1823, pp. 68–9). Malthus corrected this error in what he wrote in 1825, but he never troubled to go over all the rest of the *Essay*. Thus it would appear from Malthus that the censuses of England and Wales were made in 1800 and 1810; in fact the first Enumeration was on 10 March 1801 (when the weather was extremely bad), the second on 27 May 1811, and the third on 28 May 1821. The Parish Register Returns, however, naturally ended on the 31 December of the preceding year, which presumably led to Malthus's confusion. What is difficult to explain is Malthus's referring to Rickman's Abstracts and Observations as being published a year before they actually were; all are clearly dated, the first on 12 June 1802, the second and third merely June 1812 and June 1822 respectively.

Booth wrote of Malthus's inaccuracy in his pamphlet *Letter*: 'It appears certain, that though there are 80 pages of your Essay employed upon the Censuses, you have never seen either of the "Population Abstracts", and must have received the remarks which you published from some one of your calculating friends.' This seems unlikely; in any case, all Malthus's page references to Rickman's work are correct, and in a number of places he quotes Rickman verbatim. It is possible that Malthus's aberration was influenced by his knowledge of the American censuses, made decennially in 1790, 1800, and so on.

ROBERTSON, WILLIAM, D.D. (1721–1793), was a Presbyterian minister who first achieved fame with his *History of Scotland* in 1759. It was followed ten years later by *The History of the Reign of the Emperor Charles V*, with *A View of the Progress of Society in Europe, from the Subversion of the Roman Empire to the Beginning of the Sixteenth Century*. By this time Robertson could appear on the title-page as Principal of the University of Edinburgh and Historiographer to His Majesty for Scotland; the work itself was to give him a European reputation. In Bk I, ch. vi, Malthus quotes almost verbatim Robertson's own sonorous phrases, although without inverted commas.

Robertson's *History of America* first appeared in 1777, and was immensely popular, coinciding as it did with the American War of Independence; modern readers ought perhaps to be reminded that Robertson – like William Burke (q.v.) – took it for granted he should cover the whole continent, and he cited a number of Spanish sources. On his map Robertson shows a 'Great Space of Land unknown', between New Mexico and Louisiana.

Here again, in Bk I, ch. iv, Malthus borrows Robertson's own phrases; sometimes he omits telling words, as when he cites Bk. iv, p. 71 (n. 7): what Robertson actually wrote was: 'As hardly any restraint is imposed upon the gratification of desire, either by religion, or laws, or decency, the dissolution of their manners is sometimes excessive.'

Malthus's own four-volume octavo editions of Robertson's *Charles V* (London 1782) and *The History of America* (London 1780) are in the Malthus Library at Jesus College, Cambridge.

ROGERS, COLONEL ROBERT (1727–1800), was born at Dumbarton, New Hampshire, where his father was one of the first settlers; he distinguished himself in the war against the French, then became a soldier of fortune and died in London after many adventures. His *A Concise Account of North America*, published in London in 1765, was admired by both the young George III and the young Joseph Banks.

Malthus's quotations in Bk I, ch. iv may be amplified. The reference in n. 10 is to Rogers's statement that: 'The Indian men are remarkable for their idleness, upon which they seem to value themselves, saying, that to labour would be degrading to them, and belongs only to women; that they are formed only for war, hunting and fishing.'

In n. 104 Malthus omits passages favourable to the Indians: on pp. 209–10 Rogers wrote,

You will rarely find among the Indians a person that is in any way deformed, or that is deprived of any sense, or decrepit in any limb, notwithstanding the little care taken about the mother in the time of her pregnancy, the neglect the infant is treated with when born, and the fatigues the youth is obliged to suffer; yet generally they are of a hale, robust, and firm constitution; but spiritous liquors, of which they are insatiably fond, and the women as well as the men, have already surprizingly lessened their numbers, and will, in all probability, in one century more nearly clear the country of them.

Rogers goes on to say that the mothers are fond of their children, and look after them well.

'ROGGEWEIN', WAS JAKOB ROGGEVEEN (1659–1729), whom de Brosses (q.v.) calls Roggewin, and describes as a German from Mecklenburg, whereas he was in fact a Dutchman, and was born and died in Middelburg. His discovery of Easter Island on 6 April 1722 was made in the course of an adventurous circumnavigation of the globe when he – no sailor – was 62. The story was published posthumously, *Histoire de l'Expedition des trois Vaisseaux, employées par la Compagnie des Indes Occidentales des Provinces Unies aux Terres Australes* (La Haye 1739).

Roggeveen gives no specific number of inhabitants for Easter Island, but said that 'plusiers milliers' (several thousand) appeared on the beach, some offering chickens and root vegetables; this sounds more like a figure of speech than a statistical estimate. When the explorers disembarked, 150 strong, they were completely surrounded by curious islanders, and had to use force to push their way through the crowd. Roggeveen was much impressed by the idols of Easter Island, especially their ears, and obviously understood why these people felt they needed no other form of protection, no weapons of any kind. (De Brosses, *Histoire des Navigations aux Terres australes*, Vol. II, pp. 231–5.)

ROSE, GEORGE, M.P. (1744–1818), was a Scot brought up in London; he became an important supporter of William Pitt the Younger, who made him one of the secretaries to the Treasury. Other offices followed, and Rose was also given a seat in the House of Commons. But when Malthus revised the *Essay* in 1807, Grenville's brief Whig government was in power, so that Mr Rose was no longer 'of the Treasury'. What had 'lately been stated in Parliament' occurred during the debates on a bill proposed by Samuel Whitbread: this was a comprehensive scheme of social reform, and Whitbread, like Rose, respectfully disagreed with Malthus's opinions in the *Essay on Population*.

Rose's pamphlet to which Malthus refers was called *Observations on the Poor Laws and on the Management of the Poor in Great Britain* (London 1805). It is extremely interesting, as Rose compared the compulsory relief of the poor to the compulsory taxation imposed for the defence of the realm: neither could safely be left to private generosity. Rose wanted a large population for the fighting services, and low wages (subsidised by poor relief) for cheap competitive exports.

Rose criticised both Malthus and Sir Frederick Morton Eden (q.v.) for their remarks about Scotland. On pp. 18–19 of the pamphlet Rose wrote that

several districts in Scotland ... resorted to the legislature for provisions of a kind more entirely analogous to those which the law of England afforded, than those already recognised in the law of Scotland, or the practice under it, were supposed to allow. *A special act of parliament* was obtained in 1802, by the inhabitants of Edinburgh, and the surrounding districts, for an assessment for the support of their poor: and in Glasgow, and in parts of the counties of Lanerk and Renfrew in its vicinity ... assessments are resorted to *under the authority of the common law*, differing very little in any of its circumstances from the Poor's Rate of England.

Rose added in a footnote:

These measures were taken before the publication of Mr Malthus's book, who refers to the account of Paisley ... in the statistical account of Scotland, in which the system of English assessments for the poor is reprobated in strong terms ... but where it seems it was then adopted by the inhabitants.

In the year 1804 the whole sum expended for the poor in the city and suburbs of Glasgow was £6130, of which £5190 was raised by assessments, and £940 arose from ordinary funds in aid thereof. ... In 1800–1 the whole sum raised was £8750, of which £7880 was by assessments, and £870 by other funds.

Rose was concerned with the poor as well as with the poor-rates; in 1795 he secured the passing of an Act which gave legal recognition and tax concessions to registered Friendly Societies. He took up the cause of Savings Banks when he was over seventy, in spite of virulent opposition from Cobbett and other working-class writers. The 'act' to which Malthus refers (Bk IV, ch. xii, n. 5) was introduced in the House of Commons on 5 February 1817; the clause to which he objected laid down that a person should not be denied parish relief if he had less than £30 in a Savings Bank. This was passed by the Commons by 60 votes to 27 on 23 May. Malthus's Preface to the 1817 edition of the *Essay* is dated 7 June. He could not then have known that the clause about poor relief would be thrown out by the House of Lords on 1 July, and he omitted to alter the paragraph when he was preparing the edition of 1826.

The remainder of Rose's Bill received the Royal Assent on 12 July 1817. It was regarded as the charter of the Trustee Savings Banks, and some 150 new banks were established within 12 months of the passing of the Act.

RUBRUQUIS, GUILLAUME DE (*c*.1215–*c*.65), was a Franciscan priest from Brabant, sent by King Louis IX of France (St Louis) to convert the Tartars; this was when the Mongol Empire, under the great Khans, was at the height of its power. Rubruquis's *De Moribus Tartarorum* was translated into English and published in London in 1598, but Malthus used extracts from the collection of John Harris (q.v.). His quotation from this in Bk I, ch. vii, n. 55, is verbatim, although without inverted commas.

RUMFORD, COUNT (1753–1814), was born Benjamin Thompson, in the then Colony of Massachusetts; he showed an early interest in natural science, and at 17 became a teacher at the Academy of Rumford (now Concord) in New Hampshire. After his marriage at the age of 19 to a wealthy widow of 33, he associated with British officers, and was forced to flee in 1775.

Thompson retired from the British Army on half-pay in 1784, and with the permission of George III (who knighted him) he took service with the Elector of Bavaria. Here he completely reformed the army, and then swept all beggars from the streets of Munich by the simple process of having them arrested by his soldiers on 1 January 1790.

All the beggars and vagrants were set to work in the Institutions to which Malthus refers in Bk IV, ch. iv, n. 11. Spinning and rope-making were the principal tasks of the unskilled, but it is also recorded that at first 'they spoiled more horns than they made spoons'. These workhouses were not residential, but there was a daily dinner of a quart of 'good soup' of peas and hulled barley, with white bread, and seven ounces of rye bread, which the people usually took home for their supper. As Sir Benjamin was fascinated by the physical problems of heat, as well as social economy, the food cooked on the stoves he invented, by three women, served over a thousand workers at a cost of one-third of a penny per head.

The Elector made Thompson Count von Rumford, and as such he returned to England in 1796, when he published three volumes of *Essays, Political, Economical and Philosophical*; a fourth volume appeared in 1802. Thus it was hardly necessary for Malthus to mention Rumford by name when he referred to the reluctance of the English poor to accept unfamiliar food in times of scarcity (Bk IV, ch. viii, n. 8). 'Rumford soups', distributed by the charitable during the winter of 1800–01 were regarded as sorry substitutes for proper food, and in more dignified language Malthus agreed with them.

There seems to be no reason why the authentically lively passage against *them* was cut, apart from personal considerations. By 1806 Malthus may have been going more into London society, and associating with those who were connected with the Royal Institution, founded by Rumford in 1799; Sir Humphry Davy, the Institution's foremost professor, was one of the signatories who recommended Malthus for Fellowship of the Royal Society.

SELKIRK, THOMAS DOUGLAS, 5TH EARL OF (1771–1820), his heroic efforts to establish a colony in Manitoba after the Napoleonic wars were beset with disasters. He had published a book in 1805 (second edn, Edinburgh 1806) after successfully settling a small group on Prince Edward Island, off Nova Scotia: *Observations on the Present State of the Highlands of Scotland, with a View of the Causes and Probable Consequences of Emigration*. Lord Selkirk pointed out that it was not until the second half of the eighteenth century that the Highland proprietors appraised their land for raising money, rather than for raising fighting men, and decided that sheep-rearing was more profitable than innumerable tenant farmers practising subsistence agriculture and paying nominal rents.

According to Lord Selkirk (*op. cit.* p. 81):

After all the declamation that has been excited by the depopulation of the Highlands, the fact in reality amounts to this; that the produce of the country, instead of being consumed by a set of intrepid but indolent military retainers, is applied to the support of peaceable and industrious manufacturers ... The result is ultimately favourable to population [because more food is grown more cheaply] when we take into account that of the whole kingdom, balancing the diminution in one district by the increase in another.

Malthus's compliments to Lord Selkirk in the 1806 *Appendix* (nn. 9 and 31) are in return for Selkirk's reference on pp. 116–17 to 'the valuable work of Mr Malthus on the Principle of Population, in which these arguments are traced to such uncontrovertible general principles, and with such force of illustration, as to put scepticism at defiance'. He agreed with Malthus, that notwithstanding the drain of emigration, 'the natural tendency of population to increase has more than filled up the blank'.

SHAKESPEARE, WILLIAM (1564–1616), of Stratford-on-Avon, generally regarded as England's greatest poet and dramatist, with whose works all Malthus's readers would have been familiar. Jane Austen in *Mansfield Park* (1814) makes Henry Crawford say: 'Shakespeare one gets acquainted with without knowing how. It is part of an Englishman's constitution. His thoughts and beauties are so spread abroad that one touches them every where, one is intimate with him by instinct.'

1. Malthus's quotation in Bk III, ch. i, n. 6, seems inappropriate, which is no doubt why he expunged it in 1817. It is from one of the most famous speeches in all Shakespeare's plays (*Henry VIII*, Act iii, scene 2) when Cardinal Wolsey realises that the King has turned against him:

> Farewell, a long farewell, to all my greatness!
> This is the state of man: today he puts forth
> The tender leaves of hope; tomorrow blossoms,
> And bears his blushing honours thick upon him;
> The third day comes a frost, a killing frost,
> And, – when he thinks, good easy man, full surely
> His greatness is a-ripening, – nips his root,
> And then he falls, as I do ...
> Vain pomp and glory of this world, I hate ye ...
>                    Oh how wretched
> Is that poor man that hangs on princes' favours! ...
> And when he falls, he falls like Lucifer,
> Never to hope again.

2. Shakespeare's phrases in Bk III, ch ii, n. 2 are from *The Tempest* (Act iv, scene 1) from Prospero's much-quoted speech when Caliban threatens to disrupt his plans:

> Our revels are now ended: these our actors,
> As I foretold you, were all spirits, and
> Are melted into air, into thin air:
> And, like the baseless fabric of this vision
> The cloud-capp'd towers, the gorgeous palaces,
> The solemn temples, the great globe itself,
> Yea, all which it inherit, shall dissolve,
> And, like this insubstantial pageant faded,
> Leave not a wrack behind. We are such stuff
> As dreams are made of, and our little life
> Is rounded with a sleep.

3. The inaccurate quotation in Bk III, ch. iv, n. 12, is from Hamlet's best-known soliloquy, 'To be, or not to be' (Act iii, scene 1); he is, of course, contemplating suicide and not emigration.

> For who would bear the whips and scorns of time,
> The oppressor's wrong, the proud man's contumely,
> The pangs of despis'd love, the law's delay ...
> When he himself might his quietus make
> With a bare bodkin? ...
> But that the dread of something after death, –
> The undiscover'd country, from whose bourn
> No traveller returns, – puzzles the will,
> And makes us rather bear those ills we have
> Than fly to others that we know not of?
> Thus conscience does make cowards of us all ...

4. This reference is to Mark Antony's sarcastic speech to the crowd in *Julius Caesar* (Act iii, scene 2) which begins

> Friends, Romans, countrymen, lend me your ears;
> I come to bury Caesar, not to praise him.

There is a refrain of

> But Brutus says he was ambitious,
> And Brutus is an honourable man.

The most telling lines are, referring to Caesar:

> He hath brought many captives home to Rome,
> Whose ransoms did the general coffers fill:
> Did this in Caesar seem ambitious?
> When that the poor hath cried, Caesar hath wept:
> Ambition should be made of sterner stuff.
> Yet Brutus says he was ambitious ...

5. In Bk IV, ch. x, n. 6, Malthus's quotation is from Portia's famous speech in *The Merchant of Venice* (Act iv, scene 1). Disguised as 'a doctor of laws', she saves Antonio from having to forfeit a pound of his flesh to Shylock;

> The quality of mercy is not strain'd;
> It droppeth as the gentle rain from heaven
> Upon the place beneath: it is twice bless'd;
> It blesseth him that gives and him that takes:
> 'Tis mightiest in the mightiest; it becomes
> The throned monarch better than his crown ...

334

Malthus's memory may have been at fault here; but it is possible that he learned this speech by heart as a child from a book of extracts, in which the word *earth* was substituted for *place* – a natural mistake for someone brought up in the country.

6. In the *Appendix* of 1806 (n. 24) the quotation is from the dramatic quarrel between Brutus and Cassius in *Julius Caesar* (Act iv, scene 3). Brutus says

> There is no terror, Cassius, in your threats;
> For I am arm'd so strong in honesty
> That they pass by me as the idle wind,
> Which I respect not.

As in (5) the misquotation may be due to Malthus having learned this scene by heart as a young child.

SHORT, THOMAS, M.D. (?1690–1772), was a Scots physician who practised in Sheffield, the author of many medical works, the chief being the two quoted by Malthus, both published in London. The first appeared anonymously in two octavo volumes in 1749, *A General Chronological History of the Air, Weather, Seasons, Meteors, &c. in sundry Places and different Times; more particularly for the Space of 250 Years, Together with some of their most Remarkable Effects on Animal (especially Human) Bodies and Vegetables.* There are over 1000 pages altogether, with accounts not only of weather and diseases, but also of treatments: from p. 506 of Vol. II (which is the only volume Malthus quotes) one may learn that 'Feverish Belchings and Wind' can be cured by the application of 'warm Tiles to the Belly, with Brandy sprinkled on them'.

Malthus's quotation in Bk I, ch. vi, n. 60, is almost verbatim. In Bk II, ch. vi(a), n. 9, he hardly does justice to Short, who wrote: 'A severe mortal Epidemic is generally succeeded by an uncommon Healthiness, from the late Distemper having carried off most of the declining worn-out Constitutions.'

Short's *New Observations on Town and Country Bills of Mortality* was published under his own name in 1750 in one volume; he listed his Observations as Natural, Moral, Civil, Political and Medical, based on the work of John Graunt (q.v.). Malthus's quotation from the *New Observations* in Bk II, ch. x, n. 6, is not strictly accurate. Dr Short wrote thus:

Towns propagate a Number equal to their present Inhabitants from 24½ to 29½ years, the Country from 27½ to 29¾. One in about 57½ is married yearly, or two of 115; in the Country one of 56, or near 2 of 113.

SIMOND, LOUIS, was closely connected by marriage to Malthus's friend Francis Jeffrey of the *Edinburgh Review*. His anonymous work, the two-volume *Journal of a Tour and Residence in Great Britain during the years 1810 and 1811*, was deceptively described as being 'by a French Traveller': Simond was American, and the concealment of his true nationality – as distinct from his birth – might have been due to the fact that Britain and the United States were at war from 1812 to 1814. The *Journal* was published in Edinburgh in 1815, and there was a second edition two years later. Simond was at Albury, in Surrey, in the summer of 1811, and as this village was the home base of the Malthus family, it seems more than likely that they met.

Simond's views on the English Poor Laws coincided with Malthus's, and he wrote that a poor rate of five shillings in the pound would tend 'to put everything in common; that is, to destroy the very foundation of society, industry, national wealth, science, and everything which distinguishes the civilised from the savage life, depending on the right to property'. Simond believed that: 'The present generation of poor once provided for, those born after a certain period of years might, with justice and good policy, be left to their own exertions, as in other countries, and particularly Scotland.' (*op. cit.*, edn of 1815, Vol. I, pp. 225, 229–30.)

On p. 224 of Vol. II, however, Simond gives a different impression:

The peasants look very decent in their manners, dress and appearance. No marks of poverty about them; but they are certainly very diminutive in stature, and thin. They seem better clothed than fed. One might suspect that a certain native pride in them disdains to wear the livery of poverty, although they suffer in secret.

SINCLAIR, SIR JOHN (1754–1835), of Thurso Castle, Caithness, educated at Edinburgh, Glasgow and Oxford, called to the English Bar, some-time member of parliament, and President of the Board of Agriculture 1793–98 and 1806–13. He was known for his energy, conceit, and lack of humour, but he was a reforming force to be reckoned with.

The 21 octavo volumes of *The Statistical Account of Scotland* to which Malthus first refers in Bk I, ch. ii, n. 10, appeared at intervals from 1791 to 1799. What would now be called the survey was carried out by ministers of the Church of Scotland; in his printed letter to them, dated 25 May 1790, Sinclair explained that 'statistical' meant 'Inquiries respecting the Population, the Political Circumstances, the Productions of a Country, and other Matters of State', such as had been carried out in many parts of the Continent, particularly Germany.

Sir John drew up a list of 160 questions, but did not expect them all to be answered in every case. They concerned the extent of each parish, its situation and soil, climate and diseases, rivers, mineral springs, hills, woods, caves, migratory birds, number of horses and sheep, population, births, deaths, and marriages, rents, number of proprietors and tenants, state of the poor, language (some were Gaelic-speaking), manners and morals, and much else.

SMITH, ADAM (1723–1790), was born at Kirkcaldy, in Fife; he became Professor first of Logic, and then of Moral Philosophy, at the University of Glasgow. His *Theory of Moral Sentiments* was published in 1759, and his *Enquiry into the Nature and Causes of the Wealth of Nations* in 1776, when Malthus was ten years old. The book became a 'classic' immediately.

Malthus gives occasional references to the third edition of the *Wealth of Nations*, published in three octavo volumes in 1784, with Smith's own additions and corrections. In most cases Malthus assumes that the reader is as well acquainted with Adam Smith as he is, and gives no page references to well-known passages. The definitive Glasgow Edition of the *Wealth of Nations* (ed. Campbell, Skinner and Todd, 2 vols., Oxford University Press 1976) gives the pagination of the edition Malthus used in square brackets: thus any reader who wishes to trace his quotations will have no difficulty in finding them.

It is perhaps worth noting that in 1798 (*Essay*, p. 302) Malthus writes that he 'cannot avoid venturing a few remarks on a part of Dr Adam Smith's Wealth of Nations; speaking at the same time with that diffidence, which I ought certainly to feel, in differing from a person so justly celebrated in the political world'. By 1803, in his chapters on the Corn Laws, Malthus is disagreeing with Adam Smith on completely equal terms.

In an article on his great quarto, in the *Monthly Review* for January 1804, Malthus might have read that 'wherever, in future, any positions in political economy are discussed, his name will be associated with those of Montesquieu and Turgot, of Hume and Smith'. Until the publication of Ricardo's *Principles of Political Economy* in 1817, it was widely taken for granted that Adam Smith's mantle had fallen on Malthus, 'the foremost political economist of the age'.

SOLON (*c.*638–558 B.C.), was a Greek legislator whose revision of the constitution traditionally laid the foundations of Athenian democracy. He followed Draco who, according to legend, established a criminal code so brutal that the smallest offences were punished by death. Solon was a very gentle magistrate by contrast, and Malthus's reference to him in Bk I, ch. xiii, n. 2, might be interpreted as 'when even the kind-hearted Solon permitted the exposure of children. . . .'

SPENCE, THOMAS (1750–1814), moved to London from Newcastle-on-Tyne, and sold books and pamphlets, as well as a popular coffee-substitute called saloop, from a stall in Holborn. His basic plan for Utopia was that the land in each parish should belong to a corporation; rents would be used for all local services, including schools and libraries; after a contribution towards national expenses, the sum remaining would be divided equally among the inhabitants. Spence wrote a fable about Spensonia, a country where his scheme was put into practice; he also published a periodical miscellany called *Pig's Meat*, Edmund Burke having written in his *Reflections on the Revolution in France* that: 'Learning will be cast into the mire and trodden down under the hoofs of a swinish multitude.'

It seems strange that Malthus should have troubled to notice this rather pathetic contribution to political idealism in Bk III, ch. iii(b), n. 7. He obtained his figures from pp. 5–6 of a little pamphlet entitled *Address of the Society of Spencean Philanthropists to all Mankind on the Means of Promoting Liberty and Happiness*; it was published in 1815. The anonymous author obviously regarded the yearly bonus of £4 a head – 'after providing for every national expense, without tax, toll or custom' – as a good substantial sum. He believed that Spence's system would unite 'the enjoyment of our primary natural rights with a polished state of civilisation'.

STATISTIQUE GÉNÉRALE ET PARTICULIÈRE DE LA FRANCE ET DE SES COLONIES. This was compiled by 'une société de gens de lettres et de savans', which might be freely translated as a group of well-informed and learned men. It was published by Herbin in Paris in the year XII (22 Sept. 1803–21 Sept. 1804) in seven volumes; the statistics on the population of France may be found in pp. 115–40 of Vol. I.

War was resumed between England and France in May 1803, but the French courteously released from internment Malthus's friend Alexander Hamilton, a notable Orientalist, in order that he might take up his appointment at the East India

College in the spring of 1806. It is possible that Hamilton brought this book to England as a present for his colleague, just at the time when Malthus was revising the quarto for the first two-volume octavo edition of the *Essay*.

Malthus's n. 25 of ch. viii, Bk II, refers to the Bureau de Cadastre, which could in English be designated the Land-Surveyor's Office. Count Mathieu Depère (1746–1825) was a professional politician who began his career as a moderate revolutionary and died happily as a constitutional monarchist; in this report (p. 116) he is of course referred to as 'Le citoyen Depère' – Citizen Depère. Necker (q.v.) is 'M. Necker'.

The figures for the ratio of births to the whole population may be found on pp. 129–30; the 'curious remark' on marriages is on p. 131. Buffon (q.v.) is referred to throughout as 'le célèbre Buffon', and the calculations to which Malthus objects are on p. 136; these are elaborated on the recto: at birth a child can only expect to live for eight years, but if he survives his first 12 months he may look forward to 33 years more; a man of 30 will live for another 28 years and six months.

(The editor is greatly indebted to the Bibliothèque Nationale in Paris for the relevant photocopies of this work, through the good offices of the International Lending Section of the British Library at Boston Spa, the Oxfordshire County Libraries, and the Branch Library at Chipping Norton.)

STAUNTON, SIR GEORGE LEONARD, M.D., F.R.S. (1737–1801), was an Irishman who studied at the Jesuit College of Toulouse and qualified in medicine at Montpellier; he practised in the West Indies, and was captured by the French when they took Grenada in 1779, during the American War of Independence. While a prisoner in Paris, Staunton was invaluable to the British as a negotiator, and was thus able to embark on a new career. He became secretary to George (later Earl) Macartney, and accompanied him to India when he was made Governor of Madras in 1781; Staunton's diplomatic services were rewarded with a pension from the East India Company and an Irish baronetcy from George III. In 1792 Sir George went with Lord Macartney to China, and in 1797 published in two quarto volumes *An Authentic Account of the Earl of Macartney's Embassy from the King of Great Britain to the Emperor of China*.

Malthus in his chapter on China quotes Staunton, like his other authorities, almost verbatim, although without inverted commas. In a reference to Staunton's Vol. II, p. 157 (Bk I, ch. xii, n. 30) Malthus is perhaps not strictly accurate; Staunton wrote of Peking:

The city partakes of the regularity and interior safety of a camp; but it is subject also to its constraints. In the suburbs only, public women are registered and licensed. They are not indeed very numerous, being proportioned to the small number of single men, and of husbands absent from their families to be found in the metropolis.

On the same page Staunton wrote of those children abandoned by

the wretched authors of their being. It must have been the most dire and absolute necessity which led to this most shocking act, when first it was committed. It was reconciled, afterwards, in some measure, to the mind, by superstition coming in aid to render it a holy offering to the spirit of the adjoining river in which the infant was thrown, with a gourd suspended from its neck, to keep it from immediate drowning.

STEUART, SIR JAMES, afterwards Steuart-Denham (1712–80), was an exiled Jacobite who between 1746 and 1763 travelled all over Europe, speaking fluently French, Spanish, Italian and German. On his return to Scotland he was allowed to work unmolested on *An Inquiry into the Principles of Political Oeconomy*, which was published in 1767 (London, 2 vols. quarto). Steuart was pardoned by King George III in 1772.

Malthus's references in Bk I, ch. ix, n. 12 and Bk III, ch. vii, n. 14, hardly do justice to Sir James as a perceptive economist and a lively writer. Sir James wrote in italics, as one of his *principles*, that: 'Agriculture among a free people will augment population, in proportion only as the necessitous are put in a situation to purchase subsistence with their labour.' If there is no trade, the farmers' superfluity 'will perish like their cherries in a year of plenty; and consequently the farmers will immediately give over working'. It is the duty of 'the Statesman' to 'contrive different employments for the hands of the necessitous, that, by their labour, they may produce an equivalent which may be acceptable to the farmers, in lieu of this superfluity; for these last certainly will not raise it if they cannot dispose of it'. Population could not augment 'without an increase of food on the one hand, and of industry on the other, to make the first circulate. They must go hand in hand.'

(See the edition edited by Andrew Skinner in 2 vols., Edinburgh and London 1966, Vol. I, pp. 39, 40, 119.)

STEWART, DUGALD (1753–1828), was the son of an influential Professor of Mathematics at Edinburgh; he himself became an even more influential Professor of Moral Philosophy, at the time when Edinburgh was described as the Athens of the North. Thus, when Macvey Napier agreed with Archibald Constable to edit the *Supplement* to the fourth, fifth and sixth editions of the *Encyclopaedia Britannica*, it was natural that he should ask Dugald Stewart to write the Preliminary Dissertation.

Stewart's introductory essay was to exhibit 'A General View of the Progress of Metaphysical, Ethical, and Political Philosophy since the Revival of Letters in Europe'; the first part, which appeared at the beginning of the first volume, occupied 149 quarto pages. He reflected on the repeated reproduction of theories of cosmogony, from all countries and all ages, by modern authors 'whom it would be highly unjust to accuse of plagiarism'. Stewart continued,

One is almost tempted to suppose, that human invention is limited, like a barrel-organ, to a specific number of tunes. But is it not a fairer inference, that the province of pure Imagination, unbounded as it may at first appear, is narrow, when compared with the regions opened by truth and nature to our powers of observation and reasoning?

Stewart added in a note:

The limited number of fables, of humorous tales, and even of jests, which, it would seem, are in circulation over the face of the globe, might perhaps be alleged as additional confirmation of this idea.

Malthus was able to refer to this passage (Bk III, ch. iii(b), n. 2) in 1817 because some contributions to the *Supplement* were printed in advance of the complete set; this was not published until 1824, in six volumes; the fifth volume begins with Part II of 'Dissertation First', with an apology from Stewart dated 1821.

'DR STYLES' is EZRA STILES (1727–95), chiefly remembered as the seventh President of Yale College, which he became in 1778; in his time, his fame was such that the University of Edinburgh made him a Doctor of Divinity in 1765. One can only assume that Malthus and Richard Price (q.v.) were supplied with their notes on 'Dr Styles' by an extremely careless person; in the fifth edition of Price's *Reversionary Payments* of 1792 (Vol. II, p. 282n.) 'Dr Styles' is 'now the worthy President of the College of Yale in Connecticutt [*sic*]'.

The title-page of Dr Stiles's sermon is perfectly explicit: *A Discourse on the Christian Union*, 'the Substance of which was delivered before The Reverend Convention of the Congregational Clergy in the Colony of Rhode-Island Assembled at Bristol April 23, 1760, by Ezra Stiles, A.M., Pastor of the Second Congregational Church in Newport'.

The *Discourse* must have been considerably enlarged for publication in Boston in 1761; it amounts to 128 octavo pages; what might be called the demographic section runs from p. 102 to p. 123; Malthus's figures are taken from a note on p. 109. Dr Stiles's approach is distinctly historical, with a long account of the state of the Christians at Philippi, and a reference to recent unhappy excesses: during 'the late enthusiasm that prevailed since the year 1740 ... Multitudes were seriously, soberly and solemnly out of their wits.' His text is printed on the title-page, from Deuteronomy x, 22: 'Thy Fathers went down into Egypt with three-score and ten persons, and now the Lord thy God hath made thee as the Stars of Heaven for Multitude.' Below this is printed: 'Four Thousand British Planters settled in New England, and in 120 Years their Posterity are increased to five hundred thousand Souls.'

(The editor is indebted to the Library of Congress for the identification of 'Dr Styles'.)

SUMNER, JOHN BIRD (1780–1862) was educated at Eton and King's College, Cambridge, and finally became Archbishop of Canterbury; as Bishop of Chester he voted in the House of Lords for Catholic Emancipation in 1829 and the Reform Bill in 1832; he was a member of the Poor Law Commission of 1834.

In 1816 Sumner published *A Treatise on the Records of the Creation, and on the Moral Attributes of the Creator; with particular Reference to the Jewish History and to the Consistency of the Principle of Population with the Wisdom and Goodness of the Deity* (London, 2 vols. octavo). Sir Charles Lyell used the first volume to show that revelation and geology need not be incompatible.

The second volume began with the orthodox description of earthly life as a period of trial and discipline, intended by God for the development of the human spirit. The point Sumner wished to illustrate was

that the order of things, in which the human race arrives at the highest degree of improvement, and has the widest scope for moral and intellectual perfection, is inevitably, and with some trifling exceptions, universally established, by the operation of a SINGLE PRINCIPLE, and the instinctive force of a single natural desire.

This single principle was Malthus's principle of population:

Every exertion to which civilization can be traced, proceeds directly or indirectly from its efforts; either the actual desire of having a family, or the pressing obligation of providing for one, or from the necessity of rivalling the efforts produced by the operation of these motives in others.

According to Sumner, the duties of the affluent included 'a sound exertion of discriminating judgment ... The charity which is often employed to wipe the tear of distress, might, by a more prudent application, stop the source from which it flows.'

There was an Appendix explaining how the entire human race was descended from a single pair, Adam and Eve, in spite of differences of colour and features. The work went into seven editions.

SUPPLEMENT TO THE ENCYCLOPAEDIA BRITANNICA, *see under* William Jacob for Prussia, John Ramsay McCulloch for Corn Laws, Joshua Milne for Mortality, and Dugald Stewart for the Preliminary Dissertation.

SÜSSMILCH, JOHANN PETER (1707–1767), was the son of a prosperous corn merchant in Berlin, of a Bohemian family which had migrated to Brandenburg. He was more interested in plants and minerals than in Greek and Latin, and horrified his parents by wanting to become a doctor; they sent him to Halle to study law, but he preferred theology; he found he disliked Hebrew so much, that he went to Jena to read philosophy; there he decided that mathematics was the basis of all science.

Süssmilch then obtained a post as tutor in the household of Feldmarschall von Kalkstein, who in 1736 made him chaplain of his regiment, with an initial two years' leave to go to Holland, for yet more study before his ordination. When the Elector of Brandenburg went to war with the Duke of Silesia, Süssmilch had already written the first version of the work which made him famous, and the regimental chaplain dated his book 'on the march to Schweidnitz'.

This was in 1741, and the full title of the work was *Die göttliche Ordnung in den Veränderungen des menschlichen Geschlechts, aus der Geburt, dem Tode und der Fortpflanzung desselben erwiesen.* This might be freely translated as *God's Plan for the Development of the Human Race, as demonstrated by the Births, Deaths and Propagation of the Same.* The divine order was such that the balance of the sexes gave no sanction to polygamy, and even the devastating effects of epidemics were nullified in twenty years by an increased birth-rate; the earth was to be gradually replenished according to God's command (see the Bible, Genesis IX, 1) through the overall excess of births over deaths. It was the duty of government to assist this process: they should help couples to get married, and to be healthy and fruitful (which meant discouraging large towns), arrange for the provision of food, maintain order, and defend the country.

The second edition of 1761–62 was virtually a new book, with statistics not merely brought up to date, but added to include foreign countries – Holland, England, Switzerland, Denmark and Sweden – as well as various German states. There was a third edition, identical to the second, in 1765, in two octavo volumes, of which there is a copy in the British Library. A fourth edition appeared posthumously in 1775, with a substantial third volume compiled by Süssmilch's son-in-law, another pastor, called Christian Jacob Baumann; he corrected some of his father-in-law's arithmetical errors, but not all of them.

Malthus could not read German, and nor could Richard Price (q.v.) from whom Malthus first heard of 'Mr Susmilch'; he printed some of Süssmilch's tables, extracted from Price's *Reversionary Payments*, in the *Essay* of 1798. Thereafter the picture is one of complete confusion, and the most plausible explanation seems to be that both Price and Malthus obtained the help of several people, who extracted quotations from Süssmilch very carelessly, perhaps from different editions, or from the works of other writers not easily traceable today. Price, for instance, in the 1792 edition of *Reversionary Payments*, Vol. II, has the Kurmark of Brandenburg on p. 200 and the Churmark of Brandenburg on p. 336.

Although Malthus re-wrote his statistical chapters on fertility and epidemics in 1806, he never added any new quotations from Süssmilch to those he had used in 1803. His first reference to Süssmilch, in his chapter on Sweden, is to the final complete edition of the *Göttliche Ordnung*, published in three volumes in 1798. This may provide a clue. Malthus met Professor Nicander (q.v.) in Stockholm in 1799, and he possibly supplied his visitor with some extracts from this edition, perhaps translated into Latin, which would account for Malthus giving almost all Süssmilch's section numbers in Roman figures, whereas Süssmilch himself used Arabic. Malthus's journals for this part of his Scandinavian tour were lost, after he had lent them to his friend Edward Daniel Clarke; he had asked to borrow them to supplement his own account of the same territory. In his letter of thanks for the Swedish journals, Clarke wrote to Malthus on 4 December 1820: 'I thought I should have died with laughter at some of the Scenes you describe ... when the old Doctor seized you and Otter and kissed you on both cheeks in spite of your Latin.' (*The Travel Diaries of T. R. Malthus*, p. 21.)

Nicander at this time was 55, and he might have seemed an old man to Malthus at 33; on the other hand, there is no explicit evidence that he was the osculatory doctor. It is a little surprising to find educated men at this period communicating in Latin rather than French, but Latin was still used for mathematical and medical treatises. Unless further documents are discovered, the source of Malthus's quotations from Süssmilch is likely to remain a mystery.

(For this note the editor is greatly indebted to Dr Henry Buba, of Mount Pleasant, South Carolina, and to Dr Schneiders and his colleagues at the Bayerische Staatsbibliothek in Munich; they very kindly checked all Malthus's references to Süssmilch, but were unable to explain them.)

SYMES, MICHAEL (?1753–1809), was a soldier who went to India in 1788, and in 1795 was sent by Sir John Shore – later Lord Teignmouth – on an embassy to the ruler of Ava (Burma) to obtain permission for the appointment of an Agent in Rangoon to look after the interests of British subjects. On his return to London he published in 1800 a huge quarto entitled *An Account of an Embassy to the Kingdom of Ava sent by the Governor-General of India in 1795*.

Malthus's reference in Bk I, ch. iii, n. 4, is not quite correct, as he quotes mainly from pp. 130–1, almost verbatim. Symes's impression of the Andaman Islanders was possibly more favourable than Malthus implies. He wrote on p. 133: 'It affords, however, satisfactory reflection to find, among the most ignorant and barbarous of mankind, a confirmation of the great and pleasing truth, that all reasoning existence acknowledges a God. The half humanized Andaman invokes the luminaries that lend him light; and in that simple and spontaneous praise, he offers up the purest devotion of an unenlightened mind ... Their religion is the simple but genuine homage of nature, to the incomprehensible ruler of the universe.'

TACITUS, GAIUS CORNELIUS (*c*.A.D. 55–117), was a Roman historian. What Malthus calls *De Moribus Germanorum* (The Germans' Way of Life) was part of what is also known as *De Origine et Situ Germanorum*, which might be translated as 'On the Origins and Homeland of the Germans'. The *Germani* were the tribes living north of the Rhine and the Danube, whose chaste and hardy existence was contrasted with the luxury and corruption of Rome.

Malthus's reference to Tacitus' section xvi (Bk I, ch. vi, n. 43) deserves comment. Tacitus wrote 'Each man has an open space round his homestead, either as a protection against the risk of fire, or because they do not know how to build otherwise.' The idea that such isolation would have prevented the spread of epidemics was Malthus's own.

With regard to the beginning of section xix (n. 45), Hamilton Fyfe's translation (Oxford University Press 1908) is as follows:

So chastity is well cloistered in their lives. They are not corrupted by the allurements of the theatre or the subtle temptations of banquets. Neither men nor women know anything of clandestine correspondence ... For in Germany no one laughs at vice, nor calls mutual corruption 'the spirit of the age'.

TEMPLE, SIR WILLIAM (1628–1699), was a public servant and a man of letters; as a diplomat his most notable achievement was to make the preliminary arrangements for the marriage in 1677 of William of Orange and Mary, the elder daughter of James II of England. He is possibly better known for his courtship of Dorothy Osborne and his friendship with Swift. Malthus used a superb folio edition of Temple's *Works* in two volumes (London 1740) which was compiled by Swift himself and Sir William's long-widowed sister Martha, Lady Giffard. The citations are from an essay in eight chapters entitled *Observations upon the United Provinces of the Netherlands*.

Sir William thought that the chief cause of Holland's decline was that 'there seems to be grown too many Traders for Trade in the World, so as they can hardly live one by another. As in a great populous village, the first Grocer, or Mercer, that sets up among them, grows presently rich, having all the Custom ... At length so many fall to the Trade, that nothing is got by it; and some must give over, or all must break.' Secondly, while the Dutch East India Company found the profit on the products of the Spice Islands diminished, 'the Charge is increased by the great Wars, the Armies, and Forts, necessary to maintain, or extend, the Acquisitions of that Company in the Indies'. The third cause was the low price of corn in Poland and Prussia: 'Now the less Value those Nations receive for Corn, the less they are able to give for Spice, which is a great Loss to the Dutch.' And finally there was 'the mighty Enlargement of the City of Amsterdam, by that which is called the New Town; the Extent whereof is so spacious, and the Buildings of so much greater Beauty and Cost than the Old, that it must have employ'd a vast Proportion of that Stock which in this Country was before wholly turned to Trade'.

THAARUP, FREDERIK (1766–1845), was born in Copenhagen, where he was Professor of Statistics from 1793 to 1797; he quarrelled with his colleagues and retired to the country in Norway – then ruled by Denmark – with the office of Fogd (usually translated Sheriff) in Solör and Odal. Malthus and his friend Otter visited Thaarup on 1 August 1799, at his home near Kongsvinger, in the course of their Scandinavian tour. Speaking in French, Malthus explained 'that we had heard of his fame as a statistic writer, & had purchased his work in Copenhagen, even tho' we did not understand Danish or German'; when they 'wished to beg the favour of an answer to a few questions on the subject of his enquiries, he was so much alarmed, & seemed to feel so awkward that we were rather in pain for him'. (*The Travel Diaries of T. R. Malthus*, C.U.P. 1966, p. 208.)

The work to which Malthus refers was published in two octavo volumes in Copenhagen in 1795–96. The full title was *Versuch einer Statistik der Dänischen Monarchie*, and it had been translated into German from the second Danish edition, with the author's additions and corrections. Malthus used only the tables on pp. 4–5 of Vol. II for his chapter on Norway. Thaarup's proportion of annual deaths to the whole population of Norway was actually $1:48\frac{1}{2}$. He noted that the total population of 723 141 consisted of 658 394 country-dwellers and 64 747 town-dwellers. His proportion of marriages to this total population was $1:130\frac{1}{3}$.

THE TATLERS (later known as *The Tatler*), was a duodecimo penny periodical 'by Isaac Bickerstaff, Esq.'. He published his 'Advices and Reflections every Tuesday, Thursday and Saturday in the Week, for the Convenience of the Post', and hoped to provide 'something which may be of Entertainment to the Fair Sex, in Honour of whom I have taken the Title of this Paper'. (See 1 Timothy v, 13, in the 1611 Bible.) *The Tatlers* ran from April 1709 to January 1711, and was followed by *The Spectator*, which appeared daily from March 1711 until December 1712, and again in 1714, when 80 numbers were printed. These periodicals exerted an influence on English literature out of all proportion to their short lives; bound volumes and reprints formed part of every true gentleman's library.

The name of Isaac Bickerstaff was originally invented by Jonathan Swift (1667–1745) but it was used as a joke for the author of *The Tatlers* by Sir Richard Steele (1672–1729) aided by Joseph Addison (1672–1719).

Malthus's readers would remember that 'Isaac Bickerstaff' was led to discourse on heredity when he was concerned with the Disposal for Life of his young step-sister Jenny. An ancestor, Sir Isaac Bickerstaff, a knight of King Arthur's Round Table, was much too short and dark; so, with the 'Design of Lengthening and Whitening his Posterity', his eldest son was 'Married to a Lady who had little else to recommend her, but that she was very tall and very fair'. Later in his family history, 'Mr Bickerstaff' wrote that:

Our Race suffer'd very much about Three Hundred Years ago, by the Marriage of one of our Heiresses with an eminent Courtier, who gave us Spindle-Shanks, and Cramps in our Bones, insomuch that we did not recover our Health and Legs till Sir Walter Bickerstaff Married Maud the Milk-Maid, of whom the then Garter King at Arms (a facetious Person) said pleasantly enough, That she had spoil'd our Blood, but mended our Constitutions. (*op. cit.* No. 75, issue of 1 October 1709.)

THORNTON, HENRY, M.P. (1760–1815), was one of the 'Clapham Evangelicals'; his wealthy and philanthropic family were on terms of close friendship with William Wilberforce and prominent Directors of the East India Company, including Charles Grant, through whose influence Malthus obtained his post at the East India College in 1805.

The 'valuable publication' was *An Enquiry into the Nature and Effects of the Paper Credit of Great Britain* (London 1802). It is available to modern readers in Hayek's edition (London 1939). Professor Hayek believes that Francis Horner's summary of this work, in the first number of the *Edinburgh Review*, in October 1802, 'probably exerted as much influence as the book itself'. (p. 51.) Malthus became a close friend of Francis Horner, and it is possible that the footnote about *Paper Credit* was excised in 1806 for personal reasons, although Malthus could have decided on reflection that his criticism of Thornton was unjustified.

THUCYDIDES (*c.* 460–400 B.C.), was a soldier of the golden age of Athens, who wrote an unfinished history of his times, largely of the wars waged between Athens and Sparta, including Pericles' famous funeral oration on the fallen.

*Scythians* was the name given by the Greeks to the nomadic and warlike pastoral people who lived between the Carpathian mountains and the river Don. Malthus's reference is to Thucydides' Bk II, c.97, 6: 'Even in Asia, nation against nation, there is none which can make a stand against the Scythians if they all act in concert. However, with reference to wise counsel and intelligence about the things that belong to the enrichment of life, the Scythians are not to be compared with other nations.' (Vol. I, pp. 447–9 of the Loeb edition, 1956, trans. Charles Forster Smith.)

(The editor is indebted for this reference to Mrs Martha Kneale.)

THUNBERG, KARL PETER, M.D. (1743–1828), was a Swede employed as a physician by the Dutch East India Company; on his return to Europe he succeeded Linnaeus as Professor of Botany at Uppsala.

An English version of his *Travels in Europe, Africa and Asia made between the Years 1770 and 1779* was published in London in 1795, in four octavo volumes. 'The learned Professor', as his translator describes him, was more concerned with investigating natural productions than with delineating the manners of nations, but the Preface cited by Malthus is of interest. Thunberg wrote:

Of all the nations that inhabit the three largest parts of the globe, the Japanese deserve to rank the first, and to be compared with the Europeans; and altho in many points they must yield the palm to the latter, yet in various other respects they may with great justice be preferred to them. ... We must admire the steadiness which constitutes the national character; the immutability which reigns in the administration of their laws, and in the exercise of their public functions; the unwearied assidulity of this nation to do, and to promote what is useful, and a hundred other things of a similar nature.

... That no foreign war should have been waged for centuries past, and interior commotions should be for ever prevented; that a great variety of religious sects should live in peace and harmony together; that hunger and want should be almost unknown, or at least known but seldom, &c. All this must appear as improbable, and, to many, as impossible, as it is strictly true, and deserving of the utmost attention. (*op. cit.* Vol. III, pp. vi, vii.)

TOOKE, THOMAS (1774–1858), was born at Cronstadt, where his father William (q.v.) was chaplain to the British merchants there; he began his own commercial career at the age of 15. He drew up the London Merchants' Petition for free trade in 1820, and was one of the founder-members of the Political Economy Club: this was a monthly dining club, of which Malthus hardly missed a single meeting, from the very first on 30 April 1821 until his death.

Early in 1823 Thomas Tooke published his *Thoughts and Details on the High and Low Prices of the Last Thirty Years*, on which Malthus wrote an article for the April number of the *Quarterly Review*. In 1824 Tooke brought out a second edition, and it is to this considerably enlarged version that Malthus refers in Bk III, ch. E, nn. 16 and 18.

Thomas Tooke thought that there had been a great increase of population between 1785 and 1790; he wrote on pp. 214–15 of his second edition:

If it had so happened that in the last war we had habitually grown as much corn beyond our own consumption as we did between 1740 and 1750, and that the seasons had been equally favourable to the growth, we should have witnessed a totally different set of phenomena connected with prices. The transition from war to peace might, as was the case on several former occasions, have been attended with a rise of prices of agricultural produce, and nothing would have been heard of the distress of the landed interest as resulting from the peace, nor would a state of war be considered as the source of their prosperity.

TOOKE, REV. WILLIAM, F.R.S. (1744–1820), was a born scholar who obtained chaplaincies to the British merchant community in Russia, first at Cronstadt and then, in 1774, at St Petersburg, where he had access to the imperial library. He returned to England in 1792, on inheriting a fortune, and spent the rest of his life in London. He was one of the signatories who supported Malthus's application for Fellowship of the Royal Society in November 1817.

William Tooke's major work was *A View of the Russian Empire during the Reign of Catherine the Second and to the Close of the Present Century*; it appeared in 1799 (London, 3 vols.). Malthus used this edition, but he also refers to some tables published in the second, which came out a year later. In the second edition the title was altered to '... *the Close of the Eighteenth Century*', and the arrangement and pagination of the three volumes is quite different; those who wish to follow up Malthus's principal quotations must therefore make sure that they have the first edition of 1799.

Malthus's reference to Tooke in Bk I, ch. ix, n. 28, omits some interesting comments. For instance, on pp. 313–14 of Vol. III (1799) Tooke wrote: 'In fact the government has been as intent on converting the nomadic tribes to agriculture as to Christianity, or rather the former is not infrequently a consequence of the latter'; he wished that the herdsmen could be induced to want more commodities, so that industry would replace their injurious sloth, and promote 'trading intercourse of the nomades with more polished tribes'.

The reference made in 1806 to the 'subsequent edition' of 1800 (at the end of ch. iii of Bk I) is to pp. 550–2 of Vol. I, where Malthus quotes Tooke verbatim, but sets out the statistical summary in a different way. Malthus omits Tooke's interpretation of his figures: 'This uncommon overplus of births, unparalleled in the annals of political oeconomy, forms a characteristic feature of the russian empire (*sic*), and is an evident proof of the increasing prosperity of the inhabitants of its vast dominions ... Another striking object is the uncommonly favourable proportion which the males bear to the females, and which seems intended by nature as the foundation of the military grandeur of the russian empire.' 23 boys were born for every 20 girls.

TOTT, FRANÇOIS, BARON DE (1733–93), a French diplomat of Hungarian extraction, he was in Constantinople from 1755 to 1763, when he acquired his knowledge of the language and customs of Turkey; he returned there in 1769, after being French Consul in the Crimea, to help reorganise the army and fleet of the decaying Ottoman Empire, which the French were anxious to support against the increasing power of Russia under Catherine the Great. De Tott's *Mémoires sur les Turcs et les Tartares* (Amsterdam, 4 vols.) appeared in 1784, after he had returned to France; when the Revolution broke out, he fled to Switzerland.

The *Mémoires* are clearly put together from authentic diaries, with convincing records of conversation, and details about food, lodging and beds which inevitably concern even the most adventurous of travellers. The passage quoted by Malthus refers initially to a place de Tott calls Adgemka:

they set fire to all the stacks of corn and hay which these unhappy people had gathered ... The order was executed so rapidly, and the thatched houses blazed so quickly and fiercely, that we ourselves could not escape except through the flames ... A hundred and fifty villages were burned in the same way, and caused a cloud of ashes to stretch for twenty leagues across the border of Poland.

Some men and horses who had perished from the cold were seen by de Tott literally frozen into the ground.

TOWNSEND, REV. JOSEPH (1739–1816), was educated at Cambridge and Edinburgh, where he studied medicine before taking Orders. After some European travel, he settled down as rector of Pewsey in Wiltshire, where his congregation is said to have dwindled from 200 communicants to three, his parochial concerns being subordinate to his interest in geology, etymology, and the authenticity of Mosaic legend.

Malthus's flattering reference to 'the valuable and entertaining travels of Mr Townsend', at the end of his first chapter on France, is fully justified: the book is *A Journey Through Spain in the Years 1786 and 1787; with particular Attention to the Agriculture, Manufactures, Commerce, Population, Taxes and Revenue of that Country, and Remarks in passing through a Part of France* (3 vols. London 1791; 2nd edn 1792). Townsend had in his index 'Population, Principles of', and under this heading we may read of the mountains just beyond Leon:

Wherever a valley spreads wide enough to afford pasture for some cows, we find a village of ten, fifteen, or twenty houses; their numbers always bearing proportion to the quantity of food; and as the human race every where makes strong efforts to increase, we find the inhabitants climbing the steep ascent, to cultivate every spot where the plough can pass.

Here most evidently their numbers must be limited, because their food is so; and were they to establish a community of goods, they must either cast lots who should emigrate, or they must all starve together; unless they chose rather to agree that only two in every family

347

should marry, and when a cottage became vacant, could find means to settle, which of the expectants should unite to take possession of it. (*op. cit.* 2nd edn Vol. I, pp. 382–3.)

Townsend's *A Dissertation on the Poor Laws*, 'by a Well-Wisher to Mankind', first appeared in 1786; Malthus used the second edition of 1787, and there was a reprint in 1817. In Bk IV, ch. x, Malthus quotes what he calls 'the conclusion' of this 'admirable dissertation', but he in fact omits the final sentence – Townsend's concluding words were: 'When the poor are obliged to cultivate the friendship of the rich, the rich will never want inclination to relieve the distresses of the poor.'

The compulsory savings schemes to which Malthus objects (Bk IV, ch. xi, n. 3) were to be 'subjected to wholesome regulations'. On p. 90 Townsend wrote: 'To drive them into these societies, no man should be intitled to relief from the parochial fund who did not belong to one of these. Thus would sobriety, industry, and oeconomy take place of drunkenness, and prodigality, and due subordination would be again restored.'

TRANSACTIONS OF THE ROYAL ACADEMY OF SCIENCES AT STOCKHOLM, *see under* Nicander, Henrik.

TUCKER, REV. JOSIAH (1712–99), whose experience as a clergyman in Bristol turned his attention to politics and trade before he became Dean of Gloucester in 1758. His topical literary output was immense, on the naturalising of foreign Protestants and Jews (for which he was burnt in effigy), on theological difficulties, on the poor, on the American question and colonies generally, and on Union with Ireland. His most important book, privately printed in 1755, and circulated amongst his friends – with wide margins for their comments – was *The Elements of Commerce and Theory of Taxes*. This work in many ways anticipated Adam Smith, and in some respects showed greater foresight in describing the problems of an industrialised society. Dean Tucker was greatly in favour of increasing the population by encouraging marriage.

Towards the end of his life, Tucker corresponded with James Stanier Clarke (1765–1834) who was Chaplain and Librarian to the Prince of Wales, and the brother of Malthus's college friend, Edward Daniel Clarke (1769–1822). In 1799 James Stanier Clarke published a pamphlet on Ireland, with extracts from the writings of old Dean Tucker. The editor is unable to trace Malthus's reference to Dean Tucker's remarks on the 'plan' of Mr Pew (q.v.) and can only suggest that he heard of them through the Clarkes, possibly in a letter, possibly even in a printed circular, since Tucker believed that 'the press is still to be considered only as a more expeditious amanuensis'. (See George Shelton, *Dean Tucker and Eighteenth-Century Economic and Political Thought*, London 1981, p. 106.)

TURGOT, ANNE-ROBERT-JACQUES (1727–81), a French statesman who was Contrôleur-Général des Finances from 1774 to 1776, and advocated a policy of free trade, especially in corn. The *Oeuvres de M. Turgot, Ministre d'État*, are a selected and edited miscellany in nine octavo volumes, published in Paris in 1808, which was put together by Dupont de Nemours (q.v.).

Malthus's reference in Bk III, ch E, n. 5, is to an interesting table from the

'Extrait de la quatrième Lettre sur la Liberté du Commerce des Grains', written in 1770. In this table Turgot distinguishes between the *récolte*, or amount of grain harvested per acre, and the *produit en argent*, or yield in money. In a year of extreme scarcity, the price of a *septier* of corn might be more than double that of a good year, but the farmer's total receipts would still not cover his costs.

TURNER, CAPTAIN SAMUEL, F.R.S. (*c*.1749–1802), was a native of Gloucestershire and a kinsman of Warren Hastings; he had a distinguished career as a soldier with the East India Company. In 1783 Hastings, as Governor-General, sent Captain Turner on a mission to Tibet, to congratulate the Regency on the reincarnation of the Grand Lama. The child, by then 18 months old, listened solemnly to a long, formal address 'as though he understood every word'.

Samuel Turner wrote up his journals on his return to England, *An Account of an Embassy to the Court of the Teshoo Lama in Tibet, containing a Narrative of a Journey through Bootan and Part of Tibet*, published in London in 1800. It is a quarto of 473 pages, and an excellent example of how Malthus used his sources, picking out what he wanted for Bk I, ch. xi; in places he quotes Turner almost verbatim, as he did so often with his authorities. On p. 348 Turner refers to 'Polyandry, if I may so call it'.

After remarking on the beggars fed by the Lama's bounty (Bk I, ch. xi, n. 36) Turner goes on with the next stage of his journey; in the course of an exploratory walk after an early dinner, he found

a shallow brook, whose waters were completely frozen, and what was my joy, when I found the ice firm enough to bear my weight! My skates were immediately sent for, and I had the satisfaction of skating for two hours upon a piece of ice, which though narrow, was tolerably smooth, and above a mile in length. It was a matter of surprise to most of the spectators, to view the apparent ease and velocity with which we moved.

Malthus, as English as Turner, a cricketer, swimmer and skater, might well have done the same.

ULLOA, ADMIRAL ANTONIO (1716–1795), was a native of Seville, and one of the mathematicians employed in measuring a degree of the meridian in Peru, which he surveyed from 1735 to 1745. He was elected a Fellow of the Royal Society.

What Malthus calls simply *Voyage d'Ulloa* (Bk I, ch. iv, n. 25) was a two-volume quarto entitled *Voyage Historique de l'Amérique Méridionale fait par Ordre du Roi d'Espagne* (Amsterdam and Leipzig, 1752). This is the only 'travel book' which Malthus quoted in the 1798 *Essay* (pp. 102–3) and there is a copy in the Malthus Library at Jesus College, Cambridge. It is also the only Spanish source in Robertson's *History of America* which Malthus was able to read for himself, as none of the others were available to him in French or English translations.

VANCOUVER, CAPTAIN GEORGE, R.N. (1758–1798), was one of the few British naval officers to rise from the lower deck, like Captain Cook (q.v.) with whom he sailed as a boy of 13 on the *Resolution*. Vancouver's career culminated in the command of an expedition to Nootka Sound, formally to receive back some territory which had been annexed by the Spaniards, and also further to explore the north-west coast of

America. His ship, the *Discovery*, left Falmouth in April 1791; he rounded the Cape of Good Hope, surveyed the south-west coast of Australia (where he called the Aborigines 'the Indians of New Holland') and so by way of New Zealand and Tahiti to Nootka, to circumnavigate the Island named after him.

The work to which Malthus refers was published a few months after the author's death by his brother John, in three quarto volumes: it was called *A Voyage of Discovery to the North Pacific Ocean and Round the World in the Years 1790–1795* (London 1798). Vancouver declared he had proved conclusively that 'no internal sea, or other navigable communication whatever exists, uniting the Pacific and Atlantic Oceans'.

In Bk I, ch. iv, nn. 95 and 96, Malthus's references are correct, but his account of the diet of the people of Nootka Sound is not quite accurate: Captain Vancouver wrote of the pine-bark: 'It had a sweetish taste, was very tender, and if we may judge by their actions, it seemed by them to be considered as good food.' The party were offered pine-balls in abundance, with cockles, 'but we accepted only a few of the latter'. With regard to the halibut, what Vancouver actually wrote was, 'a very scanty supply of this species of food'.

Malthus does not point out, when quoting Vancouver's account of the South Sea Islanders' warlike propensities, that he attributed their devastating effects to the arms and ammunition traded for provisions by 'European and American visitors'. Only for weapons were the natives now inclined 'to exchange the valuable refreshments, with which there can be little doubt these islands still abound. The evil of this trade will be materially felt by vessels ... unequipped with military stores for the inhuman purpose of barter with these people.' Writing on 16 March 1792, Vancouver noted that: 'The alteration which has taken place in the several governments of these islands since their first discovery by Captain Cook, has arisen from incessant war ... which the commerce of European arms and ammunition cannot fail of encouraging to the most deplorable extent.' (*op. cit.* Vol. I, p. 187.)

VOGHT, BARON CASPAR VON (1752–1839), was a merchant of Hamburg and a connoisseur of the arts, who took refuge in Britain during the upheaval of the French Revolutionary Wars. His little book, published in London in 1796, is dated from Edinburgh, and the author was described in the Advertisement as 'a gentleman of extensive property and unlimited philanthropy'. It was entitled *An Account of the Management of the Poor in Hamburgh since the Year 1788, in a Letter to some Friends of the Poor in Great Britain*. On his return to his country house at Flottbeck, near Hamburg, Voght's advice on the building and organisation of workhouses was sought from all over Europe.

Malthus's reference to Voght's scheme in Bk IV, ch. iv, n. 11, assumed that the reader had some knowledge of it. Voght described how his committee, to reduce the number of beggars in Hamburg,

began to make an exact calculation of what each pauper wanted for bare subsistence: we went down as far as 2s a week; but in the course of our investigation about the earnings of 3500 families, we were astonished to find that we were still above the sum with which a considerable part of our poor could make a shift to live.

They took over an institution for flax-spinning:

350

Six sevenths of our poor being women and children, we pitched upon this kind of work because

1. The material is cheap;
2. The sale is always sure;
3. No nice workmanship is required …

and so on. As 'the work can be exactly ascertained *by measure*', it was not difficult to fix the rate so that no one could earn more than 1s 6d a week – that is to say, ¾ of two shillings. Children from six to sixteen spent one-third of their working time in school, and medical care was provided for the sick. Anyone in Hamburg who gave charity in the streets, or at their doors, was fined £2, but 'this wise law … was scarcely found to be necessary'. (*op. cit.* pp. 18–19, 29, 32.)

VOLNEY, CONSTANTIN-FRANÇOIS, COMTE DE CHASSEBOEUF (1755–1820), inherited a small estate, which enabled him to travel. His *Voyage en Syrie et en Egypte, pendant les Années 1783–85* was published in Paris in two octavo volumes in 1787. An English edition appeared in the same year, but Malthus used the original French, and his translations are much better than those of the official version. After being imprisoned during the Terror, Volney spent four years in America, then returned to France to hold office under both Napoleon and the Bourbons, and to write historical works.

In Bk I, ch. viii, n. 56, Malthus might have noted that the plague came to Egypt from Constantinople, and that Volney believed the subsequent famine had killed almost as many people as the pestilence itself; precise figures were impossible to obtain, because the Turks (who ruled Egypt) had 'des préjugés superstitieux' against enumerations or registers of births and deaths. (*op. cit.* Tom. 1, pp. 175–6.)

In Bk I, ch. x, n. 2 there is a strange mistake. Of the land tax, Volney wrote: 'Il paraît, malgré son caractère farouche, que ce Sultan sentit l'importance de ménager le cultivateur; car le *miri* comparé à l'étendue des terreins, se trouve dans une proportion infiniment modérée.'* He then goes on to refer to 'une foule de charges', ** which is quite different from Malthus's *changes*; possibly this is a misprint which was never noticed. *Accidental* in this context means irregular and unforeseen.

VOYAGE IN SEARCH OF PÉROUSE, *see under* Labillardière, Jacques-Julien Houton de.

WALLACE, REV. ROBERT, D.D. (1697–1771), an Edinburgh minister who in 1743 was elected Moderator of the General Assembly of the Church of Scotland; this Assembly approved a scheme which Wallace had worked out with Alexander Webster (q.v.) for establishing a fund for the widows of Scots ministers.

Malthus quotes in Bk I, ch. xiv, and in Bk II, ch iv(a), from Wallace's *Dissertation on the Numbers of Mankind in Antient and Modern Times*: 'in which the superior Populousness of Antiquity is maintained. With an Appendix containing Additional

---

* 'It appears that, in spite of his cruel disposition, the sultan recognises the importance of protecting the farmer; for the *miri*, having regard to the extent of the land, yields an exceedingly small proportion of the taxes raised.'
** 'a multitude of [additional] charges'.

Observations on the same Subject, and some Remarks on Mr Hume's Political Discourse, Of the Populousness of Antient Nations'. It was published in Edinburgh in 1753.

More important from the theoretical point of view was Wallace's *Various Prospects of Mankind, Nature and Providence*, also published in Edinburgh, in 1761. Hazlitt accused Malthus of plagiarising this work, 'perhaps without consciousness, at any rate without acknowledgment'. This is nonsense: the reason that Malthus did not refer to Wallace's *Prospects* by its title was, of course, that he took it for granted that all his readers would know about it, from the *Essay* of 1798 onwards. Godwin was familiar with the book, and realised that he had to answer the 'Objection to this system from the Principle of Population' when defending his own Utopia.

'Under a perfect government', wrote Wallace, 'the inconveniencies of having a family would be so intirely removed ... mankind would increase so prodigiously, that the earth would at last be overstocked, and become unable to support its numerous inhabitants. ... There would not even be sufficient room for containing their bodies upon the surface of the earth. ... It would be necessary, therefore ... that the earth should be continually enlarging in bulk, as an animal or vegetable body.' This would involve 'making considerable changes in the solar system'. (*op. cit.* pp. 114–16.)

WARGENTIN, PER WILHELM (1735–1783), was a Swedish mathematician and astronomer, well known for his work on Jupiter's satellites – *Observationes eclipsium secundi satellitis Jovis* – but almost ignored as a statistician. Wargentin became interested in demography after reading Halley's paper of 1693 (communicated to the Royal Society) on the mortality of Breslau. He corresponded with Süssmilch, Euler and Richard Price (qq.v.) but his work for the Swedish Central Statistical Registry, the Tabellkommission, was almost a side-line, as were the calculations he made for the Trollhätta canals.

Malthus's quotations from Wargentin's paper for the Royal Swedish Academy of Sciences, of which he was the Secretary, are from the French version. The *Mémoires Abrégés de l'Académie Royale des Sciences de Stockholm* were published in Paris in 1772, and Wargentin's contribution (presented in 1766) is entitled 'De l'homme; mortalité de l'homme en Suède, comparée à celle de la femme. Du nombre des naissances et des morts dans tous les mois de l'année.' (On man; the mortality of men in Sweden compared with that of women. On the number of births and deaths in each month of the year.)

WEBSTER, REV. ALEXANDER, D.D. (1707–1784), was an Edinburgh minister who, with the Rev. Robert Wallace (q.v.) set up a fund for the widows of the Scots clergy. Webster, being interested in mathematics, did the actuarial part of the work; he obtained statistics from all the Presbyterian ministers of Scotland, in order to make proper calculations of life expectancy. In 1753 he was elected Moderator of the General Assembly of the Church of Scotland, and was commissioned by the government to ascertain the population of the country.

This Webster did by sending a schedule of questions to every parish minister. His *Account of the Number of People in Scotland in 1755* was used later by Sir John Sinclair (q.v.) who adopted the same method for his own survey, making use of Webster's manuscript returns, which were deposited in the Advocates' Library in Edinburgh. Malthus's reference to 'Dr Webster's survey' in Bk II, ch. xii, n. 5 is to Vol. xxi of Sir John Sinclair's great compendium.

WESTMINSTER REVIEW, *see under* Mill, John Stuart.

WEYLAND, JOHN, F.R.S. (1774–1854), was a wealthy, childless man, whose wife's landed possessions, together with those he inherited, qualified him to sit as a magistrate in three counties, Oxfordshire, Berkshire and Surrey. He entered the Poor Law controversy of 1807 with two pamphlets. The first was *A Short Inquiry into the Policy, Humanity and Past Effects of the Poor Laws '. . . in which are included a few Considerations on the Questions of Political Oeconomy most intimately connected with the Subject; particularly on the Supply of Food in England'*. This he followed in the same year with a *Supplement: Observations on Mr Whitbread's Poor Bill*.

Weyland maintained that, since it was impossible to pay all labourers a wage adequate to support a large family, there must be some form of children's allowance: 'The money paid, therefore, under the operation of the Poor Laws, or of any system resembling them, may be considered in a great measure as a premium given in lieu of high wages, at once to encourage population, and to enable the manufacturer to work cheap.' (*Short Inquiry*, p. 49.)

In spite of fundamentally disagreeing with Malthus, Weyland made complimentary remarks about him in both these small works. On p. 64 of the *Supplement* he is almost fulsome: 'Mr Malthus, by profound skill in reasoning, the admirable management of his materials, and the eloquence of his style, has cast a charm around the opinions entertained by him upon this subject.' Thus Malthus's brutal criticism of Weyland's major work in the 1817 *Appendix* (Vol. II, pp. 237–49 in this edition) must have come as a shock, the more so as there is a copy of this book in the Malthus Library at Jesus College, Cambridge, inscribed 'To the Rev. T. R. Malthus. From the Author.'

The full title of Weyland's book was *The Principles of Population and Production as they are affected by the Progress of Society with a View to Moral and Political Consequences* (London 1816, octavo, 493 pp., but with much repetition). Weyland held that a society in which one-third of the people lived in towns 'had arrived at its POINT OF NON-REPRODUCTION'. Therefore it was essential 'to keep an additional set of healthy breeders for the community ... it must place them in situations most favourable to child-bearing, and to the health of children, and most favourable also to their morals, that is to say, in the country villages'. (*op. cit.* pp. 109, 172.)

Weyland's 'fifth proposition', which Malthus said he had answered in a note at the end of Bk III (Vol. II, p. 245 of this edition) was as follows:

During the alternate progress of population and subsistence, in the earliest as well as the most advanced stages of society, a *previous* increase of people is necessary to stimulate the community to a further production of food; and consequently to the healthy advancement of a country in the career of strength and prosperity. It results from this proposition that the incipient pressure of population against the *actual* means of subsistence, or, more correctly speaking, the excess of population *just beyond the plentiful supply of the people's want*, instead of being the cause of most of the miseries of human life, is in fact ... the cause of all public happiness, industry, and prosperity. (*op. cit.* p. 22.)

353

With regard to the production of food in England, Weyland could truthfully write in January 1816 that 'the actual difficulty is not how to feed the people, but how profitably to dispose of the superfluity of the food raised for their support'. (*op. cit.* p. 129.)

WILSON, WILLIAM, the unknown compiler of *A Missionary Voyage to the Southern Pacific Ocean* (London 1799).

It is interesting that Malthus felt it unnecessary to give any information about this superb quarto, so well known at the time, now so forgotten that the editor would not have been able to trace it without the assistance of Mr John Harrison of the Cambridge University Library. According to the title-page, the voyage was 'performed in the years 1796, 1797 and 1798, in the Ship Duff, commanded by Captain James Wilson', and the account was 'Compiled from Journals of the Officers and the Missionaries; and illustrated with Maps, Charts, and Views, Drawn by William Wilson, and engraved by the most eminent Artists; with a Preliminary Discourse on the Geography and History of the South Sea Islands; and an Appendix including details never before published of the natural and civil state of Otaheite; by a committee appointed for the purpose by the Directors of the Missionary Society'.

Malthus's page references do not fit any copy of the *Missionary Voyage* which the editor could find. Mr Harrison believes that the work was given out to two printers, in order that the book might be published as quickly as possible, to be sold 'for the Benefit of the Society'. Gillet's version, which Malthus may have used, is said to consist of 395 pages, but none can be traced in this country; that printed by Gosnell runs to 420 pages, and is the version which belonged to George III, Lord Grenville and others, whose copies may be admired in the British Library.

Although the *Missionary Voyage* is catalogued under Wilson's name, the moving spirit of the enterprise was the secretary of the Missionary Society, John Love (1757–1825). In 1788 he was ordained minister of the Presbyterian congregation at Crispin Street, Spitalfields, in London, where he remained for 12 years before returning to Scotland, and becoming secretary of the Glasgow Missionary Society, in addition to his duties as a minister. Love's religious fervour is shown in his posthumously published works; his practical sense in his choice of missionaries, such as a butcher and a carpenter, as well as four ordained ministers, and in his arrangements with the East India Company for the *Duff* to bring back a cargo of tea from Canton on the return voyage.

It is astonishing to read in *The Letters of the Late John Love D.D.* (Glasgow 1840) that as late as 6 June 1796 'the commercial gentlemen' among the Directors of the Missionary Society were 'much engaged about securing a proper vessel for the expedition'; the *Duff* sailed from Blackwall on 10 August. Of the missionaries, a total of 30 men, five women, and two young children were landed 'in perfect health' on three South Sea Islands. Every seaman returned to England, on 11 July 1798, 'as well as on the day he embarked'.

The *Missionary Voyage* had a long dedication to the King, and in it Malthus would have read of the previous voyages, undertaken 'to enlarge the bounds of science' or to open 'a field for commercial speculation'. The missionaries felt differently: 'On landing among these islanders, our passions were more powerfully excited to find their population greatly diminished, and, through the prevalence of vice, tending to utter extinction.' The 'Advertisement' expressed the hope that the information gathered on the voyage would 'produce some powerful impression on the minds of our countrymen; interest them more tenderly on behalf of the wretched heathen; and excite suitable efforts to repair the miseries which Europeans have in part occasioned, as well as to rescue from destruction of body and soul a gentle race of our fellow-men'.

With regard to Malthus's statements about the scarcity of women on Otaheite, see also the note on Captain Cook. The context of the reference which Malthus gives in Bk I, ch. v, n. 35, is as follows: the missionaries hear of an infant strangled at birth (no sex is given) and visit the mother,

esteemed by the natives a great beauty, which I suppose to be the inducement that tempted her to murder her child; for here the number of women bearing no proportion to the men, those esteemed handsome are courted with great gifts, and get so accustomed to change their husbands, to go with them from place to place, that rather than be debarred these pleasures, they stifle a parent's feelings, and murder their tender offspring. ... No odium whatever is attached to this unnatural deed. (*Missionary Voyage*, p. 194 in the version available.)

In his remarks on the Friendly Islands, Malthus seems to doubt the missionaries he cites (n. 49) who wrote of Tongataboo:

The murder of children, and other horrid practices, which prevail among the Otaheiteans, are unheard of here. Their children are much indulged, and old age honoured and revered.

But

Female chastity is not much esteemed among the lower orders, it being a common practice with the chiefs, in our visits to them, to offer some of their females to sleep with us; the practices of our abandoned countrymen making them believe this was a favour we could not well do without. Our first refusal seemed to excite a surprise, but has generally prevented a second temptation from the same person. Unchastity among females of rank, and especially after marriage, we have heard is punished with severity; however, we have not as yet known an instance. (*Missionary Voyage*, pp. 275–6 in the version available.)

YOUNG, ARTHUR, F.R.S. (1741–1820), the most famous of writers on agriculture, well known for his accounts of his *Tour of Ireland* in 1780, and his *Travels in France* in 1787, 1788, and 1789–90. His *Annals of Agriculture* contained contributions from other writers, including George III and Jeremy Bentham, but were written largely by himself; they extended to 45 complete volumes, published between 1784 and 1809. When William Pitt set up the Board of Agriculture, as a war-time measure, in 1793, the internationally celebrated Arthur Young was the obvious man to appoint as its Secretary; he held this office until his death, and the department was closed down shortly afterwards. In spite of their many public disagreements, Malthus and Arthur Young corresponded privately on friendly terms.

Young's *Travels in France* were published at Bury St Edmunds in 1792, then in London in 1794, in two quarto volumes. Part I, which is largely a travel diary, has been much reproduced, but 'Part Second' of General Observations – possibly of

355

greater interest today – has never been reprinted in full. It is from this Second Part, beginning on p. 281 of Vol. I, that Malthus quotes.

Malthus's reference to the Constituent Assembly's estimate of the population of France (Bk II, ch. viii, n. 7) is to the full official table printed by Arthur Young. The 83 Departments are listed in alphabetical order, in three columns, for the inhabitants of towns, of the country, and the total for each Department. On p. 465 Young explains that, since the National Assembly's 'directions for making these lists are positive and explicit, and no advantage whatever results to the people by concealing their numbers, but, on the contrary, in many instances, they are favoured in taxation, by reason of the number of their children, we may surely conclude, that these returns are the safest guides to direct our calculations'.

In Bk IV, ch. xi, Malthus is perhaps a little hard on Young. As Malthus himself pointed out in the 1806 *Appendix* (Vol. II, pp. 223–4 of this edition) there is a great difference between an employed workman having a rented plot to cultivate in his spare time, and a peasant proprietor with no other resources. The pamphlet on *Scarcity*, from which Malthus quotes extensively, was dated 14 March 1800, a year of near-famine; that on *The Propriety of Applying Waste Lands to the Better Maintenance and Support of the Poor* appeared in 1801.

By 1806, when Malthus wrote his *Reply*, Arthur Young's memories of French poverty had perhaps been overlaid by the prolonged distress of his fellow-countrymen. His attack on Malthus in No. 239 of the *Annals of Agriculture* (Vol. XLI, 1804, pp. 208–31) is a fine controversial essay: 'On the Application of the Principles [*sic*] of Population to the Question of Assigning Land to Cottages'. Young's defence of inconsistency occurs on p. 209:

A writer like myself, who has employed not a short life in the acquisition of facts, which he has been in the progressive habit of laying before the public, is not bound to reconcile such facts, or to withold any, because they militate with others that he has before communicated. He is rather bound, in candour, to the directly contrary conduct; his business is to search for important facts for public use; and though he may adduce his own conclusions and reflections, as they strike him at the moment, it ought not to be expected from him, that his ideas are to remain stationary, while he is advancing in inquiries.

Of the poor, Arthur Young wrote on pp. 219–20:

Mr Malthus says that *with land* they will increase, who doubts it? They certainly will, though perhaps not more than without it. The superfluity must emigrate [to the towns]: so they must in every case, and if there is not a demand for this superfluity, misery is the consequence. ... But will any man contend, that you shall not render 500 000 families comfortable because they will increase? Seeming to assume the false supposition, that if they are *not* comfortable they will not increase; though the proofs to the contrary are to be seen by millions.

In 1809, broken by the loss of a daughter, his unhappy marriage, and something like religious mania, Arthur Young began to go blind: he lost his sight completely in 1811. What Malthus in the 1817 *Appendix* (n. 21) courteously calls No. 270 of the *Annals of Agriculture* is in fact merely a pamphlet; at the foot of the first page of each printer's 'signature' the reader will see, in very small type, 'Vol. XLVI – No. 270', and the first page of the pamphlet is numbered 65. It is entitled *An Enquiry into the Progressive Value of Money in England, as marked by the Price of Agricultural Products* 'the *whole deduced from a great variety of authorities not before collected*. (London 1812.)

The huge footnote, from which Malthus quoted, is on pp. 90–1 of this pamphlet; it relates to a passage in the text to the effect that the price of food had risen far more than wages. After recommending a peck of wheat for a day's work, Young goes on to say that 'if the same was established at present, all complaint and clamour would be removed: the poor man would not be in the least affected by the high price of wheat; and the farmer would never complain of paying too dearly for labour, where the price was measured by that of his own production'. Later in the footnote comes the sentence: 'The common objection to such a plan, that single men would be paid as much as married ones with families, appears to have very little weight, because it is absolutely impossible on any system to avoid this inequality.'

Also in 1817, Malthus expunged an unkind passage about Arthur Young which he had published in the *Appendix* of 1806 (n. 35). The editor has been unable to find any reference to ravens, but in the *Annals of Agriculture* (Vol. XLI, p. 226) Young spoke of the 'cruel insult' of telling 'a man while in health and vigour, that *he is not to marry but to burn*', like the fellow of a college waiting 20 years for a fat living. Malthus probably also had in mind the conclusion of the 86-page pamphlet published in 1800, *The Question of Scarcity plainly stated and Remedies Considered*. Arthur Young wrote:

It is the hand of THE ALMIGHTY which has afflicted the nation … Irreligion, luxury, extravagance, and perpetual dissipation mark too many in the higher walks of life: while profligacy, idleness, immorality, vice and depredation, the sure effects of neglected education, prey amongst the lower classes. Are our poor provided for in the manner they ought to be, in a kingdom that expends forty millions per annum? … It may not be in the councils of the Almighty, that this nation should be conquered by foreign arms, or destroyed by internal commotion; but it is evidently his will that it should be chastized; or the punishment we feel at present would not have taken place.

*See also* Gourlay, Robert.

# A NOTE ON THE ORIGINAL INDEXES
## (*All page references are to the present edition*)

There are readers who invariably turn first to the end of a book, and study the Index before the Contents; they prefer to go in by the back door. Malthus's great quarto on *Population* had but 5½ pages of index, printed in two wide columns, for 604 pages of text, and the unenlightened might well have been puzzled as to the nature of the work.

The 1803 index began with '*Abnakis*, their mode of warfare', and ended with '*Zoroaster*, what he deemed meritorious acts'. [I, pp. 37 and 111). Zoroaster remained in all Malthus's subsequent indexes, but the Abnakis were dropped in 1806, among many other 1803 entries which did not survive revision. These included:

*Conduct*, ought to be governed by circumstances, II, p. 125.

*Evil*, natural and moral, instruments of divine admonition, II, p. 88.

*Gunpowder*, benefit of the invention, I, p. 71, n. 55.

*Happiness of society*, how to be attained, II, p. 105.

*Man*, has only a conditional right to subsistence, II, p. 105.

*Morals*, indigence highly unfavourable to, II, p. 105.

*Power*, has always a tendency to encroach, II, p. 125.

*Virtue and Vice*, distinction between, II, p. 90.

Malthus as historian, philosopher and theologian seems more in evidence than Malthus the economist.

Some of the entries of 1803 which did relate to political economy were also omitted or completely altered in 1806. In the quarto there were, for instance, eight sub-headings after '*England*, checks to population in'. The second is

– wealthy, and why, I, p. 395,

and the list continues

– bad effect of its national debt, I, p. 397,

– once an agricultural nation, I, p. 400,

– its corn laws, I, p. 410,

– should become more of an agricultural nation, I, p. 426,

– danger to its constitution, II, p. 124,

– more than half its people will soon become paupers, II, p. 137.

It is easy to laugh, but the modifications and qualifications which appear in the text of successive editions of the *Essay* are also reflected in the indexes, and Malthus deserves credit for his acceptance of the surprising figures given in the early census returns, and for becoming less dogmatic as he grew older; convictions, like conduct, ought to be governed by circumstances.

In 1806 the index occupied nearly 60 octavo pages, not printed in columns.

## A Note on the Original Indexes

Although it was revised with each new edition, including the Everyman of 1914, it is almost useless for the serious student today; nor was it ever of any service to the reader who wished – for example – to look up the names of the travellers from whom Malthus obtained most of the information for Books I and II. The only one given in the index was

*Bruce*, Mr; polygamy defended by,

and he was not slipped in until 1817. The statisticians fared as badly as the explorers and missionaries. There is no mention of any of them (not even Price or Süssmilch) until 1817, when we find entries for Rickman and Sir John Sinclair, although Sir John's *Statistical Account of Scotland* had contributed much to the quarto of 1803.

For modern readers, however, the strangest omission among the proper names in the index was that of Adam Smith. In 1806 and 1807 he had but one entry:

*Smith*, Dr; examination of his arguments in support of his assertion respecting the effect produced on the price of corn by a bounty upon its exportation, I, pp. 410–29.

The re-writing of the 'corn chapters' in 1817 did not really affect this entry; but Malthus, revising his great work after ten years, must have appreciated that this solitary mention of Adam Smith did not do justice to an author whose work he had constantly borne in mind throughout the whole *Essay*. Perhaps he felt that Adam Smith could be taken for granted, perhaps he could not face going through his enlarged work and picking up all the references to the *Wealth of Nations*. Whatever his reason, in 1817 Malthus removed Smith from the index altogether, and substituted Solon, a character from the quarto whose name is included in the index for the first time:

*Solon*, sanctioned the exposing of children ... his probable motives for such permission.

It would appear from the indexes that Malthus was more interested in his information than his informants. Although he dropped the Abnakis in 1806, he kept the Iroquois, and the Chiriguanes of Peru, the Kalmucks of Siberia, and other remote and fascinating peoples. There are also, as one might expect, many entries for births, marriages and deaths, the subject-matter of the early statisticians ignored in all the indexes. Surely it is significant that the only writers whose names Malthus did enter were not the collectors of facts but the exponents of theories, theories for the improvement of society. Godwin, Condorcet and Wallace, who sparked off the *Essay* of 1798, have their places in all the indexes, as do Plato and Aristotle, their schemes 'for preserving the balance of population'. Sir James Steuart, Townsend and Arthur Young also have entries, in connection with their plans for dealing with 'the poor', as does Tom Paine, though in a different category: in 1803 we have simply 'Paine's Rights of Man', but from 1806 onwards it was '*Paine*, Mr; erroneous principles of his Rights of Man'.

The only new literary names to be added to the index of 1806 were those of James Anderson, the Abbé Raynal and St Paul. All three had been cited in the quarto, not nearly as frequently as many other writers, and there seems to be no reason why they were picked out for inclusion in 1806. Five new names were fittingly inserted in 1817, because they were mentioned for the first time in this revised edition; Curwen, Owen and Rumford were added to those with projects for improving the condition of the poor, and Grahame and Weyland on account of their recent books against Malthus.

Grahame's entry read: 'examination and refutation of his misrepresentations and objections to the principles developed in this work'; Weyland merely had an 'examination of his objections'.

Not only writers were castigated in Malthus's enlarged index. A few examples must suffice:

*Encouragements*, direct, to population, futile and absurd, I, p. 125.

*Foundling Hospitals*, pernicious nature of establishments of this kind, I, p. 176.

*Parish pay-table*, disgusting picture of, II, p. 159.

In justice to Malthus one should also quote:

*Famine*, dreadful, in some of the negro nations of Africa, I, p. 89.

*Scarcity of food*, horrid in Tierra del Fuego and Van Diemen's Land, I, p. 25.

There was an improbable tradition in the Malthus family that they were all 'bone lazy', and the following item caused amusement well within living memory:

*Climbing Trees*, vast labour in, to which the natives of New Holland are compelled for the means of subsistence, I, p. 26.

These are the sort of entries which enable anyone, browsing through Malthus's index, to obtain an insight into the views of the author as well as the subjects he discussed, something not usually revealed in the indexes of today; it could be argued either way, that modern writers do not have such strong convictions, or that modern indexers (including the authors themselves) feel it their duty to be detached.

There is also an historical explanation. When Malthus wrote, the art or craft of indexing was still in its infancy, and the alphabetical index was only just beginning to take the place of a page-by-page summary, of which good examples may be found in many French works of Malthus's period; one might regard them as a cross between an index and an elaborate table of contents. Malthus's chapter headings in the *Essay* of 1798, which had no index, conformed to this pattern:

### Chap. x

Mr Godwin's system of equality. – Error of attributing all the vices of mankind to human institutions. – Mr Godwin's first answer to the difficulty arising from population totally insufficient. – Mr Godwin's beautiful system of equality supposed to be realised. – Its utter destruction simply from the principle of population in so short a time as thirty years. [pp. 173–209.]

It was natural for Malthus to compile his indexes on much the same lines.

We may take *Poor Laws* as an example. Most of these entries remain unchanged from 1806 to 1826, and began as follows:

Of Poor Laws: those of England, though they may have alleviated individual misfortune, have spread the evil over a larger surface, I, p. 348.

causes why, notwithstanding the immense sum annually collected for the poor, so much distress still exists among them, I, p. 348.

a subscription for the poor would only increase proportionably the price of provisions, I, p. 348.

– even if the produce of a country were augmented by that means, a more than proportionate increase of population would follow, I, p. 349.

no possible sacrifices of the rich could for any time prevent the recurrence of distress among the lower classes, I, p. 349.

the condition of some of the poor cannot be raised by means of money without proportionally depressing that of others, I, p. 349.

After an equally detailed summary of the next pages, Malthus went on in 1806:

– from an increased mortality among them, occasioned by the action or the ill execution of these laws, I, p. 364.

the poor laws have destroyed many more lives than they have preserved, I, p. 364.

In 1807 these last two entries were omitted; the text was not altered, but Malthus must have felt that the page references gave exaggerated prominence to opinions which could not be supported by valid statistics.

Other changes in the index show the advance of the nineteenth century. For instance, Malthus wrote in 1806:

*Banks*, some advantage might be derived in improving the condition of the poor from the establishment of small country banks ... in which they might put their savings out to interest, II, p. 182.

In 1817 he wrote with certainty 'great advantage may be derived ...'.

In 1826 *Mechanics' Institutions* appeared in the index, even though they were only mentioned in a note. We might also remark a small but significant change in the entry for *Villages*; in 1806 we find:

The general measure of mortality in single states will depend upon the proportion of the inhabitants of towns to villagers, I, p. 200.

Twenty years later this was altered to '... will depend much upon the proportion ...'. The insertion of that one word, 'much', indicates how even Malthus (who hated towns) was aware from the census returns either that urban health had improved or – possibly – that the mortality of large cities had previously been somewhat overestimated.

Whether historical change be regarded as blind evolution and regression, or as moral progress and decline, Malthus's indexes, like the *Essay on Population* itself, are a rich field for anybody who enjoys the study of mutation.

# INDEX TO THE TWO VOLUMES OF
# THIS VARIORUM EDITION*

---

* Further details of publications and authors are contained in the Alphabetical list of Authorities, vol. II, pp. 253–357

exposure of, *see* infanticide
their hours of work, I, 334
morality of, I, 21, 253, 283; in
    workhouses, I, 363
nursing of, I, 18
one's duty to propagate, II, 148
in public care, II, 164
their right to support, II, 213
sale of, I, 93, 126, 127
duty to support one's, I, 323–4, 335,
    338; II, 94–5, 102, 139, 140, 143, 148,
    150–1, 161, 219
Chili, I, 45
China (Chinese) I, 13, 62, 74, 78, 83, 119,
    121–33, 142, 297, 300, 302, 330, 386,
    387, 388, 442, 444; II, 49, 79–80, 211,
    223
Chiriguanes, I, 39
Chowarasm, I, 76, 77
Christ, II, 162–3
Christianity (Christian religion,
    Christians), II, 96, 99, 100, 101, 231,
    250; *see also* revelation
Cilicia, I, 143
Cimbri, I, 62, 65, 67
cities, *see* towns
civil liberty, II, 122–32, 202; *see also* liberty
Clarke, Edward Daniel, II, 263, 316, 342,
    348
Clarke, James Stanier, pamphlet on
    Ireland, II, 348
Claudius, I, 63
cleanliness, I, 29, 36, 288, 292, 304
*see also under* taste
climate
    and exertion, I, 87
    and population, I, 88, 122; II, 155, 231
    and production, I, 162–3
    *see also under* habits
clothing
    and diseases, I, 292
    of labourers, II, 24, 41, 85, 172
Cobbett, William, I, 372; II, 135, 232, 314
Co-le-be, I, 28, 29
Colebrook, Sir George, I, 65–6; II, 268–9
Colebrooke, Henry Thomas, *Remarks on
    ... Benegal*, II, 258, 268–9
Colebrooke, R. H., II, 258
Collins, David, *Account of ... New South
    Wales*, I, 26–7, 342; II, 269
colonies (colonization), I, 135, 293–4, 303,
    341–3; II, 33, 47, 133–4

*see also under* habits
Colquhoun, *Treatise*, II, 112, 113, 269–70
Combination Acts, 1799 and 1800, I, 375
combination of labourers
    effect on employment, I, 375
    irrational and ineffective, I, 375
    legality of, I, 375
comforts
    necessary for happiness, I, 335
    of labourers, II, 24–8, 77, 80, 85, 86,
        102, 110, 192, 210, 224, 248; *see also
        under* labourers
    of the people, I, 226
    *see also under* taste
    *see also* conveniences; decencies;
        luxuries
Comité de Mendicité (or Committee on
    Mendicity), II, 137, 146, 166, 169,
    217, 270–1
commerce
    advantages of, I, 431
    encouraged more than agriculture, I,
        407
    should not be excessive, I, 431
    growth of, II, 77–80
    and silver, value of, I, 425
    *see also under* agriculture; capital;
        condition of the labourers;
        machinery; natural; oscillations;
        profits; surplus produce of land;
        taxation; wages; war; wealth
commerce, domestic,
    its importance, I, 391
commerce, foreign
    advantages of, I, 402; II, 46, 85, 133–4;
        not permanent, II, 32–4, 43
    and commerce domestic, II, 249
    competition in, II, 32–3, 35
    and food supply, II, 32
    and foreign manufacturers, II, 35–6
    and population, I, 388
    and high prices, I, xii
    *see also under* food; money, value of;
        wages; wealth
commerce of the sexes, I, 323
    *see also* passion between the sexes
commercial system, I, 6, 389–409; II, 32–9
    its worst feature, I, 401
commotions, internal, *see* war
competition, I, 22, 251, 348, 349, 351,
    365, 373, 385, 400, 402, 426; II, 36–7,
    41–2, 46, 134, 166, 167, 169

# Index

# Index

Ostiacks, **I**, 100
Otaheite (Tahiti), **I**, xiv, 49–57, 145; **II**, 271–3
Otter, William, **II**, 262, 342, 344
Owen, Robert, **I**, xii; **II**, 82, 175–8, 260, 313–14
  *Observations on the Effect of the Manufacturing System*, **II**, 314
  *A New View of Society*, **I**, 334–9; **II**, 314
  his plan, **II**, 314

Paine, Thomas, **II**, 130, 154
  *Common Sense*, **II**, 314
  *The Rights of Man*, **II**, 126–7, 315
  *The Age of Reason*, **II**, 315
Palestine, **I**, 109, 297, 433
Paley, William, **II**, 92–3; *Moral and Political Philosophy*, **II**, 101, 107, 193, 315
  *Natural Theology*, **II**, 193, 315–16
  his altered views on population, **II**, 193, 316–16
  *see also under* luxuries
Pallas, Peter Simon
  in *Histoire des Découvertes (Découvertes Russes)*, **I**, 81, 83, 85, 101, 112, 343; **II**, 316–17
  *Voyages de ... Pallas*, **I**, 100–1, 103–7; **II**, 317
  on the history of the Mongol nations, **I**, 81
*Pamphleteer*, **II**, 272
Pannonia, **I**, 64, 65, 70
paper money
  issued by Bank of England, **I**, 353–5
  issued by country banks, **I**, 353–5
  and value of silver, **I**, 425
  and exchange rate, **I**, 354
  *see also under* corn, value of
Paraguay, **I**, 35, 39, 42
parental affection, **II**, 214
Parennim, Dominique, **I**, 131; **II**, 317
parents, veneration of, in China, **I**, 124
parish allowances (assistance, relief), **I**, 435; **II**, 67, 97
  *see also* poor laws
parish (parochial) rates, *see also* poor laws; poor's rates
Park, Mungo, *Travels in ... Africa*, **I**, 87–9, **II**, 232, 303, 317–18
Parr, Samuel, *Spital Sermon*, **II**, 163, 318
parsimony, *see* saving

passion between the sexes, **I**, 31, 44–5, 301; **II**, 90–3, 156, 239
  its irregular gratification, **II**, 92
  *see also* sexual intercourse
passions, **II**, 89, 92, 96, 97, 98, 100, 102, 105, 106, 111, 141, 158, 161, 211, 213, 214, 215, 249, 250
  *see also under* habits; natural; unnatural
pastoral nations, **I**, 74–86
pasturage, *see under* agriculture; tithes
patents, **I**, 397
Paul of Tarsus, *see* St Paul
Paulus Diaconus (Paul the Deacon), *De Gestis Longobardorum (History of the Longobards)*, **I**, 66; **II**, 319
pauperism
  causes of, **I**, 373, 379
  and food, value of, **I**, 370–1
  and taxation, **I**, 371
Peace of Amiens, **I**, 355; **II**, 72, 76
Peace of Utrecht **II**, 58
Peel, Sir Robert, the elder (1750–1830), **II**, 82
pension, meaning of the term, **I**, 374
people, the condition of, *see* condition of the labourers
Percival, Thomas, *Essays Medical, Philosophical and Experimental*, **I**, 255, 257; **II**, 319–20
perfectibility of man, **I**, 1, 306, 309–15
Persia (Persians), **I**, 62, 76, 79, 82, 108–12
Peru **I**, 39, 40, 44, 45, 293, 341
pestilence, *see* diseases
Peter I, of Russia, **I**, 104
Petronius, **I**, 96
Petty, Sir William, *Political Arithmetic(k)*, **I**, 12, 300; **II**, 320
Peuchet, Jacques
  *Essai d'une Statistique Générale de la France*, **I**, 230, 232, 234, 236, 244; **II**, 320–1
  *Statistique Élémentaire de la France*, **I**, 244–6; **II**, 321
Pew, Richard
  pamphlets on the National Debt and Taxation, **II**, 321
  *Twenty Minutes Observations on ... Providing for the Poor*, **II**, 165, 321, 348
Phaleas of Chalcedon, **I**, 138
Pheidon of Corinth, **I**, 138, 139
philosophy, moral and political, **II**, 203
physical check, **I**, 145; **II**, 231

384

# Index

# Index